WITHIN THE WHIRLWIND

Eugenia Ginzburg
Within the Whirlwind

Translated *by* IAN BOLAND • *Introduction by* HEINRICH BÖLL

A Harvest/HBJ Book
A Helen and Kurt Wolff Book
Harcourt Brace Jovanovich, Publishers
San Diego   New York   London

HBJ

Originally published in Italy: in Russian, as Krutoy Marshrut *(2)*;
in Italian, as Viaggio nella Vertigine *(2)*.

Library of Congress Cataloging in Publication Data

Ginzburg, Evgeniĭa Semenovna.
Within the whirlwind.
Translation of Krutoĭ marshrut.
(A Harvest/HBJ Book)
1. Ginzburg, Evgeniĭa Semenovna.   2. Political
prisoners–Russia–Biography.   3. Russia–Social
conditions–*1917*–   I. Title.
DK268.G47A3413   *365.6'092'4* [B]   *80-8748*
ISBN 0-15-697649-8

Printed in the United States of America

First Harvest/HBJ edition *1982*

C D E F G H I J

vi

"Don't cry in front of them"

It would be more than presumptuous to preface a publication of this kind with a description of its contents; in this book each line speaks for itself, each line says everything, leads us into that terrible and absurd cosmos which begins approximately at the 130th meridian, the archipelago of prisoners and detainees. This is a *narrative* book in the category of "autobiographical novel," and in this case the word "novel" does not imply "invented material"—not the smallest detail is invented: "novel" stands for structure, for the arranging of an immensely copious amount of direct experience; many people have lived through what Eugenia Semyonovna Ginzburg tells us here, very few can narrate it, even fewer can write about it, and it is these few who transform personal experience into testimony. What Eugenia Ginzburg gives us here is not—and this would be more than enough—an enumeration of bare facts and data; she has added other dimensions: analysis of and reflections on this archipelago of absurdity in an absurd land calling itself the U.S.S.R. A further element, which I hesitate to mention because it could be misinterpreted, is the tension arising not from titillation but from involvement, for from the very beginning every reader must wonder: *How,* in God's name, how in the world did this woman, whose autobiographical novel in two volumes runs to almost a thousand pages—a thousand pages for eighteen years of prison camps and exile—how in the world did she manage to come out alive?

It is a good idea to study an atlas or a large map before or while reading this book to obtain some notion, if only in abstract terms, of the vast regions in which all this takes place; this bit of geographical homework is necessary for a proper "visualization." Western Europe extends over some 25 degrees longitude, Eastern Europe as far as the Urals some 45 degrees, and from there, where what we call Siberia begins, there are another almost 130 degrees longitude as far as the easternmost point that almost touches Alaska. From Yakutsk, where the archipelago of the prison camps begins, it is approximately 60 degrees longitude to the far end of that archipelago. The map of

Eastern Siberia shows only a few dots, names, places. The names of the camps mentioned by Eugenia Ginzburg do not, of course, appear, except for the one that is mentioned again and again in the songs and stories of the inmates: Magadan, the capital and administrative center, dream and horror in one; lying some 500 kilometers north of the northernmost point of Sakhalin and on the Sea of Okhotsk.

Eugenia Ginzburg spent eighteen years on this prison-archipelago. She was one of the first to report on it: as early as 1967, after first being published in Italy, *Journey into the Whirlwind** appeared, a book still as fresh as on the day of publication. At the time, Eugenia Ginzburg described it as "the story of an ordinary Communist woman during the period of the personality cult," and stated: "Only Stalin—I suppose instinctively—I could not bring myself to idolize." And when a prominent theoretician, whom she knows and respects, is arrested and she expresses surprise, she receives the indignant reply: "Don't you know that he's been arrested? Can you imagine anyone's being arrested unless there's something definite against him?"

Not long after—in the period following the murder of Kirov that marks the beginning of the most appalling period of the reign of terror—she is arrested, not because she had participated *actively* in any particular action but because she did *not* denounce the recently arrested parasite, and it is this *lack* of protest on the part of Ginzburg the lecturer and editor that labels her "for all time" a "known terrorist"; the crime is then extended to "group terrorism." Thus began *Journey into the Whirlwind*, to which *Within the Whirlwind* is a sequel. A female Lazarus, a female Job, a female Ulysses, not exposed to the waves, moods, storms, and currents of a sea or the whims of its coastal population, but thrown into the chaotically organized ocean of limitless bureaucratic absurdity in which the cruelty of the system too often becomes intensified in the cruelty of an individual one is at the mercy of; a system also in which—such are the advantages of the fortuitous happenings that I would like to call Destiny—those "angels in human form" often emerge to whom in the end Eugenia Ginzburg owes her life. This experience is part of that misleading category of "tension" which in turn springs

* Published in England under the title *Into the Whirlwind*.

from Eugenia Ginzburg's brilliant gifts as a narrator who has no need to "invent" but is more likely to have "left out."

Although I have some knowledge of the Gulag Archipelago, my interest as I read this book never for an instant wavered, and this may be partly because this astonishing woman has never lost her sense of humor, never mislaid it during her enforced wanderings when she was shunted about between a number of hells and a few dots of "heaven." That in itself would be a miracle. And a further miracle is—here one can only stand in awe—that she has poetry to thank for her strength and endurance, her will to survive in even the most hopeless situations. As soon as she has but a few minutes' peace and quiet, is able to breathe, to sit, lie, take a deep breath, lines of poetry come into her mind and across her lips: Akhmatova, Pasternak, Mandelstam, as well as novels, stories, literature—in other words, everything a Russian woman of her time simply carries *with her;* a possession that cannot be confiscated, that survives all the searches—literature that in *Journey into the Whirlwind* already proved to be a vital necessity to her. In rags, enfeebled, humiliated, felling trees at a temperature of minus 49 degrees Celsius (only when the temperature dropped to minus 50 were the detainees allowed to remain in their barracks, and there were violent arguments at the thermometer with the guards!); evenings in the barracks where one would expect basic necessities such as soup, bread, warmth, dryness to be uppermost in her mind—poetry!

Could it be that poetry is among the basic necessities for this extraordinary kind of human being? After many encounters with Soviet citizens—detainees and nondetainees—I am inclined to believe this. In Western Europe the word "literature" has a slightly derogatory sound—something between luxury and vice, at any rate nonessential. For Eugenia Ginzburg it was part of life. For this "known terrorist" literature was more than literature. Poems become symbols of recognition, not in the sense of a mechanical code but in their totality: when Eugenia Ginzburg meets her son Vasya again after twelve years, she recites poems to him during the night; he carries on where she leaves off, and that is how she "recognizes" him.

Delicately, yet explicitly enough, another phenomenon is presented and analyzed in these recollections, a phenomenon that is not only part of life but part of survival: the love affairs within this archipelago of camps, relationships of the tenderest and the coarsest kind between convicts and political prisoners (the mother of one child, for instance, is a lecturer in philosophy and the father is a burglar known throughout the city of Rostov), relationships among criminals, among political prisoners; and the children of these liaisons are of course "rounded up" and classified into groups—infants, toddlers, seniors; and when the command to report for nursing resounds through the camp, these haggard, tattered apparitions come hobbling up, almost sexless in their misery, for "feeding." And, needless to say, love must be punished when it takes place during working hours, the threat of the designation "sabotage" is ever present, and the offense is then described as: "Relations between a male and a female convict involving a horse standing idle for two hours."

These human details in no way reduced the "constant presence of terror," the constant threat of change, for there was always the possibility of terror being intensified; from Camp Elgen (in the Yakut language, "corpse"), which is bad enough, she is moved to Mylga, which is appalling yet allows for a still further intensification of horror: Izvestkovaya. And within this dual hegemony of absurdity and chance lurk the "regulations," of which the breadth of interpretation, spanning sadism, corruption, and puritanism, opens up a new and limitless dimension of horror. It may be a story called "The Little Cockroach" or a radio drama "The Wolf and the Seven Little Kids," it may be someone lambasting the Nazis prematurely (perhaps in 1940, the war having not yet started for the Soviet Union and the "progressiveness" of the Hitler regime, i.e., autobahns, tackling unemployment, being beyond doubt until June 1941!), but invariably everything hangs by a brittle thread, and it is advisable not to settle too comfortably into whatever "little heaven" may have been attained. On all sides danger and threat, even when Eugenia Ginzburg is (temporarily) released—still listed in the files as a "known terrorist"—and gives KGB officers lessons in Russian and literature and awkward interpretations are unavoidable; and when, in view of the danger of being held up on her way home by criminals, she is escorted by a gallant body of KGB officers, one day it is the turn of Major Gorokhov, the very man to whom she has to report twice a month, in fear and trembling, under humiliating circumstances! With all that, though, she does learn, during a holdup by a criminal who takes her for a "colonel's wife" because of her fur coat and demands her passport, that her husband, Dr. Anton Walter, whose gift this fateful fur coat was, is regarded in the underworld as taboo; and it may have been some consolation to discover that in this chaotic world even "colonel's wives" were not safe from holdups.

Between her thirtieth and fiftieth year, Eugenia Ginzburg spends eighteen years on this ice-age archipelago. During that time her oldest son Alyosha dies of starvation in Leningrad, she loses track of her husband, who is reported to her as dead, she is separated from her four-year-old son Vasya and does not see him again until he is sixteen. After she has fought stubbornly for his entrance visa, he is brought to Magadan by free citizens; and it is in the home of these same free citizens, of these unknowingly or knowingly involved people, that she meets him again, and young Aksyonov, as deeply moved as she, whispers to her: "Don't cry in front of them." With these words a sixteen-year-old, who has been separated from his mother for twelve years, expresses more than an entire novel often can express: his allegiance. "Don't cry in front of them"— he belongs, as his mother later puts it, to "our people, that underground realm."

That underground realm comprises millions whose watchword might be: "Don't cry in front of them." Who are those people in front of whom one does not cry? The involved ones and the unknowing ones, who often enough stumble themselves; the ones lacking in imagination who have always believed that no one was ever arrested without reason; and the great mass of people, not restricted to any national boundaries, for whom "Philistines" is as good a name as any, who think in terms of perquisites and live off them— all those who will later appear in the stories and novels of Vasily Aksyonov, whose life up to his eighteenth year is also described in *Journey into the Whirlwind* and *Within the Whirlwind;* it is the same Vasya whose garish jacket and wild hair caused his mother considerable distress even after she had spent seventeen years in the "ice age": she discovers the "former Komsomol member" in herself. But Vasya, who comes to see her as a medical student, refuses to abandon either jacket or wild hair; they too are—and he is adamant about this!—even if on a secondary level, an expression of that "new age" to which he will give voice within a few years in the company of Yevtushenko, Voznesenski, Akhmadulina, and Okudzhava, a "new age" that was allowed to find public expression.

With the subsequent generation of Voinovich, Kornilov, Vladimov, and others, it was once again driven underground. Many a line in this book—such as "Don't cry in front of them"—could form the basis for whole structures of interpretation; many a sentence, many a statement introduced into the flow, is worthy of note: "The egotism of those who suffer is probably even more all-embracing than the self-regard of those who are happy," or, more significant still: "But even our own experience—let alone other people's—fails to teach us anything," or the terse yet wistful comment when the mother takes home Vasya, drunk for the first time in his life, after his graduation party: that that was the "classically Russian role"!

Then the unbelievable, of which nevertheless she had a "foreboding"—the wave of rearrests in 1949; once again, although ten or six or twelve years have been served and one has been discharged, back into prison, once again interrogations—and I try to imagine what mountains of files must have been transported back and forth on this archipelago, how many registration centers, registration officials, assistants, officers, and subalterns must have been kept busy, and what the privileges of these privileged persons must have cost!

Under the title "The Thorny Path to the Classless Society," Yakov Mikhailovich Umansky, Eugenia Ginzburg's companion in suffering, supplied a model for the "social and political order of Kolyma" and arrived at nine different social classes: "Zéks, ex-zeks without civil rights, ex-zeks with civil rights, deportees for a fixed period of time, compulsory settlers for a fixed period of time, deportee-settlers for life, settlers with special status for a fixed period of time, and settlers with special status for life. At the apex of this pyramid stood the Germans who were simultaneously compulsory settlers and Party members."

Also discernible in this record, although only by allusion, is the biography of that Dr. Anton Walter who combined within himself three lethally dangerous though not "terroristic" qualities: he is a German, a Catholic, and a homeopath, in the latter capacity suspected of mysticism, if not of sorcery, yet he of all people is called in emergencies to the bedsides of top functionaries, most of whom are suffering from liver disorders; his herbal elixirs, potions, and powders, which he brews and prepares himself, are then in great demand, and effective too. And he personifies not only that contradiction but a further one: since he is regarded as a "good person" yet is a good German, the question arises: "How can such a good

man be a German?" (The question can also be reversed!) All that
does not fit the cliché, even when one bears in mind that Engels and
Marx must have been Germans and even wrote in German. One
must never expect a minimum of logic or even the rudiments of
reason in a system in which someone who has been taken to the
mortuary by mistake but has the effrontery still to be alive is automatically considered at fault and asked what he, a living person,
thinks he is doing among the dead.

I will not conceal the fact that I am writing this attempt at an
introduction not only as a contemporary who is grateful for every
piece of information about the century in which we live: I am
writing it also as a homage to a dead woman whom I was privileged
to count among my friends. I have sat across from Eugenia Ginzburg in Moscow and Cologne, have admired her intelligence and
felt myself put to the test by those intelligent eyes in which her
skeptical humor had never been extinguished. I am writing this also
for a friend who is still alive, her son, Vasily Aksyonov the writer,
whom I meet in *Within the Whirlwind* as a youth: seeing his
mother again and parting from her again; and I am writing this in
memory of a third person whom I never met yet would so much
have liked to know: Dr. Anton Walter.

Heinrich Böll
Translated by Leila Vennewitz

Summary of the first volume of Eugenia Ginzburg's memoirs,
Journey into the Whirlwind

On December 1, 1934, S. M. Kirov was assassinated in Leningrad.
Khrushchev, among others, has hinted that Stalin engineered the
removal of a colleague whose popularity in the Party he saw as a
threat to himself. However that may be, he seized the opportunity
to launch what was ostensibly a punitive action against traitors and
saboteurs, but in reality a ruthless campaign of prophylactic terrorism. His victims included thousands of Communists who believed, and in some cases went on deluding themselves through long
years of persecution, that the Party would sooner or later "sort it
all out" and vindicate the innocent, and that Stalin was not to blame
for the cynical cruelty of policemen and jailers.

Eugenia Ginzburg, teacher, journalist, and wife of Pavel Aksyonov, an important Party official in Kazan, has described her own
experiences of 1934 through 1939 in the first volume of her memoirs,
Journey into the Whirlwind. Although she could not find it in her
to "deify Stalin" she never until the mid-thirties doubted the correctness of the Party line. Dutifully and sincerely she propagated
the official explanation of Kirov's murder and the lessons that the
Soviet people were required to draw from it. But very shortly she
herself was accused of a lack of vigilance amounting to complicity
with the "enemies of the people": she had failed to denounce her
former colleague, Professor Elvov, now unmasked as a Trotskyist,
and to condemn a publication of his on the history of the Tartar
region. She could have truckled to her persecutors; she could, as so
many did, have sought to extenuate her "guilt" by denouncing
others; she could at least have listened to her friends and withdrawn
discreetly to some remote spot where her masters might forget her.
Perhaps none of these could have saved her. But the course she
chose instead made arrest and imprisonment inevitable, and execution highly probable. By persistently demanding justice she forced
herself on the attention of the central Party organs; and so followed
NKVD disciplinary measures, including the cancellation in the autumn of 1935 of her license to teach, which brought her to the

brink of suicide but no closer to hypocritical compliance. When, in September 1936, Stalin complained that the security organs were four years behind with their work, and ordered his new Commissar for Internal Affairs, Yezhov, to make up for lost time, the contumacious Eugenia Ginzburg could obviously not remain at large much longer.

She was arrested in February 1937, after the customary formality of expulsion from the Party. Fortunately for her, her interrogation was concluded before the summer of 1937, when "new methods of investigation were introduced," which meant that earlier restrictions on the use of physical torture were abandoned. She endured nothing worse (!) than imprisonment in vile conditions, the "conveyor belt" (continuous interrogation for seven days and nights, without food or sleep, by relays of tormentors), and confrontation with fainthearted friends who supported the allegations against her.

"Well, frankly, I'm glad that some of you Communists are in jail at last," said one of her cellmates, a member of the old Socialist Revolutionary Party. "Perhaps you will learn in practice what you couldn't understand in theory." The military tribunal of the Supreme Court took seven minutes to find Eugenia guilty of "participation in a Trotskyist terrorist counter-revolutionary group," and to sentence her to ten years' imprisonment. On her way from the courtroom back to jail she was still insisting on her innocence. "I've done nothing, absolutely nothing wrong at all," she told her escort, weeping. "Of course you're not guilty!" he replied. "Would they have given you ten years if you had been? Do you know how many a day they're finishing off now? Seventy!" Eugenia, at least, could understand the charge against her and, eventually, its real political significance—unlike her neighbor on the bedshelf in the Butyrki jail, a sixty-five-year-old peasant woman totally mystified by her condemnation as a Trotskyist ("Trotskistka"). "As God's my witness I never went near one of them cursed things. I don't know how they thought of it—'trakhtistka' indeed. . . . They don't put old women like me on tractors. . . ."

Eugenia expected to spend her ten years as a "tyurzak"—in solitary confinement in a maximum security prison for political offenders—rather than in a "corrective labor" camp. She served the first year of her sentence in the harshest of Soviet prisons—that at Yaroslavl, at first in solitary confinement in a damp and mildewed cell, with its window boarded up, forbidden to take exercise, to lie down in the daytime, to sit with her back to the door, to speak, or to sing. Soon, however, Yaroslavl, like all other Soviet jails, was inundated by the rising wave of arrests, and it was Eugenia's good fortune to share a cell with Julia Karepova, who became her devoted friend and in the years to come a generous helper. In Yaroslavl Eugenia was also introduced to the punishment cells. Accused of "continuing counter-revolutionary activity in prison," she was thrown half-naked into a dark, ice-cold, rat-infested underground cell. In the next cell an Italian Communist shrieked her protests until a warden silenced her (perhaps forever) with an icy jet of water from a hose. Eugenia emerged, after five days, with frostbitten toes.

Her sufferings were aggravated by anxiety for her family. Her behavior in the two years before her arrest had strained her relations with her husband; he had wanted her to lie low "at this special stage in the history of the Party," and to forget her resentment: "You mustn't bear a grudge against the Party." (He himself would not remain at liberty much longer.) To spare her feelings Eugenia's mother wrote that all was well with her two sons. (The older, Alyosha, had been sent to a home for the children of political prisoners, and Eugenia was never to see him again. The younger, Vasya—Vasily Aksyonov—was looked after by relatives of his father.) Her parents were imprisoned for a while in 1938. After their release they found themselves homeless, destitute, and ostracized. Eugenia's father shortly died.

In July 1938 Yezhov was dismissed. Reckless and random political terror had done its work. Henceforward a carefully calculated regular cull would suffice to keep the Soviet population cowed and to replenish the slave labor force in the northern and eastern regions. For Eugenia, the "relaxation" of 1938 meant that her sentence was commuted to ten years in a forced labor camp. The journey from Yaroslavl to Vladivostok took several weeks. Eugenia was cooped up in a boxcar (labeled "Special equipment") with seventy-five others. They queued to peer through the tiny, barred window. They were forbidden to talk while passing through stations. In scorching heat they were fed on gruel made from herringtails and were given half a glass of water each, once a day. They slept on the bare boards. Of the seventy-six, at least twenty insisted that Stalin knew nothing of the "illegalities" that his underlings were committing.

In Vladivostok Eugenia learned the rudiments of camp life. A long march under escort (soldiers with guard dogs: "We'll shoot if you break formation") brought the new contingent on July 7, 1939, to the Vladivostok transit camp with its barbed wire, watch-towers, tumble-down huts and bug-ridden bed platforms. Eugenia had already discovered that class distinctions were scrupulously observed in camp society. The common criminals (those not regarded by the regime as "socially alien") were the aristocracy: they had their pick of the lighter jobs and were permitted, indeed encouraged, by the camp authorities to bully and rob political prisoners. "Counter-revolutionary terrorists" like Eugenia were the pariahs of the camps—inferior to such minor political offenders as the "joke tellers," the "careless talkers," and even the suspected spies—and were usually assigned to the heaviest tasks. Eugenia was sent to a quarry. Suffering from scurvy and dystrophic diarrhea, tortured by back-breaking work under the July sun, she could still find, in her enjoyment of poetry, of the smell of the sea, of the stars, a defense against the stupefaction that threatened all in her position.

From Vladivostok to Kolyma, her ultimate destination, the journey was by sea. In the dark, overcrowded hold of the *S.S. Dzhurma* Eugenia became seriously ill. A doctor who had known her husband saved her life by moving her to the sickbay, where men and women, politicals and criminals, sufferers from diarrhea and syphilitics, the living and the dead whom no one had yet dragged away, lay together on the same bed platform. When the *Dzhurma* put in to shore, the sick and the dead were left lying on the cold cobblestones while the rest of the contingent were marched off. It was late night before Eugenia was carried, unconscious, to the Magadan camp hospital. A woman doctor nursed her back to health, bringing her especially nourishing food from outside, perhaps trying to compensate by this act of charity for the evil that her husband did as an NKVD interrogator.

After two months, fully recovered from exhaustion and scurvy, Eugenia was sent on to a camp, and was put to shame by the bluish faces, the frostbitten noses, the hungry eyes of her fellow prisoners. "I felt as if I had betrayed them." She was quickly reduced to their level by ten days of (apparently quite useless) "land reclamation." The women prisoners were marched five kilometers before day-break to work until late evening in temperatures of minus 40 degrees, hacking with pick and shovel at the permanently frozen soil of Kolyma.

In danger of becoming a "goner" again, Eugenia bribed her way indoors; she was a cleaner in a hostel for free workers until a vigilant management chased the counter-revolutionary from this privileged post. Next, she worked as a dishwasher in the canteen of the men's camp, until the trusty in charge, outraged by her resistance to his advances, arranged for her to be posted to the dreaded Elgen, a state farm out in the taiga. There her task was tree felling. Two women were supposed to cut and trim eight cubic meters of timber a day. The bread ration was proportionate to the amount of timber cut. Eugenia seldom cut more than 20 per cent of the required amount. Nonfulfillment of the norm was treated as sabotage and punished by confinement in an icy cell, with no sanitation, not even a night bucket. The women were marched to work through the frozen forest at five in the morning, and arrived so exhausted that there was never any hope of completing their task.

Once again, Eugenia was threatened by death from malnutrition, exhaustion, and exposure. She was saved this time by a surgeon from Leningrad, who found her employment as a nurse in the home for children born in the Elgen camp. It is in the children's home that this second volume of Eugenia's reminiscences begins.

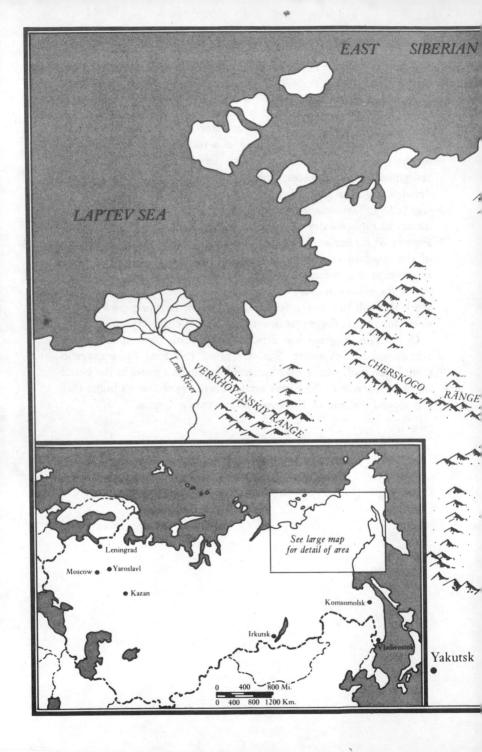

EAST   SIBERIAN

LAPTEV SEA

Lena River

VERKHOYANSKIY RANGE

CHERSKOGO   RANGE

Leningrad

Moscow ●   ● Yaroslavl

● Kazan

See large map
for detail of area

Komsomolsk ●

Irkutsk ●

Vladivostok ●

Yakutsk
●

0   400   800 Mi.

0   400   800 1200 Km.

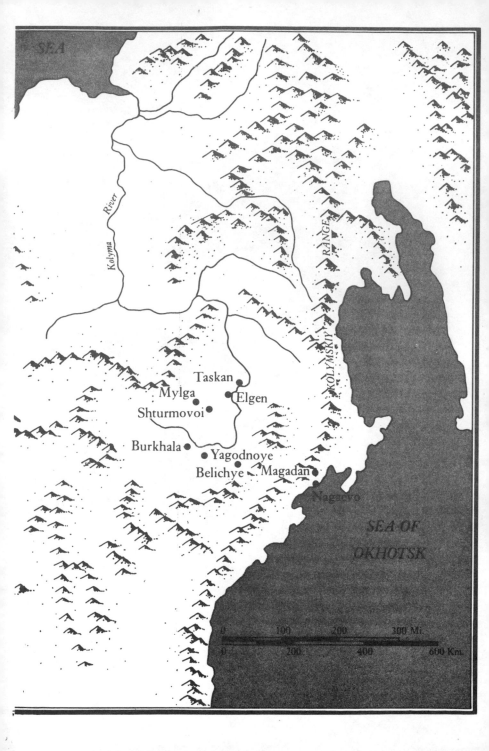

SEA

Kolyma River

RANGE

KOLYMSKIY

Taskan
Mylga   Elgen
Shturmovoi
Burkhala
Yagodnoye
Belichye   Magadan
Nagaevo

SEA OF
OKHOTSK

0   100   200   300 Mi.
0   200   400   600 Km.

Part one

Part One

1

· *Here lived children*

The children's home was also part of the camp compound. It had its own guardhouse, its own gates, its own huts, and its own barbed wire. But on the doors of what were otherwise standard camp hutments there were unusual inscriptions: "Infants' Group," "Toddlers' Group," and "Senior Group."

After a day or two I found myself with the senior group. The very fact of being there restored to me the long-lost faculty of weeping. For more than three years my eyes had smarted from tearless despair. But now, in July 1940, I sat on a low bench in a corner of this strange building and cried. I cried without stopping, sobbing like our old nurse Fima, sniffing and snuffling like a country girl. I was in a state of shock. The shock jerked me out of a paralysis that had lasted for some months. Yes, this undoubtedly was a penal camp hut. But it smelled of warm semolina and wet pants. Someone's bizarre imagination had combined the trappings of the prison world with simple, human, and touchingly familiar things now so far out of reach that they seemed no more than a dream.

Some thirty small children, about the age my Vasya was when we were separated, were tumbling and toddling about the hut, squealing, gurgling with laughter, bursting into tears. Each of them was upholding his right to a place under the Kolyma sun in a perpetual struggle with his fellows. They bashed each other's heads unmercifully, pulled each other's hair, bit each other . . .

They aroused my atavistic instincts. I wanted to gather them all together and hug them tight so that nothing could hurt them. I wanted to croon over them, like my old nurse, "My sweet little darlings, my poor little dears."

I was rescued from my trance by Anya Sholokhova, my new workmate. Anya was the embodiment of common sense and efficiency. Her married name was Sholokhova, but she was a German, a Mennonite, taught as a child that there was a right way to do everything. In the camps they called people like her "sticklers."

"Listen, Genia," she said, placing on the table a pan that gave off a heavenly aroma of something meaty, "if one of the bigwigs

4

finds you behaving like that you'll be packed off to the tree-felling site tomorrow. They'll say you're high-strung, and in this place you need nerves like steel hawsers. Pull yourself together. Anyway, it's time to feed the children. I can't do it all myself."

It would be wrong to say that the children were kept on a starvation diet. They were given as much to eat as they could manage, and by my standards at the time the food seemed quite appetizing. For some reason, though, they all ate like little convicts: hastily, with no thought for anything else, carefully wiping their tin bowls with a piece of bread, or licking them clean. I was struck by the fact that their movements were unusually well coordinated for children of their age. But when I mentioned this to Anya she made a bitter gesture of dismissal.

"Don't you believe it! That's only at mealtime, that's their struggle for existence. But hardly anyone asks for the potty—they haven't been trained to it. Their general level of development . . . well, you'll see for yourself."

I saw what she meant the following day. Yes, outwardly they did remind me painfully of Vasya. But only outwardly. Vasya at four could reel off vast chunks of Marshak and Chukovsky,* could tell one make of car from another, could draw superb battleships and the Kremlin bell tower with its stars. But these poor things! "Anya, haven't they even learned to talk yet?" Only certain of the four-year-olds could produce a few odd, unconnected words. Inarticulate howls, mimicry, and blows were the main means of communication.

"How can they be expected to speak? Who was there to teach them? Whom did they ever hear speaking?" explained Anya dispassionately. "In the infants' group they spend their whole time just lying on their cots. Nobody will pick them up, even if they cry their lungs out. It's not allowed, except to change wet diapers—when there are any dry ones available, of course. In the toddlers' group they crawl around in their playpens, all in a heap. It's all right as long as they don't kill each other or scratch each other's eyes out. Well, now you can see how it is. We're lucky if we can just get them all fed and put on the potty."

* Samuel Marshak (1887–1964): writer of children's verse, satirist, and translator. Kornei Chukovsky (1882–1969): popular and influential writer, critic, translator, and author of children's verse.

"But we ought to try and teach them something. Some songs . . . some poems . . . tell them stories."

"You can always try! By the end of the day I have barely enough strength left to climb into bed. I don't feel like telling stories."

It was true. There was so much work to do that you did not know which way to turn. Four times a day we had to lug water from the kitchen—which was at the far end of the compound—and haul back heavy pans full of food. Then, of course, there was the business of feeding the children, sitting them on their pots, changing their pants, rescuing them from the enormous whitish mosquitoes. . . . But the main preoccupation was the floors. Camp bosses everywhere had a mania for clean floors. The whiteness of the floor was the one criterion of hygiene. The fumes and the stench in the huts might be suffocating, and our rags might be stiff with dirt; but all this would pass unnoticed by the guardians of cleanliness and hygiene. Heaven help us, though, if the floors did not shine brightly enough. The same unblinking watch was kept on the "floor situation" in the children's home; the boards there were not stained, so they had to be scraped with a knife until they shone.

For all that, I did one day try to put into effect my plan for giving lessons to improve the children's speech. I unearthed a pencil stub and a scrap of paper, and I drew for them the conventional picture of a house with two little windows and a chimney with smoke coming out of it.

The first to react to my initiative were Anastas and Vera, four-year-old twins, more like normal mainland children than any of the rest. Anya told me that their mother, Sonya, was doing time as a petty offender and not as a "professional." She was some sort of cashier who had made a mistake with her books—a quiet, decent, middle-aged woman now working in the camp laundry, in other words, in one of the most privileged jobs in the camp. Two or three times a month she used to slip into the children's home, profiting from her contacts with the guards: she had an "arrangement" to launder their clothes. Once inside, sobbing quietly, she would comb Anastas's and Vera's hair for them with the remains of a comb and pop villainously red fruit drops into their mouths straight from her pocket. Outside, in the "free" world, Sonya had been childless, but here she had acquired from a casual encounter two of them at once.

"She adores her children, but just before you got here the poor girl was caught with one of the free employees. So now she's on detachment, as far away as you can get, haymaking. They've separated her from the children," Anya explained in her calm Mennonite voice.

It suddenly came to me that Anastas and Vera were the only ones in the entire group who knew the mysterious word "Mamma." Now that their mother had been sent elsewhere, they sometimes repeated the word with a sad, puzzled intonation, looking around uncomprehendingly. "Look," I said to Anastas, showing him the little house I had drawn, "what's this?"

"Hut," the little boy replied quite distinctly.

With a few pencil strokes I put a cat alongside the house. But no one recognized it, not even Anastas. They had never seen this rare animal. Then I drew a traditional rustic fence round the house.

"And what's this?"

"Compound!" Vera cried out delightedly, clapping her hands with glee.

One day I noticed the man on duty in the guardhouse playing with two small puppies. They were gamboling around on a sort of bed he had made for them on the guardhouse desk, by the telephone. Our guard was tickling the puppies around their ears and under their neck. There was such a sentimental, good-natured look on his peasant face that I plucked up my courage.

"Citizen Duty Officer! Let me have them for the children! They've never seen anything like them. Never in their lives . . . We'll feed them. Sometimes the group has leftovers. . . ."

Startled by the unexpectedness of the request, he had no time to erase the look of humanity from his face and reassume his customary mask of vigilance. I had taken him by surprise. And so, opening the door of the guardhouse a fraction, he reached out and handed me the puppies and their bedding.

"Just for a week or two . . . till they get a bit bigger. And then you must return them. Working dogs, they are."

On the porch at the entrance to the senior group's hut we created our "pets' corner." The children quivered with delight. The worst punishment imaginable now was the threat: "You are to stay away from the puppies!" And the greatest possible incentive was: "You can help me feed the puppies!" The most aggressive and the greediest of the children gladly broke off a bit of their white-bread ration for "Pail" and "Ladle." These were the names the children gave the puppies—familiar words that they heard regularly in their daily life. They understood the comic quality of these nicknames and giggled over them.

It all came to an end some five days later, amid great unpleasantness. The head doctor of the children's home, a free employee, Eudokia Ivanovna, discovered our pets' corner and was terribly upset.

A source of infection! They'd warned her that the new "fifty-eighter" was capable of anything, and how right they were!

On her orders the puppies were immediately returned to the guards, and for several days we went around with our hearts in our boots, awaiting reprisals—removal from this cushy job and assignment to haymaking or tree felling.

But just then there occurred an epidemic of diarrhea among the infants' group. The head doctor had so much on her mind that she forgot all about us.

"Well," said Anya Sholokhova, "that's over. It's no good grieving. Especially as the little dogs really are working dogs. They're the Alsatians who'll be taking us on parade when they grow up. And if necessary they'll seize any prisoner by the throat. . . ."

Yes, but that would be when they grew up. Till then . . . I remembered how our children had smiled at them just like mainland children. How they had put food aside for them, saying "that's for Pail" and "this is for Ladle." They had realized for the first time that it was possible to think of someone other than themselves.

The diarrhea outbreak proved very persistent. The infants died off in droves, although they received intensive care from both free and prisoner doctors. The conditions in which the mothers had lived during pregnancy, the high acidity of their milk, and the climate of Elgen had all taken their toll. The main trouble was that there was so little even of this milk—acidulous from their grief— and less of it with each day that passed. A few lucky infants were breast-fed for two to three months. The rest were all artificially fed. But if they were to hold out against toxic dyspepsia, nothing would help as much as even a few drops of mother's milk.

I had to take leave of my senior group. Petukhov, the prisoner-doctor who had been called in for consultation, recommended that as a "nurse with a bit of education," I should be transferred to look after the sick infants. He undertook to instruct me himself. For several days I attended the prisoners' hospital, where Petukhov worked, and he hurriedly taught me all I needed to know. I conscientiously worked through *The Medical Assistant's Handbook*, I learned to apply cupping glasses and to give injections, even intravenous solutions. I returned to the children's home a full-fledged "member of the medical staff," much encouraged by Dr. Petukhov's kind words about me.

Dr. Petukhov was rewarded for his goodness, his intelligence, and his decency with a great happiness, a unique event in those days: he was suddenly rehabilitated in that very same year, 1940, and left for Leningrad. People said that the famous flier Molokov, his brother-in-law, had personally interceded with Stalin on his relative's behalf.

The infants' little cots were pushed close together. There were so many children that to change every single diaper in quick succession would have taken an hour and a half. They all had bedsores, they were getting thinner, and they were wearing themselves out with crying. Some of them gave out a thin, plaintive wail, no longer expecting anyone to take notice. Others set up a desperate, defiant howling, vigorously fighting back. And there were those who no longer cried at all. They simply groaned as adults do.

We performed like clockwork. We fed them bottles, administered medicines, gave injections, and—our main activity—changed diapers. We endlessly folded and refolded the still-damp calico diapers. We grew giddy from constant to-ing and fro-ing for fourteen hours at a stretch and from the powerful stench given off by the enormous pile of soiled diapers. We even lost all desire to eat, we who were always hungry. We gulped down with revulsion the watery semolina left over from the children's meal, just to keep body and soul together.

But the most appalling thing of all was the arrival every three hours, with every change of shift, of the nursing mothers to "feed" their infants. Among them there were some of us—political prisoners—who had taken the risk of bringing an Elgen child into the world. They peered in through the door with an anxious question on their miserable faces, and it was hard to tell what they feared more: that the infant born in Elgen would survive or that it would die. But the vast majority of the nursing mothers were professionals. Every three hours they staged a persecution campaign against the

medical personnel. Maternal feelings are a splendid rationale for
misbehavior. They hurled themselves on our group with unre-
peatable language, cursing us and threatening to kill or maim us
the very day that little Alfred or little Eleanor (they always gave
their children exotic foreign names) died.

When I was transferred to the isolation ward, at first I was even
glad. There were, after all, fewer children there; only the complicated and acutely infectious cases. There it would be physically
possible to attend to each individual case. But the very first night
shift I did there I felt an unbearable spasm of spiritual nausea.

There they lay, little martyrs born to know nothing but suffering. The one-year-old over there, with the pleasant oval face, already had a spot on his lung. He wheezed and made convulsive
movements with his hands, which exhibited bright blue nails. What
should I say to his mother? She was Marya Ushakova from our hut.

Or take this one, on whom the sins of his father were visited.
The progeny of that cursed criminal underworld: a case of con-
genital syphilis.

Those two little girls at the end would probably die today, while
I was there. It was only the camphor that kept them alive at all.
The prisoner-doctor, Polina Lvovna, before she went out into the
compound, begged me not to forget the injections.

"If they can only hold out until nine in the morning, so that their
death throes don't come while we are on duty."

Polina Lvovna was from Poland. She had only been in Russia two
years when she was arrested. It may have been from unfamiliarity
with our ways, or simply because it was in her nature, but she was
scared of her own shadow, poor thing. Scared and absent-minded.
She was capable of holding a stethoscope to the chest of a two-
month-old baby and instructing it in a matter-of-fact way: "Patient,
breathe in. Now hold your breath!" She was a neuropathologist, and
not used to treating children.

I particularly recall one night in the isolation ward. Not just an
ordinary night but one of those "white nights" you get in the far
north. It was almost the last of the year. But it was not at all like
the ones in Leningrad: no gold-colored skies and, of course, no
huge buildings asleep beneath them. Indeed, there was something
primeval about it, a feeling of something deeply hostile to man in
that icy white flush in which normal outlines were held in quivering suspense: the bare sugar-loaf hills, the vegetation, and the

buildings. And the night was infested with the buzzing of mosquitoes. This buzzing drilled its way not only into our ears but into our hearts. No mosquito net could save you from the poisonous bites of this winged pestilence, which resembled the normal mosquitoes of our mainland about as much as a rabid tiger resembles a tabby cat.

The light suddenly went out, as so often happened, and all that remained was a small night light, dimly winking on the table. By the flickering glow of that night light I administered hourly injections to a dying baby. She was the five-month-old daughter of a twenty-year-old inside for some petty crime. The baby had been in the isolation ward for some time; whoever was on duty would say as she was relieved, "Well, that one will probably go today."

But there was still a spark of life in her. She was a skeleton clad with aged, wrinkled skin. But the face! The baby's face was such that we called her the Queen of Spades. The face of an octogenarian, wise, sardonic, full of irony. As if she knew it all—she who had stopped in our compound, in that little world of hatred and death, for a brief moment of time.

I was using the large needle for her injection, but she didn't cry. She only grunted feebly and looked straight at me with the eyes of an infinitely wise old lady. She died just before dawn, on the very borderline, when the first faint patches of pink are seen against the lifeless backcloth of Elgen's white night.

The dead body became once more that of an infant. The wrinkles smoothed themselves away. The eyes, prematurely initiated into all the mysteries, closed. There lay the emaciated body of a dead child.

"Little Sveta has passed away!" I said to the woman who was taking over from me.

"Sveta? Oh, the Queen . . ."

She broke off and glanced down at the rigidly extended little body.

"No, she doesn't look like the Queen of Spades any more. And her mother's away. . . . She's been drafted to Mylga."

They are never to be forgotten, those Elgen children. I'm not saying that there is any comparison between them and, say, the Jewish children in Hitler's empire. Not only were the Elgen children spared extermination in gas chambers, they were even given medical attention. They received all they needed by way of food. It is my duty to emphasize this so as not to depart from the truth by one jot or tittle.

And yet when one calls to mind Elgen's gray, featureless landscape, shrouded in the melancholy of nonexistence, the most fantastic, the most satanic invention of all seems to be those huts with signs saying "Infants' Group," "Toddlers' Group," and "Senior Group."

2

· *"A breeze amid the sweetbrier"*

Where had all these children come from? Why were there so many of them? Was it possible in this world of barbed wire, watchtowers, parades, inspections, curfews, solitary confinement cells, and work parties that anyone could still experience love or even primitive sexual attraction?

I remember how excited I had been in my youth—which fortunately was over before the epoch of the sexual revolution—by Hamsun's* definition of love: "What is love? A breeze rustling amid the sweetbrier, or a squall that snaps the masts of boats at sea? . . . It is a golden glow in the blood." By way of contrast, there was this cynical aphorism from one of Ehrenburg's† early characters: "Love is when people sleep together."

For Kolyma in the forties, even the second definition would have been too idealistic. When people sleep together . . . But this implies that they have a roof over their heads, the same roof; and that they have some sort of couch where they can sleep; and that they belong, in their sleep, only to themselves and to each other.

In the Kolyma camps love meant hasty, perilous meetings in some sketchy shelter at your place of work in the taiga or behind

---

* Knut Hamsun (1859–1952): Norwegian novelist, awarded Nobel prize in 1920.
† Ilya Ehrenburg (1891–1967): Russian novelist and journalist.

a soiled curtain in some "free" hut. There was always the fear of being caught, exposed to public shame, and assigned to a penal labor brigade, i.e., posted to some lethal spot; you might end up paying for your date with nothing less than your life.

Many of our comrades solved the problem not just for themselves but for everyone else in a ruling the ruthless logic of which showed them to be genuine descendants of Rakhmetov.* "Love is impossible in Kolyma," they said, "because here it expresses itself in forms offensive to human dignity. There must be no personal relationships in Kolyma since it is so easy to slip into prostitution pure and simple."

There would appear to be no room here for argument on principle. Nothing, indeed, is to be done except to illustrate the theme with scenes showing the traffic in living human bodies in Kolyma. Here, then, are some such scenes. (I should add that I am writing only of cases concerning women from the intelligentsia, imprisoned on political charges. The professional criminals are beyond the bounds of humanity. I have no desire to describe their orgies, although I had much to put up with as an involuntary witness.)

A tree-felling site at Kilometer 7 from Elgen. Our brigadier, "Crafty Kostya," was doing the rounds, not on his own, but with two of his cronies. They looked us women over as we set to with our saws and axes.

"Goners!" commented one of the cronies, with a dismissive gesture.

"They need fattening up. Where there are bones, there's bound to be some meat," philosophized Kostya.

"What about that young one over there, the small one?"

Seizing their opportunity while the guards were warming themselves at the campfire, they approached two of the youngest girls from our brigade.

"Hey, sweetie! My pal here would like to compare notes with you."

"Compare notes" was a euphemism, a concession to the proprieties. Without it not even the most case-hardened professional would open negotiations. But the fancy talk stopped there. The high contracting parties now descended to a form of speech stripped of all euphemisms.

* Principal male character in Chernyshevsky's novel *What Is to Be Done?* (1863); he represents the embodiment of positive, revolutionary virtue.

"I'm the forwarding agent at Burkhala" (one of the most terrible of the gold mines), "so I can put you in the way of sugar, butter, and white bread. I'll give you shoes, felt boots, and a really good padded jacket. I know you're a prison detainee. It doesn't matter—we can come to an arrangement with the guards. We'll have to fork out, of course! There's a shack available. About three kilometers from here . . . It's not too bad; you can toddle that far. . . ."

More often than not merchants such as these went away empty-handed. But occasionally they did get themselves a deal. However sad it may seem, it went like this. From stage to stage: at first tears, terror, indignation; then apathy; then the stomach protested more loudly, and not only the stomach but the whole body, every muscle —for trophic starvation leads to the breakdown of proteins in the body. And sometimes there was the voice of sex too, which made itself heard from time to time despite everything. And above all there was the example of one's neighbor in the bunks who had recovered her health, had acquired some sort of clothing, and had been able to exchange her sodden, tattered sandals for high felt boots.

It is hard to describe the way in which someone ground down by inhuman forms of life loses bit by bit all hold on normal notions of good and evil, of what is permissible and what is not. Otherwise how else could there have been in the children's home infants whose mother might have a diploma in philosophy, and whose father might be a well-known burglar from Rostov?

Some of the women who had short sentences or who had managed to get out of the camps before the outbreak of war but without the right to return to the mainland (often former Communists sentenced for CRTA—counter-revolutionary Trotskyist activity—which in 1935 had meant a mere five-year sentence) rushed headlong into Kolyma marriages as soon as they were through the camp gates, totally disregarding the possibility of mésalliances. I remember one such woman, Nadya, who the day before her release defiantly challenged those of her hutmates who sought to scare her off: "You will all end up as withered old maids, you pinched virgins! I'm damn well going to marry him, whatever you say! I know he spends his time playing cards. I know that he's a yokel and that I am a university graduate in Scandinavian languages. But who needs my Scandinavian languages? I'm tired out. I want my own quarters and my own fireside. And children of my own . . . New ones . . . Those back on the mainland we shall never see again. So the thing is to have some more while I can."

Sometimes the result was not heartbreak but a real comic turn. For example, there was the story of Sonya Bolts's "instantaneous" marriage.

Sonya, a quiet, unassuming textile worker from a little town in Byelorussia, had somehow managed to collect a stiff sentence for CRTA—a fact at which she herself never ceased to marvel. She had already served five of her eight years when all of a sudden a paper arrived from Moscow regrading her offense from CRTA to "negligence," and her sentence was correspondingly reduced to three years.

Sonya was beside herself with joy and so overlooked the fact that the document had been two years in transit. The main thing was that she had to proceed immediately to Yagodnoye, which was where people were released. It was there that the sacred rite of "regularizing" one's Form A, which redesignated convicts as "former prisoners," i.e., discharged prisoners, was solemnized.

At the headquarters of the Area Administration for Camps in Yagodnoye a little window like that of a ticket office opened up on certain days of the week. It was from this window that the ex-zek (ex from that very moment) received the hallowed Form A, her hands trembling with happiness. The workers at the gold mines in the vicinity always knew when the release of a contingent of women from Elgen was due to take place, and the suitors would gather there to await the event.

After folding her Form A once and once again, Sonya Bolts reverently tied it up in her kerchief. At that point a large individual in a shaggy fur hat came up to her and said in a hoarse voice: "Beg your pardon, citizen . . . You've been released? Well, that's grand. . . . I'm from Dzhelgala. My own master, as anyone will tell you. I'd like to compare notes with you."

Sonya scrutinized her suitor critically and put to him a somewhat unexpected question.

"Tell me, you are not a Jew, are you?"

"No, citizen, I can't say I am. . . . Mustn't tell a lie . . . I'm from Siberia myself, from near Kansk."

"Why do I even ask?" sighed Sonya. "Who'd ever expect to find a Polish Jew in this benighted corner of the earth! I suppose it's lucky you're not one of those . . . Karakalpaks. . . . How should I know?" And after a short pause Sonya said, "I'm willing."

The funniest thing of all was that this couple subsequently lived for many a long year in total harmony, and in 1956, after their rehabilitation, husband and wife left together for Kansk.

There was everything—from comedy to tragedy—to be encountered in our strange, primordial existence.

Love too? Love, as seen by Hamsun, that "golden glow in the blood"? I would maintain that it did sometimes put in an appearance among us. However heatedly our rigorists (and they were particularly numerous among the Mensheviks and the Social Revolutionaries) denied the possibility of pure love in Kolyma, love there was. It sometimes visited our huts unrecognized by the bystanders, humiliated, abashed, and defiled; but for all that it was love, true love—that very same "breeze amid the sweetbrier."

One of its mysterious visitations took the following form. After roll call one day the list of punishments ordered by Camp Commandant Zimmerman was read out. Zimmerman herself was an educated person, but she merely signed the orders drafted by the chief disciplinary officer. The form of the words varied: "Five days solitary, escort to work" . . . "Five days solitary, not to go to work."

Finally we heard one extract from the orders of the day which aroused laughter even from our ranks, from those who had been listening despondently with a sinking heart, wondering for which of us that night would mean not the blessed luxury of collective bunks and huts but the stinking frozen planks of the solitary confinement cell.

". . . relations between a male and a female convict," the duty guard read out, "involving a horse standing idle for two hours. . . . Five days solitary, not to be taken to work." Later on the phrase "relations between male and female convicts involving a horse standing idle for two hours" would become a popular joke in the camp. But at the time our laughter quickly died out and gave way to horror. Those two were done for. . . .

He was a former actor, who had worked with Meyerhold.* She

---

* Vsevolod Meyerhold (1874-1940): director and drama theorist; from 1923 director of the Meyerhold Theater in Moscow. Arrested and deported in 1937; died in camp.

was a ballerina. For a time their previous professions had given them a privileged position in the camp. At Magadan they had both been with the "cultural brigade." This was a serf theater that staged shows for the camp officials who were bored in those provincial backwaters. It fed its actor-prisoners on a comparatively generous scale, and under one pretext or another left them more or less free to go around without escort. The two of them managed to meet from time to time outside the camp. What happiness! It was all the more acutely felt, perhaps, for its fragility, its precariousness from one minute to the next. It was to endure for exactly five months. And then she was discovered to be pregnant. There was one well-trodden path for pregnant women in the camp; it led to Elgen, to the ranks of the nursing mothers recruited from the criminal riff-raff, to the children's home.

They were separated. The convict–nursing mother was now issued with rough boots and a third-hand quilted jacket instead of tutu and ballet slippers. Her little son died in the children's home before he was six months old.

In order to get to see her he pretended to have lost his voice. He was "unable" to act on stage any more, and so the work assigner, whom he knew, after calling him a blockhead, agreed to "fix him up" as one of a prison draft assigned to Burkhala, a gold mine located in the vicinity of Elgen.

And now in place of the happy-go-lucky life of an actor in the serf theater he endured by his own choice all the horrors of the hell on earth that was Burkhala. He worked his insides out at the mine face: he fell ill, he became a goner. After a certain time he succeeded in getting taken into the Northern Camps (Sevlag) Cultural Brigade, which from time to time came to visit us in Elgen to relieve the tedium by entertaining the camp officials with a variety show. A number of prisoners selected from the trusties and shock workers were allowed into the back rows.

They met! They actually met! Speechless with joy and anguish, she stood there beside him in the wings of the Elgen camp club hall. Old beyond her twenty-six years, all skin and bones, no longer beautiful, his heart's desire was restored to him.

Finding it hard to put the words together, she could only repeat over and over again how their little son had been him to the life, how even the tiny fingernails had been his daddy's all over again, how within three days the baby had succumbed to toxic dyspep-

sia because she had had no milk to give him and the little mite had
had to be fed on artificial milk. She couldn't stop talking and he
kissed her hands with their broken, hopelessly grimy nails and
implored her to be calm for they would have other children. And
he slipped into the pocket of her jacket a crust of bread he had
saved up and some sugar lumps with shreds of plug tobacco adhering to them.

He had good contacts in influential trusty circles and he arranged
to have her assigned to what by Elgen standards was a plum job—
carter at the stables. It was the nearest thing to happiness. Going
around without a guard, after all! She started to get well, recovered
her looks, and received notes from him regularly. But what had
they to look forward to? Each of them had a ten-year sentence plus
five years' deprivation of civil rights. But was it so imperative to
look forward? She read his notes a hundred times over and beamed
with happiness.

So why all of a sudden "five days solitary, not to be taken to
work"? It emerged that he, with the help of some people he knew
in the camp administration who were patrons of the arts, had contrived to obtain a fictitious work assignment to Elgen and had lain
in wait for her and her horse near Volchok, a spot some five kilometers from the camp compound. And then of course the two of
them had tethered the knock-kneed, stunted apology for a Yakut
horse to a tree. But some wretched creature had spotted them and
denounced them to the authorities. Hence the incident, punishable
with solitary confinement, "relations between a male and a female
convict involving a horse standing idle for two hours."

Roll call was over, and it was time for the guard to arrive to take
the culprits off to the punishment cells. "As long as they don't
take him," she said, pulling her rags around her more tightly in
anticipation of the penetrating dampness of the cell. "As long as
they don't take him. He's had chronic pleurisy ever since he was
in the gold mines."

"Where is she? I have a note for her," said a voice.

The voice belonged to Katya Rumyantseva, who was allowed
around without an escort. She had the job of bringing in the water
supply on her ox. What a splendid girl! She had managed to get a
note past the guards.

"Thank God! It's all right!" she exclaimed with joy, scanning the
letter. "Tomorrow and the day after they're putting on perform-

ances for the camp officers at Yagodnoye. So they're not sending him to the punishment cell after all, merely giving him a reprimand. . . . They need him! And as for me . . . I can stick it out. . . ."

She was the first of all those sentenced to the cells to arrive at the punishment block, making her way with her graceful ballerina's walk to spend five days in hell.

Who would not envy them!

3

· *The stick and the carrot*

The year I spent working in the children's home was a rest period in my camp curriculum vitae. I. gave thanks daily to fate and Dr. Petukhov for transforming me into a member of the medical staff. I wore a clean, warm jacket. Each morning I marched out of the central compound at Elgen with the second shift, not into the prickly mist of the frozen taiga and the December or January cold, but onto the premises of the children's home, warm and soothingly redolent of soiled diapers. Each day I received a respectable portion of manna from heaven in the form of the watery semolina slop left over from the children's meals. And finally, I lived in a hut where the warden was our dear Marya Dogadkina. It had an improvised iron stove hissing away in the evenings, and there was hot water bubbling in a large tub. I could always take shelter from the bitter cold, and before I went to sleep I could even permit myself the luxury of a companionable poetry recital—a real, solid session as the guest of Lena Yakimets up there above me, on the second tier of bunks.

We might, for instance, regale each other, in a conspiratorial whisper, with Gumilev.* What a comfort he was! What a lovely

* Nikolai Gumilev (1886–1921): poet, founder of Acmeist movement. First husband of Anna Akhmatova. Shot after defiantly confessing his involvement in an anti-Bolshevik conspiracy.

thought it was there in Elgen that a long way off on Lake Chad there lived a beautiful giraffe. There he was, the spotted beauty, roaming around as though nothing had ever happened. Then, interrupting each other, we recalled aloud from beginning to end the poem about the old raven and the ragged beggar talking over their moments of supreme bliss. That was what mattered—to be able to recall moments of bliss even while lying on upper bunks in Elgen.

> Old man raven, all of a flutter,
> Likes to tell in his fast, raucous stutter
> Of the dreams of adventure and power
> That he dreamed up there in the tower . . .

Lena was working as a roofer. Each day she was up there, repairing the roof with bark strips. She valued her work highly. It was quite different from being a general laborer. The main thing was that there were always four walls near at hand. You could always slip into the hut when your limbs were about to go numb. It was not the taiga, but nevertheless she got so paralyzed with cold by the end of the day, poor girl, that she was already nodding off as she took up the verse:

> Of how, soaring aloft in effortless flight,
> The slums of reality banished forever.
> He was reborn a swan—so gentle and white . . .

Lena fell asleep and it was my turn to take over . . .

And a Prince emerged from the horrible beggar.

It was all right for me: I was on the second shift. But Lena was with the first. At half past five in the leaden Elgen morning. The first shift included the roofers and the workers at the agricultural base and the stables. But those at the children's home, the hospital, and the state farm administration were all on the second shift. A whole hour's grace, and what a delicious interval it was, this extra hour of dozing in the morning when you could hear everything and yet at the same time every fiber in your still-warm body could luxuriate in each additional moment of half-waking repose.

"First shift!" Marya Dogadkina proclaimed. "Get up girls, whoever's on the first shift!"

And up they got, groaning, to wind their puttees; then came the clangor of their ladles as they filled their mugs with hot water. We turned over, and any faint sense of shame at having been accorded this privilege paled before the tremendous joy of being able to close our eyelids and postpone the commencement of a new day for one whole hour.

There was also a third shift. But that was for the aristocracy, billeted not here but in the hut for ancillary personnel. That was where the trusties could be found: the work assigners, the foremen, the canteen and stores personnel. They had individual trestle beds and bedside tables, instead of plank bunks, in their hut. There was a table in the middle of the hut, covered with an openwork tablecloth of freshly laundered sacking, and the bulb above the table shone so brightly that in the evening it was perfectly possible to read or sew.

The really frightening thing is that wickedness became part of the daily routine, a feature of our life. We had already grown accustomed to what has to be called, for want of better words, our way of life, and we discussed the details of our existence as if referring to something quite normal. The visions of our previous life receded further and further into the past, and the pithy saying of the professional thieves gained more and more currency: "It was long ago and never happened anyway."

There was hardly anyone who recalled, for example, who Elena Nikolaevna Sulimova, the wife of a former Chairman of the RSFSR Council of People's Commissars, was before she got put inside. A research worker, a doctor, she was now universally looked upon as on her last legs—or worse, a goner. She was never parted from her quilted jacket, which had become stiff as a board with dirt; she hid away from the communal bath routine; and she went around the canteen carrying a bucket into which she slopped all the dregs of the soup from other people's bowls. Then she sat down on the step and greedily gobbled up the slop straight from the bucket, like a sea gull. There was no point in talking to her about it. She had entirely forgotten her old self.

Then there was Marusya Ostreiko, our compound overseer, who somehow contrived even there to keep up the peroxided blondness of her tresses. She ran around the compound in a fetching little fur coat, crying out challengingly, "Come on now, girls." Marusya was clearly a superior being, irrespective of who she may have been when free.

However odd it may seem, a category of specially reserved jobs was to be met with here, too. Those who had served as work assigners, foremen, or cultural section staff normally graduated back to work as trusties, even after they had been temporarily suspended for some misdemeanor.

Our Hut Number 7, of which Marya Dogadkina was warden, catered to the third estate in the camp. Not for the trusties, nor for the "sloggers" who were permanently assigned to manual labor outside the compound. Our hut housed those who already possessed a specific camp speciality and were valued for their work. Greenhouse workers on the camp farm, carters and attendants from the stables, junior medical personnel, nurses, and cleaners.

Marya insisted that everyone bring back with her from work each day at least a small bundle of firewood. There was more than enough lying around. The difficulty at times was to make off with a bundle and smuggle it past the guards under your jacket, but it was certainly a reasonable demand. It meant that it was always warm inside the hut. And we had our pans—somehow conjured up by Marya—in which, without the guards' knowing it, we could cook in the evening wonderful preparations from frozen turnips. Each evening the bread rations were meticulously laid out on a sheet of plywood and the extra portions secured to them with slivers of wood. We took strict turns to receive the crust. Each night Marya got up several times to turn over our footwear, which was drying out next to the iron stove; by morning it was all dry for us to put on.

It was nice in our hut, especially in the evening when there was the homely smells of boiled turnips, washing, and sometimes even of cod-liver oil that the hospital personnel had contrived to smuggle out in small quantities at a time.

But our domestic bliss rested on the summit of a dormant volcano, for there was always the Registration and Distribution Section, the main executive arm of our fantastic State. At any given moment the hut door might slam to and the work assigner come in holding long scrolls of paper in his hand. These were the lists of the work-party drafts drawn up in the Registration and Distribution Section. In a special penal parade-ground voice, pitiless and brooking no question, he would proceed to bawl out one by one the names of those posted to such-and-such a site or such-and-such an area. All of us would be sitting on our bunks, as motionless as statues, and those who heard their names called out would groan quietly and curl up as if a bullet had hit them.

Many considered the shock of being drafted to a work party every bit as bad as being arrested. Or perhaps worse. If you were arrested, there was always the hope of a mistake, of some misunderstanding. If you were drafted, there could be no misunderstanding because it had been decided by the Registration and Distribution Section. You were unerringly and efficiently yanked out of the pitiful refuge in which you had been hiding, hoping to be forgotten about. No, they hadn't forgotten you. And you were ejected once more into the icy mist.

Particularly sensitive to the appearance of the Registration and Distribution Section in the huts were those prisoners who had been in Elgen in 1937–38, at a time when we, prison detainees, were behind bars in our solitary confinement cells in Yaroslavl.

"Although you prison types are supposed to be the ultimate in dangerous political prisoners, you weren't here for the worst of it, you were sitting it out in that Yaroslavl prison of yours," the old Elgen hands, Sonya Tuchina, Masha Ionovich, and Lyusya Dzhaparidze—daughter of one of the commissars who were shot in Baku—would tell us.

From their words we learned just what the arrival of a Registration and Distribution Section messenger meant in 1937, at the height of the Garanin era. Especially if he came at night.

"To Serpantinka. And nobody's ever come back from there."

Colonel Garanin was Stalin's viceroy in those frozen wastes of Kolyma, Emperor and Absolute Ruler of all Kolyma at the end of the thirties. . . . The colonel was devoted mind and soul to the cause of higher production. He felt so deeply for the gold-mining output plan that he was incapable of dissimulating his righteous wrath when he saw some enemy of the people feigning jaundice or undernourishment and failing to apply himself or herself energetically to pushing his or her wheelbarrow. And since Colonel Garanin was choleric and impulsive by nature, he would not infrequently pull out his revolver and shoot the loiterer dead—on the spot—at the mine face right where he was working.

More often, though, the colonel displayed commendable restraint and jotted down the names of the saboteurs for future reference.

A little later, the next day in fact, he would issue an order: So-and-so and so-and-so, for counter-revolutionary sabotage, in the form of systematic underfulfillment of the plan, have been sentenced to the supreme measure of punishment.

Lists along these lines were read out at morning inspection and evening roll call. The reading completed, the guards would add, "The sentence has been carried out."

Sometimes people figured on Garanin's lists without having had any personal encounter with the colonel, evidently by reason of the crimes of which they had been convicted. Again the Registration and Distribution Section courier would appear in the hut, surrounded by armed guards and camp officials.

"So-and-so, with kit! And so-and-so, with kit!"

People would jump down from their bunks and desperately, with maniacal deliberation, start searching for the damp leggings they had left by the stove to dry. The Registration and Distribution men would urge them to get moving, with transparent hints that they would hardly have any need of leggings.

Among the names of those who never returned I particularly recall that of an Old Communist, Nushik Zavaryan. The tale of her exploit had made the rounds for many years now. Our Marya Dogadkina would tell the story of Nushik to each new lodger in our hut.

"She must have got fed up with living. . . . A proud girl she was. . . . She put up with cold and hunger, but the humiliations were more than she could bear. She sat down and wrote a statement to the head of Dalstroi. 'How long,' she wrote, 'is this rule of arbitrary terror to last?' The most interesting bit was the address. Her statement was addressed: 'To the Governor General of Kolyma, from the Leninist-Bolshevik prisoner Nushik Zavaryan.' . . . They took her away to Serpantinka. . . ."

The few lucky ones out of those who fell within the orbit of Garanin's justice managed to get off with nothing worse than an additional sentence. It was called a Garanin sentence. In our hut, for example, one such ten-year sentence on top of the old one had been handed out to Liza Keshvi, a relative of the official assassin of Kirov, Nikolaev.*

* Leonid Nikolaev (shot 1936): young Party member accused of assassinating Kirov, the head of the Leningrad Party organization, in 1934, allegedly on the orders of Zinoviev, Kamenev, and Trotsky.

We former prison inmates arrived in Kolyma in 1939, after Garanin's time. But later on we learned that on Pechora there was someone called Kashketin who was Garanin's double as regards his style and methods of work. So it was quite clear: these irascible, peppery colonels, who had exceeded their authority and assisted Stalinist justice in dealing with the vast masses of saboteurs, were in no way exceptional but constituted part of a carefully elaborated general plan.

In the post-1939 period the activity of these people had, it seemed, become a thing of the past. By then visitations from the Registration and Distribution Section were often the prelude to no more than being sent off on work assignments from which it was almost impossible to emerge alive. New charges leading to the firing squad were now manufactured individually, on the strength of some informer's report to an operations officer.

Besides that, we received the enthusiastic attention not merely of the Registration and Distribution Section but also of the Cultural-Educational Section. This in itself was a progressive development, as the work of the Cultural-Educational Section was evidently based on the premise that even out-and-out enemies of the people might respond to benevolent re-education efforts.

The Cultural-Educational Section put up a lot of posters and slogans. In the canteen there were "Wash your hands before eating!" and "Pine extract helps protect you from scurvy!" In the camp club there was "Our selfless labor will restore us to the family of the workers." And at the gates to the compound there was "Let us fulfill and overfulfill the state-farm production plan for this quarter."

The political enlightenment program consisted in the main of someone loudly reading extracts from six-month-old newspapers. But in the children's home the prisoner-doctors and prisoner-nurses were permitted to attend political training sessions conducted by the head doctor, Eudokia Ivanovna, for the benefit of the free workers.

Eudokia Ivanovna was over forty before she became a doctor, and had started off as one of the auxiliary medical personnel. She was now over fifty, but she was still quietly astonished by the permanent wave she sported and by her magic ability to write out prescriptions in Latin. With her total devotion to the regime and her fanatical faith in Marxism-Leninism, she had implicity accepted as gospel truth all that she was told about terrorists and saboteurs when she signed on to work in the Dalstroi system. However, her peasant's sense of reality occasionally compelled her to take a closer look at us. She would even launch into vague remarks about dastardly agents of international imperialism who were getting to young girls, who maybe weren't all that bad in themselves, and implicating them in their own dirty work.

It was this theory of hers that inspired Eudokia Ivanovna to suggest to our Cultural-Educational Section that we—the women prisoner-employees in the children's home—should be allowed to attend her political lectures. Her carefully suppressed kindness and compassion for us were transmuted into a burning desire to re-educate us, the enemies of the people, who, quite incomprehensibly, were turning out on closer daily acquaintance to be conscientious workers and even—damn it—fine human beings. The head doctor was determined to assist our re-entry into the family of the workers. It was with precisely this in mind that she had signed on as one of the voluntary activists of our Cultural-Educational Section.

I had exactly the same feeling toward the head doctor as she had toward me. I desperately wanted to take her education in hand. Because despite all her prolix speeches about the majesty of Stalin and the wicked deeds of those enemies who had insinuated themselves into positions of command in our Party, despite the episode with the puppies that spring, I felt sympathy for this typical beneficiary of the era of adult education and women's rights who had learned to make out prescriptions in Latin. Somehow it seemed to me that my own efforts all those years ago must have contributed to the transformation of Dusya, the medical orderly, into Eudokia Ivanovna, our head doctor. Sometimes I had a clear picture of this Dusya devotedly following my lectures from one of the front rows in a large workers' education auditorium.

But since it was highly unlikely that I, a prisoner-nurse, would be entrusted with her education, I readily agreed to go and see how she would set about reindoctrinating me. It might be that as a result of the direct human contact she would start to fret a bit. If these are our enemies, she might say to herself, who are the decent people? As a good start is half the race, I made a point, even after my night shift, of attending punctiliously every one of Eudokia Ivanovna's political talks. I had further incentive because she produced for us some scraps of information from recent newspapers, to which we had no access.

I distinctly remember one such political talk. We were studying

a speech by Molotov. The speech referred to the progressive significance of the Nazi regime for the German economy. Unemployment
eliminated, highways built. Within an eight-year period Germany
had been transformed from a poverty-stricken country crushed by
the Treaty of Versailles into one of the leading European states.

Eudokia Ivanovna slightly lowered her voice at this point and
advised us in confidence that at the present stage of relations with
our powerful neighbor we should not use the term "fascists" but
say "German National Socialists." She accompanied this with a conspiratorial wink, intimating that these polite forms would shortly
bring us great benefits, of which the naïve Nazis had no inkling.

And so the year went by. It must have been the most uneventful
in my camp existence. My work was exhausting but bearable. There
was the stinking, humid heat of our wonderful Hut Number 7.
Each night I was terrified at the thought of being assigned to a work
party. I was under the aegis of the two determinant forces—the
Registration and Distribution Section and the Cultural-Education
Section.

Time went by with gathering speed. July 1941 was around the
corner.

4

· *War! War! War!*

The news spread like a Siberian forest fire.

"The Germans! The fascists! They've crossed the frontier. . . ."

"Our troops are falling back. . . ."

"It's not possible! How many years have we been saying, 'Not
a yard of our land will we give up!' "

The huts in Elgen were buzzing with the news. No one slept
that night. We had a sense of awakening from some silly, tiresome
dream. The unexpected blow had the effect of bringing us back to
reality, and we looked around us uncomprehendingly.

Why were we here? Why were we playing this devilish game
with such solemnity? Why did we say our piece, "Article number
such-and-such . . . Sentence, so many years . . . ," at each roll
call, then form lines to file past the guardhouse? How had we sunk
so low? Could we really have thought of establishing a roster to determine who got the crust?

No, we were now no longer just forestry workers, carters for
the stables, or nurses for the children's home. We had suddenly recalled with utter clarity who was who. . . .

We argued ourselves hoarse. We tried our best to discern what
lay ahead. Not just for ourselves but for everyone. We, the outcasts,
racked by four years of suffering, suddenly felt ourselves citizens of
this country of ours. We, its rejected children, now trembled for
our fatherland. Some of us had managed to lay hands on scraps of
paper and to trace a message with a stubby pencil: "I ask to be sent
to the most dangerous sector of the front. I have been a member of
the Communist Party since the age of sixteen. . . ."

Just as if the thirteen thousand kilometers of hatred, calumny,
and suffering which separated our Kolyma huts from the land of
human beings had ceased to exist.

"Perhaps 'he' has had second thoughts. He did say 'Brothers and
Sisters. . . .' That has never happened before. Perhaps his heart has
failed him."

"Hardly. A heart like his would never falter. . . . But his common sense . . . His common sense would tell him that there's no
point in keeping in prison millions of people who are ready to fight
the fascists with their bare hands. After all, in his heart of hearts
he knows what we are like."

In those feverish days and nights the person we most envied was
Masha Mironovich. Her five-year sentence would be up any day
now. And of course Masha would be dashing off to the front. Our
only worry was that she might not reach her native Byelorussia in
time—it was already caught up in the conflagration. "I'll get through.
. . . I've got my wits about me. . . . I'll keep to the byways."

One evening on our return from work we came across Masha
Mironovich lying on one of the topmost bunks. Her eyes were red
with crying and fixed immutably on one point. Marya Dogadkina,
our hut warden, was making desperate signs to all of us: "Don't ask
her any questions, say nothing, just let her be!"

We learned about it later. Masha had been summoned to the

Registration and Distribution Section, where she had had to countersign a document to the effect that she was to remain in the camp
for the duration of the war. Masha thus turned out to be the first
on the list of the new class in the camp—the "extra-termers." In the
course of the next six years the number of these continued to grow.
At first the extra term of imprisonment handed out to them was
"for the duration of the war," but later it simply became "pending
further orders."

Two days later at roll call the powerful voice of the chief disciplinary officer made itself heard. On this occasion his order was not
immediately intelligible to us: "All you Burgs, Bergs, and Steins,
fall out on the left. All you Hindenburgs and Ditgensteins and so
forth."

They were organizing a special maximum security hut for Germans. Panic ensued. As always, there were tragicomic misunder-
standings. People laid into Anya Sholokhova: How dare she hide
under a Russian surname! She—a fascist. What sort of a Russian
could her husband be? A fine Russian, to have married a fascist!

One of the girl professionals had a fit of hysteria, swearing that
she had acquired her name—Schiffmacher—with the last passport
she had stolen. How the hell was she to know that there was about
to be a war? She couldn't even get her tongue around the name
anyhow, and always pronounced it Schachermacher. And in fact her
personal data showed that she was Olga Vasilevna Karyakina. But
her old passport had been ditched long ago . . . when she first
landed in jail. "You're my fellow countrymen. You can't shove me
into a fascist hut!"

Since the disciplinary officer had been precise in his instructions
—"All you Burgs, Bergs, . . ." I automatically found myself in this
bizarre group. The guard officer—a Kazakh not exactly well versed
in the "national question"—came right up to me:

"Come on, Ginzburg!" heavily stressing the incriminating second
syllable, "get your things together and move over to the German
hut."

Luckily I managed to dash into the Registration and Distribution
office and persuade the inspector to look into the case and determine
my nationality and citizenship. It was a very near thing.

This must have been the first time in the history of the world
that being Jewish was an advantage.

Our head doctor, Eudokia Ivanovna, at the risk of her good name, kept begging the Registration and Distribution Section to grant us a reprieve, if only for a week, before taking us away from our work. To no avail! It was already clear that our hopes of a nation united—ourselves included—in the defense of the fatherland were illusions. The "enemies of the people" were not only disqualified from association with the people, but a fortiori, under wartime conditions the regime in places of detention was to be drastically tightened up. In our case—given the sort of offenses for which we had been sentenced—we were supposed to be employed solely at hard manual labor out of doors under armed guard. The head doctor was instructed to make do with the services of common criminals. It was no use for Eudokia Ivanovna to argue with tears in her eyes that these desperadoes should not be allowed within gunshot of the children. And as for free medical personnel—why, the total number of free nurses for the entire children's home was three.

The Registration and Distribution Section insisted on having its way. Terrorists, saboteurs, and spies had to be under the ever vigilant eye of the guards! Didn't the head doctor realize that there was a war on?

Good-by, children's home, my quiet little backwater. Three days later we were already being sorted according to our articles. In double-quick time, before we were even split into working groups for drafting to distant tree-felling sites, we were turned into an agricultural brigade. As far as production was concerned, we were of no use to anyone. Farm management didn't know what to do with us. But that didn't matter. What did matter was that we were under escort. The vigilance of the escort troops had improved 100 per cent. They never stopped counting and recounting, lining us up in columns of five, rechecking our personal data. In between times we did a bit of weeding or hoeing under the relentless rays of the taiga sun, trying to ward off the attacks of the mosquito swarms.

"Give us mosquito nets! We can't take any more."

"Where are they supposed to come from? Anyhow, you'll manage. . . . We have other things to think about now besides you. . . . So many decent people are dying every day for no good reason, and all you can do is . . ."

And Fedya the Tartar—a guard previously renowned for his good nature—looked at us as though it were we who had let the Nazi gangs into the fields of Byelorussia.

But after a few days of such "work" (for want of a better word) in the fields, our hands and faces were a mass of sores and fearful blisters, festering from the dust, and itching so badly that we felt like howling.

At night it was one search after another. No sooner had you closed your inflamed lids than the hut door banged and the penetrating voice of Lydia, the assistant overseer, boomed out, "On your feet! Line up!" And lowering her voice as if to deliver an aside, "Come on you women, get a move on. It's a general frisk!"

We lined up and the guards and their professional women assistants from the overseer's staff hurled themselves at our bunks, the upper and the lower ones. It was a pogrom! Feathers flew, you might say—except that there weren't any feathers to fly. For the past four years we'd been sleeping on our bundles spread on top of the straw. But our so-called personal belongings, even those received in authorized parcels, were relentlessly confiscated. All the resources of our technical genius were tossed into the rubbish bin. Look what they've been up to—frying food! All our homemade saucepans and frying pans, all the little knickknacks each of us had fashioned for herself with indestructible feminine ingenuity were destroyed beyond repair.

Photographs? Forbidden! Embroidery on lengths of sacking? Not allowed! Your own spoon? Where did you get that from? You're not supposed to have anything of your own!

It was the clash of two irreconcilable currents of thought and of feeling, two types of reaction to the war.

We were ready to forget and forgive now that the whole nation was suffering, ready to write off the injustice done to us. Just as long as we didn't have to stay there, a sitting target for sadists and a source of gratification to paranoiacs! Please let us go to the front! We're at war with the fascists, after all!

Our jailers were obsessed with tightening everything up. "What's the point of pussyfooting around with enemies of the people? There's a war on, after all, against the fascists!" This attitude was evidently the product of inertia; the inertia of set phrases, hammered into people's heads since childhood. "In answer to so-and-so's maneuver, we shall intensify . . ." and "No mercy for the enemy!" But who the enemy was, was left to be elucidated later. . . . As the result of some incomprehensible logic, the hatred directed at the Germans spilled over onto us. After all, the enemy who with each passing day was penetrating deeper into the great expanses of Russia could not be seen from Kolyma. But there were these homebred enemies of the people right here at hand. So our betters prepared to strike!

The Cultural-Educational Section had virtually ceased to function. They stopped giving us our letters and wouldn't even read last year's newspapers to us. We were told nothing, but it was amazing how somehow or other we did learn what was taking place. The most terrible thing in our terrible life was to hear the names of the captured towns. They were waiting for us in the hut when, more dead than alive, we returned from the fields. Smolensk, Minsk, Kiev. Dear Lord, Rostov gone too? It's not possible! But it was! More madness—another aspect of the madness with which this century of ours was so generously regaling us. At night Lena and I continued, despite everything, to recite poems to each other. We huddled together in the upper bunk, although the others shouted at us from time to time. More often than not it was Blok* we recited:

> The last, the foulest age of all
> Shall you and I behold.
> The lowering sky 'neath a pall of sin
> The laughter stilled on the lips of men,
> The longing for oblivion.

Blok had had a premonition. . . . It fell to us to behold the reality.

Alongside the truthful information that filtered into the camp, fantastic rumors also circulated. These were pure inventions—we called them "hallucinations."

"Have you heard? Kolyma's been sold to the Americans!"

"With or without inhabitants?"

The notion of trading in people—as things now—surprised no one.

"Let's hope the inhabitants are included!"

"Stop talking rubbish!"

"Why is it rubbish? After all, they did sell the Chinese Railway. Minus inhabitants, it's true."

Then there was a ferocious argument in the making between those who dreamed of being rescued at any price and those who—damn it —wanted to stay in their own country if it killed them. The voice of a skeptic provided a summary:

"Stop squabbling. Don't you see: even if it were true, they'd

---

* Aleksandr Blok (1880–1921): symbolist poet, considered the most important Russian poet of the twentieth century.

liquidate the lot of us before they carried out their bargain. We know too much to be sold off abroad."

Quite apart from the suffering of our country as a whole, which we outcasts experienced even more acutely, with even more bewilderment than others, we now had our own private horror. The children! Our children! For in the situation as it now was, the first to be trampled underfoot would be those orphans of ours.

Many of us had families in towns already occupied by the fascists. Within a short time we were to learn that the Hitlerites in Rostov had shot Lara, the fourteen-year-old daughter of our neighbor in the next bunk. We had always admired the photograph of this extraordinarily beautiful girl, and listened raptly to her letters when they were read out to us by her mother. As it happened, she had a rare spiritual beauty to go with her looks. Lara, who was of mixed Jewish-Ukrainian blood, had been shot because her best friend at school denounced her—a girl who was jealous of Lara's friendship with one of the boys in their class.

By now the town that appeared most often on the list was the one that tore my heart in two: Leningrad. . . . Alyosha . . . my first-born. I don't think it's just hindsight. I knew that I would lose him. I had never put it to myself in words, but I had always felt it with the infallibility of instinct. He was still alive in those first months of the war, but I was already numb with desperation. I peered into the darkness of the hut at night with my sleepless eyes. I couldn't lift a finger to ward off that disaster. I lay as rigid as a corpse. I *knew*.

In the daytime I tried to behave sensibly. For what we tend to call sensible is whatever serves to silence our one true, inner, prophetic voice. I tried to listen to the comforting assurances offered by my comrades. Of course, he wouldn't be old enough to get sent to the front. He wasn't even sixteen yet. The war would end. I volunteered that my Leningrad relations who had given Alyosha a home were good, dependable people. They would do everything humanly possible to get him evacuated in time. That was the version I tried to impress on others, and on myself, during the daytime. But at night—at night I lay there, knowing full well that this, the greatest punishment in my life, was awaiting me, and that the day, the hour, when it would be administered was at hand.

One day one of the free nurses from the children's home came walking past the field where we were busy hoeing. It was Anya, the Kolyma counterpart of Ella Shchukina,* the "gold digger": she had come to Kolyma to earn a fast buck so as later to be able to dazzle with her gowns, if not perhaps Miss Vanderbilt, then at least all the fashion-conscious young ladies of her home town of Buzuluk.

In broad-minded prewar times Anya used sometimes to come and visit me when I was on night duty in the isolation ward of the children's home; she would interrogate me at length on the sort of clothes currently worn by the wives of bigwigs in the fashionable resorts. For she herself had never been out of Buzuluk. At the same time Anya was very kindhearted and sensitive; she was given to bursting into tears of compassion for the sick children and their unfortunate mothers, and she would slip the nursing mothers sugar lumps and candy. I depended on her for one invaluable service: she used to forward my letters to Mother "through the bars." Mother was the only person I wrote to. In the case of my children and my sister, I did not want to compromise them by involving them in "links with a detainee."

I looked around. The guard was some way off. I rushed up to Anya. "Anya, dear, please send my mother a telegram! She must be half dead with anxiety. Ask her where Alyosha is, Anya!"

"I beg your pardon?" The gesture of a Roman matron—an indignant toss of her frizzy, dyed curls. "I'm a loyal Soviet woman, aren't I? A war like this, and you think I'd help the enemies of the people?"

A few steps farther on past me, and Anya suddenly swiveled around and came back toward me. The Roman matron, who had just been the beneficiary of a lesson in the highest civic virtues at her political indoctrination class, had given way to the simple girl from Buzuluk.

"Don't cry! I'll send it. I remember the address. You'll be the undoing of me. . . . The devil himself would be hard put to know who's good and who's bad around here."

At roll call Lyolya—a professional criminal—had been barged into and knocked down just outside the guard hut by a hefty young guard who was unaware of his own strength. She screamed out in a hysterical, high-pitched shriek:

"Are you supposed to be serving your country, you shit? People

* Character from the novel *The Twelve Chairs* by Ilf and Petrov; satirical embodiment of avarice.

are fighting back there, and all you can do is bash us women about and mount guard over anything in a skirt. You hero! Look at you, you blubberguts! You stinking swine!"

Lyolya was hauled straight off to the punishment cell. The guard was left literally quivering with rage. His face had gone all blotchy. He even felt the need to justify himself to such pathetic witnesses of the scene as us.

"Attention, you there," he bawled out savagely, striding along our column. "Attention, you lot! Why the hell am I stuck with you? Why did I have to get the job of guarding you degenerates? How many times have I asked to be sent to the front? They won't release me!"

Autumn was at hand and the timber-rafting season was almost upon us. Before the war the medical personnel in the camps had been able to play some sort of role in the selection of people for this heavy work; they had on occasion managed to save those most enfeebled by scurvy. But now everyone was hauled off—the only thing that counted was which article you were in for.

This time I was sent off to Sudar, a very remote tree-felling site in the taiga. It was, by all accounts, a site where they felled not just the usual variety of trees, but timber for building. People said that among the women sent there on previous work parties, suffering a prolapse of the uterus from having to lift excessive loads had become commonplace—rather like catching a cold. But among all these reports, there was one encouraging rumor: the guard commander was Artyomov, a decent man.

"This guard officer—is he really a decent type?"

"Well, they don't all have to be tarred with the same brush, do they?"

But the argument died down before it could become heated. We weren't the women we used to be. We found talking a strain. We kept our mouths shut. We straggled along, a formation of shadows from beyond the grave, just as I had described the scene in my very first verses about Kolyma:

And I stumble along in the ragged throng
Of women who are convicts.
Our backs are bent, our gaze is spent—
It's a painting by Käthe Kollwitz!*

* Käthe Kollwitz (1867–1945): antifascist German printmaker and sculptor, whose art depicts hunger, distress, and war.

5

· *Minus 49 degrees Celsius*

Minus 49 degrees Celsius was the worst possible reading of all, because the official humanity of the medical regulations could come into operation only when the thermometer read minus 50 degrees. Minus 50 degrees meant that the administration could cancel work in the forest that day. But it was futile to try getting the duty guard, nicknamed Freckles, to admit that it was reading 50 and not 49 below.

The thermometer hung on the black log wall of the guard hut. It seemed an anachronism; it was as if the universe had already succumbed to some general cataclysm, while here on earth—otherwise restored to the very first, primordial days of creation—this memento of a lost civilization had happened to survive.

"Just look! Take a look from this side. It's quite clear—minus 50," I said, holding a match up to the gleaming column of mercury.

Freckles, wearing his new white, tanned-leather jacket, which squeaked as he moved, edged closer and flicked his lighter.

"Dead on 49!"

November, December, January, February; for me, life each day began with precisely this argument: minus 49 or minus 50 degrees. And the rations grew ever smaller. Even for the top category—for the very highest felling output—the bread issue was 400 grams. But which of us could hope to fell enough to qualify for that? We could hardly stand upright!

The cold and the hunger; the hunger and the cold. This must have been the blackest, the most lethal, the most evil of all my winters in the camps.

And yet I had been relatively fortunate compared with the others. At the very last moment, just as the Sudar contingent was on the point of leaving the central compound at Elgen, while Marya Dogadkina was waving good-by to us with tears in her eyes, up rushed Lydia, the assistant overseer, and gave me a message from the Registration and Distribution Section to the effect that at Sudar they had arranged for me to be put on only half of the output norm. I was to spend half of the day sawing—and that only to get in wood for heating the huts, the guards' quarters, the kitchen, and the dispensary; and I would spend the second half of the day on medical duties. In the absence of any other medical personnel, ran the message, my year's work in the children's home had undoubtedly brought me up to the standard of medical assistant. So I should be allowed to deal with patients in the evening. And I could thank my lucky stars; after all, I was a prison detainee and it was wartime, and not everyone had the chance of loafing around and twiddling her thumbs in dispensaries.

This was the source of authority for my daily passage of arms with Freckles. The certificate exempting the prisoners from being escorted to work on certifiable days had to be signed by the guard, the work forewoman, and a medical representative. Within our reinforced, seven-man guard detachment, Freckles was in charge of weather. Our commander (whom we chose to call by his real name, Artyomov, because he really was a decent man) realized that he himself was a little too soft-hearted for that particular job. So that's how Freckles came to be chosen; he wouldn't admit to minus 50 until he could see at least minus 53.

Sudar is eighteen kilometers from the central compound at Elgen. It is a fabulously beautiful corner of the virgin taiga, with majestic stands of forest timber, treetops soaring toward the stars. There was a taiga river—a powerful presence even under its icy crust—tumbling untidily over itself beneath the lofty canopy of the sky. There were low, sugar-loaf hills, faultless in their symmetry. At night the sky blazed with galaxies that were somehow oppressively ancient, taking the imagination back to the first beginnings.

But the main thing about Sudar—that place where we were dying of hunger and cold, where we were, as we variously put it, "on our last legs," "packing it in," "waiting to kick the bucket"—was that there was an abundance of fuel and food at hand. If you looked around you could see brilliant-white ptarmigans flying overhead, swooping as they went; you could hear the cry of the woodcock. The river was full of all the local varieties of fish: grayling, katalka, omul. The snowy expanses were dotted with impenetrable thickets of raspberry and currant bushes, and there were pine nuts galore. If one only knew how; if one only dared to accept the taiga's food offerings!

Alas, we didn't know how, and we didn't dare. Even the armed guards had no time to spare for hunting or fishing. They had more

than enough to get through as it was. They had to drive us or coax
us from one place to the next, count and recount us, report on us,
and await with fear and trembling visits from their superiors. And
they had good cause to be afraid! There was no way for them to
know what to expect. If the visitors found warm, well-heated huts,
smelling comfortably of hot food, they might react with a sneer and
a hostile comment: "Very cozy indeed. Other people are dying at
the front and you've fixed yourselves up with a vacation resort!"

On the other hand, if they found icicles in the corners of the huts
and a number of sick goners groaning on their bunks under a huddle
of rags, they were capable of bursting out on a quite different note:
"You've got them dying like flies in there! You're just turning them
into so many Form A's. Suppose you tell us who'll be responsible
for fulfilling the plan if they all kick the bucket. Pushkin?" And that
would be another excuse for a reference to the heroes dying at the
front, with a candid aside about those who "entrench themselves in
order to guard the skirts" and who "sit out the war in nice warm
guard huts. . . ."

Incidentally, the reference to huts at Sudar is not meant to be
taken at face value. Only the one set aside for the guards bore any
resemblance to a proper hut. Our quarters were two sagging shacks,
barnacled with ice, overlaid with snow, and with holes in the roofs.
Every day we had to plug these holes anew with lengths torn from
old, cast-off duffle coats. The kitchen was housed in a cabin that
rattled with every gust of wind. The dispensary took the form of a
lean-to on one side of the guards' hut, which itself was equally
vulnerable to all the winds that blew. That completes the site inventory. A real Viking camp!

I did only three hours an evening in the dispensary, when the
sloggers returned from the forest. I smeared iodine on their
scratches, issued aspirins for "sore heads" and salol powder for
"stomach trouble," put ichthyol bandages on their boils, and dressed
any frostbitten parts with cod-liver oil. In addition I gave each one
of them a spoonful of cod-liver oil. I personally saw to its administration and poured it down their blissfully receptive throats. It was
a holy rite. I was paralyzed with fear lest I spill a single drop of the
treasured liquid that contained all our hopes of life.

This procedure was a source of endless self-questioning and self-
doubt for me. In fact, cod-liver oil was issued only for "severely
debilitated" cases, amounting to about half the total. But how was I

to distinguish? It was not as if there were anyone present who was not severely debilitated. My way of settling the matter ran contrary to Party teaching on the impermissibility of egalitarianism. Even if they didn't get a full spoonful each, it was to be given to them all. As long as it lasted. And thereafter . . . well, it was no good trying to guess what tomorrow might bring.

That exhausted the sum total of my medical practice. For the rest of the day, from six in the morning, I kept hard at it with a saw. In the fresh air at a Celsius reading, according to Freckles, of minus 49. Push and pull, push, pull, push and pull. Even in my sleep I continued to have visions of logs, thick or thin, unwieldy or easily handled, knotty or smooth. A lot of wood had to be brought back. Especially for the guards—they liked their warmth.

But there was no comparison between my sawing and what the others had to do in the taiga! In the first place, I had a sawhorse to hold the log steady. In the second place, all I had to do was saw the logs into lengths—not fell trees by the roots or pile wood up into cords. But the main thing was that my living quarters were close at hand. I could slip into the hut at any time and warm myself not at a bonfire with its thick, black, resinous smoke spiraling upward, but by the iron stove.

Yes, I was a privileged person. Dr. Petukhov really did save my life—dear Dr. Petukhov—when he took me on as a member of the medical staff. May he forget that such a place as Kolyma ever existed! My feeling of moral responsibility, of duty toward my comrades who were at that moment less fortunate than I, was all the more acute for that reason. I fought with Freckles for certifiable days until my throat ached.

"Fifty!"

"Forty-nine, dead on!"

"Fifty. I shall complain to the Medical Section!"

"Hah! Trying to frighten me, are you? If I put in a report, you'll be hauled off to slog it along with the rest."

There was a strict norm set down for each medical assistant to follow about exempting sloggers from work on grounds of illness, and I had already received two inspection visits from the head of the Medical Section, Kucherenko, with whom I had an extraordinary dialogue.

"An assistant who exceeds the norm for sick-leave slips won't be left kicking her heels in the Medical Section very long," Kuche-

renko said meaningfully, raising his heavy, frostbitten eyelids in my
direction. "The slogan now is 'All for the Front,'" he added in his
thick Ukrainian accent.

"But what good are they to the front if they are half dead,
Comrade Chief? It's just multiplying Form A's! And we won't get
a good mark for that either."

"Well . . . Why do you put down the same diagnosis for everyone—'alimentary dystrophy'? Don't you have any other illnesses?"

"Well, Comrade Chief, I don't actually know many diagnoses," I
answered with disarming frankness. "In my opinion, it's all the result
of starvation, the Latin name for which is alimentary dystrophy."

Oddly enough, that was in fact the case. There was no sign of
other illnesses. No inflammation of the lungs, no acute bronchitis, no
colds, which would have been natural enough, given the twelve-
hour working day out in the bitter cold. Only boils and trophic
ulcers; only the lurching gait of the sloggers, who seemed to lack
a center of gravity; only inflammation of the gums, and teeth that
could be pulled out with the fingers.

So I persisted in my primitive approach, based on the same egali-
tarian principle. It was the best I could do at the moment. Turn and
turn about, and that was all there was to it. Each evening after roll
call I visited each hut; and taking them one by one, strictly in turn,
I leaned over the first of the huddled-up figures on the bunks, and
then over the next.

"Nadya, you won't be working tomorrow. Tomorrow you're ill.
The same goes for you, Katya."

The next day I took the list with the names of those released
from work to the guard commander, Artyomov. He looked around
at his underlings and pretended to give a disapproving cough.

"What a lot of people off . . ."

Then he threw his sheepskin across his shoulders and added in
an equally stern tone of voice:

"Let's go and visit the huts. We'll check the medical situation. . . ."

The two of us emerged from the stuffy guards' hut, which reeked
of tobacco, sheepskin jackets, and some fatty-smelling stew. Above
our heads was the magical, star-strewn sky of the taiga night. All
around us was the unsullied whiteness of the snow. We walked quite
slowly down the path trodden in the snow that led from the guards'
hut to the sloggers' huts. A conversation started in which only the

words "commander" and "assistant" made it obvious where we were.

"Real trouble, assistant! Hitler's almost reached Moscow!"

"But surely he won't get through? Tell me, commander, he won't get through, will he?"

"The devil only knows! They shouldn't let him through. . . . But I wake up in the middle of the night, and I break out in a cold sweat. Is it thinkable? After all, the Soviet regime has been functioning for twenty-five years. . . . What do you think, assistant? Can we trust the Allies?"

His anxiety, confusion, and pain demanded an outlet, and there was no outlet for them in the company of Freckles and the eternally guffawing "Mongol." Thus the unheard-of thing—which flouted all the canons—occurred: he shared his nagging disquiet with a woman from the mysterious tribe of enemies of the people. Out of the depth of his fear for his country and faced with the threat of the collapse of all authority, he—a simple, wise, and kindly person—now trusted his intuition more than his official instructions.

We walked slowly down the narrow path between tall, dazzlingly white snowdrifts and suddenly saw that the sky above us was ablaze.

"Look! The northern lights!"

On further inspection it proved to be a quite undistinguished, faint red glow. But behind it there were streamers of light, pulsating in mad abandon.

Before going into the hut and donning his inscrutable mask, Artyomov concluded reflectively:

"As I see it, those who manage to get through this winter will come out of it all alive. That goes for both those here and those around Moscow. Correct?"

I didn't know. Each day I debated this same question, "Can we get through this winter?" with a real, fully qualified doctor—Olga Stepanovna Semenyak. She had been recently transferred there under escort and was assigned to general duties. This was the cruel punishment meted out to her by Zimmerman. Her offense was, as a doctor at the central compound at Elgen, to have attended prayer meetings of religious detainees in the camp boiler house. They were sectarians—Seventh-Day Adventists.

An assistant lecturer at the Kharkov Medical Institute, Olga Semenyak was a mere babe in arms where practical things were concerned. She couldn't fulfill even one-tenth of her work norm for tree felling. That meant death from starvation. We set about saving her, all of us together, as best we could, with crumbs of bread and frequent sick days.

"What do you think, Olga Stepanovna? Can we all pull through?"

"Hm . . . well, in general terms, trophic starvation, general functional disturbance, profound disturbance of the metabolism . . ."

"But the people here still don't look as if they're dying. Listen to the way they talk, the way they think. . . ."

By way of answer, Olga Semenyak quoted from the Bible about the spirit being willing but the flesh weak. Strange as it might seem, though they were not in high spirits, the women were energetic enough. Despite the damage to their organisms, they had an active inner life. They wrote interesting, thoughtful letters home and hid them under their straw mattresses, waiting for better times and an opportunity to send them along otherwise than through the camp post. They greedily lapped up the scraps of news from the front which came to them via the free employees—former prison detainees, loggers, and drivers. They recited from memory and composed poems. They even made jokes.

"Girls! Here's a riddle for you! What is the difference between Katya Kukharskaya and the rest of us? Can't anybody guess? Well, take a closer look! All of us look like Russian beggars, homeless vagabonds, while Katya looks like a *Czech* beggar." (Katya wore some weird garment, halfway between a waistcoat and a jerkin, which gave her, so it was thought, a West European look.)

Hunger. Each day the bread ration became more minute and more tantalizing. If you left half of it for morning (it was issued in the evening) you would stay awake all night. It would prevent you from getting to sleep, torment you through the straw pillow. Like lying on top of dynamite. You kept waiting for the morning to come so that you could eat it up. If you did eat it all at once in the evening, how would you manage, when you got up hungry in the morning, to stagger to work?

Some of us did adapt ourselves to permanent hunger. It was as though we had shriveled up. Others endured it more painfully, finding relief in passionate outbursts about unfair weighing of the ration or in feverish attempts to lay hands on something edible by other means.

Sometimes terrible things occurred. I remember one impenetrably black, starless night. All of a sudden the door of the dispensary burst open, and a woman with a face contorted into a dark mask tumbled in and immediately collapsed on the wooden trestle bed. I hardly recognized her. She was one of ours. In her arms she was carrying something miraculous—a large loaf of black bread. She hurled it onto the rough plank table.

"Eat it. I can't touch it. . . . At least you can have your fill, for once!"

"Where's it from? What's the matter?" I countered, already sensing that something irreparable had happened.

Long, anguished sobs, and then hysterical laughter:

"It's hell to be an intellectual! Absolute hell! After all it's not as if it were a tragedy, is it? Others do just the same to get themselves some bread. And I did it too. Earned it in the same way as thousands of other women earned it when there was no other way open to them. There was this peasant coming through the taiga. And I was sawing on my own. My workmate was out sick, you see. And the guard was a long way off at the time. What sort of peasant? I don't know. I didn't notice. I kept staring at the loaf. He pulled it out of his sack and showed it to me. He put the loaf straight down on the snow. I couldn't take my eyes off it. Now I can't even touch it."

I poured a gigantic dose of bromide into her mouth. I stroked her head. There was nothing I could say. She seemed to have gone completely numb. I remembered her as she was in our Car Number 7 of that first prison train en route to Yaroslavl. A merry, curly-haired girl, so pleased that she had managed to get her postgraduate thesis approved before her arrest.

I put my arms around her shoulders and led her into the hut. She had to be put to bed straight away and given an opportunity to forget. After her outburst of hysteria, she had become weak and could hardly put one foot in front of the other. The path from the dispensary to the hut was very narrow. It was walled in on either side by steel-blue ramparts of solid snow. We kept slipping and getting out of step with each other.

The clouds overhead suddenly parted, and far away in the firmament we saw icy, frozen stars. The stars of Sudar. There was a hard frost. It was minus 49 degrees Celsius.

6

Light in the darkness

At these tree-felling sites there was, in addition to the cook, the head
of supplies, the warden, and the medical assistant, one other person
of importance: a highly privileged person—the toolsetter. Usually he
lived in a separate cabin where a small stove purred away, giving
out a permanent red-hot glow. The toolsetter worked without any
fixed norm. He worked as need dictated, or rather, on the whole, as
he thought fit. He received extra portions from the kitchen.

As a rule the toolsetters were recruited from the veterans who
had been sucked dry at the mines and then slung out. All of them
were delighted with their soft job. Some of them grew so sleek with
the favors of the cooks that they even began taking bribes from the
sloggers, for it was the sharpness of the saws and the correctness
of their alignment that largely determined the possibility of sur-
passing the wood-cutting norm.

Our toolsetter at Sudar, Egor—or as he himself pronounced it,
Yogor—was an exception. Like the others, Egor could not have
managed general duties. All that remained of his right foot was a
short stump, and the toes of his left foot had become infected and
had started to rot; they now gave off a gangrenous smell, which accompanied him wherever he put in an appearance. But unlike the
others, he hated his job, because he had been sent to Sudar for
punishment. He had been caught red-handed by the guards at the
central compound at Elgen, carrying a pail of cabbage that had
been stolen by one of the prisoners at the state farm pickling station.
Egor, who was not under guard and had free passage through the
guardhouse, had undertaken to transport the precious cargo.

As bad luck would have it, the duty guard that day was that fine
figure of a man, Demyanenko, a tall, red-faced humorist, and the
meanest of the entire Elgen guard force.

"You've got a mighty big belly on you for such a skinny runt!
How so?" he inquired, leaning out the window of the guard room
into the passageway.

"Come on, open up your jacket! And make it snappy!"

The same evening the order for Egor's incarceration was read out at roll call. He was to do five days in the punishment cell without going out to work, followed by reassignment to Sudar. The whole episode plunged Egor into the depths of gloom. Dear me, he had really hit bottom—and from what a height! In the central compound at Elgen he had not been just one of the crowd: he had been the gravedigger.

Each evening when he visited me in the dispensary to have the dressing on his leg changed, he used to paint fabulous scenes of his free-and-easy life in his unconvoyed job. "Seriously, though, we were free to come and go past the guardhouse at any time! You could step along to the settlement and saw up a few logs and split them into firewood for the womenfolk. They'd give you a nice hunk of bread. And there's those of them not too stuck up that would even let you into their hut and give you a mugful of soup. And then in the compound too . . . You'd go and visit Polya, the cook, and she'd pour out a real large mugful of homemade beer. And you'd get as much gruel as you could manage to put away." He had lived in the hut for ancillary personnel. "And the work, well . . . it wasn't dusty . . . and you didn't have to sweat your guts out at it."

To console him I put forward objections. "Still," I said, "you had a lot of corpses to deal with and only three gravediggers, and it's no joke digging into permanently frozen ground. . . ."

Egor gave me a knowing grin and a wink. Every trade has its secrets. And, it seems, know-how is everything, even in such a delicate matter as the burial of deceased prisoners. It was winter almost the whole year, and there was snow aplenty. So . . . they would dig into one of the deeper snowdrifts without disturbing Mother Earth's stony surface, and in the spring, with the thaw, the dear departed were borne away on the spring waters—Lord rest their souls! They didn't spread infection, because they were nothing but bones, or, as you might say, pure remains.

"Aren't you ashamed, Egor?" I asked in distress, removing with my tweezers the smelly lint dressing from his frostbitten, gangrenous toes. "Here I am, doing my best for you, giving you treatment, and if I died you'd bury me in the snow. And my corpse would float away in the spring. . . . 'And the dead man floated off anew, In quest of a grave and a cross.'"

"Please, Eugenia Semyonovna," said the demoted gravedigger in a trembling voice, "do you think we haven't got any conscience at all? As if we wouldn't give our medical assistant a proper burial! Other people, well—but our medical assistant . . . we'll give you a real Christian burial, in Mother Earth, you can be sure of that. . . ."

He looked at me trustfully and disingenuously. He had a northerner's light blue eyes, devoid of lashes. His white eyebrows came together in a frown. He had just remembered that he was now retired, shorn of his plenipotentiary powers of inhumation. He heaved a sigh.

"Don't grieve about it. When they need an experienced grave-digger, they'll take you back again."

"We're both from the Tartar Republic. But I'm Orthodox myself. In the old days I lived in Elabug District, Kazan Province."

Egor's article was 58(2): armed uprising. A paragraph specially designed for collective farmers. Egor spoke calmly of his arrest, as if telling an epic story about some fire or epidemic. His only quarrel was with the unfair incidence of arrests from village to village.

"How many households were there in our village, and how many were there in Kozlovka? Nearly three times as many of them, there were, but they took the same number from both. Is that fair, I ask you?"

He seemed to find his removal from the post of camp gravedigger harder to bear than his actual arrest and sentence. I learned even more details of his blissful life in the central compound.

"Sometimes as you come back from work, the worksetter speaks to you, and it isn't just a quick hello. . . . I say to him, 'Good day to you, Sergei Vanych!' and he says to me, 'Hello there, Egor! How's tricks? How are you making out with your norm for stiffs?' and he laughs. . . . Whatever got into me to touch that cabbage? The terrible trouble I've had over that . . ."

To distract Egor, I put various questions to him.

"Where did you get your legs frostbitten, Egor? Moving from camp to camp, I suppose?"

"No, it wasn't then," Egor answered calmly. "It was when I first died. . . ."

It had happened at the Zolotisty gold mine. Egor was lying in the camp hospital. One day the medic was doing the rounds and saw that Egor had passed away—he must have given out all of a sudden. So the medic told the orderlies to take him off to the morgue. Egor, of course, didn't remember this part of it, but the men told him all about it afterward. He came to with a pain in his foot—

the one that was half chopped off now. He started groaning with pain. It stung like fire. Well, he pulled himself together and his mind began working again. He was still alive, it seemed!

The watchman at the morgue heard this horrible noise. He was one of those Turks, Chulumbei or something—or was it Kulyumbei? —he was off his rocker from that very day. It was frightening, of course. The man knew he'd stacked the stiffs tidily the night before, and then suddenly a dead man makes sounds right from the bottom of the pile. This Chulumbei of course yelled so loud that the guard heard and came running fast.

They pulled the corpses away from on top of Egor one by one. They chucked a padded jacket over him. And then they let him have it: "What business do you have, breaking into the morgue when you're alive and kicking?" they said. Why pick on him? It wasn't as though he had been playing the fool. Was it Egor's fault if the medic had blundered? Well, it was all right in the end. They really let him have it hot and strong, but they didn't beat him up, and they didn't put him in solitary. They sent him back to the hut.

Egor found hunger very hard to bear. He was thin to the point of emaciation. Even in his blissful job as a gravedigger he couldn't contrive to put the least suspicion of flesh on the large, knobbly bones of that big frame. The ravages wrought by three years at the Zolotisty gold mine were irreparable. The psychological hunger tormented him even more keenly than the physical hunger. He thought and talked of nothing but food. The only thing that forcibly distracted him at times from these thoughts was the pain caused by gangrene.

Our daily meetings for the purpose of dressing his wounds brought us closer together. We had a ritual for the spoonful of cod-liver oil, which I would pour into his mouth every evening. He was afraid to hold the spoon himself, fearing that he'd spill it, God forbid. His hands were all aquiver at the thought. This introduced a maternal note into my relationship with him, although he was ten years older than I.

It was getting on to mid-December. The end of that accursed year—1941—was approaching. I had somehow let it slip to Egor that the twentieth of December was my birthday. Would anyone remember me that day? Or was there anyone alive to remember me still? The shadow of a sudden thought flickered across Egor's face. During the next few days something came over him, something caused him to forget his usual preoccupations. He stopped hanging about the dispensary when the bandaging was over, and on these occasions he even came out with the words, "I haven't got time"— an inconceivable statement for him to make.

On the twentieth of December it was late before he appeared for his bandaging. I had already put my instruments away on the shelf and was about to go to the hut, when all of a sudden the smell of gangrene announced the arrival of Egor. In his hands he held a large, sooty cooking pot from which rose a delicate coil of warm steam. On Egor's face there was a look of beatitude.

"There, Eugenia Semyonovna," he said triumphantly, placing the pot straight down on the dispensary table, "I've come to wish you a happy birthday, see, and good health, and every kind of success. . . . And here's hoping you see your sons again. And look, we've got a present for you!"

The pot contained oat jelly. This was a dish that I associated with especially happy moments on the Elgen state farm. Its recipe was well known there long before our arrival. It was a complicated one. The oats—the kind you feed to horses—had to be put through a series of complex chemical transformations before they turned into jelly. They were soaked, squeezed out, and ground. Next you had to wait until they started to rise, and then add the leaven, then boil them. . . . The reward for all this labor was a thick, satisfying jelly of a beautiful light coffee color. It was our unanimous opinion that the taste reminded us of almond cookies. But how had this unheard-of luxury materialized there in Sudar?

It turned out that when he was getting his things ready for the move to Sudar Egor had actually managed to secrete about his person a small bag of oats stolen from the Elgen stables in his glorious grave-digging days. Luckily Demyanenko had not been on guard duty. He would have been sure to sniff it out. But Lugovskoy, as everyone knew, was slack, made no effort at all, just watched the clock. So there you were—the oats just came in handy for the assistant's red-letter day; as good as a birthday cake, in fact.

Egor's eyes sparkled. They gave off a light-blue radiance. His hands shook more than usual, from excitement. His one wish was that I should eat up all the jelly on the spot, in his presence, while he sat and enjoyed watching me. . . .

"Thank you, Egor Petrovich, thank you! Let's eat it together! You hold the spoon."

But he indignantly turned down my proposal. He merely said no, but I knew what he was thinking. He had used up his last reserve of food and had spent three days going through the complex technical processes of turning oats into this warm-smelling, velvety slop. Would he be doing all that just to eat it himself? No indeed! This peasant from Elabug, the first sign of whose presence was the smell of putrefaction coming from his "healthy," still-unamputated foot, wanted to give pleasure to a fellow creature in misfortune.

I stopped protesting. I ate up the oat jelly with the help of a bent tin spoon that smelled of cod-liver oil. He looked at me, his eyes alive with kindness and happiness. Yes, that was a moment of happiness for Egor, the former camp gravedigger, ahead of whom there lay four consecutive amputations—a piece at a time from the end of his legs—and death in that sector of the nether world which is called the "Invalid Treatment Center."

7

· *A land flowing with milk and honey*

In the early spring when, according to the state farm plan, tree-felling operations were due to end, we received orders to march back to the central compound at Elgen. This was for a new "grading" (the term "selection," as applied to human beings, had not then reached us) of the work force, those who had escaped death or dismemberment. We were then scheduled to join the "land-improvement" brigade for the summer season.

Thereupon it emerged, quite unexpectedly, that the Sudar contingent were the most productive sloggers of all those employed at tree-felling work. Real progressive workers! This unlooked-for reputation we owed to the fact that we had managed the return journey on foot. We had got back to the compound on our own two feet, after a thirty-two-kilometer march through the taiga without any losses, i.e., deaths en route. And this was at a time when

the "woodmen" of Tyoplaya Dolina, Zmeika, Kilometer 12, and
many other tree-felling sites had let their officers down so badly and
shown such base ingratitude! For they had literally had to be
dragged out of the forest, while those past being dragged had had to
have wayside graves dug for them. And of course a report had to be
made out for everyone who had been buried. You couldn't just leave
it at that—they were state property and had to be properly accounted for.

The first year of the strict wartime regime was bearing its fruit:
a sharp outbreak of illness, often fatal, and as the inevitable consequence, the failure of the Elgen state farm's economic plans. At that
point the pendulum again swung the other way. A stentorian hail
came from on high: "But who will fulfill the plan?" And after this
interpellation came acts of official humanitarianism of a sort that the
war seemed for a time to have abolished. A convalescent hut was
again inaugurated. The younger goners, whom it was hoped to rehabilitate as part of the work force, were given passes to this camp
resthouse. It had the atmosphere of Nirvana. Day and night they
all lay around on their bunks, chewing their 150 per cent bread
ration.

Even those cases of starvation not admitted to the resthouse began
to get a much more generous quota of rest days. During the lunch
break there were again goners lining up outside the dispensary, each
holding out a tin spoon. A few drops of elixir were poured into each
spoon—a nauseating, impure substitute for normal cod-liver oil,
called "fish extract."

Kucherenko, the head of our Medical Section, had now completely forgotten his recent threats ("any medical assistant who
dishes out sick-leave passes for no good reason will be whisked off
to slog it with the rest"). On the contrary, he was now loud in his
praises of the robust appearance of my Sudar patients, and compli-
mented me on "taking good care of the work force."

Then something fantastic happened. I was sent off for a month
to take over from the medical assistant at the dairy farm, who had
fallen ill.

"Zimmerman wouldn't agree to it at first," Kucherenko told me
in confidence. " 'No convicts on any unescorted assignment,' she said.
Still, I persuaded her—just for a month. It'll do you more good than
the resthouse, and you look as if you've a touch of scurvy yourself. . . . So off you go, have a good time, get yourself some cal-

ories! And then you'll be going back to the forest, to Tyoplaya Dolina."

(Kucherenko was said to be just as much of a self-made doctor as were we ordinary mortals. He had come to Kolyma as a fireman, it seems, but then had somehow become head of the Medical Section at Elgen. He was the roughest of rough diamonds, both in appearance and in conduct. But he was firmly tagged with the reputation of being not a bad man. Far from it: if he saw a chance to do good, he seized it.)

The dairy farm . . . the very words sounded to Elgen inmates like the designation of a fairy kingdom. A land flowing with milk and honey . . . The farm stood by itself, half an hour's walk from the central compound. The huts there were not fenced in, there was no guardhouse, and the guards were there only for show. People moved around unescorted from the huts to the cow barns, the calf sheds, the chicken houses, and the incubators. The calves and chickens were fed rich concentrates, fish meal, cod-liver oil, and skimmed milk, all of which the animals generously shared with their convict-overseers.

The farm was run by two free zootechnicians, Rubtsov and Orlov, who never called people terrorists, spies, or saboteurs. They made a point of referring to "our milkmaids," "our cowgirls," "our poultry hands." They greeted the women convicts first whenever they met them.

The dairy farm after Sudar and its tree felling was the equivalent of the Côte d'Azur after Kamchatka, or a cream cake after our daily gruel. And was I to be there for a whole month? I, the creature from the untouchable caste of prison detainees? To have a room all to myself, and to sleep on the iron bed standing in the corner?

The thought that I should be sleeping not on a plank bunk but in a completely separate cubbyhole of my own gave me back my dignity as a human being. Fate had granted me this happiness for only a short span; and it was all the more precious to me for that.

I remember my first night at the dairy farm. For the first time in several years I found myself alone in a room. The distant voices and the sound of steps outside the little gray window had given way to silence. Silence—what a long time since I had last heard it! How empty my soul had become in this painful chopping and changing between the tedium of hard manual labor and the torments of working as a camp medic. I seemed to have stopped reciting poems to

myself. But here I could make a new start. I should become myself
again. And in the silence the poems would come back to me. Blessed
solitude, a gift beyond treasure, especially after the fearful loneliness of compulsory, unrelieved togetherness. . . .

> O silence, thou art the sweetest sound
> Of all I've ever heard. . . .

The girls working at the dairy farm were mainly Ukrainians and
Latvians fortunate enough to have had practical experience of farm
work and to have been pulled in under the sort of articles deemed
"consonant" with working unescorted. In other words, for modest
political offenses such as CRA or SE (counter-revolutionary activity
and suspected espionage, respectively); or under 58(8–10); or for
minor misdemeanors verging on the political, such as SDE or SHE
(socially dangerous element, socially harmful element). Common
criminals were kept out, in the knowledge that they could not be
allowed anywhere near the cattle. But all elements represented there
applied themselves to their work with fantastic industry and devotion. Many of them got less than four hours' sleep a day. This
was not only because the "promised land" of the dairy farm saved
them from lethally dangerous manual labor on starvation rations, but
also because work in the dairy involved looking after living creatures
and thus tended to create an illusion of normal life. This impelled
them to abandon the obsessions bred by camp life in favor of preoccupations worthy of rational human beings.

The medical assistant had things particularly easy. She didn't
have the daily task of trying to decide which of two half-dead
prisoners should receive the last spoonful of cod-liver oil, and how
Kucherenko's medical certificates were to be distributed in such a
way that no one died of work. Here it was the other way around:
everyone was scared of being on the receiving end of a certificate.
They all did their best to put up with minor illnesses without being
ordered to bed, so as not to have to part, albeit for an hour, with
their calves and their chicks, so as not to earn a reputation for
slacking.

In the evening my main job was to massage the dairymaids' hands
and put dressings on their swollen fingers, which were chapped so
badly that they bled. The dairymaids brought with them into my
minute room the smells of the cow house, mild grouses about non-
delivery of fodder, and news of the comic names given to newly

born calves and heifers. (Each year the animals all had to have names starting with the same letter. And what inventiveness this gave rise to! I remember, for example, a bullock by the name of Beelzebub, and a beautiful little heifer called Bacchante.)

The clock on the wall ticked away. Augustina Peterson, the milkmaid, was warming her frozen hands in a tin basin and telling me in her staid Latvian farmer's voice all about a favorite cow left behind somewhere near Elgava. She spoke as if we were not in the second year of an unbelievably dreadful war, as if the ovens of Auschwitz were not burning merrily, as if there were no central compound at Elgen, a mere half-hour's walk away, no Zimmerman, no Registration and Distribution Section, no disciplinary department, no punishment cells of various shapes and sizes.

These happy days at Elgen were brightened for me by one other unexpected joy—an intense friendship that surged up almost instantly at the very first meeting, putting me in mind of the almost forgotten days of my youth and allowing me to rev up my thoroughly rusty, disused spiritual motor. My new friend was Willi Rupert—Wilhelmina Ivanovna, as everyone called her at the farm. She held the post of tally clerk, an almost unthinkable one for a prisoner, in effect that of statistician.

Willi had been terribly lucky during her investigation. For some reason or other, they had decided to deal with her—an employee of the "ideological front," a Communist with a period in the Latvian underground, the wife of a Secretary of the Party Regional Committee of Stalingrad—not according to the harsh penal regulations for people with that background, but as a member of a suspect nationality, like the other Latvian dairymaids on the farm. She was handed a mere five years under the much neglected SE article (suspected espionage). This allowed her to settle down on the beloved farm, helped by the fact that the senior zootechnician, Rubtsov, with his sharp eye for everything around him, saw that she had a very good head on her shoulders.

The year we met she was under forty, and her face was alive not only with intelligence and kindness but also with feminine charm. Her eyes, which mirrored her inner nature, were particularly remarkable: "round and hazel, hotly burning."

It was not only our common love of books that brought us together. We instantly sensed in each other an agonized need to think about life, for all its obvious lack of sanity. To hold it up to the light

and examine it, to make comparisons and derive general conclusions . . .

"What do you talk about all that time, right up to midnight?"
was the amazed reaction of Augustina Peterson, who could hear our
endless conversations through the partition wall.

What did we talk about, in fact? Well, about everything under
the sun: about war and fascism; about Buchenwald and Elgen; about
the fate of three generations, our parents', our own, and our children's; about the great riddles of the universe and the inexhaustibility
of human genius. And in the intervals we talked about how pleasant
it is to have the snow crunch under your feet when you are dashing
around Moscow in the evening, or even in Kazan or Stalingrad; of
the pleasure we used to get, when young, from marching in line
abreast in the mass parades. Little had we known then what a terrifying thing it is always to have to line up five abreast.

We were in a hurry to tell each other everything. We knew we
would soon have to go our separate ways. The unnatural presence
of a prison convict on soft, unescorted work could not last for long.

Suddenly there he was—an armed guard in the doorway of my
nice little room with its iron bed in the corner. He had a rifle over
his shoulder. He had come to escort me to Tyoplaya Dolina. This
idyllic name—"Warm Valley"—designated a remote marshland area
in the taiga, some twenty-five kilometers from the central compound, where they felled trees in winter and made hay in summer;
where there weren't even any huts; where the denizens had to live
in improvised shanties and tumble-down, drafty shacks; where, above
all, there would not be a moment's peace because they were all professional riffraff, to the very last woman.

We set out on our way, following the spring tracks in the taiga.
Once more I carried a knotted bundle over my shoulder. Once
more the boots of my temporary traveling companion squelched
through the mud, always right behind me. How I envied him those
boots: they kept out the wet. My poor old boots became totally
sodden with the first few steps I took, and, as in my prison days at
Yaroslavl, my joints were again giving me an unbearably sharp,
shooting pain. Unbearable? I would bear it, of course.

One forced march . . . and yet another. This time I was all on
my own, so there was no other prisoner even to exchange a word
with. The guard I had ended up with might as well be a deaf-mute.
He didn't even say "Come on, come on!" He just kept squelching

along, his eyes drilling into my back like the eyes of a mindless robot.

Well, enough of that, did the dairy farm really exist? Perhaps it was all a dream—those quiet evenings on the farm, my own bed, the books conjured up from somewhere by Wilhelmina, her eager, whispered confidences.

Just before we got to Tyoplaya Dolina, the guard suddenly came out with his first pronouncement of the journey. His first, and how apt it was!

"We're there," he said. "It's on the left—over there, where the animals are roaring!"

And roaring they were! A terrible wave of yelling and cursing rose from the valley into which the pack of women criminals had been herded. Snatches of their cursing and swearing, outbursts of hysterical screaming, and apelike shrieks were to be heard from far off in the taiga, serving as a landmark for travelers.

Here, thanks to the Registration and Distribution Section and Special Camp Commandant Zimmerman, I was being offered a vast field of activity on the same sardonic lines as previously: half the working day attending to the medical needs of this "production collective," and the other half doing general manual labor.

It would be hard to imagine anything more unendurable than such a combination. The position of a medical assistant among criminals is hard enough as it is. And to make their victimization of me all the easier, I had to go haymaking with them.

The first thing that happened in the morning was that well over half the women rushed over to the windbreak where all my phials were set out on a tree stump. They all demanded the same thing: "slips." When I refused to issue sick-leave certificates to those who were not ill, they screamed out fantastic curses and threatened me with all the forms of dire punishment which their pathological imaginations were capable of conjuring up. The one that most acutely engraved itself in my memory was the promise to "slash your peepers with a razor." I could picture it very clearly: I myself standing there, blind, doused in blood, my arms stretched out in front of me, encircled by this howling pack of wild beasts.

But to show how frightened you are is to sign your own death warrant. However overwhelming your instinctive terror and revulsion, you must speak to them calmly and even smile.

"Come, come, girls! I'm sure you know there's a norm for sick-leave certificates. No more than two to three a day for our entire contingent. Look how many there are of you! Why not take turns? Today you, Lida—your temperature is up—and you, Nina, because of the boil under your arm."

(My line was to speak to them politely and always use the polite second person plural form of address, whatever obscenities they might be spitting out. The unexpectedness of it sometimes helped cool them down, at least to some extent.)

A fresh outburst of curses, threats, and obscenities made the guards appear on the scene. They ordered incarceration in the punishment cell for "objectors." And after my "out-patients session" I was off to work in the fields, cheek by jowl with the same endearing patients.

But this time it was easier for me to bear it all. I knew now that somewhere, not all that far away from Tyoplaya Dolina, the promised land did exist—the dairy farm. And from time to time encouraging signals got through to me in the form of notes from Willi, or food packages containing bread and sugar. These signals came as opportunity offered, by courtesy of the supplies chief of our outpost, or of some newly arrived small contingent of prisoners. Willi's messages gave me grounds for hope: the zootechnicians were interceding with the Registration and Distribution Section on my behalf, and taking up my case with Zimmerman. They were requesting that I be assigned to the farm. Not as a member of the medical staff, but as a poultry hand. I didn't know what arguments they had deployed in support of this, but there was hope. I needed only an adequate share of patience.

I had more than a fair share of patience, enough to withstand work beyond my physical powers, starvation, and slavery. But never should I be able to put up with living among common criminals. To me they were as alien and incomprehensible as, say, the crocodiles of the Nile. I never got on terms with them. At times I even started to reproach myself. I needed to try more often to remember just what it was that had reduced them to such degradation. I thought of Dostoevsky. I kept trying to impress on myself that the characteristics of "brothers in misfortune" must surely be discernible through the outer shell of these evil people. My efforts to conjure up enlightened compassion or even a modicum of comprehension for their spiritual motions were of no avail. What was uppermost was a feeling of anguish—not for them, but for myself—that by some devilish conjuration I was condemned to a form of torture more fearful than starvation or disease, to the torture of life among subhuman creatures.

What shattered me were the "self-inflicters": those who inflicted wounds on themselves, sometimes involving horrendous physical pain. They would do this simply for the sake of not working, of taking things easy on their bunks. I remember a girl named Zoika, nicknamed Psycho. Abnormally ugly, with black pockmarks all over her, she aroused acute physical revulsion even in her neighbors on the bunks. All of a sudden she went down with a temperature of 40 degrees. She tossed about in a fever, and didn't know where she was. I was at my wits' end to know how to get her transferred from the depths of the taiga to a hospital. I was afraid that she might have typhus, which would reap its harvest here amid the overcrowding and the filth.

It was not until two days later that I paid any attention to her foot, which was bound up in rags. She put up a frenzied resistance to my efforts to unwind the rags and take a look at it.

"I told you, assistant, a self-inflicter!" exclaimed the guard commander, who had observed this scene.

He suddenly gave an almighty tug at the rags and exposed Zoika's foot to our gaze. What we saw caused even the guard to blanch. The big toe was transfixed with a large rusty nail that protruded on both sides of the bluish-black, swollen mass. In the area of the nail there was a nauseating, suppurating wound.

This was, of course, an exceptional case. But simulated abscesses produced by injecting kerosene under the skin, and cases of purulent conjunctivitis (from treating the eyes with a powder scraped from an indelible pencil) were commonplace in my medical practice at Tyoplaya Dolina.

There were moments when I feared for my own sanity. As luck would have it, one other nurse with a less compromising article than my own turned up in the Elgen area at that time. They sent her to Tyoplaya Dolina in place of me, and I was transferred to physical labor in a different sector of the taiga.

The haymaking station called Novaya Tyoplaya Dolina was located even deeper in the taiga. In fact, "station" was a misnomer. We were required to build our own shanties. By way of assistance, two knock-kneed little white Yakut horses were assigned to us. These two horses and the nature of the surrounding landscape all suggested to me a vision of our planet as it had been immediately after the Flood. And yet I was happy. In this place there was no professional riffraff. Only normal, decent people: spies, saboteurs, and terrorists!

I was handling a scythe for the first time in my life. Mowing across hummocks is a difficult job even for an expert male reaper. We went about it barefoot. We moved in line abreast, swinging our scythes from side to side, puffing and panting. We shuffled through the marshy bits and stumbled over the hummocks as best we could. At night we returned to our improvised shacks. We were soaked to the skin and plastered with mud up to the waist. Our sodden skirts clung to our legs. Those with "serviceable" boots tried at first to protect their legs from the icy water. But shod feet sank still deeper into the glacial quagmire.

After a fortnight of such work I again experienced that strange sensation of weightlessness in my body and that constant mist before my eyes which, I had known for some time, could be signs of approaching death. We no longer had the strength to fulfill our output norms. Our rations were steadily reduced. Even though underfoot there was untold wealth—clusters of honeysuckle bushes with their velvety, blue berries—we were so weak by the end of the day that we did not have strength enough to bend down and pick them. Moreover, the first frost came early and we were in danger of succumbing to the cold in our improvised shacks.

One morning I was terrified to find that for some reason or other I could not raise my head. Then I found out why, and there was no cause for alarm. It was simply that a tress of my hair had frozen solid to the straw bedding because of the snow and frosty slush that had drifted in through the cracks in the botched-up door. At that moment Kolya came into the hut, a cheerful, flirtatious guard from Vologda, who had been banished to the wilds of the taiga for the repeated offense of cohabitation with women prisoners.

"Get your things ready!" he said cheerfully, evidently happy for me. "There's an indent in for you. You're to go to the dairy farm . . . as a poultry hand!"

And he added respectfully:

"You must have been in that line of business outside, I expect. They asked for you by name. They've lost a lot of chickens. Only there's no transport—it's hoofing it or nothing. Can you manage it? I'll take you there myself. I badly need to get to the village. Can you make it? It's thirty kilometers and a bit over."

Will I get there? Dear Lord, on all fours, if need be. So the chickens have started dying off, you say? Well, who, apart from me, is capable of dealing with such a catastrophe? My dear Willi had managed this; and those golden friends of mine, Rubtsov and Orlov, the free zootechnicians. But how had they won over Zimmerman, the incorruptible Zimmerman?

I bundled up my worldly goods, now reduced to rags and bones. I urged Kolya from Vologda to get a move on. (Those from Vologda are by no means the worst of the guards to have as one's convoy, that's well known; no comparison with someone from the Ukraine or Tashkent. So if I really started losing control of my legs, Kolya would allow me to have a rest—he was a good boy.) And ahead of me was the dairy farm, the promised land, a land flowing with milk and honey.

8

· *Pallid combs*

I stood in the center of an enormous chicken house with a full pail in my hands, holding it above my head in desperation. The pail was terribly heavy. It contained mixed feed which had to be evenly distributed among the feeding troughs. But chickens, just like humans, are unable to distinguish friend from foe, and are equally ready to kill each other for the benefit of an extra beakful. I had opened the door to the chicken house only a fraction because the entire population was clustered around the door. It took all my strength to force my way in. . . . But once inside . . . inside, a frenzied cackling mass of several hundred of them hurled themselves at me, at the pail, and at the feed.

All my storybook illusions about chickens being the most harmless creatures in existence were dispelled in a trice. As the saying goes, "Even a chicken will bully the sad and the shy. . . ." And make no mistake about it, they're good at bullying—particularly the cocks. With much crowing and cackling, they pecked at my bare calves—I was not wearing stockings—and alighted on the pail, threatening to overturn it. One enormous feathered monster, resembling a Tsarist general, perched on my shoulder, from where he subjected me to insufferable insults. Another, a more down-to-earth fellow, rather like a rollicking drunken peasant, clambered on top of my head and also treated me to a flurry of ripe oaths. Idiots! I am here to give you your food. . . . What do you think you're doing?

I don't know how I would have come to terms with this winged pestilence, but aid was at hand in the shape of the senior poultry keeper, Marya Grigoryevna Andronova. She calmly took the pail from me and, in the space of two minutes, had its entire contents evenly distributed among the troughs, while giving the chickens as good as she got in the form of picturesque samples of the Russian vernacular. She sent me off to the feed point to fetch another two pails of feed.

I returned in the gloomiest possible frame of mind, carrying two more impossibly heavy pails. All was lost. Willi had kept warning me that the one important thing was to get on with Andronova. It would be no easy matter, because she simply couldn't stand women intellectuals who were good at scoffing omelettes but afraid of getting muck on their hands. A collective farm agronomist herself, she had not been able to stomach these fine ladies even then, before her arrest. Though she'd done her five years, they still wouldn't let her go back to the mainland—but she wouldn't stick up for loafers. Some might think—said Andronova—that she was giving herself airs because she had been employed as a free laborer for the past six months, with pay. It wasn't that at all! Simply—well, they were living creatures and needed to be treated properly, even though they were real stinkers, those Italian Leghorns. No comparison between them and our Russian chickens—ours had a conscience. Still, this wasn't tree felling or ditch digging. If you were on that, you looked after Number One, doing the odd stroke, not trying too hard, getting through the day as best you could. But here you had to work just as though you were on the mainland. When all was said and done, they were living creatures. . . .

Willi had already given me the gist of this. I was well aware that certain people had already got the sack for neglecting the chickens, and, more particularly, for their inability to get on with Andronova.

And there I stood, as if dead. Through my tears I observed the now pacified population eagerly pecking away at the troughs as they were supposed to, all of them formed up in orderly lines. I obviously couldn't cope with them. . . . Would this mean back to tree felling for me? Or to haymaking?

"What's there to be so upset about?" Andronova the Terrible suddenly snapped. "Not everyone can cope with these bastards straightaway. They're no ordinary birds, they're Kolyma birds. They need a special approach. And though they've got a good pedigree—they're Italian stock, you know—they've become holy terrors here in Kolyma. Foreigners can't stand our conditions, of course. You can't say they have it easy. Just look at their combs. Do you notice anything?"

Only then did I notice it. So *that* was why the entire chicken flock looked somehow washed out, with none of the usual gay profusion of color. Earlier I had thought my impression due to their all being white, without a single speckled hen or rainbow-colored cock among them. It turned out, though, that the combs of hens and cocks alike were not red, as they supposed to be, but barely pink, with a dead, dull yellow undertone.

"Vitamin deficiency," said Andronova with a frown. "And their eggs are just the same—you can't tell the yolk from the white. Any slackness on our part and they'll all croak within a week."

The same fear was shared by the vet, Kolotov, also a former prisoner, but long since released and now living right there on the farm's veterinary station. He visited us in the chicken house almost daily. He and Andronova performed their rites over the chickens and suffered together.

"Let's have a look at the one with the eye," said the vet.

What then occurred was black magic. Andronova looked at the crowd of birds for about a minute with her sharp, round, somewhat chickenlike eyes, and then with a single unerring movement plucked out by the tail the one, solitary cock with eye trouble and passed it to Kolotov. The very one he wanted out of several hundred—as white as its mates, and with the same whitish comb.

It turned out that the cock had something like a stye on its eye and that this was another side effect of vitamin deficiency. Both the poultry keeper and the veterinarian were terribly worried: What on earth would happen if the infectious diseases were to go the rounds of the chicken house? The doctor prescribed an ointment for the patient. Then the two of them proceeded to have a long consultation about possible improvements in the chickens' rations, their daily routine, or the lighting of the houses.

"If only they could just get out into the grass . . . and into the sunshine!"

So as to be able to give me some instruction on the sly, Andronova suggested that for the first week I should work night shift when the chickens were asleep. At night time there were only two requirements: to maintain the temperature, which meant lugging along wood to fill the stove; and to see to it that there was no "wastage." How was one to ensure this? The answer was to pay frequent visits from the kitchen—where you had to attend to the stove—to the building in which the chickens were languishing. As soon as you saw one of them looking "thoughtful" and about to throw in the towel, you picked up the hatchet—and off with its head!

I had never in my life had occasion to chop any head off, not even that of a chicken, and my boss's words reduced me to panic. But then I had a blinding vision of the tree felling, the haymowing, the women professionals with their "wounds," and I gave a servile smile and nodded assent. You might have thought nothing could be simpler or more natural for me than to chop off the heads of those about to pack it in.

The very first night there was a catastrophe. Even though I had not sat down for a single minute, but gone around inspecting my troops, who were peacefully dozing on their long perches, the fatal moment came when one of them started looking thoughtful and escaped my vigilance. I heard only the thud of a body dropping from its perch, then another . . . and another. . . . There they lay, inert, freezing fast on the sawdust-covered floor.

Wastage, that horrendous word! Andronova owed her reputation to there being no wastage in her domain. And now, my very first night on duty, there were three casualties. I had disgraced Marya Grigoryevna. I had disgraced Willi, who had vouched for me and gone to such pains to secure my appointment to this life-saving job. And I had destroyed myself. There was no escape for me now from manual labor.

I squatted down on the floor, like a monument of grief to the dead chickens. My state of desperation was such that the defunct trio might have been my sisters. And suddenly . . . suddenly the door creaked, and in swept Andronova with her large, rapid, almost masculine strides.

"I knew it! I just couldn't get to sleep. Even though I'm dog-tired! I'll just have a peep, I thought. . . . Quick, any hot water?"

Yes, there was. I had heated up a large panful in order to wash down the kitchen floor.

"Take the pan off the stove and put it on the floor," Andronova ordered, picking up the dead chickens.

In a second she was armed with a hatchet, and a few seconds later the three corpses had been beheaded. Now Andronova was holding up a chicken in each hand, gripping them by the tail and shaking them with all her strength. I picked up the third corpse and began to copy the motions of my boss. We kept it up until we were exhausted, but we finally succeeded: a slow trickle of blood began to come out of the carcasses.

"Harder! Harder! The more they bleed, the better. We're lucky *rigor mortis* has not yet set in. I just had a premonition, and how right I was! And now, into the boiling water with them."

Half an hour later the carcasses had been plucked clean and lay there on the stool, looking perfectly edible and reminding me for the first time in years of a butcher's slab.

Andronova wiped her forehead with her sleeve and sat down on the bench.

"Well, why have you become so silent? I suppose you're thinking in your highbrow way that that woman Andronova is a monster, because she passes off carion as top-quality meat. It may just occur to you that it's not disease they die from but vitamin deficiency. They're clean and healthy all right, poor things, but they haven't got the strength to continue living. They can't wait to become soup for the bosses. And nothing will happen to any of our lordlings as a result of eating them; they'll gobble them up as sweet as you like and pick the bones clean. We've seen it before. Look at it from another angle—the only thing our management understands is figures. What matters most to them is a dash in the wastage column. What, wastage? No, we don't have any because we're an exemplary collective, transforming nature on Kolyma. If we didn't put a dash, but a real, honest figure, there'd be hell to pay and people would be in terrible trouble. All the prisoner–poultry hands would be assigned to hard manual labor, and former prisoners, like me, for our sins would be charged with wrecking and sent back to the lock-up. It would be a black day for the chickens too. Because if they kicked us out—we who try to do a proper job—and installed some slapdash free workers in our place, then it wouldn't be a matter of two or three chickens dying each night, but of the whole lot of them dying off like flies. So that's how it is. . . . Now you know, in case anything happens. I'm to blame. . . . I did drop a hint, but you didn't catch on. . . . All right, I'm off. . . . Dog-tired, that's me. And hungry as a wolf."

This was her favorite triple formula: been sweating like an ox, tired as a dog, hungry as a wolf. She loved to "call a spade a spade," scorned all "quibbles" and "sugary sentiments." She vented all her resentment on the hens and cocks, but was none the less ready to work for them right around the clock.

"If you want to learn, keep your eyes peeled," she told me the morning after my first tragic night with the chickens.

And I decided not to go to bed after my night shift, but spent the entire day dogging her heels and studying every movement she made. My life now depended on my learning how to manage in the chicken house, and learn I did.

I found out what grip I had to use in order to hoist a sack of grain weighing over 150 pounds onto my shoulders without its toppling over; and how to shift enormous egg boxes without breaking the eggs; and how best to scrape the chicken-house floors clean of droppings; and then to take the sacks full of droppings out to the yard and empty them onto the compost heap; and the quickest way to transport fully laden water buckets without provoking Filka, the water carrier, into bad language; and many, many other things.

My working day began and ended in the dark. It ran from five in the morning to ten at night. I now made a point of sleeping on my back with my arms above my head. It was essential to have one's arms free so that they could get some rest during the short night. That was when I first fully understood the words in the folk song:

Little arms as white as snow
Ache with pain from endless work . . .

I had also taken a good long look at the chickens and learned how to ward off their attacks on the feed pail, how to distribute the food evenly among the troughs, how to collect eggs from the nests (my arms were constantly being picked until they bled), and even how to pick out from all the chickens the patients of Kolotov the vet.

I performed my duties conscientiously, even hyperconscientiously, although I felt no sympathy for my charges. The hens were forever squabbling both with their keepers and with one another. They had endless domestic altercations and kept poking their heads out of their nests like quarrelsome neighbors leaning out of the windows of their apartment block. As for the cocks, they staged roisterous, drunken brawls, drawing blood from each other's heads. For some time after a bout had ended, they flapped their wings demonstratively, and screamed out obscene curses from all over the place. So they gave one absolutely no cause to love them.

It was only when it was my turn to be on night shift, when I saw them asleep, that I sometimes felt a twinge of pity for them. I used to go around the chicken house, peering at their pitiful, ruffled figures perched on their crossbars, and at their pallid, drooping combs, and then I would remember that they were deprived of sun and green meadows, that they had no sweet meadow grasses, like their brothers and sisters on the mainland did. There was something about the crossbars that reminded me of our huts at night, our endless rows of tiered plank bunks. These living creatures in their unquiet sleep definitely had something in common with us. They too were under duress. They too were fellow sufferers from vitamin deficiency. They too had an ax permanently poised over their heads.

One night I was so absorbed by this strange feeling that I failed to notice the door opening and Andronova coming in. She made a point of looking in pretty frequently during the night—obviously not wholly trusting in my competence. On such occasions she usually bombarded me with questions. Are they all alive? Have you remembered to add cod-liver oil to their feed? Has Kolotov been here again? Have you washed the troughs down with soda?

But on this occasion she looked at me somehow more attentively, and suddenly asked:

"Feeling sorry for them, the pests—is that it? Are they worth it, the little skunks? Your hands are all bleeding from where they pecked you. . . ."

And suddenly, apropos of nothing, she told me about my predecessor in the job, Klava. I had doubtless heard that Klava had been kicked out of here because of her, Andronova? No point in being coy about it. She knew perfectly well that the intellectuals among the prison detainees had baptized her "the Fury"—and still worse names—because of that. But what they didn't know was how Klava maltreated those birds. She used to pour their feed into the troughs

without troubling to clean them. Not once did she bother to wash
the water cans, and at night all she ever did was to heat the kitchen
so as to keep herself warm—the chickens over there in the chicken
house could die of cold on their perches. Just as long as she didn't
have to fetch wood. She had to look after Number One. Those
other living creatures could keel over, as far as she was concerned—
they couldn't say anything about it anyway. . . . Those lady intellectuals could call her by any name they chose. Fury would do
fine. She was only an ordinary person, of course, a collective farm
agronomist who'd never given a university lecture in her life. But
she wouldn't allow anyone to maltreat cattle, or the birds in this
place.

A few days later, when I asked permission to dash off to the camp
canteen for lunch, Andronova growled:

"Why do you want to go and slop down that dishwater of
theirs? Take that mug, and go out and get your ration and bring it
back here. We'll liven it up with some curds and pop a beaten egg
into it. That'll make a soup fit for a prince. You won't get me into
the canteen. In the canteen for ex-prisoners it's just the same gruel,
only you have to pay good money for it!"

From then on we started taking our meals together, eating—as was
done in this camp—from the same bowl. We smothered the camp
semolina with cod-liver oil that we "borrowed" from the chickens.
We boiled up oatmeal jelly. We also had three eggs daily between
us—one in the soup and one each to be eaten raw as a special gastro-
nomic treat. (We took no more because we dared not lower the
egg productivity index, by which our work was judged.)

By the time summer came I had grown physically so much,
stronger on this diet that once again I was capable of forgetting my
own plight for a while and giving some thought to general questions. What was going to happen to our country? It was summer
1942, and the German fascists were on the Volga. The Volga! But
all these general fears merely overlaid one overwhelming, deeper
dread: a year had now passed since I had last heard from my
elder son.

Andronova the Terrible, who had become attached to me despite
my membership in the hated tribe of intellectuals, sought to comfort
me after her own manner. "They'll leave as they came," referring
to the fascists; "he'll be safe and sound—letters aren't getting
through." But in her heart of hearts she, too, worried, and in order

to comfort me went so far as to borrow books for me from the free library, and didn't complain if, on night duty, I took the odd hour off to read.

"Only do be careful not to fall asleep over your book," she warned me, "because they say our senior zootechnician pokes around at night to see whether anyone is sleeping on duty."

Rubtsov, the zootechnician, did indeed appear on my threshold one night—like Harun al-Rashid in the story.

It had been over six-years since I had had anything to do with normal free persons, other than jailers. So I was terribly excited when this free person, a specialist, a Party member who had come to Kolyma on contract, sat down on the stool with the evident intention of having a talk with me.

"What are you reading?"

I was reading Madame de Sévigné's letters, a tattered, yellowing little book issued as a free supplement to the journal *Niva* ages ago. Rubtsov barely glanced at it; he wanted to speak of other things.

"Well now. Tell me, are you happy in your work? You seem to be all right here. It's warm, there's plenty to eat and you can even fit in an hour or so's reading."

He spoke with a nervous intonation, as if requiring from me an answer to some other, unvoiced but far more important, question. It was clear that Rubtsov was not preening himself on a liberal attitude toward his slaves, but, on the contrary, was anxious lest he himself might seem to be the slaver.

(I use these terms without pretending to offer a definition of a social-economic category. It was simply that this word had by then already firmly established itself in Kolyma usage. I myself had had occasion to hear a free work foreman shouting into the telephone mouthpiece, "Send me along seven or eight slaves." True, he had laughed about it afterward and said that "slave" was simply another way of saying "slogger.")

Our zootechnician, Rubtsov, was not one of those who closed their eyes to everything. Willi used to tell me about his frequent clashes with Kaldymov, the state farm director (referred to later). And of Rubtsov's humanity toward prisoners, we ourselves had daily experience. So I replied with genuine respect.

"Thank you, here on the farm it's like being on another planet. I am glad that you are a member of the Party to which I used to belong until I became what you see me as now. I am simply very glad that there are still people in it such as you."

"But what do I see you as now? A poultry hand! An honorable occupation!"

At that point, I could restrain myself no longer.

"Of course, if it were my real profession. But as it is, it doesn't really make sense. First they educate me, give me university degrees . . . . then they send me off to fell trees, or, as an exceptional favor, to work in the chicken house. You may remember that when Famusov,* the nineteenth-century serf owner, lost his temper with his serf maidservant, he threatened her with the chicken house as a punishment: "Be off with you to the chicken coop, and make it snappy!" A whole century and more has gone by since then. And I, trained as a research worker, now find myself hauling sacks of chicken droppings, with the feeling that I'm the repository of a great trust and that if I don't justify it I may be sent back to fell trees. That's what you might call the general picture. But coming down to the particulars, I am, of course, infinitely grateful to you. I should have been done for long ago if I'd stayed in the taiga haymaking."

Rubtsov looked at me more keenly. His lean, intelligent face exhibited both attentiveness and embarrassment.

"Yes, there are many silly things . . . and incomprehensible ones too." He fell silent. "But compared to manual labor outside, you really are better off here, aren't you?"

"And how!" I laughed, and quickly flipped over the pages of Madame de Sévigné. "It's here, about the fate of the insurgents. She writes: 'Breaking on the wheel so wearied these unfortunates that hanging was sweet repose for them.' Not bad, eh?"

The senior zootechnician gave one roar of laughter. Then he held out his hand to me. "Good-by. Forgive my discourtesy. The lady should be the first to offer her hand."

"That's not essential in present circumstances. The real point is that you are breaking the rules. Free employees must not shake hands with the prisoners."

He squeezed my hand and, turning quickly about, went out.

From time to time the second zootechnician, Orlov, also looked in when I was on night duty. He was not a Party member, had

* Character in Griboyedov's play *The Misfortune of Being Clever* (1824); landowner who maintains an obstinate hatred for books and learning.

been around, and, it was said, had been in a hurry to take up employment as a free worker in Kolyma to avoid being sent here on an altogether different basis. He was from Kostroma and had the unmistakable accent of that area. He could quote Prishvin* by heart, and got all wound up when the conversation was about the countryside. Apparently the sufferings of collective farmers affected him even more painfully than what he saw here at the Elgen state farm.

"After all, it's not such a bad thing that you're doing a spell of work here on the chicken farm," he said to me one day. "You'll be released soon (he was forever asserting that everyone would be released soon), and then at least you'll have some idea of what work on a collective farm is like."

He was right. The same thought had more than once occurred to me as I stooped under the weight of some staggeringly heavy load. I did have in my past life one unforgettable incident. Some time back, somewhere about 1934, I had been sent out by my newspaper on a special assignment to a Tartar village. One day I had to take something directly from the hands of a young collective farm girl of my own age, called Mansura. I think it was some eggs she was selling, which she was counting out. But for one brief moment our hands met. And Mansura said, "Oh, your hands—they're so lovely!"

She said this quite spontaneously. She had been struck with genuine admiration for my delicate, white, manicured fingers. They showed up to advantage against her large, work-coarsened, brick-red hands with their swollen veins, chapped fingers, and broken nails. She had not meant to hurt me, but I found myself bursting into tears with these two hands—hers and mine—in close-up before me, as if in the cinema. I felt a burning sense of shame. With these delicate hands of mine, I had come to teach her how to construct Communism. Many, many times thereafter in solitary, composing and recomposing my own obituary for the umpteenth time, this recollection would come and haunt me.

But now . . . Orlov was right. Now my hands were exactly the same as Mansura's were. As a result of my year on the chicken farm at Elgen I had come to realize for the first time what a peasant's work is like. And I mean a peasant's, and not the work of a forced laborer as exemplified by the tree-felling and mowing gangs.

What a purposeful, humane life we could create for ourselves if

* Mikhail Prishvin (1873–1954): writer, mostly of lyrical prose about the countryside; friend of Maxim Gorky.

we could get out of here now! Rejecting all unmerited privileges
. . . matching our deeds to our ideas . . .

But no—this was just another illusion. In any case, we probably
wouldn't survive. Our own "pallid combs" would get the better of
us—that part of our soul bled white by vitamin deficiency and
suffering, which so yearned to let go of its perch, to fall to the floor
with a thud, and freeze into blissful oblivion.

9

· *Who is wielding the ax?*

Sometimes one hears from people who lived through the Stalin
era as free men that it was harder for them than for us. To an extent
that is true. In the first place—and this is the main point—our plight
saved us from the fearful sin of participating directly or indirectly
in the murder or maltreatment of other human beings. In the second
place, waiting for the worst is sometimes harder to bear than actual
disaster. But there's the rub: the fearful things that had already
happened to us did not exempt us from the constant, wearying expectation of new blows.

The special feature of our Elgen hell was that there was no inscription, "Abandon hope all ye that enter here," above the gate.
On the contrary, hope did exist. We were not dispatched to the gas
chamber or the gibbet. The sort of work that destined one for extinction existed alongside the sort of work that could mean survival.
Of course, chances of survival were far less than those of death, but
they did exist. Pale and tremulous though it was, like a flame in the
wind, hope flickered within us. And where there is hope there
is fear.

Therefore, we did not enjoy the prerogative of fearlessness. We
could not say that we had stopped listening for approaching steps,
that we had ceased to peer into the shadows. We could not feel
ourselves to be people who had nothing more to lose. . . . Indeed,

I most certainly did fear losing my pale-combed chickens, and my Marya Andronova, and my Willi, and the possibility of slogging from dawn to dusk—indoors and not in the open air.

And I was not the only one. Everyone and especially those who had succeeded in escaping, albeit briefly, from hard manual labor, lived in permanent terror—of being transferred, of solitary confinement, of denunciation to the operations officer, and of new charges carrying the possibility of the death penalty. . . . There was plenty to wait for and plenty to be afraid of. I had worked in the chicken house for over a year, and each day my heart contracted at the sight of officials turning up at the farm: the work assigner from the central compound, the disciplinary officer and his subordinates. Oh, that one seems to be looking at me very hard! Perhaps he's about to say, "Get your things together!" Dear Lord, let this cup pass! Oh, he's gone past. So it's not to be this time. After that, the sack on my back weighing over 150 pounds seemed negligible, a pleasurable load. It had passed. But tomorrow it would start all over again.

Andronova put in excellent reports on my work. The splendid zootechnicians had twice awarded me production bonuses for egg production, in the form of a newly issued padded jacket and a pair of decent boots. But it made no difference. . . . Our fate was not in their hands; they were not free to decide questions of life and death. It was not their hands that held the ax poised over our heads. So whose hands did?

Throughout those many years at Elgen there were two persons who effectively wielded the power of life and death over us: Kaldymov, the director of the Elgen state farm, and Zimmerman, the Elgen camp commandant.

Oddly enough, Kaldymov was a philosopher by profession: He had graduated from a philosophical faculty and taught dialectical materialism somewhere or other. He had volunteered to come to Kolyma in connection, so it was said, with a delicate family matter. His daughter, a fourteen-year-old schoolgirl, had suddenly had a baby. Kaldymov had swept up the young mother and her infant, and apparently decided to put as much distance as possible between himself and evil tongues.

He was tall and broad-shouldered, with a dark, ruddy complexion and indestructible white teeth. His whole appearance, his movements, his way of walking, the way he galloped across the state farm fields, always on his white steed—all this betrayed his Mordvin origin. He belonged to the first generation of his Mordvin peasant family to have received education. He personally involved himself, as the saying goes, in the work of the farm, and—judging from fulfillment of the plan—he made quite a respectable job of running a state farm in the taiga with its convict labor force. (A better description for it would have been "labor farce," for its members could hardly put one foot in front of the other.)

He kept this fact very much in mind, and used to run his enterprise on a work-intensive basis, relying on slave labor and a rapid turnover of "worked-out contingents." Each time his subordinates came to report to him on the latest outbreak of "wastage" among the prisoners, he would reply: "We'll get some new ones. I'll go to Magadan. We'll fix it." He reasoned that it was infinitely more efficient to go to Magadan and take delivery there of some new prison drafts than to have to bother about the half-dead remnants of the political drafts of '37 and put them on rest cures and dole out extra bread rations to such malingerers. It was the fresh contingent who were particularly advantageous during the war years, when—instead of those walking corpses of Moscow and Leningrad intellectuals—you could obtain without fuss young, healthy West Ukrainians used to working in the fields, or, failing them, young factory girls arrested for going absent without leave from their job on the production line.

He was no sadist. He derived no satisfaction from our sufferings. He was simply oblivious to them, because in the most sincere way imaginable he did not regard us as human. Wastage among the convict work force was to him no more than a routine malfunction of the production line, akin, shall we say, to the wearing out of a silage cutter. And the conclusion to be drawn in both cases was identical: get in new ones.

He was totally unaware of his own cruelty. To him these actions were simply routine. Take, for example, his dialogue with Orlov, our zootechnician, which one of our female workers who was forking manure near the dairy farm happened to overhear:

"What about this building? Why has it been left empty?" inquired Kaldymov.

"It had bulls in it," Orlov replied, "but we have had to put them elsewhere. The roof leaks, the eaves are iced up, and the rafters have rotted through, so it isn't safe to put cattle in it. We will be doing a proper repair job on it in due course."

"It's not worth wasting money on such a pile of old lumber. The best thing would be to use it as a hut for women."

"What are you saying, Comrade Director? Why, even the bulls couldn't stand it and began to fall ill here!"

"Yes, but they were bulls! No question, of course, of risking the bulls!"

This was not a joke, nor a witticism, nor even a sadistic gibe. It was simply the profound conviction of a good husbandman that bulls were the foundation of the state farm's life and that only extreme thoughtlessness on the part of Orlov had prompted him to put them on equal footing with female prisoners.

In his sanguine swinishness, his fixed belief in the solidity and infallibility of the dogmas and quotations he had learned by heart, Kaldymov would, I think, have been fearfully surprised if anyone had called him to his face a slave owner or slave driver. The Jacob's ladder that supported on its lowest rungs the prisoners and near the top the Wise and Great One, with the official cadre members like the state farm director somewhere in between, seemed to him utterly irreversible and sempiternal. His firm conviction of the unchange-ability of this world, with its hierarchy and its accepted rituals, could be sensed in every word and gesture of the director. Anything that did not form part of this world of his, to which he had been born, trained, and promoted step by step to his present position, was the work of the devil. He was a boss-man—not only on the state farm entrusted to his care, but wherever he went.

There were times when he began to miss the abstractions he had left behind on the mainland. They had become an organic part of his view of life. And so he enjoyed giving the odd lecture on theoretical questions to the free workers of the state farm. When Willi Rupert earned her discharge and was re-employed as a free statistician on contract, she had occasion to attend these lectures.

They were no worse than others of their kind. The director had a well-trained memory, and from time to time he even stopped looking at his notes to scan the audience with his cheerful blue eyes. And he got the terminology right too. "Pride" was always qualified by "legitimate." "Glory" had to be "unfading"; "patriotism," "life-giving." He knew his way around the philosophical categories.

"Theorizing" always went with the damning epithet "naked."
"Rhetoric" was "bombastic," and "empiricism" had inevitably to
be "creeping."

Nor was any mercy shown, of course, to the various deviationists
—the vulgar Mechanists, the Menshevizing idealists, and other Debo-
rinites—at these lectures. But whenever someone from the camp administration volunteered a comment to the effect that there were
some of these philosophical criminals in Elgen, too, Kaldymov
looked blank and left the remark hanging in the air. His high forehead gave away absolutely nothing. He could not manage consciously to associate the gray figures of the sloggers, stumbling along
to work under the eyes of their guards, with those formulations
that had served as his cue in combating unseen ideological oppo-
nents, whose unmaking was clearly set out paragraph by paragraph
and subparagraph by subparagraph, and that formed part of the
subject matter on which he had once examined students.

The ax that Kaldymov wielded and that was constantly suspended
over our heads struck not at persons, not at individuals, but at
whole groups of prisoners, entire detachments at a time. His order
would never be, "Ivanov to tree felling!" or "Petrov to get in hay!"
Each blow of the ax served to dispatch a large group of people. So
the instructions ran: "Fifty people to be transferred from the farm
to Tyoplaya Dolina," or "Seventy people to be transferred from
indoor work to land improvement."

He wasn't interested in whether there was anything resembling
living quarters in the given corner of the taiga, were it only the
most primitive shelter against the fury of the elements. With the
same ruddy flush on his cheeks, with the same smile revealing his
indestructible teeth, he would write off those on whose heads his
ax was in the process of falling, and take himself off to Magadan to
arrange for new penal drafts.

It was interesting that the professional criminals who were used
to giving their various bosses unprintable names, for a long time
persisted in calling him by his own name, until one day pock-marked
Lyonka, who was sometimes to be seen with a book in her hand
and loved to "have a bash" at a novel, announced for all to hear:

"His real name is not Kaldymov but simply Dymov, and Kal
['shit'] is his first name."

And that's how he got his new name.

In the case of Zimmerman, the camp commandant, the criminals sometimes called her the Pike (from the protruding teeth in her upper jaw which rested on her lower lip) and sometimes the Zimmerman-Woman. I deduced this from an absolutely unprintable ditty, composed by the same pock-marked Lyonka and much favored by the criminal riffraff, which began with the words:

> Kal Dymov sat down in the car
> The Zimmerman-Woman was driving . . .

Valentina Mikhailovna Zimmerman was a Party member of long standing, from '18 or '19. Some of our people, the older ones, even thought they recognized in her a former comrade and remembered seeing her at Party meetings in the early twenties. The recognition, truth to tell, was one-sided. Zimmerman herself refused to acknowledge anyone. For example, she never once paused in her inspection tours of the huts to say a word to Khava Malyar, when the latter was agonizing in a fearful heart attack. Yet she had been a close acquaintance of Khava's outside, and a member of the same Party organization.

The Elgen commandant was then just over forty years old, and she had retained a trim, handsome figure. In uniform, surrounded by guards and camp personnel when she proceeded on her rounds of the huts, one detected a certain resemblance to another fine figure of a woman—Ilse Koch.*

To this day, right into the seventies, arguments about Zimmerman persist. Among Elgen's "last of the Mohicans" still alive to tell the tale, there are those who feel a certain regard for Zimmerman because she was *honest*. Yes, simply honest in the literal sense of the word. She did not steal food from the prison detainees' canteen, she did not accept bribes for reassigning people from fatally dangerous work, she was not up to any tricks with the camp finances. All this set her apart, as a sort of alien body among her colleagues, who certainly did not love her.

Apart from honesty, another of her attributes was a certain asceticism. Everyone knew that Zimmerman, who was a widow, lived alone with her two sons and did not take part in any of the Kolyma binges or the orgies of the higher-ups. It was even rumored that the top brass of Sevlag (the Northern Camps Administration)

---

* Ilse Koch: wife of Karl Koch, commandant of the Nazi concentration camp at Ravensbrück.

could not stand her. Debauchees, bribe takers, and rakes sensed
something alien about her and recoiled from her, just as a wolf, so
they say, will recoil from other predators.

I, for my part (although I know that many consider me a heretic
on this score), have given a lot of thought to this problem, both
then and even more since. Of what value are virtues such as honesty,
moderation, and even incorruptibility when the person endowed
with all these qualities is performing the role of a butcher vis-à-vis
others? And who was more humane, Puzanchikov—Zimmerman's
subsequent replacement, who was far from prone to asceticism, but
who did sometimes manage to look the other way when a convict
stole a cabbage leaf from the farm to save himself from starvation—
or Zimmerman, who killed many people without any thought for
herself, acting, from her point of view, on the most idealistic of
principles?

She was accustomed to addressing everyone curtly and harshly,
but she used the polite form with us all. She would chuck straight
into the waste bin any homemade mess tins containing semolina
which had come to light during her tour of inspection, but she
watched to see that any animal fats supplied against the prison detainees' norm (on the basis of so many tenths and hundredths of a
kilogram per head) actually went into the cooking pot, and not into
the grasping hands of the trusties. In contrast to Kaldymov, she
was able to identify individuals from among the crowd of prisoners,
and her ax fell not only on groups but also on individual necks—
on mine, in particular. In doing so, she proceeded evidently again
from the same, noblest of principles, as she saw them: the struggle
for honesty, purity, and obedience.

It must be said that on the question of theft, opinion in our circle
was pretty unanimous. Only the appropriation of someone else's
personal property was considered to be theft and, as such, publicly
condemned. If we availed ourselves of products to which our jobs
gave us access, we were convinced of our complete right to do so; of
course, we lifted them on the sly, since we were not allowed to do so
openly.

"They've stolen a lot more from *me*," my Andronova used to say
to me as she broke an egg into the camp gruel in order to give it
some body. "Quite apart from the fact that I've done five years'
work here without pay, they also had to go and confiscate all my
belongings. And for no known reason. I was a young girl then, and

I could have sold them off to keep myself alive while my parents were in prison. But no, it wasn't to be—they carried off all the furniture bit by bit. And as bad luck would have it, my folks had just bought a chest of drawers—a polished one!"

"You know," Willi Rupert said to me pensively, "you and I could filch a dozen eggs a day. Nobody would ever suspect us. Highbrows like us . . ."

If we refrained from doing so and confined ourselves to taking one for the pot—meaning the cracked specimens—it was not from pangs of conscience, but only because we were worried about the egg productivity coefficient, for this was the basis on which our work was judged.

Zimmerman never let pass a single incident that came to her notice. In her indignation at the "connivance" of the production chiefs she signed countless orders for incarceration in the punishment cell of those guilty of "misappropriation" at their place of work. And her hand did not tremble. Such ideologically improper considerations as that those guilty of sacrilege against Socialist property were starving never entered her head. For she was *honest*. She never stole, and she never took bribes. How could she, the incarnation of all these virtues, fail to mete out punishment to any brazen hussy who, while working at a fresh vegetable depot, was caught gnawing one of the state's raw potatoes with such of her teeth as scurvy had spared her?

During Zimmerman's reign, Eva Krichevaya was sentenced to a further term for "stealing tomatoes from the collection point." Whenever the prisoner-doctor, Markov, submitted reports recommending the use of sulphone drugs for a prisoner suffering from severe lobar pneumonia, Zimmerman almost invariably wrote "rejected" right across the application in her precise handwriting. The sequel to one such fruitless application was the death of Asya Gudz, a talented writer and a fascinating woman. A similar fate befell Lyalya Clark, a twenty-year-old girl in the first flush of her youth, arrested while still at the university. In her case, Zimmerman wrote "rejected" with even less hesitation than usual, and explained verbally to Markov that Clark was not only an enemy of the people but, to add insult to injury, half German and half English. And sulphone, as everyone knew, was in short supply on Kolyma, and a stock of it had to be kept in reserve in case it was needed for the treatment of people valuable to the front and to the rear. She spared no effort to safeguard the principles of honesty and the sanctity of state property.

Zimmerman waged an even sterner campaign on behalf of chastity. Every time she assigned someone to a penal convoy, or sent someone else off to the punishment cells for "liaison between male and female detainees" or, still worse, for "liaison between a prison detainee and a free employee," her face expressed not merely her wrath as boss, but also heart-felt revulsion. Such libertines were an insult to the purity of her widow's weeds. She never doubted for one minute that depravity was the root cause of all such liaisons.

Perhaps it was precisely this uncompromising way of thinking that sowed the seed from which sprang in full flower the fanatical Bolshevik of the first years of revolution, the "woman in the leather jacket," as epitomized for us by the camp commandant, complete with military uniform. But the evolution of Zimmerman ought to form a special research subject for a historian, sociologist, or major writer. It is beyond me.

I sometimes thought in those days that she could not fail to grasp the tragedy of her situation, and that the camp compound at Elgen was a compound for her as it was for us. I sometimes thought that one fine day she would suddenly see herself as others saw her, and put her head in a noose.

But this was, evidently, just a highbrow's fantasies. For her later years have been perfectly serene. I am told that even now our Zimmerman-Woman, decorated with the medal "For Victory over Germany" (without ever having set foot outside Elgen!) is living out her days in "well-merited" retirement, is the recipient of a special pension, and has access to the Old Bolsheviks' canteen in Riga, where she often comes across those over whose defenseless, tortured heads she held her ax year in, year out—not only held it, but often let it fall.

10

· *Virtue triumphs!*

When you have spent years in a tragic world, you somehow come to terms with constant pain, and you even learn how to escape from it. You comfort yourself with the thought that suffering lays bare the real nature of things, that it is the price to be paid for a deeper, more truthful insight into life.

In this sense my life in camp was an enviable one. It was as if some editor kept sending me off deliberately to assemble material on the most varied circles of hell, where I might witness, sharply lighted, the conflict of characters, actions, and thoughts.

The situation became unbearable only when suffering turned into tedium, when situations already witnessed and comprehended repeated themselves. At such times all that remained was the physical torment itself, without the possibility of fresh insight to console or uplift me. This was precisely what happened every time I was posted to some remote penal outpost as medical assistant.

So it was this time too. The new location was playfully called Zmeika (the snake pit). It meant renewing my acquaintance with starvation, to which I had grown completely unaccustomed during my year with the chickens, sharing in their lavish rations. It meant again the mosquito-infested taiga, the tumble-down huts with their continuous tiers of plank bunks, and, above all, a stockade of loneliness. There was not a single soul to speak to. The girls were all common criminals, all seemingly cast from the same mold—which left only the guards, whose vocabulary extended to a few dozen stock phrases.

By now I had come to resemble Egor, the toolsetter at Sudar. He pined for the central compound at Elgen more than he did for his own native village. And I caught myself pining for the dairy farm's chicken house more than for Kazan University. This gave me a fright. It seemed to be an outward sign of spiritual emptiness, and I fervently set about filling the vacuum. Perhaps nature would be the answer.

Well sheltered from the wind, Zmeika was surrounded by tall, spreading, leafy trees. The beauty of the landscape here was dif-

ferent from that at Sudar. Sudar had a morose beauty to it, typical
of Kolyma, and Zmeika was an oasis. You do come across a few
such places in Kolyma, away from the malignant rocks and swamps
that hem in the central road. Profiting from my relative freedom
of movement in the vicinity of the penal outpost, I explored Zmeika
and discovered astonishing, simply fabulous spots. I remember one
clearing, overgrown with grayish-pink, feathery pussy willow. I
felt that there ought to be a gingerbread house hidden somewhere
in the bushes.

No such house turned up, but there was the "Old Witch" who
had entrenched herself at Zmeika in the job of supply chief. Gavrilikha was all lopsided. When she talked she sprayed saliva. Her
large, protruding upper teeth overlaid her lower lip. This touch
gave her, the ugly duckling, something in common with the beautiful Zimmerman. Gavrilikha was like a caricature of our handsome
commandant.

Just a year earlier Gavrilikha still had stood on the other side of
the barricades: she had been an employee of the Registration and
Distribution Section at the women's camp at Magadan, and her
husband had been head of the same section. But the devil had led
the poor lady astray. She had either mislaid some sort of secret
document, or else blurted out what was in it. Anyway, she had got
three years for carelessness with regard to official secrets.

As soon as she found herself a prisoner under Zimmerman's orders, she managed to read Zimmerman's character, get into her good
graces, and obtain a responsible post in the camp establishment.
Alas, the Witch, so successful at dissembling, was nevertheless
unsuccessful at overcoming her basic instincts, and in no time got
caught cheating. Her camp career plummeted downward and she
ended up in Zmeika. True, she was a storekeeper, not yet a slogger.
It was still a far cry from the central compound to this loathsome,
starving penal outpost.

The girls' hatred for Gavrilikha was so acute that I lived in
constant fear of their carrying out their daily threats of slitting the
Witch's throat. I even tried once or twice to hint delicately to
her that in this situation she ought to moderate the rapacity of her
conduct. My admonitions were quite useless. The recent Registration and Distribution Section employee was not accustomed to
going short of food, and each day her sleight of hand with the
official rations became bolder and more blatant. Sometimes, late at

night, I would wake up to hear a voluptuous champing sound coming from the direction of Gavrilikha's bunk, for only under the cover of darkness could she risk gobbling up her dishonest mite. It was 1944, and the camp ration was growing more meager by the day and by the week, even without her help. Ten grams spirited away from every ration soon resulted in a serious danger of mutiny. Those concerned in this matter were the mistresses and floozies of the professional riffraff, and the mutiny threatened to be a bloody one. The male counterparts were already sniffing around Zmeika, having been alerted to the girls' distressing plight.

Klava Baturina, the forewoman, and I tried to tell the guards about it. But they, well fed and disinclined to stir, lived by the principle: "Sufficient unto the day is the evil thereof." They enjoyed their cushy jobs far from the front and were not disposed to look for trouble.

It would all have ended very badly had the Witch not succumbed to violent stomach pains. I said to the guard commander that she ought to be taken to the hospital, for who knows? It might be typhus. The commander himself took her off to the central compound aboard a tractor that happened to be passing our way, and on his return gave orders that I should supervise the weighing out of the bread rations until she returned.

Klava and I brought along Gavrilikha's scales, which she kept in a dark corner of her so-called store, and we ensconced them on the table in the middle of the hut. I cut the bread up bit by bit and weighed it out carefully, with the girls watching me. The first honestly weighed bread ration was visibly larger than Gavrilikha's usual portion.

This unheard-of democratization of supply touched and delighted the girls. The professional thieves among them were moved to tears at the thought that there could be an honest supplies chief. "If I don't take it up with Zimmerman, my name's not Lyonka," said the pock-marked girl ecstatically, and she swore in Rostov thieves' jargon that the Witch would return only over her dead body.

They had long been planning a visit to the commandant. They had even hidden away a sample of the rations doled out by Gavrilikha. Let them weigh it, and even allowing for drying, Zimmerman would see for herself how much was stolen from each

ration. Now for comparison they would take along the straight
ration that "Genia the Med" had dished out.

I don't know quite how it was done, but within a few days I was
summoned to see Zimmerman. For the very first time the terrible
commandant looked straight at me with a calm, even benevolent,
gaze. After all, I had displayed the one quality that she valued
above all else—honesty. Honesty in the direct and narrow sense of
the word: not stealing! "I appoint you supplies chief at Zmeika."

I went cold. Responsibility for supplies in those surroundings!
Not to mention my arithmetical cretinism! I did not dare confess
this aloud, but I knew that in order to subtract 25 from 76, say,
I had to say to myself, "Take away 10, that's 66, then another
10, that's 56, then another 5 and it comes to . . ." I had received
my secondary education at a period when the young Soviet system
of schooling was experimenting with early streaming, and at the
age of thirteen I had been allowed to concentrate exclusively on
the humanities.

"I'd sooner do any sort of manual labor," I begged Zimmerman,
"no matter how hard! Anything but this . . . I shall make an addition mistake, or get the weights wrong, and the storekeepers will
cheat me unmercifully."

Suddenly, in answer to my wail of despair, something almost
impossible happened. The commandant looked at me strangely and
uttered the unthinkable words:

"Suppose I appoint you nurse in the central compound infirmary
under Dr. Herzberg?"

It couldn't be true. This was one of the top trusty jobs. Could it
possibly happen to me? To wear a clean white overall? To live in
the hut for ancillary personnel where there were individual bunks,
and where in the evening the lamp bulb gave out so much light
that it was possible to read while sitting at the table in the middle
of the hut? To work in the warmth under the direction of kindly,
gentle Polina Lvovna, whom I remembered from my time at the
children's home?

All these audacious dreams became reality. The stove crackled
peacefully in the evening in the outpatients' clinic of the central
compound of Elgen. I wore a clean overall. There was a folding
cot with two calico sheets in the hut. But none of this was of the
least concern to the clockwork figure with her mechanical move-

ments and lifeless eyes who now went by my name. Was there still a me? Could I still be alive after the most fearful of all punishments had been visited on me? After the death of my son, my first-born, my other self?

It was 1944. I had had a premonition about it. . . . I sought to conjure it away. "Lord, spare me . . . Any cup but this, let it not be this." I was not spared.

Suffering made me callous. For the thousandth time I looked at the lines of my mother's letter and failed to see that the writing had gone all awry from unbearable grief. Not until six years later, when I received notification of my mother's funeral did I dig out her letter again, and in joining the two unbearable griefs together, I realized for the first time what it had cost her to form those letters with her reluctant hand, to plunge a knife into her daughter's heart. That, however, was six years later. At the time I felt no compassion for my mother, who had lost her husband, then me, and now her elder grandson. I scanned the words of her telegram with the same dumb stupefaction. "You must stay alive. Please look after yourself for Vasya's sake. Remember, he is fatherless too." I passed over this indirect intimation of my husband's death almost unmoved. I cared for no one, absolutely no one, at that moment. . . . The egotism of those who suffer is probably even more all-embracing than the self-regard of those who are happy.

Had I not been under escort during those weeks . . . There were so many of them, all around me—those turbulent, icy booming rivers and streams of the taiga. Any one of them might have "extinguished this poor anguished memory."

But I was not left alone for a moment. The guard was constantly with me, and I was compelled to keep working. There were dozens, hundreds of people all around me. I cupped them, lanced their boils, put drops in their eyes and noses, and bandaged their frostbitten toes and fingers. In Sudar I had done all this lovingly, with deep compassion for my patients. Now my movements were those of an automaton. I frequently forgot that it was time to remove the cups, and Polina Lvovna would shake her head reproachfully. I tried to take myself in hand. I tried to concentrate. After all, outwardly I was still alive.

In the mornings when I opened my eyes, I knew myself to be alive by the sensation of acute suffering clawing at my chest. As a young girl I liked to repeat, "I think, therefore I exist." Now I could have said, "I suffer, therefore I am alive!"

The procession moved from hut to hut. It was led by the camp commandant, followed by the chief disciplinary officer, the commander of the guard attachment, the head of the Cultural-Educational Section, the work assigner, and the foreman. It was brought up in the rear by the representative of the Medical Section. Sometimes Polina Lvovna sent me in her place. It was the ceremony of daily inspection. In each hut the duty warden for that day reported, "So many, at work; so many, on their day off; so many, off sick." Sometimes, but much more seldom than at the remote taiga sites, there were a few "refuseniks." It was occasionally old Katya, from the German hut. She was seventy years old and had rheumatism. Still, she was a tough, wiry old lady, and they tried to force her out to work, if only for two or three hours. Snow clearing—she could surely help to clear the compound, at least. But old Katya wouldn't have it! She stayed put in the hut for days at a time, knitting socks from threads that she had painstakingly pulled out of American flour bags. We were now eating American cornbread, as white as cotton wool, and we got the sacks on the "old girl" network from the storeroom. We got them clean of flour, then they were washed and boiled, and after that we could embroider them, hem-stitch them, or knit from them all sorts of things— socks, mittens, collars, kerchiefs, etc. Old Katya was a past master at it.

"You must work," the higher-ups explained to her.

"*Draussen?*" Aunt Katya exclaimed indignantly, pretending she couldn't speak Russian. Then she rapidly and angrily expostulated in her *Volksdeutsch* dialect that people must be fed before they are turned out to work. Her rations were useless. A sparrow couldn't live on them. She had already been to complain to the village Soviet, and would do so again. Aunt Katya stubbornly persisted in calling our Registration and Distribution Section the village Soviet, and it was impossible to explain the difference to her.

They let her be. She was seventy, after all. Anyway, they hadn't got time for her, or for the old penal contingents in general, just at present. The tumultuous, complicated process of assimilating new labor contingents was underway. In 1943–44 the Elgen compound was stuffed to bursting with new drafts.

These drafts were the first echoes of the war to reach us: girls from the Western Ukraine, women from recently incorporated territories, young women who were the very picture of health. The transformation that their industrious hands wrought in Hut Number 2, to which they had been assigned, was simply miraculous. The floor planking was polished to a gleaming yellow. The crazy windows, made of bits of broken glass glued together, sparkled like crystal. Green branches of dwarf pine embellished the corner posts of bunks, and straw pillows were touchingly draped with embroidered hand towels. As for the production plans . . . Guess what these magicians did with our state farm plan! They simply fulfilled it, without cheating and without fuss.

The only thing that caused the bosses difficulty was the faithfulness of the "Westerners" to the church calendar. A Tuesday just like any other . . . but Hut Number 2 to a woman stayed put, not one of them went out to work on the day of the Beheading of Saint John the Baptist. The inspection procession was greeted with some well-modulated chanting of prayers.

"Why aren't you working? Are you unwell?" the chief disciplinary officer politely inquired.

"No, Citizen Chief. Nobody's sick. But today is a holy day."

The management did not want to use force. You can't drag an entire hut off to the punishment cell. Besides, these girls were shock workers. The head of the Cultural-Educational Section came forward.

"What dreadfully backward people you are," he said in aggrieved tones, shrugging his shoulders. "You're all honest working girls, and yet you believe in all that rubbish!"

"Well, that's why we're honest, because we believe in God."

For some reason all these strong-bodied, nimble girls, with their healthy southern complexions, were desperately keen to have medical treatment. During the evening office hours they crowded into our outpatients' department until there was no space to move.

"I've got a bad pain somewhere under my breasts," twenty-year-old Marika announced in her lilting Ukrainian voice, her madonna-like eyes moving from side to side. "And my stomach's feeling bad. And I've got a sickly taste in my mouth."

I tried bringing the conversation down to the practical plane.

"Are you asking to be let off work?"

"No, not that. I can work. I just want some drops, please."

An unprecedented occurrence in camp life—she did not need to be let off work! So, probably, her talk about pains "somewhere under my breasts" was her way of saying that she longed for someone to take a kindly interest in her.

"What did they pull you in for, Marika?" I ask cautiously, putting some drops of lily of the valley into the measuring glass.

After all, seven years had gone by since 1937. How did things look now against the background of the war, Nazism, and limitless, universal suffering? Surely it was all different now; surely it wasn't all done to plan; surely it wasn't just a matter of conscription for forced labor. "Well, what are you in for, Marika?"

"Thank you kindly for the drops."

"You don't want to tell me, then. You hadn't done anything, most likely."

Marika's eyes darkened, narrowed, and lost their madonnalike serenity.

"What do you mean, done nothing? They caught me red-handed pasting leaflets on fences!"

I was almost relieved to hear it. As long as there was something—a leaflet, a careless word—however severe the punishment, however disproportionate to the crime. As long as it was not just because of their profession, their nationality, their birth . . . On that basis, who knows what category might be written off next? Perhaps those whose hair is a certain color? Take redheads, for instance: isn't there something suspicious about the fieriness of their coloration?

Alas! I was soon to learn that because of Marika and her leaflets, some thirty people had been arrested just for living near her, and another hundred for having known the original thirty. No, the principle had remained unshakably the same.

Apart from the Western Ukrainians, large contingents of the "decree-infringers" arrived in Kolyma. Another wartime product: these were youngsters, in the main, sentenced under the special decree on absenteeism. In our central compound there were droves of these young women—almost schoolgirls. They were eager to tell how it had all happened to them. Their stories were always the same, save for minor variations. Things were very difficult in the factory. No food, no heating—couldn't stick it out, ran back to Mother.

"But were you really starving? Like in camp, eh?"

"And what do you mean by that? If it was like here in the camp, would I have run away? No. The bread's lovely and white here!"

We, the old hands, the prison detainees, didn't care at all for that transoceanic cornbread. It had no body to it. Our own indigenous black loaf is altogether a more solid affair. But the decree-infringers were enchanted with the sheer whiteness of the new bread. They looked at it adoringly as if it were some half-forgotten symbol of normal life. All in all, they decided, after taking their bearings, that the camp was not so bad.

"You can at least feel like a woman here," said nineteen-year-old Zina Pcholkina in her pleasant, slightly hoarse voice.

She was recovering from a chill. I had cupped her. She was lying on the outpatients' couch with some sort of coat over her, explaining why she liked Elgen. If only by comparison with Ulyanovsk, where she had lived with her mother and sisters. For there, in Ulyanovsk, there was nothing but women. There were times when you'd think that the whole world consisted of nothing but skirts. Take Mishka Vorobyev, who returned from the front—and all above board in his case; he'd left one of his legs behind. All the local beauties went into a whirl over him, and yet Mishka, even when he had had his two legs, was a sight to scare the crows. Did anyone ever look at him at school? Not likely! In Elgen it was quite different. The compound was for women only, but you'd only got to take a step the other side of the guards' hut, and there was a whole bunch of men! Kolyma must be the last place on earth where there were twice as many men as there were women, and where they still appreciated us ladies.

Zina smiled a conspiratorial smile and invited me to feel in the pocket of her jerkin. What an assortment of letters from boys! She giggled proudly, and the cups on her back tinkled melodiously as they came into contact with each other. Her blond pigtails, tied with ribbons, also quivered from her laughter. Our Mayka, my step-daughter, had also had pigtails like these.

"Don't be in too much of a hurry, my dear! Have you heard the word 'jackals' around here? Make sure those letters aren't from the jackals. And burn them. If you are caught with them on you they'll lock you up in the punishment cell."

A waste of words, of course. Within but a few months, virtually all the decree-infringers—mother's girls every one—were pregnant.

For their sentences were light ones of the kind that permitted working without a guard among the free employees.

Pregnancy was not the worst of it. Late at night, after lights out, I found myself giving secret injections. Claudia was still wearing her school uniform. She had been arrested in it. She raised her brown, pleated skirt to reveal a rosy, childish buttock, and I thrust in a large needle containing a liquid looking like thick tomato ketchup—she had syphilis.

The months rushed by. My way of life was settling down to an established routine, as if it were so ordained from the time the world began: reveille, parade, inspection, roll call, lights out. My duties as compound nurse brought me into closer contact with the camp administration. During the quiet off-peak hours, between the morning inspection and the lunch break, the wardens—and sometimes their wives—looked into the dispensary.

The Tartar warden had four small children, who had been taken ill. His wife had become a frequent visitor. She escorted me past the guard post and led me to her minute room, which smelled of chicken noodle soup and hot mutton fat. I treated her dark-skinned little children with the long-forgotten patriarchal recipes of my childhood: rubbing their chests with turpentine and applying hot compresses to their little tummies. I manufactured some passable Tartar phrases and we talked about Kazan, about the Hay Market and the TUM department store, about Arskoe Pole and new trolley bus routes.

Bit by bit, all the guards grew used to me. By now it was sufficient for me to glance in at the little window and say, "With your permission . . . ," for the long iron bolt to slide to the left and the door of the guardhouse to open before me. Only Pretty Boy Demyanenko would ask, "Are you going far?" But even he was content with the standard reply that I was off to the hospital for medicine.

I went down the road through the state farm, maneuvering with practiced skill between the petrified mounds of black mud, manure, and rubbish. Past the stables and the management offices, past the bathhouse and the hospital. I hurried to get back to the compound in time to be on duty during the lunch break. I walked warily— I didn't want to bump into one or other of the bosses, to be pulled up by a shout: "Where are you going, without an escort?"

And yet this walk was like a breath of air to my soul. Come what may, there I was walking all on my own! I was going where I wanted to—to the dairy, to visit my friends. I would see them all and have a heart-to-heart with them. And drink some milk and eat a stolen egg, laid by my own dear "pallid combs."

I had grown used to Elgen, and it no longer seemed dead-alive to me. Over there down by the stream, beside the bathhouse, some free women employees standing on crossplanks were rinsing out clothes. I paused for a minute and observed their movements with burning envy. That one there—the stubby girl with the thick calves. She was wringing out some men's calico breeches. She had worked herself to a standstill and was purple in the face. Sticking her lower lip out, she blew up at a lock of her hair that had fallen over her eyes. Soon she would finish her wash, pile it all into a basin, and make her way home to her own little shack, where her own borsch would be simmering in an earthenware pot. Her husband would come back at lunchtime and they would polish off the borsch together, from the same tin bowl. And he would tell her how that bloody foreman had done him dirty. The swine needed to be taught another lesson!

I remembered our Nadya Ilyina, a former Scandinavian languages specialist who had been released from camp without the right of returning to the mainland, and married a stevedore who had been a former kulak. Lucky girl! True, he mixed melted snow with medical spirits and tossed the lot down his throat from an old tin can. When he was drunk, so they said, he would sometimes remember his lost youth and batter Nadya about with his large fists. But at other times he would show her kindness. . . .

Once again—thank God!—I had just managed to scramble back in time. I peeped in again at the guards' window. "With your permission."

"OK, in you come." The iron bolt moved easily aside.

By this time, in the third year of the war, the camp regime had slackened off a bit, especially in the central compound. After all, the most dangerous elements had been dispersed around the remoter outposts and mobile working sites. The Cultural-Educational Section had again come into its own, was busy re-educating, reading newspapers aloud, etc. It had even managed to arrange a film show for the best workers, as a productivity bonus. We sat in an enormous, stone-cold hut, designated "the club." We burrowed deeper into our jerkins, wiggled our icy toes about in their damp socks, and watched with eyes riveted to the screen as Lyubov Orlova,

playing a champion textile worker, all in crepe-de-chine and long
ringlets, ran the gamut of her emotions in the most natural way
possible. Look, now she's having a medal pinned to her chest! The
rite was being performed by the "All-Union Headman," M. I.
Kalinin. (His wife was also somewhere in a camp, and rumors had
reached us that she had been nicknamed Mrs. Headman by her
fellow prisoners.)

The film was called *Bright Is the Path*. I kept my eyes glued to
the screen. Now the heroine was preparing to leave the building,
and we should see Moscow. I was all keyed up at the thought that
any minute now Okhotny Ryad or Revolution Square would be
there before my eyes. But the whole action took place on factory
premises resembling palaces or in palaces resembling phalansteries
from the visions of Charles Fourier.

But it did make me feel better. After seven years of forced ab-
stinence I was seeing a film again. And for us, the children of darkness, they had chosen a film about someone's bright path.

This was the reward of true virtue. This was the high living
in the central compound with which our strict but just commandant
was rewarding me for my honesty, for not stealing bread from the
starving.

My work at the central compound dispensary lasted a whole
year, until one day . . .

11

· *Vice is punished*

The crime I had committed was unprecedented in the history of
the camp. I had picked the commandant's pocket. I had removed a
piece of paper from her pocket and burned it in the stove. When
asked point-blank, I had confessed to this unheard-of deed. Actually,
the whole thing was not quite so simple.

For an entire week before this occurrence I had been beside myself with remorse. I had been unable to forget a certain nighttime summons.

"Look sharp there! Get your things on. You're needed at the farm. Something's up. . . ." Such were the orders that the duty guard, who had turned up in our hut in the dead of night, hissed at me.

What could possibly have gone wrong on the farm during the night shift? There was no dangerous machinery there. The night workers merely stoked the enormous heating ovens in the greenhouses, or turned out the peat pots that had already become fashionable in Kolyma.

But clearly something important had happened, because none other than the chief disciplinary officer was scurrying along beside me toward the farm, lighting the way with a flashlight, and there were two unfamiliar men in civilian dress with him.

"It's a doctor, not a nurse, that's wanted," said one of them. But the disciplinary officer retorted that, as he saw it, there was nothing left for the doctor to do in any case, and as for making out the report, the nurse would do still better, as she was younger and smarter than the central compound doctor.

At the entrance to the greenhouse there was a crowd of women workers from the night shift. The duty guard for the farm wouldn't let them in. But he wasn't very sure of himself and didn't refuse outright. I managed to catch the sound of sobbing and the name Polina drifting from this gathering of gray, faceless shadows.

"Go through, nurse," commanded the disciplinary officer. I was pushed forward through a low door. The large stove crackled, spat, and fizzled as it struggled with damp logs that wouldn't burn properly. Shadows cast by its uncertain blaze flickered across the dark walls like the outlines of objects perceived from the window of a moving train as night is ending. The greenhouse looked in fact just as if it were on the move, rocking and swaying as it went.

I grabbed the door frame to stop myself from pitching to the floor. Directly above a framework of open shelves with cabbage seedlings in pots arranged along it, there was a long, thin object gently swinging from the ceiling. The object ended in camp boots. They had frozen solid, and were now thawing out. A steady trickle of dirty ichor was dropping from them. The head, black and horrible, with the tongue protruding from it, bore a fantastic resemblance to the old Gogol monument. A thin nose, a lock of hair drooping over the forehead, the parting at an angle. Polina Melnikova!

"She must have been hanging there a good long while. She's gone quite cold," the duty guard explained to us.

"Why didn't you take her down?"

"Well, when we spotted her it was too late. She'd already had it. Well, I think to myself, she'd better stay up there until I get my orders. . . . Better wait for the authorities. . . ."

On the frame, just under Polina's feet, there lay a scrap of paper held by two peat pots. Next to it was a chewed blue pencil stub. . . . If I close my eyes I can still see the three sprawling words, "I've had enough."

Absolutely nothing had occurred to account for the suddenness of her decision. It had been a night like any other, the regular camp shift at the Elgen state farm. Perhaps the shadows from the oven as they glided over the walls had contrived to form some peculiarly sinister and grotesque shapes. Who can tell why someone suddenly realizes that he or she has had enough?

They cut the rope, and Polina lay on the frame among those half-incinerated peat pots, which might easily have been produced in a home for backward children. Polina Melnikova—my fellow passenger in Car Number 7; former Sinologist and translator; former woman; former person.

On the contrary, if anyone there was a former person, it was not she. She had asserted her rights to be a person by acting as she had, and she had made an efficient job of it. *I* was the former person. I, who instead of sobbing over her corpse and yelling curses at her assassins, was now writing out her death certificate, using the edge of the shelfstand as a desk. I was alive. I was living on, even after Alyosha, even after it had become clear that there was nothing more for me, ever. I hung on to that degrading existence, to those days, each of which was like a slap in the face.

Come to think of it, she had been along to the dispensary shortly before that night. I had bandaged one of her fingers for her. Abscesses were so frequent here. I had asked, "How are you getting on, Polina, and is your finger still throbbing?" But I had never asked her why not only her nose and hair but also her eyes had begun to resemble Gogol's, as seen on the old monument. Perhaps, had I asked her kindly, not like a camp nursing sister but like a real sister, a Sister of Mercy, she might have hesitated before taking up her pencil stub.

Within a few days of Polina's death, Asya Gudz died. From lobar pneumonia. The doctor wanted to get her to the infirmary somehow—by horse, or even by ox. But she couldn't manage it, so I set out with Asya on foot. I walked arm in arm with her, and we both thought that the doctor must have been mistaken—it couldn't possibly be pneumonia. Although Asya's cheeks were bright red, she smiled and even managed, between gasps, to joke. Asya was one of those who retained their femininity whatever their age or situation. How often had I seen it: at morning parade or at evening roll call Asya would suddenly pull a fragment of mirror out of her pocket, look at herself in it, put it back, and look around, beaming. As if to say: There's still a shot in the locker. And as long as a woman is attractive, there is everything to hope for.

Even lying in the morgue she was beautiful and youthful looking.

"Two in rapid succession; a third is bound to follow," superstitiously whispered the hut warden, Grandma Nastya.

And follow it did. The third was Lyalya Clark. Polina and Asya were both about forty. But little Lyalya was only twenty-five. And such a robust girl. Zimmerman wouldn't let her stay in any tolerable job: Lyalya was half German and half English. As soon as the commandant learned that Lyalya was employed in the dairy (she was a cowgirl there and did the work of three men), she immediately dispatched her to a very remote tree-felling outpost as storewoman. Lyalya set off alone through the remote taiga, lost her way, and only just escaped with her life. She had to pull the sleigh, which was loaded with provisions, out of a snowdrift. She finished up soaked through and frozen to the bone. She too caught lobar pneumonia.

The prisoner-doctor, Markov, twice asked the commandant for permission to treat her with sulphone. The answer was no. That same morning Lyalya had said, "I will be all right. I'm young." By lunchtime she was in the morgue.

The day after her death I rushed across to the dairy. They were all talking of Lyalya. There was not a single one among them—free worker or prisoner alike—who did not grieve for her. On the way back, Orlov the zootechnician slipped a letter into my hand. It was about Lyalya. He wrote of the dead girl in the saddest, sincerest, and most humane terms. Without mincing words, he called Zimmerman a murderess.

I read the letter as I walked along, and was greatly impressed by the audacity of the zootechnician. I tucked it into the pocket of my jerkin, with the idea of reading it to my friends in the compound.

All that year I had not once been searched at the guardhouse, and, as the expression goes, I had lost my vigilance. How true it is that those whom the gods wish to punish they first deprive of their reason. How frivolous I must have been to do as I did with a document of that sort.

"With your permission," I said as usual, glancing in at the guards' window.

The bolt moved aside. But before I had moved along into the passageway, I heard the voice of Demyanenko.

"Come into the guardroom!"

It wasn't that Demyanenko, that high-colored, handsome specimen, the meanest of all the guards, had decided to search my jerkin pockets for seditious literature. He had simply heard a rumor that the "lady medic" had been flitting across to the farm, so he had instituted a search in the hope of finding some contraband in the form of a bottle of milk or a couple of eggs. After going through my pockets, he was most disappointed to have found nothing of the kind. He fingered Orlov's not very legible letter, without betraying any special interest; apparently, he was just about to return it, taking it perhaps for a requisition for medicines for the dispensary. But at that moment the door at the end of the passageway creaked, and Camp Commandant Zimmerman walked into the guardroom.

"What's all this about?" she asked. Then she plucked Orlov's letter, which Demyanenko had taken from me, out of his hands, tucked it carelessly into the pocket of her fur-lined reefer, and said to me, "Get back to the dispensary. I'll be coming there for bandaging in a moment."

The fact of the matter was that the commandant's organism was also showing the effects of the Kolyma climate. She suffered from boils, though not, of course, as seriously as we did. In fact, she had a sizable boil on her stomach, and she preferred to have treatment for it not in the free hospital, but in our compound infirmary. She would come along at a time when we were not receiving prisoners, and we would dress her boils with ichthyol or rivanol. At first only

Polina Lvovna was allowed to do this. But her hand shook so badly from fright that the treatment was entrusted to me instead.

As soon as Zimmerman came into our dark little corridor, some ten minutes later, I realized that she hadn't yet read the letter. Her face was calm, even benevolent. After all, you can't help getting used to people who apply dressings to your abdomen each day. She took off her fur-lined jacket, hung it up on the nail in the corridor, and went through to that part of the hut which we proudly called the doctor's office. Polina Lvovna had gone off somewhere. We were quite alone.

"Let's get the dressing done," said the commandant, sitting down on the couch. I saw that she was well disposed toward me, as we are always well disposed toward those for whom we have performed a service. She had, after all, had me transferred from Zmeika, where I would certainly have been a goner from starvation and despair, to my present plum job. I read in her face that if the letter contained something of no particular consequence, she would not create a fuss. She would again be my benefactress. If it turned out to be some sort of romantic involvement, she might even spare me the five days in a penal cell with escort to work.

But I knew that in the pocket of her jacket there was a time bomb—the wrathful letter of a free man directed at those who had killed Lyalya and many others. I could clearly visualize the chain of events that would ensue. Our decent zootechnician at the farm would be fired. Then they would start to persecute him at meetings, and, perhaps, not only at meetings. After that they would investigate the links between the political detainees and the free specialists. Many people would suffer. They would tighten up the regime again, and all because of me.

Despair prompted me into an act of stupidity. I began to plead passionately with the commandant to return the letter without reading it. I was thirty-seven years old, but in talking to her I proceeded, just like a foolish sixteen-year-old, from the supposition that if one tries hard enough to explain how much better it is to do good, it is possible to dissuade an evil person from his evil intentions.

I laid it on thick—I still find it embarrassing to recollect! Resorting to language straight out of nineteenth-century literature, I sought to explain to her that the interests of a third person were involved. I was sure, I said, that she didn't want to pry into other people's secrets. Let me be the one—the only one—to bear full responsibility for the consequences.

"Please let me tear it up in your presence."

The thought must have occurred to Zimmerman that I had gone off my head. Beyond that, my long, passionate monologue only heightened her interest in the letter. Without saying one word in answer to my outpourings, she lay down on the couch, exposed the area where she had her boil, and said without emotion:

"Let's get the dressing done."

The instruments and drugs were located in what we called the dispensary. To get to it I had to go through the dark little corridor where the commandant's fur-lined jacket was now hanging. On my way past I slipped my hand into the pocket of the jacket. Orlov's letter lay there, safe and sound. I crumpled it up into a ball and tossed it into the stove, which was burning brightly. It was reduced to ashes instantaneously. Then I returned to the doctor's office and silently completed the bandaging.

"It seems more painful today than usual," said Zimmerman with a frown.

She left quite calmly, without checking the contents of her pockets. But within a few minutes Ninka, one of the Registration and Distribution messengers, a "reformed" common criminal, hurtled into the office. She looked at me as one might look at people consigned to Serpantinka, and, gasping with emotion, yelled out:

"Report to Zimmerman. And make it snappy."

Then she added sorrowfully that I'd be saying good-by to my cushy job, and that the commandant was beside herself with rage.

Zimmerman really had gone white with fury at such an unheard-of affront. The cigarette in her fingers trembled as violently as the tweezers had trembled in mine.

"Hand back the letter!" she hissed at me through her long teeth.

I could, of course, have said, "I don't know anything about it—perhaps you dropped it." But for some reason I put my trust in her passion for honesty.

"I've burned it."

"How vile! Picking pockets, like a common thief! Get out!"

Polina Lvovna heard out my story and almost fainted. There were tears in her eyes, tears of fear and pity for me. But she reproached me in almost the same words as Zimmerman.

"How frightful! Picking somebody's pocket, like a common criminal!"

"But the letter belonged to me, and I wasn't the first to poke into someone else's pocket!"

"We are prisoners. They were only searching you."

That is the most dreadful thing of all. Not only were those in authority convinced of their right to trample on all that is human in us, but we, too, gradually became used to being trampled upon. Seemingly, that was the way it had to be. Seemingly, that was what God created us for.

My outburst lasted only for a brief moment. For then I was seized by a clammy dread that enveloped my body in ignominious, abject sweat. What would she do to me—that woman who had been given the right to turn my pockets inside out, to dispose of me body and soul? I would be lucky if it was only the punishment cell. I won't, I won't, I won't! I can't put up with it any more! . . . (But as it turned out, I could and did—and with a great deal more besides.)

Retribution came that same night.

"Get your things together."

The work assigner who slept in the same hut as I—Farewell, personnel hut, residence of camp courtiers!—quietly explained where I was being dragged off to.

"To Izvestkovaya! There was nothing we could do. You really sent her into an almighty rage."

I remembered the rating of punishment camps familiar to us from Magadan. Elgen was the punishment area for the whole of Kolyma, Mylga for Elgen, and Izvestkovaya for Mylga. I feverishly stuffed my belongings into a bag—my rags and tatters, or such of them as had survived my various journeyings. I realized with horror that I had nothing suitable for such a journey: no quilted trousers, no stout footwear. I had been running around the compound in old overshoes from a parcel my widowed mother had sent me back in 1940. And it was now the end of November, when we got temperatures of more than 40 degrees below.

"What sort of transport are you getting?" asked Aunt Nastya, the duty warden, in a frightened whisper. "Only a tractor can get through, they say."

Not so. Our just but strict commandant had laid down a sterner form of reprisal for my crimes. I was taken there on foot. Seventy-five kilometers. Thirty to Mylga, and forty-five from Mylga to

Izvestkovaya, across virgin, almost untrod taiga. My escort changed at each stop, but I had to keep on and on. I would perhaps never have made it, if the Tartar guard whose children I had been treating had not slipped me as I was going past the guardhouse the parcel of food which he had evidently brought with him for his twenty-four-hour spell of duty. He wanted to give me money, and even repeated in Tartar: "Hold on, hold on. Here's some money. . . ." But at that moment Pretty Boy Demyanenko walked into the guardhouse, having just finished his spell of duty. He shouted merrily after me:

"Holiday's over then, nursie. Next time you'll know better than to go through other people's pockets!"

What a splendid set of teeth he had! And such a hearty laugh— like a football fan rejoicing in a goal.

The bundle contained bread, sugar, and a large hunk of cold venison.

12

· *Izvestkovaya*

My escort as far as the twelfth kilometer was evidently one of the professionals. This showed in his peculiar, shuffling gait and the bad language he lavished on me. It was an up-to-date selection from the latest underworld slang.

I held my tongue as long as I could, and then finally snapped back. Did he really think I was dawdling on purpose? Couldn't he see that I was having to walk over frozen tussocks in shoes with heels? And with a sack on my back into the bargain.

He looked down at my legs, and without pausing for breath, rained down curses on Zimmerman. "Bloody shark, sending you on foot in that state. You're a human being, after all, whatever else you may be!" Then he reflected for a moment, and asked soberly whether the soles of my shoes were intact.

At the twelfth kilometer we had our first rest break, and it emerged that the local forewoman, a common criminal pulled in on a bawdyhouse charge, had long been wanting to get her hands on something with a heel to it; my escort, whom she called Kolya, knew of this. An exchange of advantage to me was arranged. For some well-worn overshoes from the mainland—simply because they had heels—I was given some perfectly serviceable, even if patched, high felt boots. My feet, which had suffered from the cold in the Yaroslavl punishment cell and had got second-degree frostbite at the tree-felling site, were now protected.

I strode out far more boldly now, thinking as I went along what a godsend for us all the Russian character was. By then we already knew of the Nazi bestialities. I shuddered to think how fearful the combination of cruel decrees and total, unquestioning efficiency must be. It was not quite like that with us! With us there nearly always remained some loophole for ordinary human feelings. Nearly always the decree—however devilish it may have been—was mitigated by the innate good nature of its executors, by their slackness, or simply by trust in the famous Russian "maybe."

I rediscovered this when I arrived in Mylga. The person in charge there was someone called Kozichev. There were differing rumors about him. It was said that he was capable of tearing you to bits, but at times, without visible reason, would let you off scot-free. He had a sardonic face, with puffy lids and a noticeable nervous tic. He had expressed a desire to see the woman who was bound for Izvestkovaya on foot as punishment.

"So what happened back there?" he asked, looking at me with curiosity. On hearing my brief account, he gave a great guffaw. He didn't much care for his immediate boss, Zimmerman. In fact, he disliked her so much that he had no scruples about laughing at her tribulations in my presence.

It's an old truth that when oppressors fall out the oppressed can only benefit. So it was now. After he had finished laughing, Kozichev suddenly said:

"It says in the travel docket that you're to be sent straight on without breaking your journey. Never mind, you'll stay overnight here. Anyhow, we don't have a suitable convoy guard available at the moment. Go to the hut and get some rest. You can get a meal and some bread in the canteen."

An unlooked-for reprieve. Doubly so, for as it turned out the canteen cook was Zoya Maznina, one of us and an ex-companion from Car Number 7. She gave me a generous dollop of oatmeal porridge with vegetable oil. It smelled of sunflowers, and it left behind in the mouth recollections of a summer's day long ago and of the long grass in someone's front garden.

Zoya gave me her own, still unpatched, quilted trousers. Then she had a good cry over my bitter fate. People said that an ordinary person had no chance of surviving at Izvestkovaya, especially one in her eighth year inside, whose strength was giving out.

But at dawn my convoy guard and I left Mylga. This time I had acquired a gloomy old martinet as companion. No talking to prisoners under escort. He accompanied me for fourteen kilometers and then handed me over to another.

"Clink, clank. Clink, clank. Hark, the sound of fetters." What a good thing it was they hadn't got around to leg irons yet! I wondered whether they used them on women prisoners in Tsarist times. As it happened, I didn't know the answer.

What else could I think of to put fresh heart and soul into me? Well, for one thing, how fortunate I was that my parents had endowed me with such a tough constitution! In my place anyone else would have collapsed in a heap long ago. . . .

"Bear left," the guard ordered, and we switched to some side track where the going was much harder. With each step we had to pick our way between hummocks, and we slid along the solid icy crust that had formed on top of the autumn waters. In addition, a ground wind was springing up, which was the sign of an impending snow storm. Would we manage before it came to cover the fourteen kilometers to the next point, where there was to be a change of escort?

Suddenly a sharp thought flashed into my mind. I could finish off my misery quite easily, right there, that very moment. Just swerve off the path to the right . . . and run for it! I saw a vivid picture—as in the cinema—of everything that would happen then. The only thing of which I was not certain was whether the martinet would issue a warning before he fired. Or whether he would blast away in accordance with instructions: "Just one step right or left, and weapons will be used!"

Strangely enough, this thought brought me a measure of comfort.

If I should so want, I could dispose of my own life, just like that. And, if I should so want, I could wait a bit and see what the future would bring.

Beyond the turning the going became easier and our steps more rhythmical. At this pace I could recite poetry to myself, which is what I proceeded to do. . . .

On one occasion, in Moscow in the sixties, a writer told me he doubted whether in such conditions prisoners were able to repeat poems to themselves and derive mental relief from them. Yes, yes, he knew that I was not the only person to attest to this, but, well, it still seemed to him that the idea came to us after the event. The writer in question had done very well on the whole, had never had any trouble in getting his books published, regularly appeared on public platforms. Moreover, though he was only four years younger than I, he did not have much of an idea about our generation.

We were creatures of our time, of the epoch of magnificent illusions. We were not making our way to Communism via "the low road of the mines, the sickles, and the pitchforks." No, we were "flinging ourselves into Communism from the poetic heights." In effect, for all our youthful devotion to the cold formulas of dialectical materialism, we were out-and-out idealists. Under the blows of the inhuman machine that descended upon us, many of the "truths" we had been parroting all those years lost their sparkle. But no blizzards could extinguish that candle flickering in the wind, the spirituality of the Russian intelligentsia, which my generation accepted as a secret gift from the thinkers and poets of the beginning of the century who had themselves been the target of our critical shafts.

It had seemed to us that we had toppled them from their pedestals in the cause of a newly acquired truth. But in the years of trial we realized that we were flesh of their flesh. Because even the selflessness with which we sought to establish the new path came from them, from their disdain for the satisfactions of the flesh, and from their unquenchable spiritual fervor.

"But we, wise men and poets, keepers of the secrets and the faith, shall carry lighted candles down into the catacombs, into the deserts, into the caves . . ."

Actually, we were far from being wise. On the contrary, it was with the greatest difficulty that our reason, weighed down with ready-made concepts, groped toward the light of reality. Nevertheless, we did manage to carry our "lighted candles" into solitary confinement, into the huts and punishment cells, and through the blizzard-lashed marches in Kolyma. Those lamps of ours alone were what enabled us to emerge from the pitch-darkness.

Three more escorts took their turn. And I trudged on and on. I no longer remember how many days had passed, I only know that it was late in the evening, with the stars already out, when I spotted the hollow surrounded by conical hills, distinguished the outlines of the tumble-down, black, toadstoollike huts, and heard the familiar howl hovering over the site. I could even make out the tune of one of the criminals' underworld songs.

We had arrived. Izvestkovaya. The punishment center to end all punishment centers. The isle of the damned.

And here they were, the beings whose names were uttered, even in criminal circles, with superstitious dread. Take Simka the Block, an illustration from a psychiatry textbook come to life. A shiny dribble hung down from her lower lip. Her forehead jutted out like a crag over her small, bloodshot eyes. Long, heavy arms dangled on each side of the clumsy, short-legged body. Everyone knew that Simka was a killer. A killer for the sake of it, killing simply because she was "a toughy," to quote her own words. She must have already clocked up a forty-year sentence, but was constantly having it added to, because there was never enough evidence for the drop. Her partners in crime feared her like fire, and sheltered her by taking on the blame. Just so long as they didn't bring Simka the Block's wrath down on themselves. Everyone knew that it was she who had just recently murdered a sweet young girl in the punishment cells—one of the decree-infringers who had been given five days in the punishment cell for being late for morning parade. Killed her just like that. Because Simka was a toughy! She strangled the girl with her massive arms.

Or take the repulsive, goggle-eyed little toad, Zoika the Lesbian. This one was accompanied by three other lesbians of hermaphroditic aspect, with short hair, husky voices, and men's names—Edik, Sasha, and a third one. . . .

Some of the girls I recognized. They had been brought along to the compound for antisyphilitic treatment, and I had given them injections.

These humanoids lived a life of fantasy in which there was no distinction between night and day. Most of them never went out to work at all; they simply lay around all the time in their bunks. Those who did put in an appearance out of doors did so merely in order to light a campfire, crouch around it, and bawl out ribald songs. Hardly one of them slept at night. They drank various sorts of ersatz alcohol. (To this day I still don't know what the "dry spirits" with which many of them poisoned themselves could have been. Probably something like wood alcohol.) They smoked some kind of narcotic. Heaven only knows where they got the poison from.

An enormous iron barrel glowed red hot. These fiends were constantly boiling something or other on top of it, cavorting around the stove virtually naked.

The local guards were just as bad as the girls. They were a long, long way from their bosses. Not only from the mainland, but even from Magadan. And they were superbly fed on extra rations, because the contingent they were there to cope with was considered difficult. And their daily dealings with this contingent aroused the most bestial instincts in these dull, primitive soldiers.

Both the girls and the guards were at one in their instinctive recoil from me, a being from another planet. I was not allowed to rest after our trek. A pick was put into my hand the moment I appeared (I could hardly hold it), and I was told, "Get a move on, get a move on! Off to the lime quarries!" The first day my norm fulfillment was 14 per cent and I got no bread. The second day, by some miracle, I managed to work it up to 21 per cent. But that still did not entitle me to bread.

"It's not allowed," mumbled my escort. "This is a punishment site. You only get rations with 100 per cent and up."

The first few nights I spent sitting bolt upright on my bundle in the corner of the hut. There was no room on the bunks, and the girls were not inclined to make space for a "mug," a political, a career woman down on her luck. After a while, though, Raika the Bashkir remembered that I used to give her treatment in the central infirmary and moved over a fraction to let me put my bundle next to her.

I lay with my eyes open all night, nauseated by the proximity of my benefactress. Raika the Bashkir had no nose left. I knew that at this stage syphilis was no longer infectious, but the overpowering stench of putrefaction coming from Raika almost stifled me.

In Izvestkovaya, as in the most real of hells, there was not only no day and no night, there was not even any intermediate temperature to make existence bearable. It was either the glacial cold of the lime quarry or the infernal cauldron of the hut.

I was the first political to find herself in that lepers' colony. There was a special significance to that. It was not by chance that Zimmerman had exclaimed, "Picking pockets, like a common thief!" Presumably her idea was that I should be made to realize that my unprecedented action had put me on a level with common criminals. Not until a year later did I learn that she had banished me to Izvestkovaya for *no more than* one month, for—of course—a purely re-educative purpose.

The third day of my stay in Izvestkovaya, when I was too far gone to care about anything and there were gold and violet spots dancing in front of my eyes, I was suddenly given a hunk of bread. Despite the fact that my performance with the pick was getting further and further from the norm.

"Just to try you out—maybe you'll learn some sense," growled the guard commander, looking sideways at me with some unidentifiable apprehension in his eyes.

I learned later that just at that time officials from Sevlag were scouring the area, not so far from Izvestkovaya. It could not be ruled out that they might look in here too. What with the total isolation, the gluttony, the alcohol, and their constant skirmishes with the girls, our soldiers had completely lost their bearings and hardly knew what they might get it in the neck for. At any rate a death certificate was something they could do without if the management arrived. And so I came into my portion of bread, and the apparently inevitable ending of the story was postponed.

As luck would have it, officialdom passed by without looking in on us in our hollow or putting itself out to meet the troublesome contingent. Izvestkovaya could resume the life it had grown accustomed to.

That Saturday evening after lights out the door of the hut was suddenly flung wide open with such violence that it almost flew off its hinges. The entire Izvestkovaya guard force was there, all ten of them—it was a reinforced detachment. The horde of drunken soldiers irrupted into the hut so abruptly that I immediately thought: A general search! Not so. On this particular occasion they had come on private business, for a nauseating, fearful mass orgy. In all my eight years in prisons and camps I had seen nothing like it.

The thick wave of heat, smelling of red-hot metal, which was given off by the stove, mingled with the stench of spirits. The squeals of the naked girls mingled with the swearing and guffawing of the drunken, maddened yokels. They now bore no visible resemblance to soldiers or to the peasants they had once been. They were satyrs, Grand Guignol grotesques.

I pulled my quilted jacket over my head and went into a huddle, trying to disappear into thin air, to become invisible. But then . . . a violent jerk . . . Some animal's paw was tearing the jacket off me. There I lay, like a ewe lamb on the executioner's block, and a vast, red, glistening muzzle hung right over my face. In the corner of one eye, near the bridge of his nose, there was a dark mole with two little hairs sprouting from it.

We little know ourselves. If anyone had told me what I would do I would not have believed it. But facts are facts: strange behavior did sometimes occur. In the Yaroslavl punishment cell I had picked a fight with Satrapyuk, and seized him by his iron wrists. Similarly, on this occasion I lost control of myself, gave a wild yell, and hurled myself on my bestial assailant. As in a nightmare, I bit, I scratched, I kicked. I don't know, I can't recall how I managed to get away from his clutches. I must have landed him a blow on a sensitive spot, causing him to let go of me for a moment.

What came next was a miracle. Even now I am unable to explain this event in my life in terms of ordinary, common-sense logic. I hurtled out of the half-open door of the hut and dashed around the corner of the building. There was a large, frozen tree stump. I sat down on it just as I was, in my shirt. My jacket had fallen to the floor when I had jumped out of the bunk, and I hadn't had time to pick it up.

Above me there was a vast black expanse of sky with large, crystalline stars. I was not weeping. I was praying, passionately, desperately, and for one thing only: pneumonia! Lord, grant me pneumonia, lobar pneumonia—fever, delirium, oblivion, death. . . .

Behind me the walls of the hut shook. I could hear the maniacal howls coming from inside, and the sound of breaking glass as bottles were smashed. No one came to look for me, no one came out of the hut in hot pursuit. As the girls later confided to me, the beast who'd attacked me vomited out a stream of curses, howled, even wept, and finally collapsed on the floor and went to sleep. For the rest of them, I did not exist.

How many seconds or minutes I spent sitting there on the stump, I haven't the vaguest idea. All I remember was suddenly hearing a faint, rhythmical sound coming from the direction of the track that led to the taiga. Someone was coming . . . getting nearer. His steps were unhurried and even. Suddenly I saw him silhouetted against the snowdrifts. Now I could clearly distinguish a man's figure in a camp jacket, with a sack over his shoulders. He had a bundle in his hand. He came up to me.

"Who's there? Good God, can it be you, Eugenia?"

It was the voice of one of my own kind. This kindly voice so affected me that, without knowing who it was, I rushed toward my unexpected savior.

"Is this the sort of punishment they're dishing out nowadays?" he asked, clearly agitated. "Out in the frost, with nothing on?"

It was all quite matter of fact. Just a very ordinary miracle. Everything about my deliverer was perfectly normal: his article, his length of sentence, and his personal data. And now I recognized him: Uncle Senya, from the men's compound at Elgen, another of those whom I had once looked after in my nursing days. Uncle Senya had a "light" article, SDE (socially dangerous element). He was a former kulak, a past master at repairing tools of any sort. The management kept him in the central compound so as to have him close at hand, but sometimes they sent him to outlying sites when something or other needed sharpening or mending. And since his article was a light one, Uncle Senya went around unescorted. This time he'd got as far as Mylga by tractor, and then got a lift. The last stretch he'd done on his own two feet.

He picked me up and covered me with his jacket; then he took me up the hill to where the toolsetter's hut was located. He was familiar with it, as he had been there the previous year.

Uncle Senya lit the diminutive stove and boiled up some clean, melted snow in his kettle. He gave me a large hunk of bread and a lump of sugar. He stroked my head and called the local guards "dirty alley cats," and Zimmerman "that damn shark."

To the accompaniment of these kindly words I fell blissfully asleep on two planks that were the remains of a trestle bed. I did not catch cold, let alone pneumonia, from that night's adventure.

· *The jolly saint*

When the Izvestkovaya guards had had time to sleep off their orgy, Uncle Senya handed over to the commander his work schedule for mending the tools and, *en passant*, without any departure from his normal respectful tone, put the position to him. "There could be trouble," he said, "if the bosses come around on one of their visits and this political who's here for punishment suddenly blabs about the guards. . . . Well, you know what I mean. . . . Not, of course, that they're going to believe counter-revolutionaries, but then why put ideas into their heads?"

The first reaction from the commander, who was feeling like death from his hangover, was to burst into profanity and tell Uncle Senya to stick to mending picks and not to interfere in other people's business. But when evening came he called Uncle Senya and me over to see him; looking to one side, he announced that as from the next day I would not be working in the quarry any more, but at tree felling. He addressed me throughout in the polite second-person plural, and when referring to me indirectly even resorted to the superpolite third-person plural. He instructed Senya as follows:

"Give her one of the better saws, and she can get on with the sawing. . . . She's all skin and bones and won't last out in the quarry."

In that camp tree felling was considered light work. And indeed, everything is relative. After the lime quarry I myself felt that working in the taiga was almost like being on vacation, especially as Uncle Senya had equipped me with a beautifully sharp, single-handed saw.

Two weeks later Uncle Senya had completed his work schedule. Having sharpened all the picks and saws, he set off at his own leisurely pace on the return journey to Elgen, getting lifts wherever possible, carrying with him in his sack notes from me to my friends containing desperate pleas for help. As it turned out later, my friends had already gone into action even before they had received my SOS's. A sort of rescue committee had been formed, composed of both prisoners and free workers. The case was a difficult one. Only Sevlag could annul Zimmerman's order. Besides, it was now impossible for me to exist, after all that had happened, within the bounds of Zimmerman's kingdom. So, what my friends were seeking was not only the annulment of my punishment but also my transfer to another camp.

A complicated chain of contacts was set up. My friends started by looking for people acquainted with a certain highly placed personage—none other than the housecleaner of the Chief of Sevlag, no less. They sent gifts to various third parties, and even fourth parties, looking for the entrée to those in a position of influence.

On the twenty-fifth day, by which time I could barely stand on my feet, I received a note that a passing tractor driver—one of the petty-offender class—managed to slip to me. The note gave grounds for hope. My friends begged me to hold out a little longer: a special order had already been made out for me to go as nurse to the prisoners' hospital at Taskan. It was only twenty-two kilometers from Elgen, but it belonged to a different camp group and was outside Zimmerman's authority. Well, the order was at hand, but Zimmerman was not carrying out Sevlag's instructions. She had appealed against it to Magadan, to the Chief Administration of Kolyma Camps. Beside herself with fury at this interference with her sacred right to dispose of my life, she was challenging her own superiors in Sevlag.

"When Greek meets Greek . . ." I could just make out the tiny writing in the note. "Let's hope all will be well. It's hardly likely that Sevlag will allow Zimmerman to get the upper hand. So stick it out. . . ."

I was doing my very best. Especially as it was easier to stick it out at the tree-felling site than in the quarry. Although it was already December, there was, fortunately, hardly any wind. The frost had spread over everything in a quiet, thick, woolly fog. At two paces nothing could be seen. I listened all the more intently to the sounds around me, and my hearing became almost as acute as when I had been in solitary confinement.

What did I hope to hear? Above all, something wholly realistic: the crunch of snow under the feet of the bearer of good tidings— the messenger from Sevlag, which was suddenly transformed into my benefactor. Apart from that down-to-earth listening, there was another one: some bird of the taiga had just called out. Once, twice, three times . . . If there were three more calls, I would get out of here. . . . A log in the dying campfire was still aglow; if it died before I finished sawing up this tree, I would be lost forever. . . .

Such were probably the origins of signs and portents: born in the frozen solitudes amid mysterious forests.

It happened on the twenty-ninth of December, close to New Year's Day. In the envelope from Sevlag there were three items of dazzlingly good tidings. First, I was to leave Izvestkovaya. Second, I was no longer Zimmerman's slave: I was to be handed over to another, reputedly benevolent master—the Taskan food processing plant. Third, I was to be transferred straight to paradise—to the prisoners' hospital attached to the plant. . . .

There I was in paradise. Therefore, it was not peculiar that I had as my immediate boss a saint. It was surprising only that this was a very jolly saint. Anecdotes, witticisms, and wise sayings simply poured out of him.

It would have been easy to take Dr. Walter for a highly successful private practitioner, like the joker who once visited me at home when I was seven years old, and said, placing a teaspoon on my tongue, "Ah . . . ah . . . ah . . . Now, young lady, what do you mean by falling ill just before Christmas?"

And yet Anton Yakovlevich Walter had spent ten years inside, since '35. He was now on his third sentence. He had collected his second in exile in '38. The third, quite recent, one had been handed down in camp in '43. The doctor had one serious, aggravating circumstance against him: he was a German. A Crimean *Volksdeutscher* from Simferopol. At the beginning of the thirties a female linguist from Berlin had descended on the town to study the folklore of the German colonists. She had been advised to get in touch with Dr. Walter. The doctor did in fact know a great number of comic and sentimental songs and sayings from the locality. With his appreciation of clever turns of phrase and his ear for subtle peculiarities of speech, he was a gold mine to the visiting *savante*. In his sly way, flashing his unbelievably white teeth, he performed all the main hits in his repertoire, and the woman wrote them down.

The consequences of this interesting evening became apparent some three years later, when Dr. Walter was arrested and accused of being a member of a counter-revolutionary group headed by an expert on German language and literature in Leningrad, whom the doctor from Simferopol had never seen in his life and with whom his only link was a mutual acquaintance—the lady from Berlin who collected folklore.

The sentence was a light one. No more than three years' exile to Eastern Siberia. But then came 1937. All exiles were rearrested, and by '38 Anton Yakovlevich had been given a new term, this time ten years under the CRA (counter-revolutionary activity) article. His counter-revolutionary activity, in the opinion of the prosecution, had taken the form of efforts to turn his patients against the Soviet regime. For example, on such-and-such a day, when holding his office hours in the district hospital, he had said to a tubercular case: "What you need is not medicine but intensive feeding."

In Kolyma, where Walter was sent to serve his second sentence, it was relatively bearable at first. Doctors were in demand, and he was working at his own specialty. But then came the war. In Walter's case it canceled out his qualifications, his service in his profession, and all his personal qualities. The only thing that mattered now was that he was German.

Three years' hard labor in the gold mines had shattered his robust constitution. After burning his cornea he had lost the sight of one eye. The site overseers had fractured several of his ribs. Starvation had resulted in chronic dystrophy.

And all this was pure luck, his personal good fortune. For the other German doctors under detention in Kolyma were eliminated just at this time. Some of them were tried first, others informally shot "while attempting to escape." They included the famous Odessa surgeon Professor Koch, whose name was venerated by the thousands of people he had saved.

Anton Yakovlevich had got off lightly, with no more than an additional ten-year sentence. The stoolies at the camp had testified against him. Of course, he was credited with statements that we might lose the war. It subsequently emerged that one of the "witnesses" at this third "trial" was the same Krivitsky who had been working as a doctor on board the *S.S. Dzhurma*, and who had rescued me from death during my sea journey under armed convoy. But more of this later.

The year before my arrival at Taskan, Walter had been dragged out of the fearful Dzhelgala gold mine more dead than alive and put back to work as a doctor. By the time I saw him he no longer resembled a goner. Within the space of a year he had overcome the effects of starvation and physical exhaustion, and, more important, had rapidly, eagerly recovered his high spirits. Only the bags under his eyes and his constantly swollen legs spoke of the irreparable damage done to his body. When we met he was forty-six years old.

We were doing the rounds, with all due solemnity, just as they do in real hospitals. Dr. Walter, the senior medical orderly, Grigory Petrovich (nicknamed Confucius), and I, the new nurse. From ward to ward, from patient to patient; and for each of them the doctor had a joke. At first I failed to understand, and was rather angry with him. What was the point of pretending that all was normal, that these gloomy holes, barely protected from the Kolyma weather, were really hospital wards? That these human wrecks really did have a chance of recovery?

Here we were at Britkin's bedside. After his second stroke he had lost the power of speech. Walter smiled at him as if to say it's all just a trifle. Take your pills, listen to what the doctors have to say, and it will all get better.

"And good day to you, my friend. What have you to say to me today?"

"Bu . . . bu . . . ndra . . . ly . . ."

"Well, well! Not quite Cicero yet, but an improvement on yesterday! He was, you see, a collective farm chairman before he got here. So he's quite used to making speeches. . . . Don't take it too hard, Britkin. You'll soon be able to talk. But you must get in a bit more practice. How about saying hello to our new nurse here: 'How do you do . . .' Try saying it!"

Britkin growled and moaned. He was convulsed by his efforts. The doctor smiled and said to Confucius and me:

"A long time ago I used to read Marshak to my daughters— the bit about how the little girl tried to teach the kitten to speak. 'Pussy dear, say e-lec-tric-i-ty.' . . . But the kitten replies, 'Miaow!' "

I could stand it no longer, and I gave a gentle twitch at Walter's white overall. You mustn't . . . the patient might take it amiss.

The doctor clearly knew his patients better than I did. Britkin gave him a look of devotion and tried still harder. His mouth and cheeks twitched in fearsome spasms as he struggled to surmount the insurmountable. He went purple in the face and finally coughed out a few syllables sounding vaguely like "doo-ay. . . ."

"There you are, you see!" Walter exclaimed delightedly. "Now you've said hello nicely to our nurse. You can manage 'Good day' already. 'Electricity' we'll leave till next time."

Then there was Kuzovlev, an ex-sailor, the parchment skin stretched so tightly over his skeletal frame that you could study his bone structure through it. His stomach might have been glued to the vertebrae. But the sailor had not lost his liveliness and natural sociability. He told his neighbors long stories of various kinds, all of which started with a set opening: "As we were going through the Straits of La Pérouse," or "We were going through the Straits of Tartary." You would never have dreamed that within the next few days he was destined to sail for an unknown destination in another world. Far from it: he was fully occupied with the here and now, and he dismissed his long-drawn-out agony as an "indisposition."

"How are you feeling, Kuzovlev?"

"Not too bad, doctor . . . Of course I'm still indisposed. . . . My legs ache a bit, doctor, and my bowels are giving me trouble. I've had to go to the head six times today already. Why should that be?"

"It's because you're overweight," Walter explained hyperseriously, feeling the parchment skin adhering to the bones.

Kuzovlev gave him a broad grin. He understood these jokes, and enjoyed them.

When Walter got to Berezov's bed he became all serious and very learned. He had a long discussion with the patient about the latest methods of treating tuberculosis, and about the curative powers of the pneumothorax we could try as soon as his temperature dropped.

Berezov was a former diplomat, one of Litvinov's close collaborators, and had lived for many years in England. He listened closely to Walter, anxious not to lose a single word. How trusting we are! Dear Lord, how trusting we are when given grounds for hope! It was a good thing Berezov had not seen a mirror for years. Otherwise none of the doctor's fairy tales about the wonder-working powers of pneumothorax would put any hope into him. If he were to see his own face—his hollow cheeks, his sunken chest, his eyes that burned not only with a high temperature but also with a frenzied desire to stay alive . . .

We went on. The round was full of fascination for me. These people were the waste product of the Kolyma gold fields. They had been squeezed dry, chewed up, and spat out by the mines. Most of them were male politicals with the same tough articles as us, the women of Elgen. I had seen no men of this sort, our sort—the intellectuals, the country's former establishment—since transit camp. The men at Elgen were a different kind, with a different social background, and correspondingly lighter articles. The men here were like us. Here was Nathan Steinberger, a German Communist from Berlin. Next to him was Trushnov, a professor of language and literature from somewhere along the Volga, and over there by the window lay Arutyunyan, a former civil engineer from Leningrad. Dear God, if only they knew what they looked like.

By some sixth sense they immediately divined that I was one of them and rewarded me with warm, friendly, interested glances. They were just as interesting to me. These were the people I used to know in my former life. Now after all the circuits I had completed, each of them seemed like an unread book, and I was eager to read them. The trouble was that every one of these books would have a tragic epilogue.

But maybe . . . maybe we could manage to save somebody. Perhaps the active, positive goodness that inspired every word, every action of this astonishing doctor would triumph over death, which lorded it within these walls, would prevail over starvation and exhaustion and the shortage of medicines.

On the subject of medicines, I realized with dismay that I was hearing for the first time many of the names that the doctor dictated to Confucius, who jotted them down in a little book, with an affirmative nod of his spherical, Asiatic head. What did this mean? I thought I had acquired a pretty good working knowledge of camp medicine, but here each word was a riddle. . . . Would I be able to cope? Confucius noted my confusion.

"Don't be alarmed if you don't know all the prescriptions," he whispered. "You'll be able to work it out later. You see, our doctor's a . . ."

Confucius glanced around and announced as if confiding some fearful secret, ". . . he's a homeopath!"

There were, of course, no homeopathic medicines at Taskan, but

Walter used to prepare various distillations from the herbs of the
taiga; he would use them together with small doses of ordinary
medicines, in combinations decided on by himself. He and Confucius
kept their alchemy a strict secret. The Medical Section of Sevlag
would have gone into a holy frenzy if they had ever learned of this
disrespect for all medical dogma. Rumors had reached the Medical
Section that certain miracles had been performed by Dr. Walter, but
no one had inquired into the reasons for them. For example, everyone had heard that a dysentery epidemic, which had recently galloped through the camps and carried off hundreds of victims, had
for some reason missed the Taskan food plant. Confucius was the
only person to know that the doctor had poured into the official
antiscorbutic potion prepared from pine extract a minute dose of
sublimate solution at a strength of one part in several thousand, or
perhaps even one part in a million.

"What's the point of risking your head?" grumbled kindly old
Confucius. "Heaven help us if they sniff it out. They'll put you up
against a wall and shoot you! Especially as it's sublimate—just try
telling them that in small doses it's a cure! And you're a German too.
How are you going to persuade them that you're not a fascist, not
an assassin? . . ."

At the end of the hut that served as a hospital there were two
minute rooms. Walter and Confucius both slept in the rear one.
The front one was the dispensary.

"And laboratory," the Doctor proudly declared, showing me
the room.

Sure enough, I spotted a rickety table and on it a strange, not
to say fantastic, glass and metal structure, topped by a long pipe
resembling Paganelli's telescope.

"Our microscope," Walter said proudly. "Yes, yes, don't be surprised! You know, of course, the Christian name of the inventor of
the microscope was Anton: Anton van Leeuwenhoek. Well, this
particular microscope was invented and personally put together by
another Anton, Anton Walter!"

He had built this touchingly ramshackle miracle from various
rejected materials he had acquired from the miniature repair workshop nearby.

"All right, laugh! But who, other than us, can perform a urine
test in a camp hospital? Or do an E.S.T.?"

I shortly saw the truth of this myself and acquired profound

respect for a microscope that resembled its factory-produced counterparts in about the same degree that Max Linder's boneshaker
resembles a modern car. But aloud, I made fun of this instrument
and its author. And its author gave me as good as he got, teasing
me in turn.

"Suppose just you and I and a few humanoid apes survive a third
world war. I should make a start immediately on their education.
I'd explain to them the motive power of steam, the principle of
electricity, radio . . . But I wonder what you would pass on to
them of your own prewar experience? Blok's poetry?"

The doctor's dazzling white teeth, which had by some miracle
survived all the avitaminosis, glinted provocatively. They contrasted
comically with his bald head, as bald as a billiard ball. "When God
handed out teeth," he said, "I was first in the queue, but when it
came to hair, somebody else took my place."

This was my first time at evening office hours, and I attended
as an onlooker. I was told to watch Confucius' work carefully as I
should later on be doubling for him.

I watched carefully. In front of him the doctor had a large tin
bowl over which he performed his manipulations. He was armed,
rather like a butcher, with some form of primitive instrument
which, it turned out, doctors called Luer's pliers. With these he
swiftly snipped off frostbitten fingers and toes; then Confucius
bandaged the exposed stumps and cleared up the scene of operations.
Here this was considered light outpatient work. When the office
was closed, the bowl, full to the brim with rotten, fetid human
flesh, was removed by two orderlies.

Later that same evening the tired doctor scrubbed his hands and
prepared to go out somewhere. He was freely allowed out by the
guards at any time.

"There's one of the free employees who has promised to let me
have a bottle of port. I'm treating his children. It's Berezov who
really needs it. And then there's Kalchenko . . . do you remember
him? No? He's the joker lying in the far corner. He'll die tomorrow
before dinnertime. Today he was sighing, 'How nice it would be to
have just one drink before I die!' One must humor a dying man's
last wish. . . ."

Just before lights out Nathan Steinberger, the Berlin Communist
and a friend of the doctor's, dashed in from his camp hut. He spoke

such beautiful German that Walter could listen to him for hours
on end.

Today Nathan was in trouble. He had again got two of his
partially amputated toes frostbitten, the same ones that had already
been successfully treated and had healed over.

"This is no good," the doctor grumbled, unwinding the tattered
camp puttees from Nathan's leg. Then, quite casually, the doctor
pulled from his own legs the woolen socks that had been given to
him by a grateful free patient and handed them to a reluctant·
Nathan. After performing this classic act of kindness, the doctor
also managed to slip in a joke or two and tease Nathan about how
terrified the latter had been, when outside, of his formidable wife.
Nathan half-seriously reproached the doctor: he shouldn't take
unfair advantage of admissions made in confidence.

Then, pulling the doctor's socks over his long-suffering legs,
Nathan left. Before we went to bed, the doctor entertained Confucius and me with some amusing incidents from the pre-prison life
of "that Marxist theoretician and well-known henpecked husband."
Nathan's wife, of course, was also in a camp by now, though not
in Kolyma.

Apart from treating the goners, the doctor's responsibilities also
included performing autopsies on the numerous corpses, and recording the results of his dissections.

Walter stood over the dissecting table, cutting (he was an artist
in matters anatomical) and dictating to Confucius and me. We were
taking down notes on the autopsy.

"And where is the immortal soul?" I said pensively on one occasion, when the processing of the corpse was finished.

The doctor raised his eyes and gave me a close look. He became
unusually serious.

"It's a good thing that you're asking yourself the question. It
would be a bad thing if you imagined that the immortal soul were
necessarily located in one of the imperfect organs of our body."

Confucius tapped me softly under the elbow, nodded in the doctor's direction and whispered:

"A Catholic . . . a devout Catholic . . ."

The jolly saint was to become my second husband. Our love grew
amid the stench of putrefying flesh, against the darkness of the

arctic night. For fifteen years we marched together across all the abysses, through all the blizzards.

Today that unusual and brilliant world of his and all the riches of his soul lie below a modest mound of earth in the Kuzminskoye Cemetery in Moscow. Or am I, perhaps, making the very mistake against which he sought to caution me? Am I again seeking the immortal soul where there is only an imperfect body now reduced to dust and ashes?

14

· *Paradise under the microscope*

There were no two opinions about the Taskan food processing plant: it was a paradise for prisoners. Especially for women. There were not many of them—one woman to five men—and they were all in decent jobs in the hospital, the crèche, the greenhouses, and the pig farm. In a word, they were *indoors!* Not outside in the keen air, 40 degrees below.

The women's hut lay outside the compound. It had only one armed guard on duty, who looked the other way if the women went off to the free village to do some laundry or wash down floors—in other words, earn some money on the side.

As for the men, one great recommendation for Taskan was that it was not a gold-mining site or a quarry. Taskan was considered a camp for semi-invalids, with everyone on light work.

I still had a keen recollection of Izvestkovaya, so I was loud in my praises of Taskan. This amused the doctor and also slightly irritated him.

"I see that you need to take a closer look at our paradise—under the microscope, even a homemade one like ours."

We collected Confucius, and all three of us set out for one of the work sites. This did not mean that we were on our way to the premises of the food processing plant. No, the work force there was made up of free workers and discharged prisoners now domiciled in Kolyma. Our destination was the large sugar-loaf hill that was the work site of our goners. Armed with small hatchets and with sacks across their backs they climbed up the slope of the hill in pairs to cut branches of the low-growing dwarf pine. Then they bundled the branches into the sacks and hauled them off to the reception point of the food plant. These branches were the raw material from which antiscorbutic liquids and pastes were prepared by boiling.

The goners worked without convoy guard. Where could they run to? The very idea of escaping did not fit in with these bizarre, almost otherworldly figures climbing up the hill like unknown insects propelling themselves caterpillar fashion.

"There you have before you the main population of paradise. Let's take one specimen and examine him under a microscope. . . . How are things, Balashov?"

Doing the rounds of the sloggers who were engaged on what was called productive activity also turned out to be part of our duties. It was called a prophylactic measure, and was regarded as a manifestation of humanitarianism. In practice it was directed toward preventing deaths during working hours. For some odd reason, officialdom was exceptionally touchy on this subject. People were supposed to die in infirmary beds, or if need be on their bunks in the huts, but certainly not out there on the hill. If someone were to fall into a snowdrift, you could look for hours, you'd have to raise the alarm for an escaped prisoner, and you'd have to account for the occurrence.

Walter was very adept at exploiting the management's fears on this score, so he was able to exceed the day's fixed norm for certificates.

"Do you feel sick, Balashov?" asked the doctor.

"Just a shade, you might say," Balashov mumbled, almost inaudibly, approaching us with the weird, shambling gait that seemed to defy gravity.

Walter took his arm and felt for his pulse. Suddenly I saw Balashov's figure in close-up, just as if I had focused the microscope on him. He was like a Martian, with his enormous head wrapped up in a bundle of rags, his protuberant eyes, and the purple circles of their sockets.

"Go to the hut! Don't you hear me? I say, go to the hut, you Stakhanovite!* Tell the guard there that I've released you from work. Go and rest till evening, then report to the infirmary."

Balashov's lips, covered with sores, parted to reveal black stumps of teeth. He was pleased! He was smiling!

"How old would you say he is?" the doctor asked me, following the Stakhanovite with his eyes.

"I don't know. A hundred, five hundred. Surely he's beyond having an age by now?"

"Good gracious me! According to his personal record, at least, he's thirty-four years old. Eight years ago when they arrested him he was a student at Kiev University—a keen athlete; boxing was his favorite sport. He spent nearly five years in a gold mine—that's a record!"

"And what diagnosis would you put down for him?" asked Confucius, lingering over the learned word. He loved to stress that he was a properly trained medical orderly, unlike me, a nurse who had received her training in the camps. I should add that as soon as he realized that I knew my place and was not seeking to compete with him, he was generous in sharing his secrets.

"What diagnosis? Alimentary dystrophy, I presume. It's not as if I don't know what our main diagnosis is."

"Starvation," the doctor added. "Trophic starvation. Destruction of the tissue."

If you looked not at the individual worker, but at the production process as a whole, it resembled an animated cartoon. The sloggers flexed their knees and elbows like marionettes cut out of plywood. These prisoners were also disturbed mentally. They were all touchy and quick to tears, like children. Many of them had completely lost their memory.

Day in, day out at roll call we had the same comic scene with Baigildeev. He was quite incapable of remembering the article that had kept him inside for nine years. He had no trouble remembering the length of his sentence—ten years, and five years' deprivation of civil rights—but he couldn't manage the article, not if you were to kill him for it. Still, his article was a pretty difficult one: ASMC (anti-Soviet military conspiracy).

"Baigildeev!" shouted the guard who was called the Beast,

* Worker who regularly surpasses his production quota; named after G. Stakhanov, Soviet efficiency expert.

raising the personal data card of the military conspirator to his
shortsighted eyes.

"Abdurakhman Yuakirzyanovich!" the former Kazakh collective farmer rattled off confidently, "born 1909! Article . . . Article . . ."

He wiped his forehead. The veins in his temple swelled like
knotted cords from the effort of concentration. A few seconds'
intense struggle; then finally a desperate admission.

"I've forgotten the article . . . forgotten again. . . ."

The Beast called him unprintable names. He was fed up with this
farce. Each day he had to stand there and freeze because this donkey
couldn't even remember his own personal data. "Now listen, you
non-Russian devil! For the umpteenth and last time, get it into
your thick skull: ASMC! Got it? He doesn't understand plain Russian."

Hearing these honking noises—they were so familiar, but constantly eluded him—Abdurakhman was as pleased as a little child. He
reacted as if he had found a lost toy.

"ASMC! ASMC! Oh, thank you! Thank you!"

The Beast threatened that if Baigildeev forgot his article again
tomorrow he would find himself spending the night in a punishment cell. No one believed these threats, because the Beast, despite
his nickname, was not particularly hard on the goners: he simply
resorted to bad language . . . and they all laughed. But Walter
ordered Baigildeev to report to his office.

"His heart is hanging by a thread. And after all the fun and games
every evening he gets attacks of paroxysmal tachycardia. His pulse
went up to 150 yesterday. How are we going to beat this damned
article into his brain? . . . Perhaps by hypnosis . . ."

The inhabitants of Taskan were unlike those of the real paradise
up above in that their thoughts never strayed from their daily bread.
Her Majesty the Ration. They caressed it, polished it, pined for it,
argued over it. They bequeathed it to their friends before they died.
. . . Such bequests were often made in my presence; I have even
acted as a sort of notary, taking down the last wish of a dying man.

"Look, nurse . . . If I go before supper, give my ration to Sergei.
There's a lot of jackals in our ward. You never know—they might
steal it."

These bequests were strictly observed. General condemnation and
sometimes physical reprisal were meted out to those jackals who

looked for a chance to steal a dying man's bread ration. That was, of course, assuming there were people in the ward who still had serviceable fists. When anyone was dying—not in the infirmary, but in the hut—they endeavored to conceal the death from the authorities as long as they could so that the deceased's bread ration would keep coming. Sometimes they even paraded the corpse at roll call, placing him in the back row, propping him up with their shoulders on either side, and replying for him to the question about his personal data.

And yet even the most hopeless cases among them, the true goners, considered Taskan a paradise. They really did. Because it was not the mine or the quarry. Because here they got treatment and frequent "off-work" certificates. Because here they were hardly ever put in the cells. In other words, this was a semi-invalid site at which one could enjoy all the prerogatives offered to the dying by our humane medical service.

I savored to the full all the benefits of paradise. I had been put smack in the middle of a hospital. I slept on a couch in the dispensary. I was allowed to come and go past the guardhouse when I wished. We ate all together as one family, the doctor, Confucius, Sakhno the orderly, and I. The cook put extra spoonfuls of oatmeal in the way of the medics. The doctor chipped in with the odd lump of fat bacon or sponge cakes that he got from the free employees.

We received our spiritual nourishment from precisely the same quarter and in just the same modest doses. The doctor brought along undemanding little books that had been gathering dust on the bookshelves of the free citizens of Taskan village. After supper, when the patients were resting, we read aloud. Confucius lived up to his nickname by developing various arguments to prove the unprovable: for example, that joy and sorrow were, in essence, one and the same thing because both were transitory. Philosophy was meat and drink to him. The poor man was fearfully let down when he found that the doctor and I tended to want to be on our own. Sakhno did not question Confucius' philosophical constructions—he simply drifted peacefully off to sleep.

Summer came. Walter and I often went out into the taiga to collect herbal grasses. The brief flowering of the taiga is a wonderful thing. It awoke in us an almost forgotten delight in the world around us, in the meadowsweet, which had now made its appearance with the melting of the snow, and in the elegant flowers of the willow herb, which resembled tall-stemmed purple goblets. The doctor bent down, picked the herb, and named it in three languages: Russian, German, and Latin. That evening we would perform magic rites over the brick oven and brew decoctions to be administered in the proportion of one spoonful of medicine to one barrelful of impossible dreams.

Our friendship grew stronger, and our conversations more intimate, with each walk we took. He was the only person to whom I could talk about Alyosha, and that alone made him different from all others. He somehow steered our conversation so that there seemed to be no difference between those who had departed and we who were still on earth, as though we were all—the quick and the dead—droplets in the same stream. And I had the disturbing but comforting feeling that I could still do something for Alyosha, that I was even duty-bound to do something for him. Strangely, this helped to soften and reduce the constant pain. Sometimes the doctor would suddenly mention my suffering in connection with our ordinary, everyday concerns.

"You must take the occasion to go and see Sergei Kondratevich in the second ward during the night. He is a mere boy, very afraid of death. I sometimes visit him at night, but the important thing is for a woman to do it. Just go up to him quietly, put your hand on his forehead, and tuck him in gently. For Alyosha's sake . . ."

The doctor went about his courtship with old-fashioned courtesy and gentleness. He told me about his childhood. He told me about his scientific hypotheses. He patiently endured the torrent of poetry that I launched at him. When it was no longer possible to be silent, his declaration of love was not in oral but in written form.

The occasion selected for this was his trip to a distant camp site, where he had been sent to inspect the local goners.

It was the second winter since I had started working at Taskan. I was no longer an outpatients' nurse but a proper ward nurse. I had learned all the secrets of the art: I could perform with a scalpel and I could give intravenous fluids. On that particular morning I was giving Sergei Kondratevich a calcium chloride drip (for he had gone on to make a wonderful recovery), when Zavodnik, a prisoner who had been Mikoyan's deputy at the Ministry of the Food Industry, came into the hospital. He was working as supplies chief at the camp and was constantly touring the various sites.

"I've brought you a letter from Dr. Walter," he said, with a trace of something mysterious in his voice.

"Put it down on the shelf. I haven't got a free hand."

"Hmm . . . I think it's something personal and important. The doctor asked me to give it to you direct. I'd better wait until you are free."

The letter contained his declaration—a surprising one, I might even say a unique one. For it was written in Latin. Later on, Anton explained to me, laughing, why he had resorted on this occasion to the language of ancient Rome. He had had no proper envelope, so he had folded the letter up, as if he were making a receptacle for powder. And he had no confidence in the courier's being a pure and perfect knight. The comrade had rather more of the Artful Dodger about him. He almost certainly knew German. Therefore, Anton hit on the idea of using Latin.

I had never learned Latin, but by analogy with French I could make something of it (Anton later joked that I could make a silk purse from a sow's ear) and now, turning away from Confucius and Sakhno toward the window, which reflected the glittering, bluish light of the Kolyma snow, I peered, full of emotion, at the pointed gothic script of the doctor and deciphered the high-flown, almost bombastic words: "Amor mea, mea vita, mea spes."

Judging by the interest with which Zavodnik was watching me—he was showing no signs of being in any hurry to leave—it was reasonable to suppose that this learned Jew was not completely ignorant of Latin either.

"Tell the duke there will be no answer. Or rather, tell him the answer will be delivered to him personally on his return. Good night, viscount."

(I long doubted whether it was appropriate to write of such a personal matter in a book of memoirs devoted to our shared sufferings and common shame. But Anton Walter was so much an integral part of the later years of my Kolyma existence that it would be impossible to carry the story forward without explaining how and why he had come into my life. The main thing is that I wanted to show through his image that the victim of inhumanity can remain the bearer of all that is good, of forbearance, and of brotherly feelings toward his fellow man.)

Of course, I could not respond in kind to Anton's high epistolary

style. So I resorted to a joke, camouflaging my feelings toward him
in homemade verse. In it I portrayed us going for a walk in Rome:

How beautiful is the Capitol! What wonderful old stone.
A perfect day, a happy day, and now we are alone.
The bad is clean forgotten beneath the sky's blue rays.
You whisper, "amor mea, mea vita, mea spes."
Life is sweet, I ask you and ask again, my dove,
Only in Latin, always in Latin, speak to me of love.

There was a loud knock at the door. Sakhno, half-awake, shiver-
ing, and yawning convulsively, whispered urgently:
"Get up, nurse! I can't manage on my own. There's been an ac-
cident! There's a whole lot of the bosses in the corridor."
Heavens, they would kill off all the patients! The outer door
was wide open and the frosty December fog was creeping straight
into our wards. A truck was parked outside the infirmary hut. In
the back I could make out the figure of a prisoner. The guards
dragged him out. There was quite a crowd of officers in the corridor: the chief disciplinary officer, the guard commander, and two
other smart young men, doubtless operations officers.
"The syringe," ordered Confucius. "He has thermal shock. We'll
be giving him a glucose drip and . . ."
We busied ourselves around the frozen prisoner, bringing him
back to consciousness; but the officers, for some reason, stayed put.
Far from showing any signs of wanting to leave, they paid close
attention to what we were doing, and the chief disciplinary officer
repeated from time to time:
"We want him alive. He mustn't peg out before his time!"
Finally the prisoner opened his eyes. They were quite bright and
completely empty, glassy.
"What's your name?" Confucius asked him. But the man was
silent. His long, thin mouth twisted in silent convulsions.
"His name's Kulesh," said the disciplinary officer. "He's Kulesh.
And this is his supper."
He held out to me a black, charred pot, brimful with some sort
of food.
"Let's have a medical opinion on what sort of meat this is."
I looked into the pot and could hardly refrain from retching.
The fibers of this meat were minute, unlike anything I was accus-

tomed to seeing. The skin, which was still sticking to some of the
lumps, had a covering of black, matted hair.

Kulesh was a former blacksmith, from the Poltava district. He
had been the camp workmate of someone called Tsenturashvili,
who had spent an entire six months as a patient in our hospital.
Tsenturashvili—a former Party Secretary in a rural area in Georgia—
had only one more month to do before being released from camp.
His papers were already with the administration, and impatient letters kept coming in from his family. Anton had been keeping a
particularly close eye on Tsenturashvili, whom he had managed
to rescue from his apparently inevitable end. He had constantly
summoned him to the office, given him certificates for release from
work, and counted with him the days remaining until his departure.

Then suddenly, to everyone's astonishment, Tsenturashvili had
disappeared. The guards searched the hills and took down the
testimony of his workmate, Kulesh, that the last time he had seen
Tsenturashvili was by the campfire. Kulesh had gone off to work
and Tsenturashvili had stayed behind to warm up. When Kulesh had
returned to the campfire, Tsenturashvili was no longer there. Who
knew where he'd gone? Maybe he had fallen into a snowdrift and
died. He was a bit of a weakling. . . .

The guards continued with their search for a day or two and
then declared that Tsenturashvili had run away, though among
themselves they couldn't figure out why anyone should want to
try to escape when he had hardly any time left to serve. . . .

In the presence of all the officers, I gave Kulesh a glucose injection. He didn't wince. His large, whitish eyes stared straight at me.

"What are you goggling at the medic for, you degenerate?" said
the disciplinary officer contemptuously. "She'd doubtless make more
tender cutlets than Tsenturashvili, is that it? . . ."

A cannibal! The person to whom I was giving a glucose injection
was a cannibal. Our bosses had ordered Confucius and me to save
his life so that he could stand trial. The officers deplored the absence of the doctor; the swine simply had to be brought to court,
so as to discourage others.

I felt so ill, physically and mentally, that I could hardly stand
on my feet. Were we to save him so that he could be shot? To save
this nonhuman being for humanity's sake? Why not let him die
there and then: vanish, evaporate, like a marsh phantom, like some
form of vampire? I caught myself thinking that for the first time in

all these years, at that moment, I was perhaps closer to the bosses than to a prisoner. At that moment I had something in common with the disciplinary officer: we both felt the same revulsion toward the two-legged wolf who had overstepped the bounds of what is human.

"But who brought him to it? Who destroyed him by starvation?" Confucius said in a barely audible mutter.

Yes, but all the same, what sort of a person do you have to be, to be capable of being reduced to *this?*

The people in Kulesh's hut had recently begun to notice him brewing something on the iron stove. And the smell coming from the stove seemed to be that of boiled meat. Their suspicions were confirmed: late at night, when everyone else was asleep, he boiled up his meat broth. They demanded to know where he had got it from. He said he had wangled a hunk of deer meat off some cronies working at the gold mine. His hutmates hated him for it: you might have given us a spoonful, you rat! Someone informed on him to the MGB. And they got the truth out of him. . . .

The scenario of the crime was as follows: Kulesh had gone up to Tsenturashvili, who was warming himself at the campfire, and had killed him by hitting him on the neck with an ax. Then he had removed the dead man's clothes and burned them in the fire. After that he had methodically cut the corpse up into chunks and buried them in the snow in various places, marking each cache with a special sign. Just the day before, they had found the dead man's thigh in a snow drift under two short logs placed crisscross.

In the morning our doctor returned from his trip. He already knew what had happened. He said a quick hello and went immediately into the ward where Kulesh was lying. The whole day Anton said not a word. He even completed the rounds in silence.

Later in the evening, when we were on our own in the dispensary, he looked at me and placed his hand over mine.

"It's been a terrible day, my dearest. But don't despair. True, man has a beast in him, but the beast cannot triumph over man in the end."

It was the first time he had addressed me as "dearest."

15

The most fantastic part of it all was that a domestic routine of sorts did emerge amid the chaos of that mad world. The morning began with the sound of Sakhno shuffling around in his homemade slippers.

"Breakfast," he would triumphantly announce. "Get up, doctors! The meal is on the table."

"And what is there for breakfast?" Confucius would ask in his sleepy, early morning voice, with genuine curiosity—as if our breakfast menu could vary.

"Soup and tea," Sakhno retorted. It was very pleasant to hear him calling the gruel "soup," and the hot water "tea."

Everything had its appointed time: a time for work, a time for reading, and a time for writing letters to mainland addresses. We always read aloud, since the number of books that came our way was quite small. Letter writing was also performed as a joint operation, as one had to devise ingenious formulas to ensure that the contents were both intelligible to one's relatives and acceptable to the censor. Sakhno's letters, in particular, required a great deal of discussion, for although his wife, a milkmaid at a collective farm near Voronezh, was a first-class worker, she was—as Sakhno put it— "not very bright upstairs." Sakhno always asked us to "put it to her simple." He kept insisting on this, and his lips trembled with anguished affection, no hint of which must appear in the letter. His physical debilities and the fact that at forty he looked like a man of sixty were also things he never so much as hinted at.

In the evenings Anton and I used even to go visiting. Yes, visiting! We visited the one person who had the right, if not to invite us, then certainly to summon us to his apartment: Camp Commandant Timoshkin.

Our boss was a peculiar specimen, a former juvenile delinquent, remodeled as custodian of the law. His head was stuffed with all sorts of nonsense, but he had the kindest of hearts. He had handed over the entire punishment system to the chief disciplinary officer, as he couldn't bear seeing goners crying. He threw himself enthusiastically into the running of the camp. He did his best to slip extra supplies into the camp's cooking pot; to achieve this he deployed all his resourcefulness, drawing on the know-how acquired in his misguided youth.

Anton was personally treating Timoshkin and his peaches-and-cream Dutch doll of a wife, Valya, for illnesses real and imaginary, and they thought the world of the attentive doctor. In the evening Timoshkin would telephone the guard and issue strict orders that the doctor be sent over immediately to render medical aid to the commandant's family. An hour later the phone in the guardroom would ring again. This time it was the nurse whom the commandant wanted, and she must remember to take the needles along with her for the injections. I used to leave the needles in the dispensary—as they were, of course, not necessary—and hurry off to join them at table, where they were awaiting me.

Anton and I didn't try to conceal our relationship from Timoshkin and his wife. The two of them—who despite everything had retained their simple humanity—did their best to make our position easier.

In long conversations around the table, Anton used to try to satisfy the childlike curiosity of the commandant, who had spent his school years huddled next to tar boilers in the streets of Moscow. The varied information acquired in these conversations would elicit from him either a pleasurably astonished "What do you know!" or a skeptical "You don't say!" On one occasion, when he learned from the doctor that the world was a globe revolving on its own axis, his reaction was, in fact: "You don't say!"

He also respected me for my learning. In his job he had to do quite a lot of paperwork, and he decided to teach himself grammar by signing up for a correspondence course. When it came to doing the written work for this course, he used to drive me crazy with questions about how to write this or that letter. He would give me a sly grin, cover the page of the Russian language textbook for twelve-year-olds with his palm, and openly compare my answers with those given in the textbook. If he found no discrepancies, he would give his wife a look of triumph. There, you see, what do you think of our medical assistant now!

In medicine I had made solid progress. By now I was lancing boils and abscesses without any trouble, and I was administering sulfate drips. Indeed, when it came to intravenous injections, I had overtaken not only the doctor but also the senior orderly, for they already needed glasses; I had comparatively good sight, and could get into the vein almost unerringly.

Anton had also trained me to write up case histories, since this part of his duties gave him terrible trouble. In his way of working and his general approach he was a typical general practitioner or country doctor. He was ready to spend hours caring for his patients, talking them around, comforting them. But any kind of paperwork truly got him down. In addition, although he spoke Russian almost without accent, his written compositions patently betrayed his German origins. He would pile one unwieldy sentence on another with the auxiliary verbs at the end; he would waste vast amounts of time carefully tracing out spiky, quasi-Gothic letters. But there could be no question of neglecting the documentation, because it was the sole basis on which the numerous bosses and inspectors judged the work of the hospital. When we buried our patients at the foot of the hill, we were required to do it "according to the strict rules of the art."

When he came across my first attempts at writing out case histories, Anton was delighted.

"Wonderful, Genia! Why don't we make a pact: I'll do the treatment without wasting time on that nonsense, and you do the writing. O.K.? It's no bother for you students of the humanities to cover an extra page or two with all those big words. It's second nature to you. . . ."

This was true. I was five times as fast as Anton at writing into the case history sheets various combinations of the rigidly set formulas. But I could not say that I found it easy—especially the death certificates and the records of autopsies. While my hand jotted down the details automatically ("At 12:17 he died with symptoms of growing cardiac weakness"), I had always before my eyes the actual picture of that moment I was dispassionately recording. The black cavern of the mouth frozen in the final agony; the fear of death fixed in the eyes; the last words of the dying man . . .

I always endeavored to commit to memory the very last words spoken by the patient. It could, after all, happen that I would be asked about him by those for whom, in their torment of love and pain, this hospital bed space represented their own dear Vanya. Of course, anything of real importance—about his past life, about injustices done to him, about his nearest and dearest—was usually raised by the patient before Death had sidled right up to his bedside. But when it made its last fearful appearance, those who were in a hurry to set out on their final, distant journey nearly always had some trifling thing at the front of their mind: one man would ask how soon supper would be, in the pathetic hope of being in time to tuck away a few extra spoonfuls of the thick hospital gruel; another would suddenly start a feverish search for the bag containing his spare puttees.

So the documentation of camp illnesses was by no means simple. Sometimes mad thoughts occurred to me: What about crossing out the words "History of Illness," instead writing at the top "History of Murder"? But I, of course, did not have spirit enough to do that. Besides, whom would it have helped?

Our hospital was always overcrowded. There were people lying about not only in the so-called wards but also in the crooked corridor that was subject to all the winds of Kolyma. Each day we had to settle the agonizing question: Which of the sick people seeking admission were we to admit, and which must we send off to the hut with a treasured certificate of release from work in his pocket? Those who remained in their hut did not receive the extra rations, so everyone longed to be admitted to the hospital.

It was with this difficult question—whether or not to take in certain patients—that one ill-fated day in my life began. Anton and Confucius had left earlier that morning to visit outlying sites. I had remained behind, as the sole medic in charge.

"No places left!" Sakhno was endeavoring to help me by refusing entry to the sick men who were trying to push their way through into the office. "Not one, and that's final. Nowhere to put you! Of course, there's a tiny place in the women's ward. . . . But how can we give you a bed there?"

Then I had my brainstorm. Why not, if it came to that, in the women's ward? There were only a few women in our camp, and they rarely fell ill; so there were frequently one or two unoccupied places in the women's ward. Supposing we were to put, say Mizintsev there? . . . Why not? Could anyone suppose that such a walking shadow still had a sex?

With my practiced eye I could see immediately that he would be dead by evening. Why not let him rest on a bed instead of on those plank bunks in the mud and the cold? I would give him a morphine injection so that he would get some relief from the pain.

"Put him in the women's ward, Sakhno, next to the door. . . ."
"But won't we get caught?" asked our highly experienced orderly, doubtfully. "Well, yes, he's a skeleton for sure. You'd have a hard time of it guessing his sex. . . ."

But the authorities did! It just *had* to be on that day that there arrived a commission from Yagodnoye. And their eyes just *had* to alight on Mizintsev's bluish, balding head!

"A man in the women's ward!"

A look of pious indignation lit up their leader's well-nourished face. It seems he had been hearing for some time that Taskan was one great brothel. What else could you expect when women prisoners lived outside the compound and were free to come and go in the village without escort?

Without listening to my explanations, he went through into the office, where another startling fact came to light: the nurse, despite her patently feminine sex, was living side by side with the doctor and the senior orderly, with only a plywood partition between them. . . . And some people were still surprised that the children's home was full to bursting with illegitimate children! . . .

He was swift to act. The very next day brought instructions that put an end to all the traditional Taskan liberties. As evidence of their constant concern for raising the moral standards of the inhabitants of the free settlement, Sevlag proposed that the women prisoners be immediately lodged inside the compound, that the women's hut outside the compound be liquidated, and that the women be put under close guard when escorted to work. The offending medical assistant was to be dispatched immediately to Elgen under escort. The actual crime was set out quite explicitly: "She attempted to create conditions for vice by means of hospitalizing a prisoner of the male sex in a ward for prisoners of the female sex."

"Give me some poison, Anton! Please . . . just in case. I won't take it unless I need to . . . only if Zimmerman thinks up something utterly unbearable. . . ."

Anton indignantly refused my request. I hadn't brought myself into this world, and it was not for me to take my own life. Everyone was called on to go through whatever was in store for him. But it was too soon to be talking of these things. First he would go and try to pull strings.

The doctor did have some possibilities of pulling strings. His patients had included not only Timoshkin, the camp commandant, but also the director of the Taskan food processing plant, Nina Dmitrievna Kamennova. He could count on Timoshkin's support. Timoshkin could not, of course, refuse outright to comply with the order from Sevlag, but it was in his power to put off my dispatch for several days. Anton went to see Kamennova. She was a woman of about forty-five, a typical representative of the emancipated womanhood of the twenties, a self-taught person who made up for her interrupted education in common sense and efficiency. She managed her enterprise skillfully, avoiding the reefs and rocks of Kolyma's peculiar ways. Her common sense told her that excessive severity was no help in fulfilling production plans. The rationale to which she ascribed her kindness was: "You can't ask corpses to help fulfill the plan!" A sense of gratitude was not alien to her: she treated Anton, who had attended all her family, like a close friend. In one of their heart-to-hearts, she announced to him "once and for all" that she didn't consider him a German because "How can such a good man be a German?"

Anton now implored her to go to Yagodnoye and utilize her numerous contacts there to save me. If it were absolutely impossible for me to remain where I was, then let me be sent to a different camp, not to Elgen. . . . For me to fall into Zimmerman's hands again would be tantamount to a death sentence.

Nina Dmitrievna did have some very good contacts. It being wartime, food supplies were pretty tight, even for the free workers; the Taskan food plant produced not only vitamin drinks but also such seductive items as condensed milk and powdered eggs.

She did it for her doctor—she went all the way to Yagodnoye. She got the order for my dispatch to Elgen canceled. True, the powers that be would not agree to let me stay on at Taskan; they had already kicked up such a fuss about the "man in the women's ward" and taken such credit for uncovering the incident and dealing with it. But at the request of Kamennova, with whom they saw no point in quarreling, they issued a special order. I was to be transferred as nurse to the Sevlag Central Hospital in the village of Belichye.

Quite illogically, this posting was actually a step up on the ladder of my camp "career"; from the wilds of the taiga I was now going to the regional center. Belichye was only four kilometers from Yagodnoye. The posting rescued me from the threat of Elgen and from the vengeance of Zimmerman; but my separation from Anton was an unalterable fact.

Not only our patients, not only Confucius and Sakhno, wiped away their tears when they looked at us; the camp commandant himself, Timoshkin, heartily cursed the Yagodnoye officials under his breath. He swore to exchange me for someone else at the very first opportunity—even for a heating engineer or an electrician! He would go to any lengths. . . . We must just wait a while, until the whole affair was more or less forgotten.

Anton and I spent the whole night sitting on a couch in the office, recalling the past. We reminded each other in detail how we first met and what we had thought of each other then; how Zavodnik had brought me the letter in Latin; and how we had looked for herbal grasses in the taiga. We even had a laugh about the time I had overheated the needles—every single needle—because I was engrossed in our conversation and did not notice that the sterilizer had long since run dry. We had despaired at first of finding any new needles out in the taiga; but then Pogrebnoy, from the veterinary station, had come to our rescue. Unlike us, as it turned out, he had a large stock of needles. The doctor went on teasing me long afterward for my forgetfulness.

In retrospect, the year we had gone through seemed magically happy. We were astonishingly strong . . . for we had gone through it all together.

"Get your things together!"

The escort, specially sent from Yagodnoye, had arrived to take me away. His summons—"Get your things together!"—was like the voice of Doom. Once again some dispassionate, inexorable hand was moving a pawn on the chessboard.

Sakhno was weeping quite openly, sobbing like a woman. All the patients who were capable of standing on their legs had gathered in the corridor. Through the depths of my despair, the thought penetrated: Look, they're fond of me, so my year in the camp was not wasted—I was needed by my fellow human beings.

The last moment. In a second I would cross the threshold of my bitter, hungry, fearful, and wonderful paradise. Farewell, my dears! Farewell, Anton!

"No, not farewell, au revoir! And remember, we are always with you. . . ."

We embraced in full view of the patients and of the escort from

Yagodnoye. It became very quiet. Even the outsider—the guard, who of course had more than once dragged people off to the cells "for liaison between a female and a male prisoner"—succumbed to the silence. He stood there patiently, leaning against the doorjamb. Not once did he say, "Come on, come on!"

16

· PD's, SC's, and KB's

At first sight the grounds of the Sevlag Central Hospital in Belichye made it look like a rest home or sanitorium. Luxuriant larches were dotted about the slope in picturesque clumps. The paths between the buildings had been raked clean and sprinkled with gravel. There were even flower beds here, raised ones that were edged with turf. True, in August, when I first turned up, the flowers had already been nipped by the first frost, and the white, dried-out stalks lay flat on the earth, ready to be at one with it. None the less, the very thought that they planted flowers here inspired strange hopes.

The two-story buildings dazzled me with their resemblance to mainland buildings. The other buildings, although in fact normal huts, were clean and well cared for, a striking contrast to what I was used to in Elgen and Taskan.

"Well, have you had a good look at the Pearl of Kolyma? I dare say you're glad to have left the wilds of the taiga," said the local work assigner pleasantly.

"Isn't this taiga, then?"

"I suppose it is. But there's taiga and there's taiga. You mustn't go by the label. Our Belichye is an oasis in the desert. Especially for the women. There are only two women prisoners here in all. You'll make the third. So you realize how much attention you're going to get. Let's go and have a look around. I'll take you to the head doctor, and on the way I'll show you the whole setup: the management's office, the laboratory, the chemists, the morgue . . ."

He took me by the arm, as if he were a hospitable landowner. This long-nosed, lanky person with the face of a fawn and a sly way of speaking went by the name Aleksandr Pushkin. Before his imprisonment he had held a supply post in the provinces; but he had gone in for some large-scale embezzlement and had been given a solid ten-year sentence as far back as '36. He immediately started to tell me all about it, boasting of his prescience and resourcefulness. In his version he had, as it were, deliberately got himself put away "in good time and on an excellent nonpolitical charge." Had he missed the boat with his economic machinations and left them until '37, he would have found himself—no doubt about it—up on a charge of terrorism or sabotage. Small chance he would then have had of landing the job as work assigner at Belichye! It was a big job; but he was not arrogant, and he was always glad to help politicals to the extent of his powers. So far as he could, you understand . . . especially the ladies, of whom he had a proper appreciation . . . Not to mention the doctors, whose help he needed; he had a stomach ulcer.

"Why do you look as if you have all the cares of the world on your shoulders?" He had finally noticed my look of depression. "Oh, yes . . . I did hear something. . . . An emotional separation? The German doctor from Taskan? Hmm . . . Anybody can see at once that you're not very practical: war with Germany and you choose a German. . . . Wouldn't it have been more sensible to pick a Russian? If it had to be a prisoner, why not the sort who could make sure you got enough to eat? . . . What are you frowning at? With the conditions we live under, getting enough to eat is the major problem. Still, if the new man of your choice was one of the prisoners, he could provide mental compatibility and share the world's worries with you."

He was a consumate rascal, like Captain Lebyadkin.* He had taken me on a roundabout tour in order to prolong our chitchat, yet he had not offered to relieve me of my heavy wooden trunk, which was the handiwork of the Elgen gravedigger, Egor. Pushkin continued to deluge me with suggestive witticisms that he called "folklore"—something, he said, much prized by his great namesake.

We arrived eventually at the main office building. Pushkin personally conducted me into the presence of the chief, where I was subjected to the gaze of her penetrating and minatory eyes. In offi-

* Character in Dostoevsky's novel *The Possessed* (1872).

cial documents the local chatelaine bore a very prosaic title—head doctor of the Sevlag Central Hospital. But she was also head of the camp. Her authority over the bodies and souls of the prisoners in her care was all the more absolute in that the overall boss of the province—the head of the Northern Mining Administration, Gavkaev—was a fellow countryman and close friend of'our head doctor. They were both from Ossetia.

Her name was Nina Vladimirovna Savoeva. As it later turned out, fate was to be kind to her. Her subsequent life so shaped itself as to bring out the best sides of her nature, and, conversely, to suppress the tyrannical and arbitrary instincts that were originally part of her character. She fell in love with a laboratory technician who was a prisoner, and later she married him. After Stalin's death she worked as an ordinary doctor in the Magadan hospital. If she chanced to meet Anton and me in the streets of Magadan, she would greet us amiably and pass some remark such as "I see there's a good film on today in the Gornyak Cinema. . . ." It was difficult to believe that only a few years before she had exercised the power of life and death. In those days she would walk out of her inner apartments with the bearing of Queen Tamara.* She spoke in a curt snarl and used to order her female acolytes to bathe her and anoint her rather clumsy and shapeless body with various aromatic substances.

I come back once more to the hackneyed thought that absolute power corrupts absolutely. Not a vicious person by nature, Nina Savoeva had done many things to be ashamed of under the tutelage of Gavkaev, the local Stalin of whose cruelty there were constant rumors. How fortunate it was for Savoeva that love for a man so dramatically changed her life. Given a few more years of power at Belichye, she would have been lost for good, turned into a butcher.

When I first came into her terrifying presence she was still in the full plenitude of her power. Lightning flashed from her black Caucasian eyes. Her broad, stubby hand, bedecked with rings, rose and fell in imperious gestures. "Take her off to the tuberculosis block," she said to Pushkin, ignoring me. "She can live there, in the cubbyhole. She must have her own eating things—warn her that the patients are acutely infectious, so she needs to be careful. . . ."

The head doctor uttered these considerate words so disdainfully

---

* Queen of Georgia, 1184–1212. During her reign Georgia reached the peak of its political power.

that I wanted to burst into tears. Evidently, such treatment was the local custom. An underling like myself was never addressed directly by the all-powerful ruler. I longingly recalled our evening tea-drinking sessions with the Taskan commandant, Timoshkin, and our blissful, improving talks with him about how the world rotates on its axis. ("It was hard for Uncle Tom to get used to Mr. Legree's plantations after the kind Mr. St. Clare and his daughter . . .")

The tuberculosis block stood on a slope at some distance from the other buildings. It was a hut divided into two wards. In one of them lay those who were infected by the Koch bacillus*—the KB ward. In the other were those who had no visible traces of the Koch bacillus—the "clean" ward. This division was somewhat arbitrary and the classification of the patients flexible, because the lab analyses were, to say the least, imperfect; the mortality rate of the denizens of the "clean" ward at times overtook that of the KB's. There was no women's ward.

The cubbyhole intended for me adjoined the KB ward, from which it was separated by a plywood partition that failed to reach the ceiling. I had difficulty getting rid of Pushkin, who insisted on explaining to me at great length and in vivid detail that this dangerous ward had its advantages: the guards were afraid of getting infected and seldom looked in; the bosses were even less inclined to do so.

The patients were lying on fairly solid trestle beds with reasonably substantial mattresses. No goners, no skeletons, no invalids, but normal-looking, predominantly young men. They were vastly different from our Taskan patients, who were so helplessly and inexorably floating toward that unknown shore. Here lay people who had been healthy until quite recently, who were used to putting up active resistance to the powers of death. Their resistance had been broken down not by prolonged starvation or by grinding toil, but by an acute and rapidly progressing illness. Prisoners in the old sense of the word were in the minority here. The majority belonged to the new postwar Kolyma class, the "special contingent," or SC.

It was my first meeting with people who had been brought here from that other hell—the war against Nazism. They fell into several,

* Tuberculosis bacillus, identified in 1882 by the German doctor Robert Koch (1843–1910).

widely varied, categories. To the question why they were inside, some would answer: "For not committing suicide." Others—Latvians, Estonians, Lithuanians—had been mobilized into the German army during Hitler's occupation of the Baltic states. Yet others had escaped from POW camps or had been deported from areas liberated by us.

The SC's were divided into those with six-year sentences and those sentenced to an indefinite term "pending special orders." Their regime was considered to be a more lenient one than ours. However, those who were now lying in the tuberculosis block had been through the famous Burkhala gold mine, where the young workers used to fall ill, first with inflammation of the lungs, then with galloping consumption. This degeneration was particularly rapid in the case of the hefty Balts: they needed a lot of calories.

The first days of my life there were sheer misery. I could not get to sleep at night, tossing about on my short couch (a longer one wouldn't fit in) until I was stupefied with exhaustion. Constant coughing—dry coughs, catarrhal coughs, suppressed coughing, paroxysmal coughing—rent the air. There was a multilingual babel of groans, hoarse curses, and sometimes simply crying, particularly among the younger ones. I would have to get used to it all.

In the morning I started giving injections of calcium chloride to all the patients, one after another; I would sit down on the edge of the bed and search for the vein. I formed a close, almost familial relationship with the young Latvian lads—in each of them I saw my own Alyosha. They were almost his contemporaries, just a year or two older. They were tall, like him, with the same feathery eyelashes and trusting, still chubby, young lips. They should have had life before them, but they were dying—every day, every night, fighting desperately to keep death at bay, but succumbing to it. Their places were taken by new contingents of boys just as young, and they too died, bit by bit and one by one. In the end, they either put up a desperate struggle against extinction or else gave up, and before the end came they called out for Mother. Later on I tried to work out how many of them had died in my arms. How many last sighs had I heard? It came to something like a thousand. . . .

The tuberculosis wards were in the charge of a prisoner-doctor, Dr. Barkan. He looked like an impoverished and washed-out Baltic baron, and he had symmetrical bags under his eyes. He was preoccupied with his own concerns and scarcely reacted to external stimuli. He had only a few months left to do in camp, and getting out was the only thing he could talk about or even think of.

It took me a long time to get used to his style of work. He was not unconscientious; not at all. He carried out his daytime and nighttime rounds punctiliously; he listened to his patients' heartbeats, tapped their chests, and prescribed courses of treatment based on the modest resources of our dispensary. But not a single one of the patients so much as guessed that he, too, was a prisoner, and they all called him "Citizen Doctor." On one occasion during my first month there, I burst in on him at night, shouting, "Andris is dying! Andris, the boy by the door . . ." He answered calmly, "Yes, I imagined it would be today." The thought of getting out of bed had never occurred to him. I remembered how Anton used to rush around the village, hunting for spirits for a tramp who longed for a drink before he died; and how he had sat for nights on end at the bedside of a young man afraid of the dark. I recalled this and said, "Forgive me, Citizen Doctor." And I left. I never tried to wake him after that.

There were two orderlies in our tuberculosis wards. The older one, Nikolai Aleksandrovich, had been an accountant in civilian life, and even here he contrived to retain a sort of countinghouse appearance. He wore spectacles and was extremely efficient and systematic in his work. He was responsible for all our dealings with the outside. He brought our food from the canteen, our medicines from the dispensary, and our orders and instructions from the management. He thought highly of his work, and considered himself a sharp operator for having fixed things up for himself so well: after all, he was drawing rations for dangerous work with infectious cases, but in fact he hardly came into contact with the patients at all.

The really hard, dirty, and unrelenting work was done by the junior orderly, Gritsko. He was then only eighteen years old, but he had experienced enough for three adults. In 1942, when Hitler's army was quartered in his town, Gritsko had been little more than a boy, though so tall that from the back you would have thought him five years older.

"How was I to know that it would turn out that way?" he asked bitterly each time he began telling me the story of his odyssey.

His mother used to tell him not to go outdoors, but he paid no attention. One day when the local boys were playing around with a kite, he went out to have a look. And there were the Germans.

Up they came on this nice big covered truck, beckoning to him, in a friendly way. *"Komm, Junge, komm her."* Well, they helped Gritsko into the nice big truck, and off it went with him inside. Mother still didn't know where her son had gone. . . . But he'd really been around! Gritsko was hauled the length and breadth of Europe working for the army near the front.

He always narrated his travel impressions in strict order. His main criterion for assessing this or that country was the quality of the local grub.

"In Poland, nurse, the grub was really awful . . . dishwater. . . . In Czechoslovakia it was a bit better. But in Italy! What a country! The sort of grub you get in Italy is beyond our wildest dreams. . . ."

Gritsko had arrived in Kolyma directly from Rome. Actually, he had been homesick in Italy, for all its fantastic grub. And as soon as Soviet officers put in an appearance near where he was working and beckoned him home, Gritsko didn't think twice.

"These officers brought a poster to show us. There was a really beautiful woman on it, stretching out her arms and saying, 'Come home, dearest son, your motherland calls you.' " Of course, people said all sorts of things: some said they'd put you in camp for having served the Germans. But Gritsko didn't believe it. It wasn't as if he had chosen to go over to the Germans; they had hauled him off by force. . . .

"Yes, nurse, if you only knew what a lovely send-off they gave us. There was a brass band playing! Our own Soviet officers made speeches. . . . But then as soon as we got to our frontier we had to change trains. All of us were loaded into boxcars and the doors padlocked. No more music, no more bands!"

Gritsko had come to the tuberculosis ward by the same route as the Baltic youths: the Burkhala gold mine, inflammation of the lungs, tuberculosis, and so on. But from then on, Gritsko provided an illustration of our proverb, "What is death to a German is bread and meat to a Russian." Although he was in precisely the same condition as the Balts, he managed to get well again. The cavity healed over with scar tissue, and no Koch bacillus was discovered. He was almost due for another posting to Burkhala when his fortunes took a sharp turn for the better.

As soon as he became a walking patient, Gritsko had begun to help the orderlies of his own free will. For all his traveling around Europe, the habits of his childhood died hard. When he saw the appalling filth in the tuberculosis hut, Gritsko used his initiative. In some mysterious way he contrived to exchange his ration for a bucket of dry whitewash. He improvised a brush and set to work cleaning up the walls of the hut. Just then the head doctor was tipped off that an influential commission had already set out and would be inspecting all the hospital blocks, including the isolation ward. Remembering the state of filth and neglect prevailing there, Savoeva rushed over on the warpath, all ready to punish the first "guilty party" she came across.

"What are you doing?" she exclaimed when she found Gritsko finishing his whitewashing of the last patch of wall in the KB ward.

"Nothing special . . . Just giving the old cottage a touch of paint . . . it was very dirty," was Gritsko's epic explanation.

Savoeva said nothing for a moment; then she turned briskly to Barkan:

"He's not to be discharged! He's to stay on here as orderly. . . ."

And so the habits of a childhood spent in a "little cottage in a cherry orchard" saved our Ukrainian boy from being sent to Burkhala, saved him from another attack of pneumonia and from certain death.

The patients—the PD's (prison detainees), the SC's, and the KB's—all adored the young orderly. They looked to him for help. He'd get a patient a drink of water at night; help him out of bed and take him to relieve himself outside; or simply sit by him and talk to help him through a moment of blank despair. If only I could have brought him and Anton together. What a wonderful pair of healers they would have made. . . .

The only aspect of Gritsko's character that was influenced by camp life was his gluttony for bread. We got plenty of bread in the tuberculosis block: patients who were dying ate very little, and they were all issued with extra large rations. But this didn't deter Gritsko from drying bread, hoarding it, hiding it, devising all sorts of barter deals, and constantly urging me not to report a death until the patient's rations for the day had come in.

"Why not, nurse? The trusties will take it anyway, and they get enough already. Why shouldn't we keep a bit in stock?"

Even when it came to the death of Andris, with whom Gritsko had exchanged pledges of eternal friendship, he still pleaded, with tears running down his cheeks:

"Don't go to the office yet awhile, please! After we've drawn Andris's bread and gruel, that will be the time to go. . . ."

The dirt of camp life failed to adhere to Gritsko. He was affable, and he never used filthy language—unlike many of the former intellectuals. I only once saw him in a fit of ungovernable rage. That, too, was connected with Andris, or rather with Andris's death.

On his index finger Andris used to wear a massive cameo ring. He had held on to it through all the various searches and was never separated from it, since he considered it his talisman. Before his death he had taken the ring off and handed it to Gritsko with a request that it be sent to his mother in Daugavpils in Latvia.

Gritsko and I had a long, whispered discussion as to how we should set about it. We ourselves had, of course, no access whatsoever to the postal service. To keep the ring in our possession for any period of time was dangerous: it might be confiscated. So we decided to approach Pushkin, the job assigner. He had freedom of movement and a host of contacts. He could very easily send the ring to Andris's mother.

"He's a real rogue, that Pushkin, but maybe he won't bother about such a trifle," Gritsko mused.

Pushkin willingly took charge of the handsome little trifle. He dropped it casually into his pocket, but said that he would certainly do as asked; anything to do with a mother was sacred. Two weeks went by; then one day Gritsko came across Andris's ring on the filthy, calloused finger of one of the criminal riffraff who worked behind the counter in our food shop.

"For half a pound of butter and two cans of pilchards in tomato sauce," hissed Gritsko in an unrecognizable voice.

A few days later, when Pushkin walked into our hut to write down the names of the new arrivals and departures, I couldn't restrain myself from asking, with feigned calmness, whether he had by now sent the ring off to Latvia.

"Of course! Ages ago!" Pushkin said readily.

"You're lying in your throat, you scum!" exclaimed Gritsko, and hurling himself at the thin, puny figure of the work assigner, he began to throttle him in earnest. He had to be pried away by some of the walking cases.

For the whole of the next week I trembled each time I heard the door open. Were they coming for Gritsko? But Pushkin refrained from putting in a complaint—perhaps because of his own ignoble role in the affair, or perhaps because his ulcer had of late been giving him acute pain. It tormented him, distracted him from what was going on around him, and concentrated his attention on what was going on inside him.

With the onset of winter we began to suffer severely from the cold. The tuberculosis block was even more exposed than the hospital at Taskan to all the winds that blew, and the management gave us very little firewood. For some unknown reason wood was in short supply in the forest. The surgical and therapeutic departments were issued with it, but we were considered, reasonably enough, to be today's or tomorrow's dead who were quite beyond being harmed by the cold.

However, we proceeded to organize ourselves in defense of our sick patients and of ourselves. An illegal exchange mart was set in operation under the direction of our senior orderly, the former accountant. At night various suspicious characters used cautiously to unload what were clearly stolen logs and beams alongside the rear wall of our hut and take away in exchange sacks of dry bread and pails containing the leftovers. In the complete darkness of early morning, before inspection, Gritsko and I used to saw up all the lengths of wood and hide them away in a special place.

There was no question of our starving, with the extra rations issued to us. In addition, from time to time I received food parcels by third hand from Anton. So, to all intents, everything was going tolerably well, especially as only a finite period—a year and a half—remained to the expiry of my ten-year term (if I could believe the wording of the sentence). But despite all this, in Belichye I frequently experienced fits of insurmountable despair.

I was not able to bear the load of these daily agonies, these clashes with death in which death always came out the victor. And I was also tormented by the cynicism with which the outward respectability and decorum of our establishment served to cloak the horror within. The little gravel paths and flower beds, the new X-ray unit . . . the clean kitchen and the chefs in their white hats . . . There were even scientific conferences of prisoner-doctors. But beneath the veneer of respectability lay each day's discharge of half-dead patients, those fit for return to murderous Burkhala.

Day and night the Belichye morgue functioned without respite, ever improving its production capacity. The morgue was run by the criminal riffraff, out-and-out thugs. They were too lazy to sew the corpses up after the autopsies, or to dig graves large enough to take them. So they trimmed them, chopped them up into sections, and then tipped them into a shallow pit behind the larch-covered hillock.

One morning at dawn when I was having to pay a hasty, off-hours visit to the dispensary, I came face to face with such a funeral cortege. Three thugs were hauling a long Yakut sleigh laden with cuts of human flesh. Frozen, bluish "hams" stuck out obscenely from this heap. Chopped-off arms trailed in the snow. Now and then parts of the entrails spilled over onto the ground. The sacks in which the corpses of the prisoners were supposed to be buried were sensibly utilized by these riffraff "anatomists" for various barter deals. So I beheld the Belichye funeral rites in all their brutal glory.

For the first and only time in my life I had something like a hysterical fit. The words that came to mind were the ones often used to describe our corrective labor camps—"the mincing machine." At the sight of this laden Yakut sleigh, the figurative meaning of the word was suddenly replaced by the all-too-solid literal reality. There they were: chunks of human flesh cut up ready for the gigantic mincer. With horror and astonishment I heard the outburst of my own choking laughter, my own loud sobbing. Then I started to vomit uncontrollably. I don't recall how I managed to stumble back to my block.

The very same day we had a sudden visitation from a commission of the top brass. Not merely officials from the Medical Administration but even the head of Sevlag, Colonel Seleznev, in person. With a large retinue in attendance, he marched straight into our infectious ward, where at that moment Gritsko was washing the floor, being careful to swab under the beds with his rag.

"Is this a PD or an SC ward?" asked Seleznev.

I didn't have time to open my mouth to answer; Gritsko got there before me. Wringing his rag mop out with rapid, almost feminine movements, he gave a loud sigh and said unceremoniously:

"As if it mattered whether they're PD's or SC's. They're out-and-out KB's, every one of them!"

"What? What?" The head's brows rose abruptly in bewilderment.

"KB's—that is, Koch's bacillus cases," I hastened to explain. I was afraid he might get furious with Gritsko and send him off to Burkhala. "What the orderly has in mind is that the patients in the ward are grouped not in terms of their personal file, but according to their medical history. Here we have acutely infectious cases who secrete bacillus Kochii."

The head abruptly let go of the door handle, and looked apprehensively at his palms, as if expecting to find bacteria jumping about there. Turning to our head doctor, he said angrily:

"Why disturb such very sick people? It would be better if you showed me your new X-ray unit. . . ."

17

· *Mea culpa*

Is the need for repentance and confession an integral part of the human soul? This was something that Anton and I had discussed at length in our endless, whispered conversations during those nights in Taskan. We were surrounded by a world that seemed to refute any notion that not by bread alone . . . Here the quick, the half-dead, and even the all-but-dead lived by bread, by bread alone, by the goddess of the bread ration. Perhaps we ourselves, though we talked about such things because we were intellectuals and couldn't break the habit, were in fact as morally dead as the rest. I used to parade before Anton a whole string of arguments to prove that our society had reverted to barbarism. True, the new barbarians were divided into the active and the passive, that is, into butchers and victims; but this division did not invest the victims with moral superiority, for slavery had corrupted their souls.

Anton was horrified to hear these ideas from me, and was passionately concerned to refute them. I was glad when he succeeded in demolishing my arguments. My only purpose in flinging these hard sayings at him, sayings that I myself loathed, was to get him to prove me wrong. I hoped that a gleam of the astonishing serenity with which every particle of his being was infused might also illumine my soul.

There in Belichye I found myself brought up against facts that
tended to confirm Anton's ideas. As a result of certain painful, but
at the same time comforting encounters, I saw for myself how from
the depths of moral savagery there suddenly arose the cry *"mea
maxima culpa,"* and how with this cry the patient recovered the
right to call himself a human being.

The first encounter was with Dr. Liek. One evening, in the icy
January twilight, two people who were not patients knocked at the
door of the tuberculosis ward. One of them I recognized; Anton had
introduced us at Taskan. He was also a doctor but a free man,
having been released on expiry of his sentence. He was now employed at one of the gold mines and looked as though he was doing
very well. In his mainland overcoat with its astrakhan collar and
with his curly black beard (also reminiscent of lambswool) his
whole appearance served, as it were, to underline the pitiful status
of his companion. The latter resembled an ostrich, with his height,
his small head, and the frayed camp sandals on his long feet. He had
reached that stage of emaciation at which even the most conscientious of Medical Section heads write: "Light work only."

This was Dr. Liek, through whose help Anton had five years
previously, in the first year of the wàr, lost the sight of his right
eye. At that time all Germans, including doctors, were employed
exclusively at hard manual labor. There were not enough protective
glasses to go around, so the unrelenting ultraviolet rays of the Far
East, reflected in the whiteness of the primeval snows, had burned
Anton's eye. There was no question of anyone ever being released
from work. A corneal cyst developed. Vision in the affected eye
grew worse and worse. Anton went for the second time to visit the
dispensary attached to the gold-mining camp. The doctor in the
dispensary was a prisoner, Dr. Liek. It is difficult to say why he had
been allowed to remain in his medical job despite being a full-
blooded German. Was it an oversight, or did Liek have special
services to his credit? No matter; the fact was that, at a time when
a mass witch hunt against German doctors was in progress, Liek
continued in charge of the prisoners' hospital at this mine.

"Yes," he said to Anton, "it's a cyst on the cornea." But he
couldn't put him in the hospital, because Anton Walter was a German and a doctor. Liek could then be accused—almost certainly
would be accused—of seeking to save his fellow countrymen.

Anton said nothing for a moment and then asked discreetly

whether his colleague realized that parasympathetic infection of the second eye was possible, and as a result, total blindness. Yes, Liek did realize this. In a frenzied whisper he replied in German that if he had to choose between Liek's life and Walter's sight, he would choose the former.

I had long known about this from Anton; now my unexpected guest repeated it all exactly as I had heard it and in virtually the same words. He spoke almost without emotion, in the slow way that is characteristic of dystrophics. Sometimes he repeated the same sentence, as if afraid of leaving out something important. His un-shaven face, covered with a reddish stubble, retained an unnatural composure.

"Why did you decide to tell me all this?"

"Because I can't sleep. I'm not yet forty and I have incurable insomnia. Of course I should go and speak to Walter himself. But I'm under escort, so I've no way of getting there. They brought me here under guard to attend a doctors' conference. And here I met this colleague of mine who's now being released, and he told me of you. I want you to tell Walter . . ."

"But we've been separated. I'm also under guard. I don't know whether I shall ever see him again."

"You have only a little more than a year left to serve. You'll see him. But I have a twenty-five-year sentence; I still have sixteen and a half years left to do. So I beg you to tell him . . ."

Then Liek's deceptively calm face twitched desperately with a nervous tic. But I called to mind the thick cataract on the pupil of Anton's right eye, and I asked him relentlessly:

"Tell him what, exactly?"

And then he shrieked out loud:

"Tell him that I am a shit! That I am a greater shit than even the butchers themselves. At least they are honest murderers. . . . Tell him I ought to be stripped of my doctor's diploma. . . . And tell him too that I can't sleep. And that I have nightmares even when I am awake."

He had a very unpleasant, squeaky falsetto. And the grimace that distorted his face was quite revolting. But there was so much suffering and self-accusation in his cry that I suddenly touched his sleeve and said:

"The diameter of the cataract has grown smaller over the past year. He is treating it by homeopathic means. He can now see a little with that eye."

Another of the Belichye encounters, similar to this one, was still more painful for me. This time the person in question was someone who had helped me in '39, but who two years later had become a witness in the new case against Walter.

I have already written about him. It was Krivitsky, who used to work as a doctor on board the convoy ship *S S. Dzhurma*, the same man who had saved my life by putting me in the isolation ward in the *Dzhurma*'s hold and hospitalized me on arrival in Magadan. But by '41, at the Dzhelgala gold mine, he had become an informer, and at the dictation of the local MGB representative, Fyodorov, had signed the deposition giving "particulars of the anti-Soviet agitation by Walter in the prisoners' hut." This served as the basis for a new trial and a new sentence—his third! In court Krivitsky brazenly repeated all his incriminating fabrications to Anton's face and made it much easier for the court to hand down a further ten-year sentence. In fact, this unhappy man must have slid much farther down his appalling path; in Moscow during the sixties I was to come across the name Krivitsky when I read the camp memoirs of Varlam Shalamov. In them he figures in the same despicable role.

I don't know whether he's alive now. It's hardly likely. Even then, in the winter of '46, he had been brought into Belichye after a stroke, suffering paralysis of the leg and arm, and partial aphasia. When he learned I was there, he sent me a note through the orderly. In atrocious squiggles, evidently writing with his left hand, he asked me to visit him. He didn't know, of course, that I had anything to do with Anton Walter. He cannot, evidently, have supposed that I knew about his feats of treachery.

For more than a week I put off visiting him, merely sending him my sugar ration, care of Gritsko. Then Dr. Barkan, who had been called over to look at him, said to me with a wry grin:

"Why do you want to speed up Krivitsky's death? He's going out of his mind because of your not visiting him. And after a stroke of that sort, the least upset . . ."

I went to see him. The power of speech had returned to him a few days before. It was confused and difficult to follow, but nevertheless speech. He was in a state of acute excitability. He talked without stopping . . . in denunciation of me! For my shameful, black ingratitude. If it hadn't been for him, what chance would I have had of surviving aboard the *Dzhurma?* And now when he was in trouble, I didn't want to visit him! I'd waited three weeks before putting in an appearance. . . .

What was I to reply? To explain the reason for my black ingratitude would have meant causing a deterioration in his physical condition. To say nothing? That would have been unbearable. His present appearance, as much as my knowledge of his past, made me shrink from him as from something slimy. His lackluster eyes, already on the point of glazing over, even now conveyed cunning and deceit. His mouth was contorted, not merely with paralysis but also with profound malice. I put the food package down on his bedside table and left without saying a word.

A few days went by and I learned that Krivitsky had had a second stroke. He was once more unable to speak and almost unable to move. Only his left hand was still capable of movement, and with it he had written me another note. As he handed it over, our senior orderly said to me:

"Some new patients have let the cat out of the bag—he knows you know who gave Dr. Walter his third sentence."

Among the three of us we tried to decipher the note. It was a pretty lengthy one, but it was almost impossible to make sense of his hieroglyphics—the only words we could read were "forgive" and "I shall die tomorrow."

His left hand was still mobile. It plucked feverishly at the hem of my gown. It clawed at the blanket. It had an extraordinary expressiveness about it. It was his hand that told me he was asking forgiveness; his eyes were shut. I sat down on the stool, leaned toward him, and whispered:

"You did me a good turn. I remember that. As to the rest . . . I am glad you are asking forgiveness. I am sure Walter will forgive you when I tell him how you suffered. I curse those who took advantage of your weakness. . . .

One of his eyes opened. Tears poured from it, and it was alive, not spiteful or unhappy.

On yet another occasion at Belichye I saw how a man can be racked by the pangs of conscience, and how prison, starvation, and even, perhaps, death are nothing in comparison with this torment.

A patient named Fichtenholz had been brought to us with the

last contingent from Burkhala. About thirty years old, he was
ethereally handsome, with a pale, soft-skinned beauty. From his
documents it appeared that Fichtenholz was a special contingent
detainee who had been sentenced to resettlement until further orders; and he was identified as an Estonian from Tartu. But the odd
thing was that he had great difficulty making himself understood in
Estonian.

"What sort of Estonian is he?" our old Estonian patients muttered,
with hostility. "He can't even ask for bread in Estonian!"

He knew hardly a word of Russian, either. It soon came out that
Joseph Fichtenholz was Estonian only on his father's side, and he
had lost his father early on in his childhood. On his mother's side he
was German, and his native language was German.

He was very ill indeed. His temperature refused to drop. At
nights he would gasp for breath, fall into a delirium, and toss about
frantically on his bunk.

The Baltic eyes of our Dr. Barkan looked more and more distantly
on the world immediately around him as the date of his release approached. He didn't bother too much about diagnostic differentia-
tion. All our patients were considered to be tubercular before they
came to us and they were all given the same treatment—calcium
chloride injections. But one day, on Barkan's day off, the rounds
were made by Dr. Kalambet, the spit and image of Taras Bulba;*
even here in camp the doctor had contrived to retain his portly
figure. When he arrived in our antechamber to the morgue, life itself
seemed to enter with him. Kalambet, who always filled out his diagnoses with jingles, funny faces, and Ukrainian proverbs, thus cheer-
ing up many of his patients, had only this to say about Joseph
Fichtenholz:

"He's not your patient, he's mine. He's got bronchial pneumonia.
Tell Barkan to transfer him to us in the main block."

But this caused Barkan to mount his high horse. His diagnosis
could not be wrong. He continued to prescribe the same pointless
treatment for Joseph.

One night Gritsko woke me up.

"You'd better come and see the cherub. . . . It looks as if he's
on his way. . . ."

* Jolly, fat, mustachioed Cossack, hero of novella (1842) by Gogol.

Fichtenholz was completely doubled up, barely able to breathe. His light blue eyes were bulging from their sockets; cold sweat was streaming down his face.

"*Ich kann nicht mehr.* . . . *Bitte* . . . *Luftembolie* . . . *Machen Sie Luftembolie um Gotteswillen.* . . ."

I didn't at first realize what was meant by *Luftembolie*. When I did, I shuddered. I had heard that this particular form of murder was practiced by doctors in Hitler's Germany: when a syringe that is filled with air is introduced into the vein it causes an air bubble and death. And he wanted me to do just that!

"You're mad! We're not fascists. We don't murder our patients, we treat them."

Yes, but he was beyond treatment by now. So the nurse shouldn't prolong his agony; he was at the end of his tether.

What was to be done? It was quite useless to run for Barkan. Kalambet wouldn't come either—he wouldn't want to get on the wrong side of Barkan. Then I put to myself the question that had more than once come to my aid here in Belichye. What would Anton have done in similar circumstances?

The sick man had an emphysema. He must be bled. Under camp conditions, the old methods of letting blood had more than once saved people in the Taskan hospital.

There was nothing to lose by it. . . . I put the bowl in position and introduced a large needle into the vein. The blood started to trickle into the bowl in large, slow drops like red currants and spread out over its white base in rivulets. My heart beat frantically. Was I doing something wrong? How many grams of blood had Anton taken using this method?

The sick man stopped groaning, and even seemed to have fallen asleep. With trembling hands I gave him a camphor injection. What else was there? Ah yes, hot, sweet tea, the stronger the better. . . .

In short, I managed to save him. And on our rounds of inspection the following morning, Barkan said to me sarcastically:

"Now do you see? You and Kalambet doubted my diagnosis. See how the patient's condition has improved on calcium chloride."

I don't know whether Fichtenholz understood this remark, but in any case it had been decided between us—without any form of words, simply by an exchange of glances—not to say anything to Barkan about the previous night's bloodletting or about my not giving him the calcium chloride injection.

He became dear to me, as the fruits of our efforts always are dear to us. When he was put on the convalescent list and his temperature returned to normal (37 degrees), I deliberately wrote down 38 degrees on his chart. I wanted to give him a chance to get stronger and keep him away from Burkhala as long as possible. I used to slip him half my ration. It wasn't all that difficult, because what with the exhausting work and the stuffy atmosphere I had almost entirely lost my appetite. But he ate with the keen appetite of a condemned man restored to the land of the living. He was visibly recovering his health.

He repaid my attentions with silent adoration. He was generally taciturn, and would not talk about himself, even when I put questions to him in German. But one evening our senior orderly, Nikolai Aleksandrovich, after collecting the supper from the canteen—the place where all the Belichye news circulated from mouth to mouth—brought back some distressing information about Joseph Fichtenholz.

"He's a Nazi officer! Just think of it! And he's been here on the same footing as our boys who fought honorably and were guilty only of having been taken prisoner. . . ."

It was a blow for me. It would seem that I had saved a murderer, perhaps a member of the SS!

"How did you learn of it?"

"They all say so. . . ."

The source was far from reliable. It was well known how camp rumors got distorted out of all proportion in the telling. I said nothing to Fichtenholz, but began to keep a critical eye on his behavior. It was impeccable. He tried his level best to be useful to the block. "Neat and tidy" were the approving comments of Gritsko, whom he helped with the cleaning. He worked particularly hard on the floor in my little room, scrubbing the pine planks until they were pristine. In addition, he used to present me with little wooden figures he had made himself. By some miracle he had retained a small penknife; with it he used to carve amazing objects from chunks of wood—gawkily graceful little figures, full of thought and talent. Once he brought me two small cherubs, similar to those at the foot of the Sistine Madonna.

"They're for you," he said, giving me a look of utter devotion, "because you are an angel."

We were alone together. I found myself saying some terrible things which would probably have been better left unsaid:

"I, an angel? What do you mean? I'm just an ordinary person. But if you had met me three years ago and in different circumstances, you would have burned me alive, poisoned me in a gas chamber, or hanged me on the gallows. . . ."

"I? You?" His handsome face broke out in dark red blotches. "But why?"

"Because I'm a Jew. And you are a Nazi officer, aren't you?"

He went ashen white and fell to his knees. I had the impression that he was afraid of being denounced, and I struck again.

"Don't be afraid. If they don't know about you, I won't be the one to denounce you. . . ."

He cried out as if a bullet had hit him. And I realized my mistake. It was not fear, but pangs of conscience that were tormenting him. Those excruciating pangs that will break a man down far more effectively than any form of physical pain. To this day I still don't know whether he had been in the service of the Nazis and in what precise capacity. But it was evident that he had something to repent of.

Poleaxed by the unexpectedness of the blow, he forgot his normal restraint and caution. Kneeling before me, he burst into loud sobs like a child, grabbed at my hands, and tried to kiss them, endlessly repeating one and the same thing: "I'm a Christian. . . . It wasn't as if I wanted to! It wasn't as if I wanted to!"

There was such profound anguish in all this that for a fraction of a second I was sorry I had struggled so hard to save his life. Perhaps it would have been better for him to die than to live with such a burden on his soul. I don't know—perhaps he was a fascist monster, perhaps merely a blind executant of inhuman orders. In any event, as of that moment, in that supreme anguish of his, he had become a man.

People may reply that it is more common to come across cases of those who loudly protest their innocence while seeking to put the blame on the era they live in, on their neighbors, or on their own youthfulness and inexperience. . . . And that is so. Yet, I am all but convinced that the very loudness of these protestations is meant to drown the quiet and inexorable inner voice that keeps reminding a man of his guilt.

Today, as I near the end of my allotted span, I know for certain that Anton Walter was right. *Mea culpa* knocks at everyone's heart and the only question is when that person will hear these words resounding deep within him.

These two words are easy to hear during sleepless periods when you look back on your life with loathing, when you tremble and curse. When you can't sleep, the knowledge that you did not directly take part in the murders and betrayals is no consolation. After all, the assassin is not only he who struck the blow, but whoever supported evil, no matter how: by thoughtless repetition of dangerous political theories; by silently raising his right hand; by faint-heartedly writing half-truths. *Mea culpa* . . . and it occurs to me more and more frequently that even eighteen years of hell on earth is insufficient expiation for the guilt.

18

· *Crime and punishment again*

In 1939, when we were sitting out our second year in a Yaroslavl punishment cell for two, Julia reminded me of a couplet from a book, the title of which I have forgotten:

> And while we are talking here like this
> Ten years slip past like a thin gray mist.

We had a good laugh. In those days, ten years—the period to which we had been sentenced—seemed to us quite unreal, a price subject to negotiation. During that time, according to our learned calculations, one of two things was bound to happen: either the Big Bad Wolf would die or the Little Pig would perish.

We were wrong. Ten years turned out to be real enough. Now they were coming to an end. It was February 15, 1946. There was exactly a year to go to the expiry of my sentence, and things were perfectly stable: our beloved Big Bad Wolf, despite all the vicissitudes of history, was still alive and kicking, and the Little Pigs were still hauling their loads along the remote tracks of our nether world.

I had very little hope of being released when the calendar period was up. The number of "extra-termers" who had counter-signed on the dotted line the papers sentencing them to be re-imprisoned "pending special instructions" was constantly on the increase, as I could see for myself. Nevertheless, the thought that I had got it down to the last year somehow gave me fresh heart. The important thing now was to avoid getting assigned to lethally danger-ous work during that period, to stay put with my KB's. All the more so, in that I had turned out to be amazingly resistant to tu-bercular infection. Dr. Kalambet had been giving me a monthly X-ray check-up, and all was in order.

Alas, spring brought great changes to our Belichye, and they af-fected me painfully on the rebound. I don't know what higher considerations were behind it, but Savoeva was moved elsewhere. And her place as head doctor was taken by a stout lady named Volkova, nicknamed the She-Wolf. The day of her arrival, the work assigner, Pushkin, said to me in a malignant whisper:

"She hates women! She's caused the death of more than one woman prisoner. Savoeva will seem to us like our own long-lost mother after her. . . ."

"Why only women? For what reason?"

"Who knows? But it's a fact. She treats men O.K., but the women . . . maybe because she's got a glass eye."

Oddly enough, Pushkin turned out to be right. With our new chief the women prisoners had to mind their P's and Q's. Who could tell what importunate dreams kept causing our new head doctor to get up in the middle of the night and set out on a hunt for clandestine lovers? Why did she derive so much comfort from her furious campaign for purity? Why was she so fond of sending to certain death women prisoners who had an affair in camp? Why did she spare the men and punish the women? Who could tell . . . ? But I felt the oppressive weight of her suspicious and hostile glance the first time I met her; not only her good eye but even the glass one seemed to bore right through me.

One night I was awakened by heavy thuds on the little door of my cabin.

"Open up! At once! Or we'll break the door down!"

Half asleep as I was, I couldn't immediately lay hands on my slippers and dressing gown.

"Very well, then . . ."

There was a splintering sound from the makeshift plywood door and I was confronted by two armed guards under the leadership of our new head doctor, the She-Wolf. Her hair was all awry. Her face—which must once have been attractive, but was now droopy and heavily jowled—was white.

"Search under the bed," she commanded.

It was awkward for the guards. They had known me now for a whole year, and they respected me for "being hot on science," as they put it. I had more than once lent them a helping hand with their homework for the night-school courses that many of them were taking. On one occasion I had made an impression on them by being able to answer straight off the cuff the question about when and where Stalin had first met Lenin. Trying not to look at me, they were now making a very halfhearted search under the bed.

When the action was over and I was left on my own again, Gritsko looked in on me, terrified out of his wits. He reported that he had heard one of the guards, on his way out, saying to the She-Wolf about me: "A serious, educated woman . . . never been known to have any fancy men."

Nevertheless, within a week Volkova decided to make yet another raid. Likewise to no effect . . . But then one night . . .

It was already two in the morning when someone tapped softly at my window. I jumped up, and in the pale moonlight I made out Anton's face. Yes, it was he! Our benefactor, the commandant of Taskan camp, our kindly master Timoshkin, seeing how his court physician was pining away with grief, had hit on a pretext that would give him a chance to see me. It was by no means all that simple to get authorization for a prisoner-doctor to undertake a duty trip unescorted, but Timoshkin got it. It took Anton an entire day and night to cover the one hundred kilometers between Taskan and Belichye. He got a lift from a driver he knew who was nursing his lumbering, massive Lend-Lease Diamond-T truck along the highway. Although it was the beginning of April, in our northern sector we were still exposed to 40-degree frosts and winds too. Anton was frozen stiff in his thin jacket. Part of the way he walked beside the Diamond, trying to get ahead of it.

Could I possibly have refused to let him in? I realized that the She-Wolf might descend on me at any moment. I could have hidden Anton in the orderly's little den or in the ward and passed him off as one of the patients. But how can you think of the dangers, how can you think calmly and logically at all when a miracle is happening, when the person of whom you have been thinking every waking moment for a year is suddenly standing there outside your window, as if he had fallen from the sky, and says, "Genia dear, it's me."

The She-Wolf was really in luck this time! She came in just as we were kissing each other. Her face beamed with joy, grew animated, became attractive. What a successful hunt!

"I am the head doctor of the Belichye Hospital," she pronounced triumphantly, looking at Anton.

"Forgive me, colleague, for infringing the regulations. I also am a doctor. I am a prisoner. I beg you to understand: this is my wife. We haven't seen each other for an entire year."

"Draw up a report," ordered the She-Wolf, turning to the guards. "The woman prisoner has been caught red-handed. She is receiving men at night, and using official premises for immoral purposes."

I was descending farther and farther down the slippery path of vice. I had been dismissed from Taskan for "attempting to create conditions for vice by means of hospitalizing a prisoner of the male sex in a ward for prisoners of the female sex." This time it was a matter of my own immoral conduct, set down in black and white in the decree committing me once again to Elgen—the inevitable receptacle of all who were penalized for breaking the rules of Kolyma, more particularly, of all loose women.

Belichye was over. With my bundle in hand, I stood once more at the voracious gates of the Elgen camp compound. I was turning back on my tracks.

But the first piece of local news was reassuring. Zimmerman, I heard, was no longer here. Major Puzanchikov was now in charge. The general opinion of him was that he was someone you could live with: he was neither cruel nor kind—he didn't give a damn about the prisoners. His main object was to serve out his time, to be credited with the 100 per cent northern area increments, and to return to the mainland.

Inside the hut it was as if I had returned to my own family. Oh, this feeling of prison kinship! It is perhaps the strongest of all human relationships. Even now, many years later, as I am writing these memoirs, all of us who have tasted of the blood of the lamb are members of one family. Even the stranger whom you meet on your travels, or at a health spa, or at somone else's house, immediately becomes near and dear to you when you learn that he was *there*. In other words, he knows things that are beyond the comprehension of people who have not been there, even the most noble and kind-hearted among them.

I had not been in Elgen for two years; during that time I had seen nothing of my former traveling companions from Yaroslavl, from Butyrki, from the penal convoys. I avidly absorbed the news. Willi Rupert had been released, Mina Malskaya had died, Galya Stadnikova's children, who were born in camps, were being brought up in the children's home. One group of extra-termers had been released. The work assigner now was Anya Barkhash, a political.

All this was important to me. It excited me, depressed me, or gladdened me by turns. And in the evening returned the much-missed pleasure of a heart-to-heart conversation with people who shared my own interests, my own obsessive passion for literature. The She-Wolf of Belichye would doubtless have considered me abnormal if she could have seen Berta Babina and me sitting down beside the stove to recite poems to one another the moment we met. And how furious it would have made the She-Wolf to see the warmth of the welcome given me that first night at terrible Elgen. Each woman, as she returned from work, was greeted with a shout: "Genia's back!"

Early the next morning, following Anya Barkhash's advice, I queued up to see the new camp commandant. Behind the desk that used to be Zimmerman's sat a dignified, handsome blond man of about thirty-five; he bore a slight resemblance, with his short side whiskers, the luminosity of his eyes, and the immaculate perfection of his uniform, to the engraving of Tsar Nicholas I. But unlike the Tsar, Puzanchikov clearly had no particular enthusiasm for his duties. He gave me an absent-minded glance, and paid no attention to what I was saying to him, nor even to Anya Barkhash's recommendation. Under our carefully thought out plan she was supposed to speak of me in a tone of bored indifference. Here she is . . . come to us from Belichye (not a word as to the reason why—and Puzanchikov showed no disposition to ask questions), an experienced nurse, but then we haven't any vacancies on the medical side at the moment. . . . Very little time left to serve, she's down to her last year . . . How about sending her to the camp farm?

Anya acted her part to perfection. We had decided between us that after burning my boats at Belichye, the best thing for me was to remain in the shadows, on general physical labor. Puzanchikov nodded unconcernedly by way of assent—the farm it was to be.

This was physical drudgery, but of the bearable sort. One could survive with employment of this kind. The agricultural workers lived in the central compound and were less liable to be posted to distant places. At the farm there were always vegetable tops and tails about the place to chew, which meant that you could keep scurvy at arm's length. The job they gave me was thinning out cabbage seedlings. I have completely forgotten by now what precisely it was that we did. All I can remember is certain automatic, monotonous motions with my hands over the open frame, and the nagging pain in my feet, which swelled up badly by the time evening came. Not being used to it, I found it difficult enough to stay upright for twelve hours at a stretch. I was positively relieved when a fragment of glass from the greenhouse roof was dislodged and embedded itself in my arm like a dagger, causing an arterial hemorrhage that brought me three days' sick leave.

I was lying on the plank bunk, enjoying the blessed feeling of having nothing to do, when Anya Barkhash came into the empty hut and asked excitedly whether, with my wounded arm, I could get my things together quickly.

"Am I being posted?"

"Sort of . . . but you needn't turn pale. You're going to Taskan, back to your doctor. You're in luck! They've swapped you for a stovesetter. Hurry up, though. . . . The guard's waiting."

We spread out on the floor the old flannel shawl belonging to my nurse, Fima, which had already done me yeoman service in all my journeyings under escort, and started piling up my worldly goods on top of it. Then we tied it all up in one large bundle. The pain in my arm and the thudding of my heart tended to blot out Anya's disjointed account, but I nevertheless got the gist of it. Our benefactor, the kindly squire at Taskan, had kept his promise.

"He came into the Registration and Distribution Section," Anya explained. "And there, by a stroke of luck, they were trying to light the stove and the place was full of smoke. 'What's this?' he asks our Puzanchikov. 'You don't mean to say you haven't got a decent

stovesetter? If you like, I'll let you have mine. He'll put all your
stoves right. . . . All I want in exchange for him is one of your
women. . . .' And Puzanchikov replies: 'Take half a dozen of them.
I'm snowed under with them as it is. . . . Well, do at least take
three, or else I shall feel bad about it. It'll seem an unfair exchange.'
. . . To cut a long story short, they shook hands on it. Timoshkin
himself has gone off, but has left a guard behind to escort you. The
guard's in a great hurry. . . . Run over to the guardhouse!"

It was all like a fairy tale. My most farfetched dreams had come
true. I found myself sitting on top of my bundle in the rear com-
partment of a jolting truck, breathing deep into my lungs the vapor
of the naked earth, which had now shed its winter covering. Spring
had come. . . . In Anton's note, passed on to me in the most high-
flown manner imaginable, via the guard(!), he mentioned that it was
the third day of the Catholic Easter.

Drip, drip . . . a large icicle fell from the roof of the state farm
headquarters. It landed on the fur cap of a passer-by. He swore, then
laughed and brushed off the ice crystals. The guard and I also
laughed. The guard was in the best of moods. He lit a cigarette,
hummed "Katyusha," and gazed at the diffidently blue Kolyma horizon. What was he thinking of? Probably the same thing I was thinking of: that we had lived, after all, to see in one more spring. . . .
When you come to think of it, with the war still to be won, his
chances of living were perhaps no greater than mine. But we had
both survived so far. My padded jacket and his greatcoat were both
bespattered with mud whenever a wheel found a pothole. We shook
ourselves and brushed ourselves clean; our shared discomfort made
us feel still closer.

Someone ahead was thumbing a lift. We let him climb aboard.
What a day of miracles it was! He turned out to be someone I knew,
Ivan Isaev, once "the young Moscow author." By now he was not
so very young: he had served his eight-year sentence and stayed on
with free status as some sort of economist out here in the taiga. Instead of leaving for the mainland he was waiting for the arrival of
his fiancée. And his fiancée was Galya Voronskaya, the daughter
of Aleksandr Voronsky: she was an extra-termer who had been resentenced pending special instructions.

After running through the latest camp news, we suddenly became
engrossed in discussing literary events of ten years before. Isaev,
it was clear, had grown frantically bored with the company of the

clerical staff of Kolyma. He welcomed the opportunity of talking like this, and we conversed without stopping until our guard thoughtfully summed up:

"The devil if I understand! You seem to be Russian . . . and that's Russian you're muttering . . . but I can't understand a damn thing! All those highfalutin words you use . . ."

We had arrived! There they were, the sacred gates of Taskan Paradise! I was led into the compound. As it happened Commandant Timoshkin was standing in the middle of the courtyard.

"Oh, oh, oh!" he exclaimed, pretending to be amazed. "You here again? I didn't even know you had been assigned here. . . ."

That was for the benefit of whoever might be passing by. But for me there was a conspiratorial twinkle in his narrow eyes. Timoshkin was radiant. It feels good to do good deeds.

Anton was already racing toward me from the hospital porch, and the tail of his white overall flapped in the spring breeze.

If only the She-Wolf of Belichye, that champion of superior morals, had been there to see us!

19

· *From the opening bell to close of play*

The extent to which, year in, year out, arbitrary practices had been on the increase could be gauged even from the change of meaning of the everyday camp expression: "From the opening bell to close of play."

Previously, this expression had been used in a pejorative sense. Look, they said, so-and-so has not benefited from any acts of clemency: no amnesty, no remissions for good work, no premature release. He's had to serve out the full term to which he was sentenced, "from the opening bell to close of play."

At this time, in the tenth year of my voyagings, with the war over and us victorious, just when we were all expecting unprecedented clemency from the government, the expression "from the opening bell . . ." started to be used in the reverse sense, with a positive connotation. Look, they said, so-and-so has been released on the dot; he's lucky, he has not been shot for sabotage, resentenced, or kept on as an extra-termer.

The numbers of the extra-termers grew from day to day as the calendar took us to the tenth anniversary of the mass purges of '37. No one could understand on what principle he or she had become an extra-termer; why some—the minority—were released grudgingly, as if under duress, but still released; while others were consigned to the fearful category of those held in camps "pending special orders."

In the huts people debated these subjects until they were blue in the face, but they got no nearer to identifying the modalities. Someone had just proved brilliantly that those who were held "pending special orders" were the ones with a T on their papers—T for Trotskyism, the brand of the devil. But then Marusya Bychkova, who had this fateful letter on hers, was suddenly released, whereas Katya Sosnovskaya, who didn't, had to countersign a document resentencing her, "pending . . ." Of course, that was it . . . they weren't releasing people who had been abroad. But then the following day the playful minds of officialdom demolished this hypothesis, too.

I had long since made up my own mind that in our world the normal chain of cause and effect had been broken. At that time I had read neither Kafka nor Orwell, so I did not yet perceive the logic underlying the apparent paralogisms. With an ever fainter heart I counted off the months and the days to that fateful date for me—February 15, 1947. I did not try to marshal my hopes and fears into any sort of logical pattern. What's the point of looking ahead when you're playing chess with an orangutan?

So I simply did my guessing on a heads-and-tails basis. It mostly came out No, they won't. By now I could scarcely imagine what it was like to be free; the idea was too vague, too abstract. As to the idea of leaving Kolyma, I simply could not get it into my head. I was absolutely sure that Stalin would never pardon those to whom he had done such a fearful wrong. I knew that no one who had fallen into that machine would ever get out of it. It could only be a question of a breathing space or a temporary relaxation, or of simply being allowed outside the barbed wire. And that was what I dreamed of avidly.

No sooner did some of our people get out of camp than they set off for the mainland, without pausing to think that what they had in their possession were not ordinary internal passports, but "wolves' passports." Many of them I tried to dissuade. It would be better, I said, to have their children sent out to them. Back on the mainland, even in the most remote spot, a new arrest would inevitably follow, however quietly you hid in your hole. Many people called me a pessimist for my forecasts; but life was to show that, on the contrary, I had been overoptimistic in my hope that we would be permitted to remain in peace, there in Kolyma, with the status of exiles, for within a few years the wave of rearrests had reached all the way to Kolyma.

In any event, I had firmly resolved not to return to the mainland. I was, of course, tortured by the thought of not seeing my mother again. But I hoped to be able to arrange for Vasya, the last surviving flesh of my flesh, to come here. The peak of my hopes was to have a small room in the free settlement of Taskan, where Vasya and I could wait for Anton's release. There was another six years to wait.

In the meantime I was peacefully sitting out my last months in camp, sheltered from storms, under Timoshkin's protection. He had assigned me as nurse to the free children's kindergarten.

The insufficiency of sunshine and vitamins had left its imprint even on the free children of Kolyma. They were slow for their age, not as high-spirited as they should have been, and they were often ill. However, these were children with a home, whose mothers and fathers brought them to and from school each day, who did not pluck at your heart strings as did the children of the prisoners at the Elgen children's home.

I was the only prisoner on the staff of the kindergarten. The others were Komsomol girls whose hearts had bid them come to Kolyma and help develop the Far North. That didn't mean, as they said themselves, that any of them didn't have other, additional ideas about finding a husband. After the war fiancés were worth their weight in gold on the mainland, while here they were everywhere to be had. In fact, there was an acutely felt shortage of women, especially free ones. One after the other, in rapid succession, the Komsomol girls went and got married to the guards, to the camp operations personnel, and to people in the administration of the camps and mines. Some of them, the headstrong ones, immediately earned them-

selves reprimands, or even expulsion from the Komsomol, by defy-
ing the categorical ban on love affairs with former prisoners.

The girls whom I came across in the Taskan kindergarten looked
at me rather apprehensively during the first few days. But after that
their healthy sense of reality got the upper hand: they preferred
to believe what they saw with their own eyes rather than what they
had been told at their special briefings. They saw that I worked
without sparing myself, that I was always ready to stand in for any
one of them. After all, I had nowhere to rush off to: the guard
brought me there each day at 8 A.M. and came to collect me at 8 P.M.
The previous free-and-easy ways had not been reintroduced in
Taskan. Nowadays the disciplinary officer took good care that
women prisoners did not walk around the village unguarded.

In charge of the kindergarten was the wife of the guard detachment commander, a woman about thirty-five years old, very proud
of the fact that she had graduated from a training school for kindergarten teachers. She'd refer to this each morning at our staff gather-
ings, when she would give a blow-by-blow account of how she
got where she was from "humble beginnings." At one time, so she
said, she couldn't even speak properly. She used always to say not
"harmony" but "armony," not "hawk" but "awk." The head smiled
prettily at the thought of her past ignorance, and added proudly that
now she knew better: not "awk" but "hawk," not "eagle" but
"heagle."

The head was not well disposed to me at first. I even heard her
complaining in a loud whisper to the cook about Timoshkin's eccentricities. "What a crazy idea of his it was to put a 'counter' in
charge of the children! I shouldn't like any trouble with him, though,
since he's my husband's boss."

My way to the head's heart lay through the piano, which until
my arrival had stood locked and shrouded in its rigid protective
cover. The head would not allow Katya, one of the Komsomol girls,
to touch it—for she could play only by ear. No question of letting
it be used for mere tinkling. The piano was only to be opened up
for someone who could sight-read the contents of the album *Songs
for the Under-Sevens*. I offered my services. The ice was broken.
And within a month my standing was such as to allow me to draw
up in the head's name plans of children's concerts on red-letter days.
Locally she won a lot of praise for this. The free population of

Taskan looked dotingly on the spectacle of their children singing to the accompaniment of the piano, and performing in dramatized fairy tales.

(I was surprised to discover, incidentally, that Anton absolutely adored listening to little children reciting, and was thrilled to find what a well-trained pianist I was. Using his privileged access as a doctor, he never missed a single concert, and could be just as comical in his sentimental enthusiasm as were the children's parents. These naïve patriarchal traits revealed a new, touchingly funny side to his character. What was surprising was that by the evening he had become his usual, acutely intelligent self, and often replied to my questions before I had even asked them. These laconic evening conversations of ours in Taskan remained among my most treasured recollections, as if the dream of wordless communion had come true.)

The year 1947 was approaching. We could now count not only the months but even the weeks and days remaining to the "close of play" for me. Anton had proposed organizing a New Year's Eve party in his office. But the chief disciplinary officer had said categorically that he would not let a woman, i.e. me, into the men's compound at night. Anton had then found a way out: we'd see the New Year in at 8 A.M., local time. For that would be midnight on the mainland. And it was New Year on the mainland, not in Kolyma, that mattered to us.

Our celebration did take place. I heated up on the hospital gas ring some precooked piroshki Siberian style (stuffed with chopped venison). Confucius triumphantly placed a bottle of port wine, held in reserve for just such an occasion, on the operating table. Sakhno laid the table, with measuring glasses for the wine and tin bowls for the hors d'oeuvres. The wintry light of the Kolyma dawn had not yet filtered through the windows, and to make things more cheerful we plugged in an extra-powerful bulb, borrowed from the morgue, where it had illuminated the table used for autopsies.

We were six in all at our New Year's feast: Anton, Confucius, Sakhno, Berezov—the ex-diplomat who had now become the medical statistician at our hospital—and Pentegov, our free guest, an ex-professor of chemistry, a former detainee, and now an engineer at the food plant. I was the only woman at the table. Now, more than twenty years later, I am the only one of the six still alive. Slutsky puts it very well in his poem: "Where the old women bend with the wind, the old men keel over." Of course we were not old people then, but the phrase holds good for men and women of all ages.

Our poor male companions! The weaker sex . . . For it was they who keeled over dead where we merely bent with the wind while we stayed the course. They were better than we at using an ax, pick, or wheelbarrow, but they were greatly inferior in their ability to withstand torture.

We raised our measuring glasses to freedom. We longed for it with a desperate, passionate, insatiable yearning. It was this longing for freedom that made us all brothers and sisters in misfortune.

And the very next day—the first of January—we again had cause to feel ourselves to be mere objects in the process of being transferred from one sack to another by some anonymous being. The order from Sevlag for the liquidation of the women's section of the Taskan camp and the reassignment of all eighteen women prisoners came like a bolt out of the blue. What was our destination to be? Elgen, of course!

"It's only a month and a half, Genia," Anton said to reassure me, clasping my hands in his. "Six weeks. They'll go by without your noticing. Then it'll be the fifteenth of February, and you'll be free. We can afford to be patient. . . . After all, the Zimmerman-Woman is no longer there. I've already arranged with Pertsulenko—the head doctor of the Elgen free hospital—that you'll be working for him as nurse. Meanwhile, I'll look around here in Taskan for a room for you. And you'll be coming back here right after your release."

He went into great detail about our arrangements for the future, in an effort to conceal the dread that the specter of extra time inspired in him.

The Taskan women, all eighteen of us, were loaded onto the back of a truck. The twenty-two kilometers that had flown by last spring seemed endless now that I was heading back to Elgen. The January frost chilled us to the bone. Our eyelashes were frozen stiff, and our cheeks tingled. The notorious Elgen camp gates stayed shut for a good half hour after our arrival; someone in the Registration and Distribution Section was late in processing our documentation, and we had to sit there in the open truck, frozen into virtual unconsciousness.

After our ordeal I found sleep quite beyond me that night, and, lying there on the second tier of bunks, I tossed and turned in a succession of half-delirious waking reveries. I was haunted by the thought that my life was like a game of croquet—a favorite pastime of mine as a child. Just when you have negotiated the most difficult hoops of all, wham! You are croqueted; your opponent steadies your ball with his foot and then makes it cannon against the peg. And that's that! Begin again! And here I was, being bashed into the Elgen peg yet again. But it was only six weeks to the fifteenth of February, after all; or, rather, six weeks less one day.

Dr. Pertsulenko, an acquaintance and admirer of Anton's, kept his word. I became a nurse at the free hospital. I worked feverishly without pausing to rest. I immediately acquired the reputation of being a slogger. But intense work without any sort of respite was the only means by which I could preserve some sort of equilibrium, considering my constant oscillation between hope and despair.

The moment I got back inside the compound after finishing work I rushed off to the ancillary staff hut where Anya Barkhash, the work assigner, was living. What news was there? What lists had come in today—lists of those to be discharged or of those to be kept back? Usually these lists arrived from Sevlag some ten days before the date of expiry of one's calendar term. With a patient sigh, Anya told me all the news, and the two of us began trying to penetrate the higher realms of official thinking. We had nothing but our woefully inadequate five senses to rely on. We had, of course, long since put from us any thought of law or justice. Nowadays the only criterion was: What would *they* deem most advantageous? But the result was still the same topsy-turvy one. Tanya was being released, although she had lived in France for a long time. But Nina was being kept behind, although she had never really been anywhere except Saratov. Katya was being released, although she had a *T;* while her sister, who did not, had been kept on, "pending . . ."

The nearer it got to the date for my release, the less able I was to control my nerves. I was literally in a fever with my constantly seesawing expectations.

But one day . . . Early one morning, before roll call, the hut door squeaked on a special, new note. Anya Barkhash stood there panting from her headlong sprint, and could hardly get a word out. But she did manage two: "It's come!"

The order for my release had arrived. My name was on one of the regular lists of those due to leave the camp. I scarcely remember how those last two weeks went by. All I do remember is Anton's phone calls during my night shift in the hospital, his telling me to keep myself under control, and, heaven forbid, not to make any slip-up in dealing with the patients at the hospital.

At last the day had come! The previous day, at evening roll call, I had already been warned not to parade for work but to report to the Registration and Distribution Section at 9 A.M.

It was still quite dark. The searchlights from the watchtowers illuminated the minute flakes of driving, slanting, stinging snow. It was difficult to keep one's footing on the filthy ice, which was patterned by the sewage seeping out from the latrines.

There was a professional recidivist ahead of me in the queue waiting to see Linkova, the head of Registration and Distribution. Linkova was in a bad mood. Her pretty, vapid face was swollen and her lids were puffy. She must have been having a bad time of it at home.

"Well now, how long are you leaving us for this time?" Linkova asked the girl in a bored tone of voice, showing her with one bright-red polished nail where to countersign the order of release. "Are we to expect you back shortly with a new sentence?"

"Who knows?" the other replied, equally indifferent, scrawling on the documents with an unpracticed hand. "All depends on Lady Luck. . . . I'm thinking of going over to the mainland when the boats start, so if I get nabbed it won't be Kolyma anyway, but Potma or one of the Mari camps or somewhere. . . ."

My turn now. The same indifferent glance from Linkova. She gave an open-mouthed yawn, which made her doll's eyes water.

"Sign here. You fifty-eighters get Form A in Yagodnoye, not here. For the time being here's a temporary identity document to show the militia. And sign again here. . . ."

I reverently folded the document in four, as our old nurse Fima used to do with her identity papers. Where was I to put this treasure? My first personal document in ten years, my pass to get out of Elgen. After a moment's hesitation, I put it carefully and cautiously inside my bodice, against my breast.

The hut warden, Grandma Nastya, whom I had known from Butyrki days, had already assembled my things before I got back. She quickly made the sign of the cross over me. "God be with you! I'll give you a hand with your things as far as the guardhouse. . . . Where are you spending the night? In the free hospital, I suppose?"

"Not likely! I'm off to Taskan this very minute. Anton Yakovlevich has already rented a room for me in the free settlement."

"And him . . . will they be releasing him soon?"

"Another six years to go."

Grandma Nastya looked grim.

"You're a silly girl! You've done your time, and now you choose to spend another six years waiting outside the guardhouse! There's no shortage of men! You'd do better to find a free one before you're too old!"

The guard on duty at the entrance that day was Lugovskoy. He had known me since 1940 and had always treated me well. He looked at me, astonished, through the little window.

"Where are you off to with your belongings?"

"I've been released. I'm leaving for good."

"Well, well! How come?"

"It's quite simple. My ten years are up. From the opening bell to close of play."

He was beside himself at hearing my news. People got used to one another, despite everything. And he was a decent man. One of those about whom Korolenko wrote: "Decent people in a foul place."

Lugovskoy came out of the guardhouse into the cold passageway where I was standing with my bundle, my wooden trunk, and the magical document that could open these doors.

"Well, if that's how it is, I congratulate you," he said, holding out his hand to me. Then he shook his head despondently, and with saintly simplicity came out in all seriousness with the famous phrase from Pogodin's* play:

"The best people are leaving us, you know. . . . Soon nothing but recidivists will remain. The sort of people we'll have to work with then! Well, O.K. So long, then. . . ."

"What do you mean?" I exclaimed in horror. "What do you mean? How can you say such a thing? It isn't so long, it's good-by! Good-by forever!"

"I didn't mean anything," he muttered, rather hurt, and he reluctantly jerked back the large iron bolt.

I emerged from the guardhouse. The anemic bluish light of dawn merged with the wan rays of the searchlights. From somewhere far

* Nikolai Pogodin (1900–1962): playwright; author of *Aristocrats* (1937), which deals with the "rehabilitation" of criminals through labor in the camps.

off came the barking of Alsatians. Along the track ambled an ox-drawn watercart and its driver.

"Up you get with your things! I can take you as far as the bath-house, anyway," the driver offered good-naturedly.

"No, no. Who wants to crawl along like that stupid ox of yours?"

I hurried past and left the ox a long way behind me. I was almost running, oblivious of the weight of my belongings and of the cold, which made breathing difficult.

There's an end to everything in this world. Even to Elgen.

Part two

1

· *The Firebird's tail*

In 1947 releases from camp were by no means on such a mass scale as they presumably ought to have been. This was, after all, the tenth anniversary of 1937, and for thousands of people the calendar year for the expiry of the sentences handed down to them by the Military Collegium, the Tribunal, the Special Conference, or one of the many other courts. And yet . . .

Although the chink through which people squeezed out of the camps became a little wider, the number of people released constituted only an insignificant percentage of those who nervously awaited their "close of play," trusting in the sanctity of the law.

The higher thinking that guided officialdom was utterly beyond the grasp even of prisoners who were particularly well up on Marxism and who had retained the habit of dialectical thought. Ordinary human reason could not solve the mystery of why certain people figured in the lists of those down for release, while most were invited to sign for a further spell in camp "pending special orders," thus bereft even of the comfort of counting the months and weeks remaining to the end of their legal, judicially imposed sentence.

One might think that this atmosphere of officially imposed arbitrariness would elicit in those remaining in camp a feeling of hostility toward those scheduled for release. And yet I can testify with complete assurance that *no one envied those who had been released*. I do not want to give an idealized picture. It would be foolish for me to imply that prisoners were more humane than the free population. How often had I witnessed faces contorted with hatred at the sight of other unfortunates receiving an extra ten grams of bread or getting off with less injurious conditions of work. I had seen displays of undisguised covetousness over someone else's newly issued sandals, or over a vacant place on the lower tier of bunks. For in camp people's faces were naked and not protected by conventional masks.

But they did not envy those who had been released. All nastiness and pettiness disappeared as if by magic where freedom was concerned, even the pitiful, meager simulacrum of freedom represented by the status of free employee in Kolyma. (For the higher thinking reached out even to those who had emerged from camp: some were allowed to leave for the mainland, whereas others had to remain behind in the taiga.)

Yes, it was there, inside the barbed wire, that I came across this gift for sharing the happiness of others, something far more precious and difficult to attain than a gift for sharing their sorrows. A paradox, you say? Maybe, after all, it's not such a paradox. For example, from my childhood days onward I had always noticed that people's faces light up when they are watching some little wild animal that has strayed into a built-up area. A hedgehog or a squirrel, say . . . How their faces are transformed! A sort of childlike simplicity is visible behind their irritable, gloomy, city-dweller expressions. An astonishing glow lights up their faces, piercing through the malevolent mask.

The same transformation occurred in the faces of prisoners when one of their number was being released and getting his things together for the last time—not to move on to another camp, but to be discharged. It was an expression of selfless joy. It's probably in people's nature to glow inwardly when they make contact with their natural heritage. To see a squirrel or a hedgehog that by some miracle has strayed into a town garden is to make contact with nature. To see someone emerging on the far side of the barbed wire was to make contact with freedom. When freedom appeared, all ignoble sentiments were hushed. There was no question of envying the man who at that given moment personified freedom. He had to be conducted reverentially to the gates to ensure that he didn't spill the precious gift he had recovered.

On the chilly morning of February 15, 1947, I was the vessel of the precious gift. I was the chalice of freedom.

No sooner had I appeared outside the Elgen free hospital, where I had served out my last two months as a prisoner, than I was surrounded by all the prisoners on the hospital staff. And I could read the same expression in all their faces. They loved me at that moment simply because I personified for them the thought that it was, after all, *possible* to get out of there!

They all wanted to do something for me. Aunt Marfusha, a sixty-year-old ward orderly—who was a Seventh-Day Adventist—reached under her overall, and a mess tin full of porridge materialized. She thrust it into my hands and insisted that I eat it all up there and then, in front of her. She recited in a high-pitched monotone, as if she were telling my fortune, that now I had lived to see the great day of transfiguration, which, God willing, all might live to see.

The laboratory technician, Matilda Zhurnakova, ran a critical eye over my jacket, and shrugged her shoulders. She found my appearance quite unacceptable for life outside and steered the conversation around to the suggestion that I take her dress and stockings without further ado. We could think about an overcoat later. . . . Matilda's wardrobe was something all Elgen knew about, because Matilda by some miracle still had a husband outside, and she constantly received parcels from home. With the same fanaticism that Marfusha had shown in prophesying the advent of the "twelfth day," Matilda now sought to impress on me the need to return to my academic work. That was her set theme. All her years in detention she had tormented herself about her thesis, which she had just completed when she was arrested. She had even been given a date for her oral examination.

Harif, the boiler man, who was doing time under Article 59(3)— banditry—weighed in with a pressing invitation to visit his folks in Azerbaidzhan as soon as I got my passport. Once they learned that I had shared the sorrows of their brother, they would feed and cherish me for the rest of my days.

We were all so electrified that even the senior orderly, Kolya, a painful stutterer, came out with several sentences one after another, without the least sign of hesitation.

"Quick! The telephone! Taskan's on the line. It's the third time he's called. . . . He's going out of his mind. . . . He's beside himself. . . ."

The receiver was vibrating, clicking with anxiety, reluctant to ask the one decisive question. It merely kept repeating on an interrogatory note: "Is that you? Is that you?"

"Yes, yes, yes! Yes, I've been released! Yes, I've signed the form to say I've been discharged. . . ."

In its emotion the receiver lapsed into German, and in my emotion I suddenly lost all power to tie up into a meaningful whole all those *um*s, *ab*s, *nach*s, and *geworden werden*s.

"Speak Russian! I can remember only Russian words today. Tell me, when are you coming to fetch me?"

We had a long-standing arrangement: immediately after I was discharged and had left the compound I was to go to the free hospital to await a phone call from Taskan. I was to confirm my release (our doubts on that score persisted up to the last minute, for there had been cases of people having their release canceled at the eleventh hour) and then Anton would come to fetch me. Timoshkin, the commandant at Taskan, had promised to provide a horse and sleigh.

Anton switched to Russian, but I still had difficulty understanding what he was trying to say. Something about the weather . . .

"Force ten . . . And a temperature of . . . The forecast for the next three days is . . . We'll have to . . ."

"I don't understand a thing. Something about a weather forecast . . . I can hardly hear you. Just say when you're coming to fetch me. . . . Speak up!"

The receiver howled and groaned and crackled and gurgled. Finally it went dead on me.

I struggled with that antediluvian wooden telephone for a solid half hour. I cranked it up and put in desperate appeals for the operator. . . . At last the head doctor of the free hospital, Dr. Pertsulenko, came into the guardhouse. He was one of those free people who kept a close eye on the life of the prisoners, one of those who had not been afraid to make friends with the imprisoned German doctor. He shook my hand, congratulated me, and predicted unbelievable success in my new life. But he had come mainly to offer hospitality for three days.

"You haven't been lucky with the weather. Dr. Walter has just got through on the telephone to my house. He asked me to give you a message: there's a blizzard blowing up and the wind's from the south. The forecast for the next three days is dreadful. No horse would get through. It'd be dangerous to try it on foot. My wife and I would like to suggest that you spend these three days with us. That's what Dr. Walter and I agreed. And as soon as the bad weather stops he'll come for you. . . ."

The head doctor's kind words, so irrelevant to my state of mind, could not have affected me if they had reached me from the bottom of the sea. From all he had said I took in only one thing: Anton was advising me to stay on another three days in Elgen. To stay on three more days in Elgen *of my own free will*.

I felt an unbearable hurt. Dear Lord, how unhappy I was. Less than two hours of my free life had gone by and along came this blow. And who was its author? The person nearest and dearest to me. How could he bring himself to utter such things? Telling me to stay behind in Elgen for three days! Three hours, three minutes, would be too long.

Pertsulenko tried once more to appeal to my good sense. It was only three days. What was that compared to ten years? And I would be not in camp, but in a free apartment. . . . It was ridiculous to go through all I had gone through, simply in order to freeze to death on the taiga track. The Kolyma blizzards were no joke; I should know that as well as anyone.

I did know, of course. How could I not know? . . . How many tales both of individuals and of whole parties under escort meeting their death in blizzards had I heard in my time? But then, it was only twenty-two kilometers. What were twenty-two miserable kilometers to me, an old taiga wolf, especially on a straight road, with no need to turn off? And then, how does one know when the blizzard will come? . . . Weather forecasts can be off by as much as a whole day. We all know about the infallibility of our forecasters.

Slipping on my jacket, I rushed out into the hospital courtyard. There you are—it was all an old wives' tale—just a normal sort of day! There was the thermometer: no more than minus 35 degrees! A really nice day . . . The sun was even trying to get through!

My decision was quickly taken. All I had to do was slip away without anyone's spotting me. Harif, the boiler man, was splitting logs beside the front entrance. He knew nothing of the weather office's forecast or of my conversation with Pertsulenko.

"Harif, be a good boy and get my things out of the lobby for me. I'm on my way."

"Where are you making for?"

"I'm going to Taskan. I've got a job with the kindergarten there, as a free worker."

At my own words I was suddenly gripped by a fit of sheer anguish. My first day of freedom, of which I had nurtured countless dreams, and for which I had prayed for so many years, and now suddenly turned to ashes! To stick around in Elgen for three more days? To be afraid of a snow storm dreamed up by some forecaster or other? To confess myself unable to manage twenty-two kilometers? I, who had such distances behind me, so many cruelties: Elgen, Mylga, Izvestkovaya. . . . And this was Anton's advice!

At that moment my exasperation with him knew no bounds. What had become of our famous mutual understanding? What of the evenings when he used to reply to questions that I had not put into words, and to thoughts that had only just surfaced in my mind?

So . . . I was going to Taskan solely because I had got a job there, wasn't I? Right! I had to work, after all. I had to send money to Vasya and Mother. And work I would—but not here, not in Elgen. They'd ridden roughshod over me too often here. The very air reeked of the rank breath of jailers. For the last seven years all that was most inhuman, most-demoniacal, most lethal, had been summed up for me in the word "Elgen." Let the blizzard scour all traces of it from my person, let me be cleansed by the gusty wind and the driven snow.

Harif was not in the least surprised that I should be hauling my case and my bundle all by myself for a whole twenty-two kilometers. In his time he had got used to seeing women haul three-meter pit props and fell full-grown timber. He made no fuss whatsoever about helping me hitch my bundle up onto my shoulders.

"Well, off you go, and all the best! Just do the odd spot of work until the rivers open for shipping again, and when the spring comes go and visit Azerbaidzhan! I'll give you a letter and they'll greet you like a long-lost sister. Good luck!"

Here I was, on the highway, with the Elgen buildings behind me. Each step took me farther away from the watchtowers in the compound. I was on my way. The snow crackled under my feet with dry finality. You could fit words to its rhythm: "nev-er a-gain, nev-er a-gain. . . ." I was quite resolved to forget that such a place as Elgen ever existed. I recall how one of the wartime parcels sent to me by my mother went astray. My poor mother kept asking me in her letters: "Perhaps I got the address wrong. Perhaps there's some other place, also called Elgen." I replied: "No, Mamma. Fortunately for mankind we have only one Elgen."

I had been making good progress for half an hour or so and the going was easy. I was so used to it all. What a lot of kilometers tramping through the taiga I must have clocked up: Sudar, Tyoplaya Dolina, Zmeika, Mylga, Izvestkovaya . . . through the virgin taiga. Whereas here I was on the highway.

The walking calmed me down. The thought that I was now a free person, that I could go where I chose, taking orders from no one, pleased me vastly. Twenty-two kilometers, only twenty-two. If I could keep going at this speed, I should be at Taskan before it got light, and I felt quite smug at the thought of how surprised the ogre would be when he saw me. "So much for your weather forecasters!" I would say and, without waiting for an answer, proceed disdainfully to my work place. He would have to run after me and ask my pardon—in Russian and in German.

If it were not for all this baggage . . . The fingers gripping the improvised rough iron handle of my wooden case were swollen, gone numb. Why not stop for a break, especially as I didn't feel at all cold in myself? It was just my hands, and those I could rub with snow.

I sat down on my trunk, rubbed some feeling back into my fingers, and pulled a frozen loaf—a parting present from Garifulla—out of the pocket of my jacket. I was about to take a bite when suddenly a piercing whistle shrilled peremptorily in my ears. My whole body felt it. With the instinct of an old taiga hand I sensed that this was it. No, I had to dismiss the thought. Lots of things can produce a whistling sound. Perhaps I had simply turned my head too abruptly. The sky was still a clear grayish blue, and the wind was no stronger than usual.

I tried hard to reassure myself, but inwardly I was all keyed up. I peered at the sky again. Though the clouds were still small, there was a new, leaden tinge to their outlines. And the fine snowy dust sweeping across my face was getting more prickly every minute. Worst of all, the highway was totally silent and empty. Could it be that everyone except me had believed the forecast?

Well, there was no point in settling down for a long siesta on my trunk, of course. I must press on as fast as I could so as to get at least as far as the Taskan electricity station while it was still light. If necessary I could spend the night there.

I strode out resolutely once more. But the sound my boots now made was not "nev-er a-gain." It was a different sound, something like: "All was darkness in that blizzard," as in *The Captain's Daughter*. Darkness and blizzard. And, sure enough, it had gone darker.

The ground wind was already blowing furiously, and overhead the snow was tumbling down faster than ever. The whole of my face was now encrusted with tingling particles of snow. They were becoming ever sharper and more penetrating.

The Kolyma blizzard is distinguished from all other blizzards not only by its intensity. Most important, it conveys a feeling of man's primeval defenselessness: as if a whole host of demons were on the prowl; as if the embodiment of some diabolic force were there, rampaging, howling, looking for a chance to knock you down. It evokes a sort of atavistic memory, a sort of Neanderthal anguish. You are indeed naked on the naked earth.

I had learned this long ago. Back in '41, when I was on a short journey with one of the penal drafts, I had composed some verses "In Imitation of Longfellow," which advanced the rhetorical questions "What do you know of the snow?" and "What do you know of the wind?"

> The primal fury, wildly raging,
>   spews destruction from its mouth;
> The mighty seas, the boundless oceans
>   tremble at its gusting wrath;
> The mountain summits shake with anguish,
>   north and south and east and west;
> But you who know the gentle breezes
>   know nothing of the wind's excess!
> Our road of pain, our road of horror—
>   never was it yours to know;
> But we, like Picts and Goths of old,
>   had cause to dread the ice and snow.

These verses of mine now came to mind. I was gasping with the effort I was making, determined to hold out, come what might, against the onslaught of the icy wind and against my own growing sense of inner panic.

It was hard to say how long ago I had left Elgen. I had, of course, no watch with me. How many kilometers had I done? How many were there left to do? If only I didn't have that damned trunk. Suppose I were to abandon it? In fact, all it contained was rags. . . . No, it was not possible. My mother had sent me the rags. My starving, wretched, heroic mother. She had sat in some miserable box in Rybinsk, the town to which she had been evacuated, and darned those ancient mittens, sewn buttons on that prehistoric jacket with coarse thread. No, I couldn't get rid of the trunk.

The clear patches between the dark clouds were disappearing with tragic speed. The wind blew ever faster and more ferociously. The farther I went, the more I was gripped by a feeling of the hostility of the elements and of utter solitude. I clung desperately to one comforting thought: each step was taking me farther from Elgen. All the same, I began to feel my strength ebbing away.

Onward, onward . . . If only I knew how much was left to do!

By now I must have come halfway. I put my trunk down on the
ground again and started to rub my frozen fingers. And then . . .

At first I thought I was seeing a mirage in the snowy desert:
the silhouette of someone walking toward me from somewhere a
long way off. It kept disappearing from my field of vision and then
reappearing in the white haze.

The feelings of the traveler on the Kolyma highway upon seeing
another person walking in his direction are complex. The first im-
pulse is to rejoice. You are no longer alone, confronting hostile
nature. A fellow creature is at hand, and you feel reassured by his
presence. But that lasts only a second. Your delight soon gives way
to a feeling of abject terror which pervades you from tip to toe.
A human being! No ordinary human being, but one from Kolyma.
A man. He could be a runaway convict who will cut you up and
use you as provision for his journey. He could be a soldier, a convoy
guard, driven wild by the endless convoying of male prisoners, by
this lost wilderness of the taiga, by his sexual deprivation. He will
come at you like a wild beast and rape you. Or, finally, he could be
a jackal, a man on his last legs who will confine himself to taking
your bread and your warm clothes.

Worst of all, there is no escape. To turn off the highway means
to drown in an ocean of snow, to lose your way. Turn back? If you
do, he will catch up with you. And in any case, in that direction
lies Elgen. So you have to go on, even into the jaws of the wolf.

There was no doubt about it now: someone was coming toward
me. At times he staggered sideways, buffeted by the wind. Sometimes he turned about, with his back to the wind and to me, and
took a breather. It was harder for him; I had the wind behind me.

It was only when he was quite close, a few meters away, that I
first got the impression of something familiar about the gait of the
lonely traveler. Dear Lord—was it possible? . . .

Yes, it was he, Dr. Walter in person, in his padded jacket and his
cape. I even recognized his gauntlets—splendid leather gauntlets that
Timoshkin, the camp commandant, had given him off his own hands.

"I knew it! I just knew it! That's what happens when a girl has
not received a proper German education! She's capable of any
folly!"

He snatched the wretched trunk from my hand, simultaneously
drying my tears with his elegant leather gauntlet. The tears froze
to it as they fell.

"Show me your hands! Frostbitten, of course . . . Stop there!"
He put the trunk down and, picking up a handful of snow, set about
rubbing my fingers as hard as he could. This was sheer torture, and
it gave me an honorable excuse to howl at the top of my voice,
saying in a high whine:

"It must be pretty evident that Elgen is not the sort of place
where one stays of one's own free will! Even if it's only a matter
of three days! Fancy you being afraid of bad weather!"

It was intoxicatingly enjoyable, after such infinite solitude, to
know that now there was someone who was sorry for me, who
would scold me, who would expose my foolish actions for what
they were. And I had someone to shout at, to accuse of all sorts of
things, each more unjust than the last.

"You weren't in any hurry, of course you weren't," I repeated,
like a nagging wife. "I was supposed to stay in Elgen and you were
afraid to stick your nose out of the hut because the weather wasn't
too good."

"The weather is indeed not at its best," he said, with comic solemnity. Only then did I notice that his figure was completely
frosted over. He had been walking into the wind. . . .

"This must be our first married quarrel! It's really quite pleasant.
I sense a really stable domestic atmosphere! *Aber beruhigen Sie sich,
gnädige Frau!*"

And there and then in that maniacal wind, with the elements
howling around us, he recited some humorous German couplets,
each of which ended with the refrain *"Ich habe zu viel Angst vor
meiner Frau."*

We both found ourselves laughing. How easy the going had become!

"It's quite a different matter when the wind's at your back,"
said he.

"Without the trunk I feel as if I've just come out for a walk,"
said I.

We marched side by side. We were heading for freedom. We
left Elgen farther and farther behind, and suddenly I felt a sharp
paroxysm of happiness coursing through me. Not joy, not pleasure,
but happiness. That irresistible uplift of the spirit with which all
your anxieties, fears, terrors, even the most deeply hidden ones,
fly away and you are borne upward as if you were holding on to the

tail of the legendary Firebird. You have managed to grab him at last!

That moment remains with you for the rest of your life.

In my life, as in anyone else's, there were, of course, moments of joy: the birth of my sons, success at work, distractions, love affairs, books. But these joys were always laced with the keen anticipation of forthcoming sorrow. When I search my memory for moments of real, unthinking happiness, I can recall only two. It happened once in Sochi. For no particular reason—simply that I was twenty-two and waltzing on the veranda of the sanatorium with a professor of dialectical materialism, who was some twenty-five years older than I, and with whom our entire class had fallen in love. The second time I managed to grab the Firebird by the tail was the day I have just described, February 15, 1947, on the Elgen–Taskan highway in a blizzard.

We almost flew along, carried by the wind. Sometimes we stopped for a moment and exchanged a frozen kiss. We held on to each other tightly, and the Firebird dutifully conducted us along its fantastic route.

Dawn had not yet broken and the storm was still raging when we finally entered a ramshackle wooden hut where prison detainees who had just got out of camp could nearly always find shelter.

"Here you are," said Anton, putting my trunk slap-bang on top of a snowdrift. "This is where I've rented a room for you. At Aunt Marusya's."

It was a two-story hut. At first sight it looked as if the upper story was keeling over and waiting for the wind to complete the process. The tattered, broken-down door put up a brave resistance to our joint efforts to open it, as if it were a wild animal. This was a historic moment in my life: I entered my very first free lodgings after ten years in official places of residence.

"Still alive?" Aunt Marusya inquired hoarsely. She, too, was a former prison detainee, who had done ten years inside for murder from jealousy.

"Well, *cum Deo!*" Anton solemnly pronounced the words that he used before starting on the operations he was always having to perform—although he was not a surgeon—because he was the only "pair of hands" in the camp hospital.

2

Our friend in exile, Aleksei Astakhov, an engineer who would have made a very fine writer, sometimes used to entertain us with his colorful vignettes of Kolyma life. His repertoire included the story of how "Nick the Nugget" (alias "Fountain Pen," "Moscow," "Goldfinger") from the gold mines behaved after his release, while he was enjoying his first taste of freedom.

In exchange for two bread rations Nick had an iron-handled plywood case (called a coffin) specially made for him and acquired a free pillow, made from four colored mosquito nets and an old padded jacket. Then he put on all his "free togs," which meant a newly issued camp jacket with a strip of squirrel fur tacked round the neck and a Cossack hat made up from the tails of a camp guard's sheepskin. Then Nick would amble blissfully and aimlessly up and down the path between the free canteen and the free shop, stopping to shake hands with the camp guard commander every time they met.

It sounds foolish, but in this unique situation certain general psychological laws seem to be at work. Though the irony of it did not escape me, I found that my behavior when I first left the camp almost exactly reflected that of Nick the Nugget as a free worker. My trunk was the spit and image of his "coffin." My pillow, or rather the pillowcase, was likewise confected from four colored mosquito nets. I had fitted my newly issued camp jacket, if not with a proper fur collar, then at least with a strip of some sort of cat fur. And the main thing I had in common with Nick was that I, too, had a blissful feeling each time I visited the so-called shop (a wooden booth, reeking of kerosene), the canteen, and especially the post office.

Behind the shop counter was our landlady, Aunt Marusya, a good-natured barrel of a woman with a husky voice. To look at her, you would find it almost impossible to imagine that she had killed her husband in a fit of jealousy.

Marusya rocked with laughter when she saw that so far as prices were concerned I was completely lost, and that I had not the least idea as to how to go about buying and selling.

"Look, now," she explained indulgently. "Look. I won't cheat you. Here, have these men's trousers. I'll let you have them without coupons, just between the two of us. You can slit them up the seams, dye them red, and fix yourself up with a skirt that will last you for your entire five years in exile. It'll even see you back to the mainland. So help me, I'll treat you right."

It emerged that all the goods were issued against coupons. Aunt Marusya almost burst her sides laughing upon discovering that I was ignorant of the meaning of the phrase "to trade in," much in use among the free population.

"What are we going to do with you?" she exclaimed, amid fits of raucous guffawing. "Listen here! Supposing you've got coupon 43b. What's it worth? On market day it's not worth a lousy kopeck! But all of a sudden I hang up a notice on the shop door 'Coupon 43b can be traded in for half a kilo of crushed barley,' or '. . . for macaroni.' At that point your 43b becomes valuable. You can swap it or sell it, or else go and get that half kilo for yourself and polish it off. Understand?"

Even such details of free living as these enthralled me. After all, they were attributes of a free existence, and they incorporated an element of personal choice. If I wanted to, I could swap my 43b for something else; if I wanted to, I could trade it in and go back and cook some macaroni on the stove.

I was particularly fond of going to the post. In Taskan we did not have any post office; we had to go four kilometers farther on, to what was called Second Taskan. I used to go there to find out how much it would cost to transfer so many rubles to Vasya and to Rybinsk, where my mother had stayed on after her evacuation from Leningrad. I was not due to receive the money in question—my first wages—for a month. But I had to prepare myself for the great day when I could freely and openly send my family money from my own earnings.

Meanwhile I sent off registered letters to the mainland and took pleasure in writing down my return address. No more "Care of Box Number . . ." but simply "House Number . . . Street Number. . . ." After handing in my letters I stood beside the counter for some while, pretending to be waiting for someone or something, but in fact simply enjoying the smell of ink and hot sealing wax. At the post office I felt nearer to the mainland; there was less of the sense of being an island castaway. (We all knew that Kolyma was not an island, but we insisted on calling it one, and on calling the rest the mainland. It was not merely a question of terminology—we were completely convinced that this was so.)

My work in the kindergarten here in no way differed from the similar work I had previously done as a prisoner. But there was the inexpressible joy of going to work without a guard in tow, or of dashing home during the lunch break to my own room, finding Anton already there, and then sitting down together to eat soup and gruel cooked the night before. It gave me the illusion of family life, and I began to forget that in fact only I was free, while Anton was still a convict, and that there were still six years to go before the end of his third sentence.

He tended to forget about this himself, especially as his situation in Taskan was an unusual one: he could walk freely through the settlement without a guard, and he attended free patients. He could even visit Marusya's shop. It was only overnight that he had to stay in the camp compound.

By and large it was a wonderful time for me, when every small detail of everyday life—even of such a meager existence as ours in Taskan—gave rise to pleasure and gratitude. It took me two months before I noticed that my room failed to retain the heat, that I used up an appalling quantity of wood and yet in the morning it was still frosty. Next I realized that it was quite a chore to lug water up to the second floor, and above all, that to be so isolated in my room was somewhat scary. My door was far away from Aunt Marusya's room, and the released criminals who were waiting for navigation to begin so that they could leave for the mainland were up to their tricks again. But then, what did I have that was worth stealing?

I was on speaking terms with two of these released criminals. One of them, an old man from Siberia who looked like Rasputin, had a reputation as a fortune teller. Aunt Marusya had brought him to see me the first time, and since then he had dropped in on his own now and again. I welcomed his visits. Why? Because after slipping his iron-frame spectacles onto his nose, he would study the lines of my left hand at great length and in meticulous detail, and then declare:

"Say what you will, but I don't see any deaths among your children there. Mark my words, your eldest son has gone off somewhere. . . . But he's alive. I don't see his death. . . . No, that I don't!" These mumblings were enough to outweigh all the precisely

worded telegrams, official reports, and answers to inquiries of which
I had already been the sorrowful recipient. I was visited at night
by wild and desperate visions of Alyosha's fate and of his miraculous
salvation. I spoke of this to no one, not even Anton. It was a secret
between me and this half-mad old man. I gave him things to eat; and
I totally disregarded the eternal verities so steadfastly drummed into
me at the university, giving myself up to dreams of the impossible.

Well, let those to whom God has been kind, who have never lost
a child, sit in judgment on my credulity.

My second convict visitor was the supplies man. He brought me
my firewood; this big bundle was the largest single item on my daily
budget. But I was pleased that he came so regularly, and I didn't try
to haggle him down. Quite the reverse, I gave him such valuable
presents as a wooden spoon and a tin bowl. He shed tears of gratitude for my thoughtfulness; he really didn't have anything to put
any hot food into, if it should ever come his way. On occasion I
even gave him a helping of soup and gruel. He used to squat in the
doorway and gulp it down straight from the bowl, forgetting all
about the spoon. When he left, he would shower me with profuse
thanks. Sometimes when I looked at his eyes, so trustingly bent on
me, I would even feel certain faint pangs of conscience at having
always experienced throughout my long camp life nothing but a
feeling of revulsion for these common criminals. Obviously, criminals, like everyone else, were not all the same. This one, for example,
was surely incapable of doing me any harm. . . .

One day in the kindergarten there was an urgent call for sulphone
for a child who had been taken ill. There was no sulphone in the
dispensary, but I did have some at home. So I dashed off at an unaccustomed, unscheduled hour to fetch the medicine.

The key somehow stuck in the lock and I couldn't manage to
move it one way or the other. As I was wrestling with the door,
getting more and more annoyed, I suddenly sensed a lurking menace
behind me. I looked around and froze with terror. Behind me there
stood my supplies man, my wood merchant, my goner, holding a
heavy log over my head. Another second and I would have been
felled to the ground. I thrust him away from me with a yell and
hurtled down the staircase, calling for help. But before people came
to my rescue, my trustworthy friend had managed to get away.

"Don't you know his name? At least his first name?" Anton kept
asking that evening.

But I didn't know. I could only give a description of his special characteristics: a thin, bluish nose like a teapot spout, a slight limp.

"It's Kiselev," Anton deduced. After all, Anton was the person who treated all the common criminals and was responsible for "certifying" them. "I'm off to see justice done."

It was no use asking him to overlook it. Kiselev wouldn't try it a second time. But when it came to dealing with the criminal world, Anton stuck resolutely to his principle—never complain to the authorities, but never let a single act of insolence escape unpunished.

"I'll deal with him personally," Anton promised. And these were no empty words: the doctor had fists of iron, which he had evidently inherited from several generations of *Grossbauern*, while his intellectual profile came to him from the solitary chemist or alchemist who had infiltrated the family.

The following day the doctor burst into the kindergarten entrance, dragging behind him a goner who was much the worse for wear.

"Is this the one?" bellowed the doctor in a voice of thunder, holding his victim by the collar.

"No," I said, at first uncertainly, and then, when I heard the voice of the accused, with horror. "It's definitely not him!"

"Lordy," sobbed the innocent victim, sniffling into his fur hat, "what are you hitting me for, Anton Yakovlevich? Cross my heart—it's not me! I wouldn't lie to you. I swear it! It's Toporkov you want. . . ."

"Why did you say with a nose like a spout?" Anton, very annoyed, was trying to shift his judicial error onto my shoulders. "Well, it's not the end! We'll square accounts with Toporkov. . . . As for you, Kiselev, I'll fix you up with a certificate and get you shipped off to the mainland. . . ."

He kept his word. After giving Toporkov a drubbing, both these precious rogues were certified. They were typical representatives of the Kolyma tribe of jackals. Though so emaciated that they could hardly stand upright, they couldn't resist thieving and, if opportunity offered, would get themselves riproaringly drunk. And now their cherished dream was being realized: they were to be transferred on health grounds, first, from the taiga to Magadan, and then, to where they most longed to be—the mainland. Before leaving, they looked in to say good-by, to express their thanks for the lesson, and, more particularly, for the certification.

Torporkov confessed of his own free will that what had led him into temptation was my padded pillow with its quadruple mosquito net pillowcase. He terribly wanted to sleep on something soft.

After this incident Anton determined on a change of lodging for me. He moved me shortly afterward to a decent little house, inhabited by the economist at the food plant, Yarotsky. Yarotsky had served out his eight-year sentence and was now living as a free man with his family around him, having arranged for his wife and daughter to join him from the mainland.

I had to hold my breath when I saw the living quarters, and above all my new room. It had been a long time since I had experienced such a degree of sophistication; there was even indoor plumbing. Best of all, the Yarotsky family had put a writing table and a whole pile of books at my disposal. Each time I returned from work, I used to pause on the threshold of my room, spellbound at the magic sight of a pile of books on a desk.

We forgot, we quite forgot, that Anton was still a prisoner. Until one unhappy day . . .

"They're replacing Timoshkin," Yarotsky announced, coming into the room.

This was a blow from an unexpected quarter. It came as a surprise to Timoshkin himself—the Taskan camp commandant who had treated all the prisoners, and Anton and me in particular, so well. Formally, his removal from Taskan did not mean that he had been sacked, only that they had suddenly decided to post him to some twelve-month promotion course in Magadan. But there were rumors emanating from the director of the food processing plant, Kamennova, that there was more to it, that somebody had evidently informed the bosses in Magadan about the Taskan paradise and Timoshkin's rotten liberalism.

The parting was painful. What most concerned our kindly but now landless squire was the fate of his dependents, to whom, unlike the landowners of the last century, he could not give freedom.

"We'll get by!" he said with more confidence than he felt, looking wistfully around his comfortable quarters. "We'll get by! We'll be O.K., isn't that so, Valya? We merely have to stick around in Magadan for a year—not what you'd call hardship. Not bad at all: a house of culture, the public baths, two cinemas . . . But I'm very worried about the doctor. Supposing they do him dirty while I'm away . . ."

Then he shook my hand and expressed his hope that I would be "a true companion for life" and not one of those flibbertigibbets who changed husbands at each camp. . . . And if—touch wood—the new management should pack the doctor off to the gold mines, I was to go with him, even though I'd got my discharge already.

The day of his departure he was so worried that he drank too much, and Anton had, for the last time, to get him back into shape.

"How can we get by without you?" he mumbled, shaking the curly head that held so much stuff and nonsense, but at the same time so many generous, bold, truly Russian impulses.

"It's true, isn't it, Valya? We've got used to you, you're like a father to us."

The peaches-and-cream Valya, all in tears, threw herself around the doctor's neck just as if she were really his daughter. We helped them get their things together and load them onto the truck, and went as far as Second Taskan to see them off. When bidding good-by to me, Timoshkin said, with touching familiarity:

"I know I can rely on you, my dear. Don't abandon the doctor in his hour of need."

We walked the four kilometers back in silence, depressed by having had to part from these kind people, and haunted by gloomy forebodings.

When we learned that the new commandant at Taskan was to be Puzanchikov, whom I had known at Elgen, I began to reassure Anton, and myself too. A stable person, without sadistic outbursts, he simply got on with his job, just as if he were serving behind a counter. All he cared about was making sure of his increments. Remember how readily he had exchanged me for a stovesetter! He knew his business, that Puzanchikov.

And so it was . . . for a time. The first days, even weeks, of the new regime brought about no changes of substance in our way of life. Anton continued to leave the camp compound as he pleased, to visit the free patients in the settlement and to have lunch and supper with me in the apartment.

It was not until about a month and a half later that the first small thunderclouds appeared on the horizon. The trouble was Puzan-chikov's wife, Eugenia Leontyevna, a doctor who had become head of the camp Medical Section, therefore Anton's immediate boss. She was a small, energetic woman of about thirty with a pleasant face and manicured fingers (no simple thing to arrange in the taiga).

She used to address Anton by his first name and patronymic, and always concurred in his diagnoses and prescriptions. But when the grandson of the director of the food plant, Kamennova, fell ill and she phoned the Medical Section as usual, asking for Walter to come and see the boy, Eugenia Leontyevna graciously replied that she would come herself.

She prescribed a course of treatment for the boy, but the illness did not respond to it, and Kamennova started to insist that they should send Walter, who had been attending her entire family for some years now. Eugenia Leontyevna gave her a sweet smile and explained that Dr. Walter was indeed quite a good diagnostician, but seeing that he had been in camp for twelve years, he could not hope to keep up with the latest developments in medicine.

"I must try and cut down my visits to my free patients," Anton said anxiously. "But how can I do it without offending them?"

A few more weeks went by, and one day I met our doctor in the local shop. She had just returned from some meeting or other in Yagodnoye.

"How are you?" she asked me kindly. "Well, I hope? But I'm afraid I have bad news for you. They're taking Dr. Walter away from us. He is to go to Shturmovoi, to the mine. A new camp has been opened there and they're in desperate need of a doctor. The Medical Administration simply turned it into an auction. 'Who would like new equipment and grants in exchange for one decent prison doctor?' I held out as long as I could. . . ."

"But you knocked him down to the highest bidder, all the same?"

She pretended to take my remark as a joke. Anton was so stricken by the news that I had to play the role of optimist.

"Listen, even at the gold mines people manage to live. . . . You're fit and healthy. . . . I will come and join you—that much they can't deny me. . . ."

Alas, this was precisely what they were bent on denying me, and Anton knew it. How lame and feeble the powers of imagination of nineteenth-century jailers seemed in comparison with the flights of administrative fantasy of which our bosses were capable. It turned out that the new gold mine, Shturmovoi, had been organized on special lines: it was to be populated solely by prisoners, plus camp and production officials. Ordinary free employees, especially if they were ex-prisoners, could not be registered for domicile in this special settlement and work was not available to them there. I was thus deprived of the right to follow Anton and take up residence in the free settlement attached to the mine, as we had originally planned.

Our make-believe family life had collapsed. Just a little while ago we had sat with our landlord and his wife, drinking tea, joking, and talking about books; we had felt like human beings. Now here we were again: the slave market, the gold mine, separation, eternal uncertainty, the black pit.

The Yarotskys were shattered by our misfortune—especially Marya Pavlovna, a denizen of the mainland, for whom it was the first encounter with Kolyma ways. She had only to look at us to start crying, and she kept on repeating in bewilderment:

"How has it come about? It simply can't be. . . ."

Anton was taken away alone, on a special warrant, not as one of a party. The Taskan escort was to take him to Elgen, and there hand him over to another guard for the second leg of the journey.

I tried getting into the camp compound to help him assemble his things. But now that Timoshkin had left, the guards wouldn't let me through.

"Free employees are not allowed in!"

"What, me? A free employee? . . ."

"What else? . . . You're not down on the list, and that's that!"

We said good-by at 11:30 P.M. He was due to be back in the compound by midnight at the latest. This time we did not try to cheer each other up as we had done on previous occasions when they had taken me away from him. We now faced a yawning gulf of six years before his sentence ended: six years without seeing each other, perhaps even without being able to write to each other.

He left. I sat down on the chair and remained there until morning came. It was a white night in June. By five o'clock objects around me had lost their hazy nighttime silhouettes and recovered their sharpness of outline. Suddenly my eye descried a well-defined hand and the sleeve of a military tunic at the window. The hand knocked on the pane, and a voice with a Ukrainian accent ordered: "Come to the door!"

I rushed out. There was a truck outside the house. Anton was there, sitting in the rear on some boxes. One of the Taskan guards, who went by the nickname Mamai the Cossack, fired off instructions at me.

"Come and sit in front, lady! And as soon as we get onto the

highway you can slip into the back and have a nice chat, just the
pair of you. . . ."

I obeyed unquestioningly. And sure enough, as soon as the truck
had left the settlement behind, Mamai told the driver to stop and
personally helped me clamber up into the back of the truck, where
Anton was.

In this unlooked-for farewell ride together, in the kindness of
Mamai the Cossack—who had allowed us to see each other once
again after we had said our last good-bys, perhaps forever—we superstitiously detected a good omen. Without our expecting it, a
kind soul had intervened. And that would-set the pattern. You come
across good where you least expect it. We would see each other
again, we were certain of it. And for the time being, I must go to
Magadan and stay with Julia.

Julia, my cellmate from Yaroslavl, my faithful man Friday, was
now, since her return from camp, living in Magadan, where she
worked as forewoman in a workshop of some kind. She had written
to me in Taskan more than once, saying how lucky she had been
in her job and her apartment, and asking me to come and stay . . .
promising to fix me up in the capital of Kolyma. Not counting
Anton, Julia was the only person I felt close to in that part of the
world. We looked on each other as sisters, baptized in the same
Yaroslavl font.

The going was hard and the truck kept skidding. The crates,
piled up any old how, shuddered, clattered, and bumped into our
legs. But we wanted this, our last tryst, to go on as long as possible;
so we welcomed the discomfort of the journey. From time to time
Mamai would open the small communicating door, poke his head
through, and peep at us. He was obviously sorry for us; in order to
hide his prohibited feelings, he would take his cap off, wipe the
inside of it with his handkerchief, and then use the same handkerchief to mop his receding forehead and his short-cropped, jet-black
hair with the Cossack forelock that had earned him his nickname.

We spent the whole journey saying good-by to each other, sense-
lessly repeating over and over again Julia's address in Magadan which
had become our only landmark in the impenetrable darkness that
would lie between us.

The actual moment of our final parting came on us unexpectedly
soon and was over in an instant. It transpired that the truck with the

prisoners for delivery to Shturmovoi had already been hanging around for some time outside the Elgen headquarters office, unable to start only because Anton was late and the escort was a prisoner short. The guards, who had come on from elsewhere, were cursing and swearing. They shoved me aside unceremoniously, and instantly pushed Anton into the canvas-topped truck, which was already tightly packed with some fifty men. I could no longer pick him out. Above the coughing of the engine, I did just manage to catch his final words:

"Wait for me! You must wait!" he shouted in German.

My Taskan boss, the kindergarten head, held out for a long time against releasing me. She began by trying to coax me out of it, promising to give me a priority coupon for five meters of calico. Then she resorted to threats. "So, if you want to be difficult, I'll make things hot for you in Magadan." All she had to do was phone her friend so-and-so, who would have a word with her husband, and I would not get work in Magadan as long as I lived.

Finally, faced with my stubborn obduracy, the head gave way, and we reached a compromise: she would release me, not immediately, but in a month. And during that month I was to teach Katya, the Komsomol girl, to play on the piano the entire contents of the *Pre-School Songs* album. Katya would learn it by touch—she had a good ear.

That month was unbearably long. As I went to and from work I would look around me in bewilderment: Was this the Taskan paradise that had been my goal for years on end, that I had dreamed of at Belichye and Elgen? . . . Why, it was nothing but a dismal hole in the taiga, with clouds of mosquitoes and horseflies; it was a settlement surrounded by swamps, with thickets of poisonous reeds. (Anton used to say that this type of reed—water hemlock—contained a deadly posion.)

All my thoughts were now focused on Magadan. On the capital! The center of Kolyma civilization. Timoshkin was right! "A house of culture, the public baths, and two cinemas!" And the main thing was: Julia was there. Anton had her address. At that address I might receive a paper triangle covered with Russian lettering that none the less looked Gothic: small, angular letters that sometimes reminded me of a crane dipping its beak into a well.

The free employees at Taskan poured salt into my wounds. I had only to put in an appearance on the village street for someone to

come up and ask did I know what the doctor had used that time to
cure Ivan the redhead so speedily? Or Vladimir the hairdresser, or
some other patient? Perhaps he had left the prescription with me?
No? What a wretched business! Sending a man like that away. Who
would pull us through now that he was gone?

They all condoled with me: "They've split up your family." And
Fedka, the food plant driver, a former professional thief, who had
now transformed himself into a model worker, said to me:

"Hey, I'll take you to Magadan. . . . Get your glad rags together! I know what's right. If it weren't for your Walter, I'd be
kicking up the turf with my ankle tagged and my face to the east;
or at least I'd be hopping around on a crutch. . . . Know what
diagnosis I was sick with?"

And proudly and faultlessly he trotted out, as if it were a title of
nobility: "Ob - lit - er - a - tive en - do - ar - te - ri - tis!"

3

· *The city of gold*

On my way to Magadan, I was obliged to make a stop at Yagodnoye. The temporary certificate of release from camp issued me by
the Elgen Operations Section had run out long ago. It had to be
exchanged for Form A; in return they were supposed to give me,
sooner or later, an internal passport valid for one year. The only
place to get this Form A was Yagodnoye.

My driver, Fedka, "Black Spot," Anton's grateful patient, agreed
to make this detour although it was well out of his way. He flatly
refused to accept any money from me.

"What the hell do I want with your bits of paper?" he asked
mournfully. "I've got nothing to spend it on anyway. That doctor
of yours, you know what he said to me when he left? 'Remember,'
he said, 'Fyodor, every drop and every puff you take,' he said, 'is

just another nail in your coffin. So watch it! It's no joke what you've got. It's obliterative endoarteritis.' "

Fedka looked in my direction proudly.

We were on our way . . . almost flying along. Fedka knew those Kolyma highways like the back of his hand. He knew all the narrow parts and the turnings, where it was all right to break the journey, and where it wasn't.

"Tired? We'll carry on to the turning, and then it'll be time for a break. You can put your legs up and take things easy."

We got down from the truck, made ourselves comfortable in a silent, moss-covered dell, and laid out the potato pies, thoughtfully provided for the journey by Fedka's wife, on newspaper. His wife was not one of the professionals but a "mug," one of the women hauled in for a disciplinary offense. The pies had a homely village smell. Fedka's wife had been punished for taking a few ears of corn or cabbage stalks, which counted as state property. The devil had led her astray in that year of wartime starvation and famine. And so she had landed in Kolyma.

But what wonderful kvass she made! She was a real magician! Fedka poured some into my mug from a sooty pot wrapped up in a clean sleeve that had been torn from an old shirt of his.

"I'm glad I brought that!" said Fedka, with a sly glint. "With a missus like that you don't have to bother about drivers' canteens."

There was only one thing that I found exhausting: while we were on our way, Fedka constantly demanded that I tell him stories. We were only halfway to Yagodnoye and I had already treated him to rambling biographies of Athos, Porthos, and Aramis. I had by now switched to the triumphs and misadventures of the illustrious Viscount de Bragelonne.*

About every five or six kilometers my story was interrupted by the checkpoints, at each of which there was a guard who asked to see our documents. Every one of them interrogated me severely as to why my certificate was out of date, and why I had no Form A. I explained in a bored tone of voice that I had been compelled to stay behind at my workplace and had therefore not been able to make the journey to Yagodnoye to get my Form A, and that I was now on my way there for precisely that purpose. The patrolmen wrote down the number of the truck, the number of my certificate,

* Athos, Porthos, Aramis, de Bragelonne: characters from Dumas's novel *The Three Musketeers* and its sequels.

and the number of my still brand-new labor book. Then they reluctantly let us go. Fedka was amazed.

"You've a real head on your shoulders. . . . What a lot of stories you know. But then you go and tell the fuzz the whole truth! Can't you tart it up for them a bit? You might say: 'Well, Mr. Patrolman, I'm not too bothered about Form A because I'm expecting full rehabilitation any day now. Comrade Voroshilov, or Comrade Molotov, has been looking into my case,' tell 'em, 'and made a personal report to Comrade Stalin. And Comrade Stalin says he'll have the hide off anybody who ill-treats this innocent lady. . . . Says they'd better look into things more carefully.' "

Fedka guffawed, exposing his yellow, horsy teeth. In his right upper jaw he had a large tusklike gold tooth, and he was only a shade less proud of it than of his obliterative endoarteritis.

At Yagodnoye men from the gold mines were jostling about in front of a small building painted a blushing pink. It was the headquarters of Sevlag. The little window on the left of the entrance was where they handed out the longed-for Form A.

Fedka explained to me that we had best go into the building together, preferably arm in arm. Then it would be clear to everybody that there was no vacancy. Otherwise all the jackals would pitch in. Look at them there, waiting. . . . Who were all those people, pushing and shoving? The suitors from the mines, of course, waiting for a free woman to come their way. With Form A you can even get married in the registry office.

I had heard a lot and have already said something about this Kolyma wedding market. It was amusing to see it first hand. In essence, if one thought it over and took a closer look at those whom Fedka called jackals, this longing for family life revealed a very human instinct, an instinct not that of a jackal. Each of these suitors had had a shadowy past. And what they had in common was that all of them—ex-criminals, ex-kulaks, ex-embezzlers, and purloiners of nationalized cabbage heads, and even the most desperate criminals among them—wanted to get married, not just to find a mistress. They wanted everything to be aboveboard, through the registry office and with the bride changing her name.

Suddenly I spotted the inscription SHTURMOVOI GOLD MINE on one of the stationary trucks. With total disregard for the rules of Kolyma etiquette, I flung myself into the throng of suitors, shouting, "Is there anybody here from Shturmovoi?"

I was surely born under a lucky star! What a fantastic stroke of good fortune: this store clerk from Shturmovoi had seen Anton only yesterday. He stood before me in his riding breeches—held up with string instead of a belt—and scratching his hairy, tattooed chest, gave me a detailed account of the conditions in which Anton was now living.

"The thing is, he's on detachment in a closed, meaning a guarded, sector, seven kilometers from the central compound. They don't let anybody in. But they say the bread ration is better than ours— a whole hundred grams better. So there's no need to worry! He'll see the winter out, mark my words."

"How could you have seen him if it's a closed sector?" I asked, doubting him.

"In the central compound—one of the bosses started caving in. Well, they fetched the doctor to bring him around. They say the doctor is really clever, he can pull anyone through. Your doctor will be making a few more trips to the central compound before the goon gets his second wind. So scribble a line for him, and I'll see he gets it, so help me. I've got a pal there, an orderly. . . . Don't fret yourself. Which kind of husband is he, though? Is he your Kolyma or your mainland husband?"

While I was writing, he peeped inquisitively over my shoulder, but I outwitted him. Playing havoc with articles and case endings, I scribbled off a message in German, full of optimism: "On my way to Magadan. I've all but got my Form A. I got a letter from Julia. She's more or less found me a job in Magadan. But do look after yourself. I'll be waiting, never fear."

The window through which documents were handed out was so deeply recessed that looking at the man sitting there was like looking through binoculars from the wrong end. He rummaged around for a good while, leafed through my papers, and muttered something indistinguishable when I asked how to set about obtaining an internal passport. Then he barked out:

"Hand!"

"What?"

"Your hand!"

I didn't understand. Could they have introduced anything so human as a ritual handshake to congratulate people on their release?

Half facing him, I diffidently introduced my hand into the tunnel, although it clearly wouldn't reach all the way.

"Ten years you've done inside and you still don't know the ropes!" roared the official. "Where are you putting your hand? Haven't you got eyes? On your right!"

I went crimson with shame and fury. I hadn't noticed the small table to the right of the window. There was a man in military uniform behind the table, and on it was the entire apparatus for taking fingerprints.

"Time to play the piano," glumly observed Fedka, who was standing nearby.

What was there to be surprised at, idiot that I was? Why, even corpses were fingerprinted! My throat contracted in an acute spasm. I'd been imagining that I was free. All my release meant was that I could come and go without escort for the time being. I was stuck with my jailers for life, forever. Even now, after ten years as a prisoner, they wanted my fingerprints all over again, wanted to harass and persecute me to my dying day. You could spin around in this accursed wheel till every bone in your body was ground to bits.

The man in uniform, without looking at me, passed a special ink roller over a clean sheet of paper. Then with practiced ease he pressed one of my fingers against the surface.

I could see why the professionals called the procedure playing the piano.

My fingers were black and sticky.

"Now where am I supposed to wash my hands?" I asked, no longer capable of containing my exasperation. The soldier shrugged indifferently.

At last I had the long-awaited Form A in my hands, in my inky fingers. I held it gingerly by the edge and read it. The certificate confirmed that I had been ten years in corrective labor camps (not a word about solitary confinement in prison) for this and that state crime (membership in an underground terrorist organization, the aim of which was, etc., etc.) and that I had been released from camp on the completion of my term of sentence, subject to deprivation of civil rights for a further five years. In addition it said at the bottom: "Not renewable if lost." On the right, instead of my photograph, there was my thumbprint.

An enviable document, no doubt about it: I was a free citizen, re-educated in the corrective labor camps and restored to the monolithic family of the workers.

We emerged from the little pink house. I bent over the gutter, and Fedka poured what remained of the kvass in the canteen over my hands. Then he passed me a rag smelling of benzine, and I wiped my hands with it.

"Let's go," said Fedka, lunging at the pedals and at the same time directing a protuberant, bloodshot ʾeye in my direction. He seemed to understand how I was feeling and to sympathize. He seemed to want to comfort me by driving fast, so as to create an illusion of freedom, an illusion of being our own masters.

"I've got a pal at the seventy-second kilometer before you get to Magadan. He's at the glass factory. It's his second year outside. What a woman he's found himself! Wow! And she's got education —she's a manicurist. We'll stop by there. You can have a wash and get your hands nice and clean, and spruce yourself up. We'll make our entry into Magadan, and you'll be a real stunner!"

He was too tactful to notice the tears coursing down my dusty cheeks.

"How about another story?" he suggested cheerfully. "What about that Viscount what's-his-name? De Barzhillon—that's him! Did he settle accounts with the fuzz? Or, if you don't feel like a story, let's have a song."

And in an unimaginable voice, nurtured on pure alcohol, he launched into the song "My Beloved Capital City." He meant Magadan, not Moscow. What he sang was:

> It's always a matter for pity
> When I don't fulfill double the plan.
> My beloved capital city,
> My city of gold, Magadan!

"Who put those words to it?"

"Who what? If you must know, I did. . . ."

In point of fact, by 1947 the romantic label, "The capital of golden Kolyma" formed part of the stock-in-trade of clichés and euphemisms with which the newspaper *Sovietskaya Kolyma* was riddled. The label was poetical, and from another point of view, it vaguely hinted at the major industry of the region. The newspaper was not permitted to refer directly to the gold mines. For this reason, in leading articles devoted to the fulfillment of production plans the words "mine" and "gold" were replaced by the words "enterprise" and "product" (later, "metal").

Fedka liked the phrase about the capital, and now responded to all questions put to him at the innumerable checkpoints (they increased in number the nearer we got to Magadan) with the formula: "The truck is proceeding to the capital of golden Kolyma."

At the seventy-second kilometer everything turned out exactly as Fedka had promised. The pal and his educated manicurist wife greeted us with the warmth one so often encounters among people who, after being wanderers on the face of the earth for so many long years, have finally settled down in their own little house. We were treated to homemade cloudberry pie. They filled a tub with boiling water for me, and I enjoyed a good soak that enabled me to get off all the dirt of the central highway. When my driver told our hosts of how upset I had been by having my fingerprints taken, the manicurist exclaimed:

"I hope they choke! They're not worth crying over. Have a real good scrub at those hands of yours. Then I'll give you a manicure that'll take the wind out of your enemies. When you get to Magadan they won't be able to tell you from the colonel's wife!"

The highway merged with the main street of Magadan. There was a street nameplate on one of the houses: "Kolyma Avenue." I nearly swooned with surprise and admiration. After seven years in the backwoods I was entering what was almost a real, genuine city. Multistory buildings, limousines, bustling streets—at least that was how it all appeared to me. It was only some weeks later that I noticed you could count the big buildings on your fingers. But at the time it really was a great metropolis for me.

How strange is the heart of man! My whole soul cursed those who had thought up the idea of building a town in this permafrost, thawing out the ground with the blood and tears of innocent people. Yet at the same time I was aware of a sort of ridiculous pride. . . . How it had grown, and how handsome it had become during my seven years' absence, our Magadan! Quite unrecognizable. I admired each street lamp, each section of asphalt, and even the poster announcing that the house of culture was presenting the operetta *The Dollar Princess*. We treasure each fragment of our life, even the bitterest.

We turned onto the second main thoroughfare. It looked even more luxurious than Kolyma Avenue and was called, of course, Stalin Street. There was House Number 1, a five-story brick apartment house, almost the first brick building in the town. It had been built by our penal draft. I, too, had been here then, lugging hod-loads of frozen bricks along the rickety scaffolding. The house of culture was a stone's throw away; it looked like a real theater. Nearby was the secondary school, which had also been built in my time. But in those days it had seemed a giant against the backcloth of our stunted, tumble-down huts. Since then it had shrunk into proportion by the addition of buildings on either side of it.

"Well, how do you like the capital of Kolyma the golden?" asked Fedka, playing the proud host.

"A nice place . . . only . . ."

"Only what?"

"Well, a lot of Russians left their bones behind here. . . ."

"I know more than you do about that. When you were still trip-ping along the Moscow boulevards I was slogging away here. I've seen it all. Russians, you say? No, no, they weren't all Russians. There were all sorts. It was a real brotherhood of the nations!"

And bending toward my ear, he added:

"He didn't even spare his own lot. There's plenty of Georgians laid to rest here, God help us. . . ."

Julia's street was called Stary Sangorodok. Here there was nothing to remind us of the two central thoroughfares we had just traversed. This was the old, ramshackle, unpaved Magadan of earlier days. I recognized it: this was the place where the prisoners' hospital used to be, where I had landed half dead from my sea journey, where I had spent a long time getting back my strength. Now all these huts had been made over for living accommodations and they had number-plates nailed to them. There was Julia's number.

We found a badly lighted, dirty corridor with about twenty doors opening onto it. In front of each door there was a mound of rags, boxes, pails, and brooms. A pervasive smell of burned grease filled the air.

"Hey, you inside there!" Fedka shouted.

From nearly every door a head poked out.

"Who do you want?"

They all knew Julia. They also knew me, without ever having seen me, because she had left instructions: "Come and get me the moment she arrives!" Julia was at her workplace, just across the way, where you could see the sign "Communal Enterprise Handicrafts."

Fedka rushed off to get Julia. He wanted to be the bearer of good news, to hand me over safe and sound, so that if the opportunity arose, he could tell Anton about it.

Julia bounced in with cries of joy and open arms. In no time at all she was pouring out reminiscences.

"Do you remember? In Yaroslavl? Did we ever think that we'd live to see this day? How we dreamed of walking free down the street! We're going to the cinema today. I've got the tickets. . . . Do you remember how we used to long for vegetables? Let's go into my room—I've prepared some borsch."

Julia was at the top of her form. My faithful Friday, my inexhaustible Micawber.

I laughingly quoted to her my old prison hexameters:

Mighty Vesuvius buries Pompeii in torrents of lava,
Save for our Julia who's pickling her gherkins above the disaster.

Fedka beamed affectionately at us.

"So here you are, together again, my dears. How many years has it been?"

"Eight," we replied in unison. And that's how long it had been since the day when the S.S. *Dzhurma* carried me away to Kolyma, while Julia, who was ill, had been separated from our draft and had then gone through a series of camps that didn't happen to coincide with mine. She had escaped Elgen. She had been in Susman, and in various other places. Then she had landed in the golden capital. I had heard that Julia had organized some sort of workshop in Magadan with a fantastic line of goods something like the Hooves and Horns Trading Emporium from Ilf and Petrov's *Twelve Chairs*. Anyway, many former inmates of camps and prisons had found a refuge from lethal outdoor labor, from cold and hunger, in the workshop. My enterprising little Julia had rescued a lot of people.

She led me along the corridor, and before we reached her room she managed to explain that her enterprise was called a "reprocessing workshop," and that she procured various kinds of industrial waste from other production centers and turned out all sorts of odds and ends from it: toys, lampshades, rugs.

"Who's your deputy manager?" I asked.

She gave me a sly wink, leaving me to understand that it was all in order. She flung the door to her room open with a regal flourish, as if she expected me to be struck dumb by the riches disclosed to my gaze. Julia then became alarmingly solemn and told me that I must consider myself mistress, no less than she was, of all the splendor I was now surveying.

A camp bed had already been set up for me in a rather narrow little room of some seven square meters; the table was covered with a carefully ironed white rag (from the reprocessing workshop), and spread for a feast. How nice to arrive where such a kind welcome awaits you!

The three of us tucked into a borsch so thick that the spoon stood up in it, and so heavily peppered that even Fedka found himself sneezing. Straight after the meal my faithful driver was ready to take his leave. He had to go and collect a load from the food plant. I was sorry to have to say good-by to him. When you thought about it, it was probably the first time in ten years I'd met a professional thug (ex-thug, it's true) who had remained a human being.

After his departure, Julia and I settled down in the very same posture we used to assume in our Yaroslavl solitary: each on her own bunk, facing one another. Now, as then, we talked about everything at once. In our eight years of traipsing from camp to camp each of us had accumulated a heap of stories of major disasters and minuscule successes, of heroic resistance to the onset of death and of miraculous escapes from it.

I noted that whatever subject we turned to, Julia always brought the conversation around to her workshop. What a miraculous transformation! She really lived for her work. It was not only that the workshop enabled her to help people, to save from certain death many who were spiritually valiant but physically feeble. No, strange to say, Julia was inspired by the work itself, stupid and trivial as it might seem. She liked showing what a good manager she was, making things work in an almost impossible situation, outwitting our bosses, making them look silly while apparently treating them with respect. In short, the spirit of private enterprise and private initiative, genetically programed into Julia by her resourceful Volga trader ancestors, had suddenly come to life here in these unforeseen circumstances.

Sinner that I am, I enjoyed observing Julia in her new Magadan

role as Vassa Zheleznova, and I mentally compared her present
animation, her bubbling energy, and her zest for life with her de-
jected looks at the university the last year before her arrest. Now
she was lively and witty; what she said was pithy and amusing.
Whereas then her unfortunate fellow undergraduates had died a
thousand deaths each time she regurgitated for their benefit the
prescribed dose of philosophical orthodoxy. She had been afraid of
each word she let slip, and she was forever looking around her with
fright. For there lying in wait for her on all sides were the vipers of
Menshevist idealism, not to mention the hyenas of vulgar materialism and the snakes of insidious empiricism.

We spent the whole evening strolling up and down the main
thoroughfare of Magadan, our golden city. Julia showed me everything and explained it all to me, putting on at times the patronizing
airs of an inhabitant of the capital entertaining a country cousin.
I was not offended. I had indeed grown unaccustomed to such
things in my seven years in the taiga. I kept making mistakes—getting into the wrong queue, sitting down in the wrong row. Julia
wanted me to be thrilled by everything, and she was quite hurt by
my lack of enthusiasm about the cinema, where we saw a quite
incomprehensible film about spies.

I was much more interested in the street scene than in the cinema.
The whole of the Magadan beau monde was parading up and down
Stalin Street that summer evening. The big bosses, for some reason,
confined their perambulations to the right-hand side of the street,
from the house of culture up to Kolyma Avenue.

The calendar said July, but there was a cold bite to the air and
a sharp, penetrating wind from the sea. In such weather all the
great ones of this world were dressed—as if it were a uniform—in
gray gabardine. Their padded shoulders jutted out proudly. This
imparted a certain majesty to their bearing, making the men all look
like the (toppled) monument to Alexander III in Leningrad. As for
the ladies, with their inordinate addiction to silver-fox furs, they
reminded me of a picture in a German textbook, showing a hunter
with the skins of dead foxes draped around his shoulders. The
inscription read: "*Der Jäger*."

Those who perambulated on the left-hand side of the street, from
the school to the corner, were neither as respectable nor as uniform
as the right-handers. Their class composition was quite different.
Here you would find run-of-the-mill employees of the lesser breeds,

so to speak—bookkeepers, technicians from the automobile works, and Komsomol nurses: small fry of all descriptions. You might even spot former prisoners among them. By now they had filled out physically and they had decent clothes on their back. But for all that, I could identify them unerringly by the exaggerated casualness of their movements and by the way in which they sometimes forgot themselves and drew their head down into their shoulders. They were still not used to strolling up and down the main thoroughfare of a city.

In one of the large windows of a brick building, an apartment house where the bosses lived, I suddenly saw my reflection. What a sight I was! It must have been the devil's prompting that caused me to sew that strip of moulting cat fur onto the collar of my jacket! Anybody could see from a mile away that I was an ex-convict. The hell with them! I hope their fox furs smother them. Cat fur's good enough for me.

Julia read my thoughts.

"Not that it matters a bit, but with you looking like that nobody will give you a job. So tomorrow morning early we'll go along to the flea market and buy you an overcoat."

Suddenly I caught the sound of some strange melody, of people singing in unison. The long-familiar tune sounded odd. I looked around. Columns of short men in what might have been either military uniform or prison uniform were marching down the road in rank abreast. Russian soldiers, with rifles at the port, were guarding them on all four sides.

"Japanese prisoners of war," Julia explained. "They're good workers. They've already built several large blocks. At the moment they're putting the finishing touches on the new cinema. Can you make out what they're singing? It's 'Through the valleys and over the hills. . . .'"

Julia laughed and told me how individual Japanese officers were sometimes to be seen about the town peddling their wares: they sold warm mittens and socks, which they knitted very skillfully themselves. It was a mystery where they got such excellent wool from—they probably unpicked their own woolen underwear. One of them even came to visit Julia in her workshop, offering his wares for sale, and had some comic things to say in his pidgin Russian about life in Magadan: "Japanese soldiers walk down road; Russian soldiers guard. We understand—war! Russian ladies walk down road; Russian soldiers guard. We not understand." This was his reaction to the numerous women's penal drafts trudging along the streets of our capital, disembarking in a constant flow of new arrivals, as if there were an inexhaustible supply of female law-breakers in our towns and villages.

Yes, there was a lot that was new in Magadan since I had last been there several years earlier, but the one fundamental remained unshakable—the endless columns of prisoners in transit.

Certain of the street scenes moved me almost to tears—for example, the sight of old men and of teenagers. They hadn't existed here before. There were still none in the taiga, or at least I hadn't seen either category during my ten years there. No prisoner ever lived to old age. In the old days local officials had never brought their parents out to this region; and the only children in Kolyma had been those who were born there. There had been hardly any teenagers. But by now a whole clutch of juveniles from the mainland had been brought to the center of Kolyma.

I avidly studied each young boy of school age, comparing him with my sons. This one, for example, must be fourteen already. I had not been there to see Alyosha at that age. Vasya was now fifteen. I couldn't picture him.

Here came an old lady leading a little girl by the hand. What a nice looking old lady, neatly dressed, with a pleasant oval face! Just like our old nurse, Fima. And the little girl resembled her: probably grandmother and granddaughter. When was the last time I had seen anything like that? In which of my dreams?

I was also greatly moved by the sight of dogs. In the taiga I had all but reached the point of hating the entire canine race. The only dogs in the camps were Alsatians—the faithful servants of the prison staff. Our savage enemies. I had forgotten that there were other dogs in the world—cheerful, harmless mongrels, eccentric dachshunds, and skittish Pomeranians. I laughed with joy when I heard Julia's guard dog, Dropdead, one of a long line of mongrel house dogs, greeting us with a hoarse bark. Not the sort of dog that goes for your throat, but one that goodheartedly wags its tail. If you think of it, there's something human about that. He, poor soul, is as little to blame for the misdeeds of his cousins patrolling the barbed-wire fences, as we, two-legged house dogs, are for the savagery of the two-legged Alsatians. I ran my hand through Drop-dead's coat and inwardly made peace with the canine race.

Julia suddenly remembered that she hadn't bought any bread, and we turned into what was called Shop Number 1.

Bread was rationed. The shelves were empty except for packages of "health" coffee. There were posters on the walls, vividly portraying blushing hams, slabs of dairy butter, whole Dutch cheeses. Inscriptions underneath told us that by 1950 we should be getting so much meat, so much butter, and so much sugar per head of population.

I was totally confused. Had I come there to live on Julia's rations?

"Oh, of course, I've got some pies," I said, happily remembering the gift of the manicurist at the seventy-second kilometer. "They're wonderful, made with rye flour."

"Well, have you ever seen anything like our splendid shop?" Julia asked bitterly. She added, "Did you notice how bloated the 'gabardine' types look?"

"But they have their own special restricted-access stores. Look, there's loads of vodka here!"

"That's not vodka—it doesn't pay to ship it here. That's pure alcohol. And they toss it down almost undiluted."

Indeed, there were drunks lying about in the street outside the shop, like so many corpses. And there were quite a few women among them.

I suddenly felt infinitely tired.

"Let's go home, Julia! I think I've had enough of Magadan scenery to last me a good long while. . . ."

Near the public baths, where, as in our time, there was a medical screening point for prisoners, we came across an enormous male prison draft that had just disembarked. The men were sitting in the roadway, squatting on their heels, surrounded by convoy guards and Alsatians. I felt as if the last seven years had never been. She hadn't changed, my capital of gold. She had put on a pretty dress, given her blood-stained hands a manicure, and draped silver-fox furs around her plump shoulders. But when you got down to essentials, she had not changed.

I was visited by an unbearable, burning sense of shame for the idiotic euphoria that I had felt as I rode into the town, hypnotized by the multistory buildings and the operetta posters.

And what of those who didn't have my experience? How easy it must be to pull the wool over their eyes if those like me, who knew it all from the inside, at times let themselves be dazzled by the pompous façades of these mock skyscrapers.

About 3 A.M. Julia suddenly woke up, turned on the light, and looked at me carefully.

"I knew it. She's lying there with her eyes wide open and taking all the cares of the world upon her. What a disposition! Hold on a moment, I'll give you some veronal and that'll put you straight off to sleep."

The veronal helped. I gradually fell asleep. In my dreams I saw Fedka turning the wheel of the truck and heard him singing— singing that patriotic, professionals' song:

It's always a matter for pity
When I don't fulfill double the plan.
My beloved capital city,
My city of gold, Magadan!

4

· Honest labor

Julia had a job in her workshop all set up for me. She had already arranged it with the management; this was by no means simple, given the sort of documentation I possessed. Julia was very proud that on arrival in Magadan I had found everything ready and waiting for me. Lodgings and a job—she had found it all for me.

So it was a long time before I could bring myself even to hint that I was less than delighted with the prospect of backbreaking work, day in and day out, in a dusty basement, converting stiffened gauze into de luxe lampshades for the idyllic domestic foyers of Kolyma.

I cherished a different, virtually unrealizable dream: to work with children once again. Why? Well, because it was a unique form of escape—escape from the Kolyma graft, from the all-pervasive smell of criminality, and even, to some extent, from humiliation. For children were the only people who didn't want to know what was written about me in my personal file. They merely responded to my treatment of them. In addition, despite all the red tape prevailing in children's establishments, they were still a diametrical contrast to the world of prisons and camps. Good or bad, the kindergarten's aim was not to torture and humiliate human beings, but to nurture and rear them. And there was one more thing—a secret from everyone, including Anton. Even to myself I didn't define it clearly. Somehow when I found myself in the company of children, the relentless torments of grief for Alyosha were somewhat eased. For me the relief was not a result of the firm and consistent Christian principles that made Anton tell me to help a patient "for Alyosha's sake." It was simply that my work in the kindergarten had helped me to get back to my life outside, which had been so pitilessly interrupted in '37. Even the mechanical repetitiveness of our basic daily chores had given me illusory relief from the knowledge that my role as a mother had been cynically and brutally trampled upon.

I realized that I had little hope of obtaining employment in an institution for children. Julia had already explained to me in detail that in the capital of Kolyma there could be no such patriarchal survivals as in the depths of the taiga, where the natural kindness of such people in the administration as Timoshkin or Mamai the Cossack could sometimes get the better of inhuman articles and regulations. "Here the personnel departments are even more rigorous than on the mainland," explained Julia.

For all that, I decided to visit the Medical Administration, which had charge of all the children's institutions, and brazenly offer my services. Perhaps the excellent recommendation given me on my departure by the Taskan administration would compensate for my term of imprisonment and my articles—and maybe even for the entries recorded against me in my secret file.

But to tell Julia of my plan would be to display rank ingratitude.

An unexpected occurrence helped me in my project. It was quite dark, dawn had barely broken, when we heard a timid, intermittent rapping at our door. It was Elena Mikhailovna Tager, whom we knew from our camps and penal drafts.

"What's happened? Why are you here at this hour?"

"I've been released!" our visitor replied in a quavering voice; then she subsided helplessly onto the couch. We were on the point of congratulating her when we suddenly noticed that she looked quite ill. After giving her some lily-of-the-valley drops and putting a cold compress on her forehead, we finally learned what it was all about.

"My friends, my dear friends . . . Don't be too surprised at what I am about to say. And please don't try to argue. . . . It's appalling, but it's a fact. The thing is that I, I . . . I can't face living outside. I . . . I want to stay in camp."

Elena Mikhailovna really could look on us as friends. True, in age she was nearer to our parents' generation than to ours, and we hadn't seen her for several years. But at various points on our journeying from prison to camp, from camp to prison, our paths had crossed and we had had a very close and deep relationship with her.

A Leningrad literary figure in her own right, a woman in whom great nobility of character went with unusual helplessness in practical matters, she was always in need of people to look after her. And there were many of us younger ones who were glad to help her. In return, she rendered us a far more inestimable service: by sharing her experiences with us, she helped keep alight the barely flickering flame of our spiritual life. Perched somewhere up on the top tier of bunks, she would talk to us till late in the night of her meetings with Blok, with Akhmatova, and with Mandelstam. When morning came we would start piloting her around like a child, showing her where to dry her sandals, how to conceal from the searchers the things we were not supposed to have in our possession, and how to keep the thugs at arm's length.

Elena Mikhailovna had often been worked onto her last legs at some land-reclamation or tree-felling site. But three years ago she had reached what in camp passed as a haven of peace. She had been certified unfit; they had recognized her right to do only light work on the grounds of her age and state of health. She had thus attained the summit of camp happiness: she had become duty warden in the hut of the girls from the Western Ukraine. She grew accustomed to the daily round of her uncomplicated duties: keeping the stove going and sweeping the floor. She became fond of the girls, the more so because by then all her own family had died in the Leningrad blockade. And the girls had grown fond of her. They saw to it that she didn't have to do any especially hard work. They split the firewood for her and washed down the floors. Many of them even started calling Elena Mikhailovna "Mamma."

"They're wonderful girls. . . . It's been a whole month since I countersigned my release documents in the Registration and Distribution Section—a whole month since my rations have been stopped. But I haven't noticed any difference. The girls feed me. . . ."

"What do you mean, a month? Why are you still there?"

"Where am I to go? You know, the longest trip I've made these past three years has been from the hut to the hot-water tap. As for this city, it's a desert to me. It terrifies me."

Elena Mikhailovna's story, as she told it, ran as follows.

She had twice ventured outside the compound during that month, looking for a place of refuge in this incomprehensible free anthill, where rations were not doled out every morning and where you didn't have a place of your own on the bunk platform. She had found nothing, had met none of her former comrades from inside. She returned despondent to camp. The guard had let her in, for old times' sake. The girls had made a great fuss of her the whole night long and had dashed to the dispensary to get lily-of-the-valley drops for her. During that month she had been repeatedly warned that she must leave the compound. "Free people aren't allowed to live in camp," she was told. And now today . . . Oh yes, she had almost forgotten—yesterday the chief disciplinary officer in person had turned up at roll call and categorically ordered her to leave the camp at once. The girls had started crying, begging him to allow their adopted mother to stay. It didn't matter if she wasn't given rations, they would be responsible for her. Elena herself had burst into tears. The disciplinary officer, deeply moved, had shown that he had a heart, not a stone in his breast. It was, of course, not in his power to let the old lady stay on, but he did put it to her nicely: "Listen, Citizen," he said, "you've been here ten years, right? Right. And no one's interfered with you. Why do you suppose that is? Because then it was all right, that's why. Now it's all over. You can't stay any more. It's against orders."

And then one of the girls had given Elena Mikhailovna Julia's address. The reputation of Julia's workshop, where even people sentenced under the most troublesome articles were found indoor work, had spread far and wide through the convict world.

"It'll be all right, Elena Mikhailovna," said Julia with such certainty that our guest turned to her with a look of childlike devotion and began carrying out all Julia's orders unquestioningly. She re-

ceived the usual wonder-working veronal from Julia's hands, obe-
diently lay down on the folding bed, and was soon fast asleep. In
her sleep she snuffled and sighed like a child; Julia and I, lying side
by side on a narrow iron bed, found it quite impossible to get to
sleep, although the dawn had still not really broken.

"Do you remember, Genia, the poem you made up in Yaroslavl?"

Who would have thought that Julia would still remember my improvised prison poem "Apprehension"?

> Lest within these walls of stone,
> Where our wings were clipped off short,
> We grow used—for all our groans—
> To being incapable of flight.

"I think Elena Mikhailovna will get over it. You'll see, Julia, she'll
get over it."

(Happily my hopes were justified. Elena Mikhailovna did recover
from her inertial helplessness. She lived to see herself rehabilitated
and returned to Leningrad. She even went on to write a perceptive
book about Mandelstam, excerpts from which appear in the preface
to a two-volume edition of Mandelstam published in the United
States. Elena Mikhailovna died at the beginning of the sixties.)

This unexpected occurrence meant that I could surrender my
place in the famous reprocessing workshop without any fear of offending Julia.

"So what will you do?"

"I'll go along to the Medical Administration. I'll try for a place
in a kindergarten."

Julia shook her head skeptically.

"You think it's the same here as in the taiga. You could get away
with that sort of thing there, where the bosses can't see you.
But not here in the capital. Anyway, nurses grow on trees here—
not only former prisoners on light sentences, but Komsomol girls
on contract."

Julia was right, as always. But my incredible good luck came
into play. It had put in several capricious appearances at various
points in my wanderings and had rescued me from the most
hopeless of situations.

As soon as I entered the Medical Administration—a single-story,
ramshackle building painted in their favorite shocking pink—I
bumped into Dr. Pertsulenko, the head doctor of the Elgen free

hospital, in a dimly lighted corridor. I had worked out my last six weeks in camp under his orders. He was a friend of Anton's.

He took me by the hand and led me straight to the office of the head of children's establishments. This turned out to be Dr. Gorbatova, a handsome forty-year-old blonde with a pleasant, tired face. Pertsulenko introduced me in terms that obliged me to avert my gaze. "She's this . . . and that . . . none better . . ."

"Would you be interested in teaching?" asked Gorbatova, giving me a friendly look. "We have a surplus of nurses, but we're desperate for teachers. There's an acute shortage of trained personnel. No one wants to take it on—it's too much of a strain. We have a very specific cross section of children."

Would I be interested? It was more than I had dared to dream of. But I realized that the illusions of these two goodhearted free employees would shatter to smithereens at the first cursory look they took at my documents. With a deep sigh, I put my Form A, with my thumbprint in lieu of a photograph, down on Gorbatova's desk. She subjected it to a long, sorrowful examination; but then she got resolutely to her feet and said, "I'll go and see the personnel department."

The personnel department was next door. Through the thin partition Pertsulenko and I could make out snatches of the dialogue between Gorbatova and Podushkin, the head of personnel.

"Buzz, buzz, buzz . . . She's a graduate teacher," Gorbatova urged.

"Buzz, buzz . . . The ideological front . . . group terrorism . . ." the head of personnel countered.

He probably had white eyebrows and chubby hands, with a wristwatch on a gold band.

"Buzz, buzz . . . Three short in Kindergarten Number 3 . . . Why not take her on temporarily . . ."

"Buzz, buzz . . . If only she hadn't been in jail as well. . . . I can't do it on my own responsibility. Try Shcherbakov? By all means . . . If the order comes from him . . ."

The door cracked and we heard the sound of steps.

"They've gone to see the head of the Medical Administration, Shcherbakov," commented Pertsulenko. He added, noticing how depressed I was looking: "You stay here and I'll go and see him myself. He's a sensible fellow. We'll talk him around. . . ."

And another of those miracles occurred. Half an hour later, when I emerged from the pink building, I was the bearer of a document attesting that I was assigned to work as a teacher at Number 3 Full-day Kindergarten.

At that time, 1947, the Magadan kindergartens differed greatly from one another in social make-up. There was a kindergarten for the children of senior officials. Spruce little boys and girls were brought along on toboggans by their nurses and domestic servants (male servants were often recruited from among the prisoners). Entry into this establishment was pretty firmly barred to children from the families of former prisoners. There were also kindergartens for the less exalted sectors of the population of Magadan.

Kindergarten Number 3, to which I had been assigned, was in all essentials a preschool boarding establishment or a children's home. Only the children of former prisoners lived there. Many of the children had been born in prison or in camp; their way in life had started in the Elgen children's home.

My kindergarten was quite near the house in which Julia and I had our lodgings. It was located in a two-story wooden building of hutlike appearance, painted the inevitable pink. The chimney stack of the boiler house stood next to this building; it huffed and puffed and vomited sooty fumes straight onto the exercise yard, enveloping the children's faces in clouds of acrid smoke. In the winter the soot turned the snow-covered exercise yard black.

I was appointed instructor to the senior group. I had thirty-eight children aged six and seven entrusted to my care. I only needed two hours with them to understand why the Medical Administration experienced so acute a shortage of instructors and why they had had to resort even to the services of a criminal like me—a terrorist sentenced by the Military Collegium.

They were difficult children. Thirty-eight infant neurotics, some high-strung and overexcitable, others subdued and silent. Some were painfully thin and pale, with blue rings around their eyes; others had grown disproportionately fat from a diet too rich in carbohydrates and deficient in vitamins. They were difficult collectively and difficult individually.

"We have a very specific cross section of children." So said the kindergarten head, repeating Gorbatova's words. "I advise you to adopt right from the start a completely dispassionate tone with them. Excessive severity or driving them too hard can give rise to scenes; too much leniency or kindness, and you'll lose control of them and find it impossible to get it back."

She was doubtless right and was basing herself on the experience of other instructors. But she didn't know and couldn't know that it was quite impossible for me to be dispassionate toward these children. I could not look upon them as strangers. These infants had grown up in Elgen, they were my fellow travelers within the whirlwind. How could I be a dispassionate, coolly methodical teacher—albeit from the highest of motives—with these child-martyrs who had known Elgen?

These children knew a lot less than their mainland counterparts. They were what one calls backward. But they had an intuitive understanding of many things (without being able to put a name to them) usually known only to old people. Such children could tire you out dreadfully, could send you into a fury, could drive you to despair. But it was impossible to remain indifferent to them. The feeling I had for them could hardly be called love in the strict sense of the word; it would be more accurate, perhaps, to call it a feeling of solidarity, of kinship, or something of that kind.

Apart from me, all the instructors were on contract; many of them were quite recent arrivals from the mainland. There were nice people among them, and I was grateful to them for their tact, for not making a point of my pariah status. But I did not feel up to making friends with them. They all seemed to me more like children than the children in our care. Despite the fact that they had been through it all—the war, evacuation, and hunger—that was the sum total of their knowledge. Their naïve trust in official propaganda was so strong that they simply refused to believe what their own eyes told them about the realities of Kolyma. Anything that appeared in the newspaper carried more conviction with them than what they saw in the street. They went into a sort of religious ecstasy when they were teaching the children the popular song "Lenin is our first eagle and Stalin is our second." In any event, they had far less sense of reality than, say, Lida Chashechkina, who had been born in Elgen, had twice been forcibly separated from her mother, and, just six years old, had seen so many meters of barbed wire and dozens of guard dogs and watchtowers.

My enthusiasm for my exalted post distinctly waned when I saw the kindergarten curriculum on which we had to base our educational activities. We were required to study the syllabus in depth and to draw up quarterly, monthly, weekly, and daily plans of educational work. We were supervised in this by experts on teaching methods from the Preschool Methodology Center. This meant I had to read and keep rereading the voluminous program for training our country's young citizens.

In the section "Training in Patriotism," the teacher was required to cultivate not only the feeling of love for the Soviet homeland but also the feeling of *hatred* for its enemies.

In the section on speech training, one had to study the poem "I'm a little girl, I sing and I play / I haven't seen Stalin but I love him each day."

At the music periods taught personally by the head, Claudia Vasilevna, the children had to learn by heart, in addition to the "Two Eagles" song referred to above, various other songs on the same inexhaustible theme: "If Stalin were to visit us . . ." And then there was the song of the young sailors: "Dear Comrade Stalin, the days will soon go by . . ."

On hearing that I played the piano, Claudia Vasilevna was overjoyed and told me to watch how she conducted the lesson. When she had administrative chores to attend to, I might sometimes be allowed to take her place at the piano.

Attendance at the Preschool Methodology Center was obligatory. At the very first seminar I listened to a very solid report on methodology by Aleksandra Mikhailovna Shilnikova. She gave an assessment of a May Day matinee concert at one of the kindergartens' and quoted the children's reactions on this festive occasion:

"We love Comrade Stalin more than Mommy or Daddy," the children were supposed to have said. Then they had shouted in chorus:

"May Comrade Stalin live to be a hundred! No, two hundred! No, three hundred!"

And one of the little boys, Vladimir, was so proficient in politics that he had cried out:

"May Comrade Stalin live forever!"

At this point the methodologist, Shilnikova, paused and glanced down at her audience with a look that was both triumphant and charged with emotion. We teachers, so well disciplined, hastened to take down in our neat notebooks everything she said.

These were the unforeseen aspects of the work with children, which I had so long sought. During my ten years' absence various trends in normal, everyday life had gone much further: the deification of the immortal Father of the People, and His penetration into every nook and cranny where there was the least flutter of life. The insurmountable problem was that of avoiding complicity in his feats. This problem arose even in so innocent a matter as the bringing up of small children.

What was I to do? My first few days at work I was frequently in despair, and the thought kept flickering through my mind: Perhaps I should go to Julia, repent of all I had done, and beg her to give me a place in her workshop. Maybe the drudgery of making table lamps would purge me of the unbearable feeling of guilt and complicity.

But about that time I noticed the affectionate twist given by the children to my first name and patronymic. It was Eugenichka instead of Eugenia and Semyonochka instead of Semyonovna. And not only to my face but also behind my back, when they spoke of me in the third person and thought I was not listening. This was their way of distinguishing the teachers they loved from those they hated. They used the two kinds of diminutive endings: the affectionate Annochka and Tamarochka for those they loved, and the pejorative Zoika and Elenka for those whom they had taken against.

"Eugenichka Semyonochka" was too much for me. After all, it had been ten years since I had last seen any of my own family. I started to show them how to project a silhouette story onto the wall —"Puss in Boots." I could see how much pleasure it gave them. I also derived comfort from our frequent rambles up the hill, going out picking cranberries, and from the lively interest of the children when I recited Chukovsky or Marshak to them. My recitations were, of course, from memory. There were no books of that kind in the kindergarten.

I was also critical of myself for lacking in *sang-froid*, moderation, and objectivity. I found myself acquiring favorites; it took a great effort on my part to conceal this fact. For example, I immediately singled out Edik Klimov from all the other children. He was a Yakut boy—or at least his mother was Yakut. His father, as with the majority of the children, was lost in the mists of the unknown. It is quite possible that Edik was a hybrid, for his intelligent, ruddy

face with the slanting Mongol eyes was lighter in complexion than
his mother's. Moreover, Edik's hair was light brown. His mother
had done time in a camp on a charge of "deer stealing" (like so
many Yakuts), and she was now working as a truck driver, ferrying
equipment to the gold mines. She was a striking woman, what with
her physical strength, her general ruggedness, and the total impas-
sivity of her face—she was like some stone statue erected on the
Great Mongol Highway leading to the palace of the Dalai Lama.
She visited her son infrequently. When she came she would sit
sedately on a chair in the corridor, unfold a man's handkerchief,
take a fruit drop or cookie out of it, and hand it over, unsmilingly,
to Edik. Her invariable response to the questions with which he
assailed her was to give a loud cough and say with great dignity:
"When you grow up you'll learn all about it." After that she
relapsed into immobility.

But Edik did not want to wait until he grew up. His narrow
little eyes sparkled with curiosity.

"Who built that place?" he asked when we passed on our walk
the recently completed building that housed the Gornyak Cinema.

"Well, it took all sorts of craftsmen: bricklayers, roofers, erectors,
carpenters . . ."

"That's not what I mean," Edik retorted. "I'm asking who built
it: lags or Japs?"

He got an exhaustive answer from Volodya Radkin, a retarded
seven-year-old. Volodya had seen a lot of things in his short life,
because on Sundays his mother, a raucous elderly professional
rejigged to serve in a grocery store, took him home with her.

"How could lags cope with a cinema like that," Volodya said
patronizingly, "on the grub they get? The Japs, though, are well
fed. . . . They're allowed to eat their fill. And they're good
workers, too."

Edik's sharp eye was constantly fastening on various features
of the world about him and picking out contradictions that required elucidation.

"Who's that?"

His question related to the portrait of Engels, brightly festooned
with red streamers and electric bulbs. It was obvious that he was
getting at something.

"Who do you mean?"

My interjection was meant simply to gain time.

"The second one in line. The first is Marx, the third Lenin, and the fourth Stalin. But I've forgotten who the second is."

"It's Engels."

"But is he . . . is he . . . ?"

Edik hesitated, uncertain as to how to put it delicately. He must have heard something unfavorable about Engels. And he couldn't reconcile it with the streamers and the bulbs.

"But is he . . . Russian?"

"Uh . . . He's from Western Europe. . . ."

Edik understood that I too was trying not to utter the obscenely insulting word "German" with reference to a man whose portrait hung alongside those of Lenin and Stalin. But he could not rest until he had got to the bottom of the matter. . . .

"But are there Germans who are on our side? Engels—he's on our side, isn't he?"

"Certainly, he's definitely on our side."

A heavy sigh. No, the question that plagued him had not been resolved.

"Eugenichka Semyonochka, bend down, I want to whisper in your ear."

He put his chubby little arms around my neck and whispered urgently straight into my ear.

"Volodya said silly things about Engels. . . . He said that he was a German. He shouldn't tell such fibs, should he? We've killed all the Germans, haven't we? And Engels is on our side, so he's a Russian, isn't he?"

The girl who relieved me each day, Anna Ivanovna, an excellent teacher who loved children, nevertheless advised me:

"Do try not to get too involved in conversations with Edik Klimov. He'll wear you out with it. And he'll get a big head."

But I was convinced that he would not end up a show-off, and that all the things he asked about really interested him. He wasn't trying to be clever or to score off people. It was simply that he wanted to determine his own attitude to life in all its various aspects. A six-year-old person was searching for harmony and was unable to hold his tongue when he saw something that didn't fit into the rational world depicted to him by his instructors.

On one occasion we were walking in our soot-spattered yard. Just outside, in the street, there were some Japanese POW's digging trenches. Edik threw a tin soldier high up in the air. It sailed over the fence and disappeared from sight into the depths of one of the trenches. A nimble young Japanese hopped into the trench and handed the soldier out to Edik through the boards of the fence.

"Say thank you to the kind man," I urged him.

"He's not a man. He's a Jap."

"A Japanese. But the Japanese too are men and women. And if he is not a woman, then he has to be a man."

Confronted with this faultless logic, Edik paused for thought.

"But he fought against our people."

"Correct! But his officers were to blame for that. He had his orders and he was afraid to disobey them. He himself probably didn't want to fight. He probably has a little boy just like you at home, and he must have been very sad to leave him."

Edik hesitated a little longer and then clambered onto the top bar of the fence and shouted out:

"Mr. Man! Mr. Japanese! Thank you for saving my soldier. But another time you must not obey your commander and must not fight us. You'd best go home to your own little boy."

The Japanese POW understood the familiar words "thank you." He came right up to the fence, and rattled off a whole string of Japanese words, displaying large yellow teeth. Then he slipped his hand through the fence and hesitantly stroked Edik's sleeve.

"You probably look like his little boy," I said. I suddenly noticed that, indeed, Edik's slanted, Asiatic eyes were exactly like those of the Japanese soldier.

When I was on night shift I was supposed to stay in the dormitory until the children were all asleep. I had to creep up and down the dormitory in slippers to see that the children were not talking after the bell had sounded, that their pillows were in the right position, and their hands outside the blankets. I loved those evenings. In their beds they immediately became ordinary little boys and girls, and their merciless past was somehow left behind. I could hear sleepy sighs; someone said "good night" for the third or fourth time. . . . These quiet minutes took me back to a distant past gone forever. Contrary to all the methodological norms, I would stroke one and then another on the hand and say, "Go to sleep, my little one."

Many of them had never been addressed in that way, and it had a hypnotic effect even on the worst desperadoes among them. They sensed in my maternal greeting an echo from a different world, one with which they were unfamiliar. They quieted down and sometimes pressed their cheeks against my hand for a moment; then they dropped peacefully off to sleep.

I always wanted very much to sit down on the edge of Edik's bed and kiss him good night; I regretted that it was not allowed. But the cunning little fellow got by the rule himself. After waiting until most of the children were sound asleep, he would sit up in bed and say in a whisper:

"My throat's sore."

He knew that if anyone complained of feeling ill, the teacher was supposed to go and attend to him. And when I tucked him in and sat down on the edge of the bed, he gave a little laugh and whispered into my ear:

"I did it on purpose. I haven't got a sore throat. I only wanted to ask you . . ."

There followed a string of artless whys that were almost always difficult to answer. He was fearfully observant, that boy! The discrepancy between the rules implanted in the kindergarten and what he saw in daily life gave him no peace.

"The teachers always say that you mustn't sit on the ground, because you may catch a cold and make yourself all dirty. . . ."

"Of course," I replied, already vaguely sensing the trap behind this innocent remark. I was not mistaken. Edik had seen for himself in the street a guard shouting "Sit down!" at the convicts in a newly arrived penal draft, and they had all sat down on the ground. A moment before there had been rain, so some of the convicts flopped down straight into a puddle. "Wouldn't they catch a cold? He must have been a bad guard, wouldn't you say?"

Mostly I avoided answering such questions. I changed the subject. Did Edik remember, for example, how he had been asking me the day before what trees grew in Africa and whether one could teach a monkey to speak, if one trained it over a period of time and with great care. . . . Sometimes my ruse succeeded in diverting the little fellow's thoughts elsewhere. But on this occasion he stuck to his guns.

"He was a bad guard, wasn't he?"

I conceded the point.

"Yes, of course, a good man wouldn't make people sit down on the freezing ground, in puddles. Of course, they're liable to catch cold. But the worst thing about it is that it's insulting. Now go to sleep; no more questions!"

I went once more around the half-dark dormitory. What had I done? Tomorrow he would be bound to report my words somewhere or other. . . . So I compounded my faux pas with a second one—I went up to Edik and asked him very softly indeed:

"Don't tell anyone about our conversation, O.K.?"

"Of course! I'm not a fool, you know!" exclaimed Edik, with the intonation of a thirteen-year-old.

The Methodological Center continued to make progress with its plan for improving teachers' qualifications. We worked through subject after subject and went through the routine of "exchanging experience." Each of our collective exercises showed me for the umpteenth time what an anachronism I, a relic of the thirties, was amid these new people and new customs. The example of this miniature world of preschool pedagogy was a frightening demonstration to me of how far we had progressed in the art of lies and falsehood during my ten years' absence.

I particularly well remember the "creative games" there. Between the afternoon snack and supper there was a one-hour period for so-called creative games. The children were left to play as they wished, while the teachers, seated to one side, were supposed simply to keep the children's ebullience within bounds, supervise the use of communal toys, and above all, write down later in the report column what they played and how their feelings of Soviet patriotism, hatred for enemies, and so on, manifested themselves in their games.

With the aim of "exchanging experience," I was attached to the group directed by Elena Vasilevna, who was officially recognized as the best teacher in the kindergarten. Everyone was in raptures over her ability to obtain silence and total obedience. I was intrigued to know why, in the circumstances, the children called her Elenka Vasilka behind her back.

They were scared of her. Hence the creative games were conducted in a whisper. Nevertheless, I managed to make out that they were playing at having a bath. The Magadan public baths, recently reconstructed from part of the old medical screening point for prisoners, was one of the seven wonders of the city and had won very high praise among the population.

In our kindergarten the children were washed in bowls, and we were terribly economical with the water, which had to be brought in by hand from the yard. For this reason the children whose mothers came to collect them on Saturdays and then took them off to the baths were left with an enduring impression of hot taps, showers, and the smell of the kvass that was available in the changing rooms.

The girls who were playing mothers were giving their daughters a thorough lathering with imaginary soap as if to the manner born, splashing water all over them, refilling their bowls, and imitating the hissing of hot water. They got so caught up in this that at times their whispered exchanges turned into a loud quarrel.

"I always go to the baths. My Aunt Zina is the cashier there."

"You're lying. How can your aunt be the cashier? She's a convict! And they only employ free people at cash desks."

"That's not so. They'll take Aunt Zina on anywhere. Because Uncle Fedya's one of the guards. . . ."

Elena Vasilevna, flattered by my having come along to benefit from her experience, held out the beautifully ruled notebook she used for plans and reports.

"You can see from that how to keep a record of the creative games. I've written down today's on this page."

"What, already? But they're still playing!"

"I've never yet missed out on a report. I write it up in the morning, together with the plan."

In the plan column under the current date, it read:

"From 1700 hours to 1815 hours creative games on the initiative of the children." In the report column, set out in the same calligraphic handwriting, was: "Today the children played at military hospital. The boys pretended to be wounded soldiers and the girls nurses. The girls bound up the boys' wounds (using play material prepared by the teacher) and said that the soldiers were their defenders and had saved the fatherland from the German invaders. The boys replied that they were doing it in the service of the Soviet Union."

"Do you understand now how to write a report?" Elena Vasilevna asked me in the same condescending way.

I did, indeed I did. I fully understood. Elena Vasilevna wanted to explain further, but at that moment the children, who were pretending to be taking a shower, became too boisterous and burst into uncontrollable giggles.

Elena Vasilevna rapped out in an icy voice:
"Kotov, go and stand by the desk! Dorofeyeva, come here! Reznichenko, leave the room."
There was immediate and total silence. Elena Vasilevna glanced at her watch:
"Six fifteen! Group, form up in pairs!"
The children in my group also frequently played "bathhouse" and "Number 1 Department Store" (with some of them giving very lifelike performances as drunks lolling about at the entrance to the store). They also played "music lessons," "school," and "Magadan Park of Rest and Culture," where the main attraction for the children was the bears' cage. The Kolyma drunks used to try to get them—Mishka, the brown bear, and Yulka, the white she-bear—tipsy by plying them with diluted surgical alcohol from a bottle, and the rascals derived much amusement from the way the bears took to it. The first time I took the children to see the bears' cage, I was nonplussed by the question from one of the children: "Why aren't bears allowed to drink champagne?" It turned out that there was on the cage an official notice that I had failed to spot: "It is strictly forbidden to give bears champagne."
I was inordinately pleased when the children used in their charades characters they had learned about from me, as when they played at Moidodyr, or the brave Vanya Vasilchikov, or the Leningrad Postman.*
One day they were playing "What will I be when I grow up?" They had entered enthusiastically into the spirit of the game. They all shouted out: "To be a pilot is best." They all wanted to be pilots, like those whom they knew in Magadan as the greatest of heroes. For it was the pilots who flew people off to the fabulous mainland.
Suddenly, sulky Lida Chashechkina came out with: "When I grow up I'm going to be Nikishov. And everyone will be afraid of me."
The name of the head of the Building Administration Far East (Dalstroi), Nikishov, was known to all of them. When we went out on our walk, each time we passed by a large block surrounded by a high fence and with sentries on guard, the children never failed to explain to me that this was where Nikishov lived.

* Characters from children's stories by Chukovsky and by Marshak.

"How can you be Nikishov, if you're a girl?" was Edik Klimov's reaction to Lida's brazen pretension.

"Well, I will!" insisted Lida.

"No, you won't," Edik interrupted. But, having a kind heart, he added: "At the most you could become Comrade Gridasova."

Aleksandra Romanovna Gridasova was the young and beautiful wife of old General Nikishov. For her sake he had abandoned his previous family and gone through some unpleasantness in Moscow, but now at least he had this handsome lady living with him in the house with the high fence round it. The women convicts who were fortunate enough to be part of the household of the uncrowned Queen of Kolyma were forever telling stories of her jewelry boxes full of priceless objects, of her lavish banquets, and of how Aleksandra Romanovna had more dresses than the long-dead Empress Elizaveta Petrovna.

All these conversations and many others besides came to the ears of the children. When their mothers arrived on Sundays to rescue them from the clinically sterile life of the kindergarten, presided over by the Methodology Center, they would take the children not only to their lodgings but also to the low joints near their homes. Many of the children with brains or a moral sense, like Edik, began to guess at the existence of the big lie.

Each day it became harder to decide what to tell the children, and how to reconcile the information emanating from the Methodology Center with the scenes of Magadan life. How was I to contrive in these circumstances to instill even a tincture of humanity into them and to teach them to tell good from evil?

Julia spotted that something was wrong and invited me from time to time to return to her workshop.

"Well, how goes your honest labor?" she would ask in the evening, scrutinizing my face. "You eat meat broth every day, but you get thinner and thinner. . . . We've now switched from lamp shades to handkerchiefs. Just hemming and embroidering. Do you want to try it?"

But I felt ill at the very thought of having to leave the children. Perhaps I could ask to be transferred to the junior group, the three-year-olds. But that wouldn't help: "training in patriotism," including "inculcation of hatred for our enemies," was part of their syllabus, too.

I parried Julia's questions with a joke, but I had more and more difficulty sleeping at night. My own personal worries were, of course, also nagging at me. But no small role in my insomnia was played by the form of honest labor in which I was engaged. These were the pedagogic problems of a Kolyma teacher, which are unlikely to have come to the attention of Ushinsky, Pestalozzi, or Comenius.

5

Provisionally freed

Almost every day I came across people I knew in the street: acquaintances from Kazan or Moscow; from Butyrki and Lefortovo; from Elgen and Taskan.

In 1947 many inhabitants of Gulag's Empire, despite all the limitations and delays with which their release was hedged about, succeeded in getting out of camp, obtaining Form A, and making the transition from slave to freedman. Many of them came to Magadan. For some of them this was the springboard for their return to the mainland; for others it was a place where they might get a better job and make their escape from the wilds of the taiga.

Meeting old friends and acquaintances was a source both of joy and of pain. The reunions were a source of joy because these people were the living embodiment of my past. Their very presence was an answer to the question: Did such-and-such a little boy exist? Yes, of course, he did! And so, too, did the mainland, the university, family, friends. There *had* been such things as books, concerts, thoughts, arguments. . . . The man to whom I was talking had known my parents. This woman had done her postgraduate studies with me. They at least knew for a fact that I had not been born on a camp bunk and that my name had not always had attached to it the barbarous word "tyurzak."*

---

* Someone sentenced to confinement in a prison rather than a camp.

But how pitilessly time had changed their faces. They were like the spars from some shipwreck, like shavings whirled along in an all-powerful, malign wind ever nearer the final abyss.

None of them looked genuinely old. The majority of those who emerged alive from that decade were then about forty or slightly over. It was not age that had contorted their features but the inhuman experience through which they had all passed. I peered anxiously and expectantly into the faces of old friends, as I might into a mirror. I too must have that same crease at the corners of my lips, that same look—the omniscient look of a snake.

Hardly anyone harbored any illusions. There was no question and would be no question of genuine freedom. We were hostages. It didn't need any real storm clouds—a spiral of blue smoke from the pipe of a special, all-too-well-known pipe smoker would be enough to drive us back behind barbed wire.

Those who were waiting for transport back to the mainland took their stand on the despairing formula: "What will be, will be! I'll get to see my family, and after that . . ." Those who remained behind did their utmost to find themselves an opening in manual labor or in some form of craft. Hardly anyone, except the doctors, worked at or even wanted to work at his old profession. The animal hatred of the authorities for the intelligentsia was all too familiar from our own experience of our years in camp. The thing to do was to be a tailor, a cobbler, a cabinet maker, a laundress—to crawl into some quiet, warm nook, so that it would never occur to anyone that once upon a time you read seditious literature.

Many people accused me of imprudence. How could I go and work in a children's establishment, where "they" would be able to keep tabs on me? "They" were that much more likely to wake up to the fact that they should never have let me out.

When I got home I used to tell Julia about these encounters and share with her the bitter anguish of my forebodings. Julia would reproach me: now that I had taken up my present work there was no point in seeking to unravel the future! The great thing was to derive satisfaction from the small, everyday joys that had so long eluded us. Julia's favorite formula was "Just remember Yaroslavl!"

Julia sought to impress on me, with all the force of her truly Flemish *joie de vivre*, that we had been devilishly lucky throughout this saga. We had cheated death and were alive and kicking, looking not too bad for our forty years, and still receiving letters from men who loved us. And as for food . . .

"Just remember the 'shrapnel' they used to give us at Yaroslavl. You can thank your lucky stars that the kindergarten gives you a three-course lunch: soup, main course, and stewed fruit."

To round off her hymn to the fruits of the earth, Julia recalled a bit of poetry:

How much beauty there is in the world.
Take, for instance, the cabbage!

"Dear Julia, you are right as usual," I replied, laughing. "But I've never really learned to live by cabbage alone."

One day I met an old friend from Kazan—Gimranova, from the university library—in the street. Her husband, the former rector of the Pedagogical Institute, had set out on his road to Calvary very early on, in about '33. He had been accused of Tartar nationalism. Up to the time of her own arrest, in '37, she had observed a self-imposed silence, keeping a firm rein on her grief, since she had her two sons to bring up.

She threw herself on my shoulder, sobbing, ignoring the file of children I was taking for a walk.

"How lucky you are! How lucky you are!" she insisted.

"I? Lucky? Haven't you heard? My Alyosha . . ."

"I know. But Vasya's still alive! Oh, how lucky you are that your Vasya's alive. My two . . . both of them . . ." (The human stump who had lost both legs envied the one-legged man with a crutch.)

Yes, I was lucky. My Vasya was alive. And I was also lucky because my present job allowed me to send him a lot more money than hitherto. Very soon the kindergarten would be taking the children for a holiday in the country, and we would be paid one and a half times our wages during this "health campaign." Then I should be able to buy Vasya a winter coat. He said in his letters that he was going around in a sleeveless jacket.

Julia kept harping on my forthcoming excursion as if it were something quite out of the ordinary. "Just think . . . you're going to a real holiday resort! You'll have to leave the cares of the world behind this time, won't you?"

At the twenty-third kilometer from Magadan, where the central prisoners' hospital used to be, there was now a Pioneer camp, the "Northern Artek." In the summer months children of school age took their holidays there, and from the end of August infants from all the kindergartens and crèches were sent to the camp.

Several days were spent in meticulous, exhausting preparations. We bathed the children; we packed utensils, clothing, toys. At last the bus was outside in the yard, and Elena Vasilevna, that stern disciplinarian, was counting in her quiet, hypnotic voice: "Fifth pair . . . tenth pair . . . Gavrilov, look in front of you! Kalinina, hold Viktorov's hand!"

Two more days went on settling ourselves in, rearranging the beds and the chairs, quieting down the children, who were all excited after their journey.

After that, blessed peace ensued. September is the best month in Magadan and the surrounding area. Summer—which is always windy and rainy—gives way to the clear, tranquil days of early autumn. A slow, diffident sun floated over the conical hills where the cranberry bushes with their red fruit looked like coral reefs. The branches of dwarf pine were weighed down with ripe cones. The woodland paths along which we strolled with the children were covered with a thick layer of pine needles. We glided effortlessly along as if it were the pile of a thick carpet. But what we loved most were the chipmunks. There were lots of them around and, knowing nothing of man's perfidy, they were extraordinarily bold. They darted fearlessly under our feet; sometimes, perched on tree stumps, and with a curiosity to match that of the children, they stared openly at us with their black, beady eyes.

The proximity of nature made the children gentler, quieter, friendlier. In addition, all classes had been canceled for the month. All we did was go for walks, sing songs, recite poems, pick cranberries, and collect cones.

This was the first time I had been able to commune freely with the sky and the trees, with the grass and the little wild animals, for almost eleven years. I strolled along with the children, trying to be as carefree as they. For the odd moment I almost succeeded. I suddenly felt reconciled to life. I accepted everything. We must be grateful to life for everything, and life will give generously in return.

I accept the deserted hamlets,
The man-made craters of the cities,
The luminous expanse of the heavens
And the anguished toil of the slaves.

I had lived to see it at last—the heavens' luminous expanse. Not, perhaps, for long but come it had for all that, to take the place of the slaves' anguished toil.

It was only on Sundays that I felt particularly uncomfortable. All the other teachers had their husbands and children coming out from town to see them. Thus I was reminded all over again that all the ordinary human joys were not for me. There was no one to visit me. *It was not within my rights.* I was in a different category. On Sundays all my griefs came back to torment me more savagely than usual. There was one pain beyond remedy—my grief for Alyosha—and two living sources of pain which I must do something about—Vasya and Anton. With both of them, things were going badly, very badly.

I had received a letter about Vasya from Motya Aksyonova, a relation of his on his father's side, with whose family he had been living all the years of his orphanhood, after they had traced him down to the Kostroma children's home for prisoners' children. Motya wrote that Vasya was difficult. Lately he had got in with some bad boys, had been playing truant and larking around on the boulevards and in the "fleapits" during school hours. In fact, it was impossible to come to terms with him. One could put up with it all so long as there was nothing else to be done, that is, while his mother was in prison. But now that she had been released, was there any good reason why she should not come and collect him? Perhaps his mother considered that the money she had been sending was adequate compensation for all the labor and nervous energy expended on Vasya. If so, she was quite mistaken!

At the end of her letter Motya put the question point-blank: Why was I staying on in Magadan now that I had been released? Why did I not return and take charge of my son, so that I could look after him myself? There followed some pretty transparent hints suggesting that I was a woman who had put my own female interests before my duty as a mother.

How could I hope to explain—especially in a letter—all the peculiar features of my "freedom" to this denizen of another planet?

What I absolutely had to do was to have Vasya sent out to Magadan. I had arranged it all with Julia. She had even told her bosses that her nephew was coming to stay with her, and they had promised to exchange our present seven-square-meter room for a twelve-square-meter one in the next building.

But he had to have a permit to come to Kolyma. And permission had to be given by the Dalstroi personnel department. It was easier for a camel to go through the eye of a needle than for someone who had been imprisoned as a terrorist to obtain a permit for a relative. The person in charge of all this was Colonel Franko, who was noted for his vigilance toward enemies of the people.

People with experience in the matter advised me to try a special method of approach that many had found effective. They called it the "never-say-die" or "endless belt" method. It consisted of putting in application after application, a fresh one every time you received a refusal. You might have had ten refusals. But never mind, slap in another application! Finally, according to the law of averages, your pass would emerge by some lucky fluke from the bureaucratic machine. You never know! Your next application might arrive while Colonel Franko was on leave. Or his clerks might make a bloomer.

I followed this advice, and by autumn I had received two refusals, one after another. I submitted a third application and simultaneously put my name down for an interview with Colonel Franko, hoping to mollify him by telling my story in person. Perhaps when he saw me he would appreciate that the danger of terrorist acts from me or my fifteen-year-old son was not all that great.

I sent off desperate letters to the Aksyonov family, begging them to be patient a little longer. I would take Vasya over very, very soon. I also wrote to Vasya, that mysterious stranger of whom I had a dual picture in my mind's eye. I tried to imagine him as a self-willed teenager with awkward habits, but the chubby face of a little four-year-old rascal in his nurse's arms kept getting in the way.

I wrote to my mother as well, asking her to think about it objectively and tell me whether there was much danger of Vasya getting completely out of hand and dropping out of school. Mother replied that I should, of course, have Vasya sent out. In general, he was an intelligent and quite good-looking boy. But his personality . . . well, I should see for myself. . . .

I began having disturbing dreams about Vasya again. I would wake up in a cold sweat, with my pulse racing. I dreamed that he had given up school and fallen in with criminals, and that I met him in a camp.

Things were no better with Anton. I had had only two brief messages from him sent to Julia's address. The first was a letter sent through the post and stamped by the camp censor. It contained a detailed description of the scenery around the Shturmovoi mine but only one laconic reference to Anton himself—that he was well. The second was a bag of cedar nuts, handed over by a supply agent from Shturmovoi who had come to Magadan on business. Unfortunately, neither I nor Julia was at home at the time, so he had left the bag with the neighbors, saying merely that it was from Dr. Walter. We picked over the nuts one by one and finally discovered among them a note on rolled-up cigarette paper. It contained just a few words in German. It was clear from them that he was at a strict regime site, that there was no contact with any free employees, and that the future was wreathed in gloom.

So I had no reason to love Sundays, which nearly all the other inmates of our children's rest and recuperation camp awaited with impatience. On normal days my bitter musings were kept at bay by work, by constant nervous activity, by the need to see to it that my thirty-eight charges were all healthy, clean, well fed, and happy. But on Sundays I was left with some seven or eight kids, all of them just as homeless and hapless as myself. The others were all collected by their mothers, or in some cases by fathers or uncles; the children went away with them in little family groups.

I tried to make my waifs forget their natural feelings of envy, of their own inferiority and unwantedness. I used to take them out on long walks, away from the camp, setting out first thing in the morning. Besides, I myself didn't want to see my free fellow teachers chatting happily to their husbands and children as they arrived.

During our long hikes I would ignore the program drawn up by the methodology experts. To amuse them and myself I told my waifs stories from the books of my childhood. They learned all about how Little Lord Fauntleroy was torn from his mother by his cruel grandfather. And about the misadventures of the little princess, Sarah Crewe, who had been so maltreated by bad people that she made friends with a rat called Melchizedek. As time went by I started telling them about David Copperfield and his cruel stepfather, about young Dombey's early death, and about Little Dorrit.

At the end of the walk, when I sat down exhausted on a tree stump, my indefatigable companions went on circling around me like gnomes, rewarding me for my stories with clusters of ripe cranberries. They would drop them into my lap and then we would eat them together. There were some good moments during those lonely walks of ours when I felt that the children were grateful to me and fond of me.

Nevertheless I was infinitely glad when one Sunday, almost at the end of our holidays, I heard the voice of Anna Ivanovna, who was taking over from me at the end of my shift:

"You've got visitors! Two men . . ."

For a moment I had the fleeting thought: Could it be Anton, by some miracle? But the two men waiting outside the door were unknown to me—an old man and someone of about forty. They introduced themselves. The old man was Yakov Mikhailovich Umansky and his companion was Vasily Nikitich Kuprianov. From my first, cursory glance I could tell they were both ex-prisoners. How did they come to be here and what were they doing? Until now I had been entirely on my own in the kingdom of the free.

It turned out to be quite straightforward. Both my guests were pathologists. When the site of what was now the Northern Artek Pioneer camp had been the central hospital for prisoners they had worked there and lived in a small room attached to the morgue. This hut was now located outside the boundary of the Pioneer camp. In October the two of them were due to be transferred to Magadan to work in the morgue of the free hospital there. For the present they had been given the task of compiling a secret report for Sevlag on mortality among prisoners. And that was why they were living next door to us.

"We heard that there was one of us among the teachers and so we came along," Kuprianov said. "It must be a bit rough for you on your own among all those free teachers. Nobody to talk to. Let's go for a walk and have a chat."

At last, at long last I had acquired relatives of my own. It was my turn to transfer the children to the care of another teacher and go off with *my relatives*.

We set off in the direction of a distant hill. We talked incessantly, interrupting one another. We talked like friends meeting after a long time apart. We were not plagued by that nasty feeling of uncertainty about the people you are speaking to, by the fear of betrayal which had so often and so long (for decades, in fact) poisoned many budding friendships.

Umansky, the old man, displayed from the moment we met his passion for philosophizing, for explaining what was going on in theoretical terms. At our first meeting he talked about everything under the sun: about the tragic quality of our epoch, about its apocalyptic character; about the hidden role of irrational forces of evil in our personal life and in the making of history; about fascism, that spiritual sickness of mankind, and about its contagiousness.

Everything Vasily Kuprianov said was steeped in bitterness. A former Communist—and a passionate believer, at that—who had gone through all the circles of the inferno, he was now living through the inevitable twilight of the gods, and this was leading him to deny that Good had any strength on its side at all. He was by now convinced that all that was honorable and good was fated to perish. He had shown brilliant promise as a young intellectual in the thirties, but now he spoke of the collapse of humanist culture, and quoted Herzen's prophecy about what happens when the invading hordes of Genghis Khan are equipped with modern communications.

His words belied his looks: Kuprianov was a fine, upstanding figure of a man, a white-skinned Viking; a typical, blue-eyed, straight-nosed, high-foreheaded northerner. He was a native of Archangel.

"You're just like Rurik, Sineus, and Truvor,"* I said to him, laughing.

Umansky, the contemplative philosopher, was an expert on the Bible, a polyglot, and a devourer of poetry. His background was a very diverse one. It included a penurious childhood in a Jewish-Ukrainian *shtetl*, and a long migration and education in France and in Switzerland.

Umansky's slightly protuberant, quite undimmed, blue eyes, and every wrinkle and bump in his aging face exuded goodness. His way of speaking, heavily larded as it was with quotations, was highly individual, full of a gentle humor with a faintly Jewish flavor. Yakov Mikhailovich's memory was simply phenomenal for

* Legendary Viking princes who founded the earliest Russian state in the ninth century.

his age. He could quote at length any writer you could mention—
Lucretius, Plekhanov, Byron, Burliuk.*

It was a perfectly clear September day. We strolled about the hill
for several hours, arguing ourselves hoarse. Finally we sat down on
the slope to rest and eat cranberries, which were at their juiciest.
We ate them by the handful, tipping them straight into our mouths.
My two cavaliers kept me supplied with green sprigs laden with
ripe berries.

"No more, thank you, Yakov Mikhailovich. You've done
enough. . . . Let Vasily Nikitich take over, he's younger."

"I'm not all that old," Umansky mildly protested. He added:
"Not of course that I'm young. The Bible says the age of man
is three-score years and ten and anything over that is due to
stamina. So I'm already living on stamina. . . ."

I have never forgotten the sheer joy that my encounter with
these newly acquired "relatives" brought me. How close we were
on that sunny day: in our sufferings, our thoughts, our desires, and
our hopes. Is there any closer relationship than that?

People somehow derive special pleasure from discerning that they
are all subject to the same psychological laws. My guests and I were
gratified to find that under conditions of identical sufferings and
humiliation our thoughts and feelings had developed in the same
direction and had brought us more often than not to identical
conclusions.

From the merest hint they were able to grasp all the immediate
concrete difficulties of my existence as a free contract worker.

"When Vasya arrives," said Umansky in the tone of someone
who had known Vasya from birth, "I will help him with his math
and his languages, so that he can catch up on what he's missed, the
young scamp!"

Kuprianov, in contradiction to his all-embracing pessimism, tried
to put my mind at rest about the permit.

"You've got the right idea, applying over and over again. Keep
it up! According to the bureaucratic law of averages, the machine
will eventually come up with the answer yes. There's no logic
about it—you can't expect anything of that sort. It operates on the

* Georgi Plekhanov (1856–1918): Marxist philosopher; influenced Lenin but
opposed Bolshevik revolution. Lived forty years in exile, chiefly in Geneva.
David Burliuk (1882–1967): poet and artist, one of the founders of the futurist
movement in Russia. Emigrated to Japan in 1920 and to the U.S. in 1922.

law of illogic. But give up the idea of seeing the gang boss himself. It's better all around if they don't know you personally."

In 1937 Kuprianov had lost two of his nearest and dearest: his wife and a close friend with whom he had kept up from childhood to the day of his arrest. His wife had died in her second year of imprisonment in the Women's Camp for Wives of Traitors to the Fatherland, in Tomsk. The case of his friend was worse. Not only had he become a witness for the prosecution against Vasily Nikitich; not only had he appeared at a confrontation and repeated that Kuprianov had had criminal contacts with sailors from foreign ships that had put in at Archangel; he had also filched Kuprianov's all-but-completed graduate thesis, and had now been given a university chair. One would think that he could at least have helped out his old friend's mother, who was now working as a cleaning woman and bringing up her fourteen-year-old grandson, Vasily Nikitich's only child.

"I have to go there. I don't doubt for an instant that they'll put me behind bars again. But there's nothing else for it. I may be able to keep afloat and support them for a year."

I remember distinctly the strange, almost mystic feeling that suddenly took hold of me: I could foresee Kuprianov's subsequent fate. I knew that he would perish. But I also knew that it was useless to try to dissuade him from his journey to the mainland.

Umansky, it appeared, had come to Kolyma as a free doctor on contract.

"Think what you will, but I came here for the money. Double salary and percentage increments. I had two daughters, both of marriageable age—Susanna and Liza. I had brought them up without their mother; my wife died young."

But Yakov Mikhailovich's life had taken an unexpected turn when in '37 the free doctors of Magadan were summoned to a meeting to express in public their wrathful indignation at the anti-Soviet, amoral actions of Professor Pletnev, who had been arrested in Moscow.

Dr. Umansky, who had come to Kolyma with the aim of getting together a dowry for his daughters, got to his feet and said: "I know nothing of Professor Pletnev's political views: I have never discussed them with him. But I have worked in his clinic, and I can assure you that all these stories about his having tried to rape a patient are absolute and utter rubbish. And anyone who knows

Professor Pletnev at all will say the same thing. I personally am unable to vote in favor of such groundless accusations."

That put an end to the process of accumulating a dowry for the Misses Umansky. He was arrested the next day. He was given a ten-year sentence by the Special Collegium under the CRA article (counter-revolutionary activity). He had served the sentence in full and had been released only quite recently.

Toward the end of our walk Yakov Mikhailovich suddenly launched into a passionate argument on hearing me call former prisoners freedmen.

"A quite inappropriate term," he snapped. "Two completely irreconcilable categories! I can quote you a dozen examples of released Roman slaves who later became personae gratae. And in any case they were never in any danger of re-enslavement. Can you say that for us? Any former prison detainee is also a future prison detainee. What do you think, Vasily Nikitich?"

Kuprianov smiled bitterly.

"What am I, the pessimist, supposed to say when the optimist among us comes out with such forecasts? Let's not take the terminological argument any further. I will say only one thing: it's apparent to me that our unescorted walk today was one of the smiles bestowed on us by Lady Luck in the interval between two prison cycles. Our Dearly Beloved Father never forgives those to whom he has done so great a wrong. . . ."

"I surrender," I announced. "It's true, 'freedman' is not the right word. What would the panel say to another current term: 'provisionally freed prisoners'?"

"That's better," the old man agreed. "But all the same, while fully aware of what it means, we have to live as if we really believed in our freedom. Otherwise all the charm of those provisionally free days and months would be lost."

"But in view of all that, should you put the boy at risk?" Kuprianov asked reflectively. "Perhaps it would be better for you to apply for permission to go back to the mainland."

"But who would give it to her with her record as a terrorist prison detainee? And what would she feed young Vasya on? Here she's been fixed up with a decent teaching job, but there they wouldn't take her on even as a cleaning woman. No, Vasya has to come here—that's for sure. God willing, he may manage to complete his schooling while his mother is provisionally free. And if not, he can still grow up to be an honorable person when he has seen the Kolyma reality for himself."

How ready they were to shoulder other people's sufferings! How kind they were, these people who, one would have said, had gone through more than anyone was capable of enduring.

By now they are all dead. Kuprianov went off to Archangel in '48 and it was not until '50 that we heard he had died on a penal draft on his way to Eastern Siberia, after his second arrest. Umansky was completely shattered with grief. "Why not I?" he kept repeating. "After all, Vasily Nikitich had almost another thirty years to go before attaining the age assigned to man in Holy Writ. And such a brain—he could have been a second Pasteur or Wassermann. But he died of diarrhea brought on by starvation."

As it happened, Yakov Mikhailovich was himself not long to survive his young friend. But I shall come to that later. . . .

6

· *In favor, out of favor**

Grimly, inexorably, 1948 advanced on Magadan, forcing a way through the twilight of its icy haze, through the morose embitterment of its inhabitants.

The explosive charge of hatred was this time vented not so much on the prisoners and former prison detainees as on the free population. The monetary reform of the end of 1947 hit them, the Kolyma conquistadors, the run-of-the-mill Soviet millionaires, harder than it did the inhabitants of any other part of the country. In the highest stratum of contract personnel, the numbers of these Socialist millionaires were already quite substantial. But even the middle-ranking free workers who had been in Kolyma for a number of

* Comment made by Liza, the maidservant, in Griboyedov's *The Misfortune of Being Clever* (1824).

years had accumulated hundreds and hundreds of thousands of rubles in savings bank accounts.

All these people, who were used to thinking of themselves as the favorite children of the Soviet regime, were dazed by the blow that descended on them. How could it be that they, who formed the regime's bulwark in this region teeming with enemies of the people, should be treated in this way? They, who had lived through countless frozen winters, depriving their organism of vitamins!

For many people the reform was the beginning of the end of the dream world in which they had lived and which seemed to them impeccably organized. I recall a conversation with the ex-commander of the Taskan guard detachment. I had met this acquaintance on the street, on my way to work, and he had kept me there for quite some time as the involuntary recipient of the avalanche of words that poured out of him. And what words! Extraordinary ones! The commander's voice hissed, gurgled, and stuttered with emotion.

"Call that justice! Seven years I worked my guts out like a madman! Risked my life . . . The tough eggs I had to guard! My wife left the kids to manage as best they could while she rushed out to work to accumulate some of those special increments. And now! We've just signed off from Dalstroi and fixed ourselves passage to the mainland. Right, we thought, we'll buy ourselves a cottage in the Poltava area, get a few things together . . . strut around the resorts a bit. And now we've had it! We can't afford . . . sweet nothing!"

I jumped at the chance to brief my unusual interlocutor on the current situation. It's the war and all that, I told him. Inflation . . . We must get the economy in better shape.

"Stop it! It's all right for paupers like you to prattle on about the economy! You've got nothing to lose. . . . Anyway, you don't give a damn about anything. You gave no thought to your own children, let alone your pockets, or you wouldn't have taken up with the enemies of the people. . . ."

He suddenly stopped short, looked hard at me, made a gesture with his hand, and burst out: "Maybe they lied about you too! The devil only knows!"

The free workers were further upset by the appearance of fresh drafts of prisoners newly convicted of fraud in connection with the currency reform. They had been sentenced under the article "economic counter-revolution," which meant that they too fell into the category of enemies of the people. There were such cases even among the inhabitants of Magadan.

People whispered apprehensively in corners, passing on sensational news of monetary operations big and small. The nature of these operations was absolutely incomprehensible to me: A had given B some advance information, C had sold D something, E had withdrawn his savings just in time, or, on the contrary, chosen the best moment to make a deposit. But these stories had a standard ending: ten, or in some cases eight, years' imprisonment for economic counter-revolution.

Julia was delighted that we had not suffered in any way from the monetary reform, not by a single brass kopeck. "I'm O.K. I'm an orphan," she joked. "I do have some sort of intuition. . . . Something told me to buy a second camp bed."

We had made this investment against Vasya's impending arrival. But for the time being that was all in the realm of idle dreams: by the end of '48 I had had eight—*eight!*—applications for a permit for my son to enter Magadan turned down by the Dalstroi personnel department.

I had worked out with maximum precision the whole technique of self-renewing applications. I emerged from one office, where I had been told that my application had been refused, only to dive into the one next door and hand in a new application prepared in advance. New applications were accepted automatically and without question. Each time they would say, "Come back on such-and-such a day for an answer." After the circuit despair yielded yet again to self-deluding hopes.

Yes, my hope of reunion with Vasya was still alive, because I was still getting letters from him. Terse and infrequent, but none the less letters. In them he wrote with interest of the distant journey ahead, the first such in his life.

As for Anton, the thought of what might become of him woke me up in the middle of the night like a jolt to the heart. It left me bathed in cold sweat. It brought a haze before my eyes.

After the bag of cedar nuts long months went by without any sort of news or any sign of life. I was frantically active. I kept writing to all of our people who had lived in the vicinity of Yagodnoye or Shturmovoi after their release. And then, just before New Year's, I received an answer that was as bad as could be. One of the women I had known from Elgen had made thorough inquiries and wrote to let me know that Anton had not been at Shturmovoi for some time now. He had been sent off under escort in very strange circumstances—in the strictest secrecy, without having committed any disciplinary offense. He had been sent off all on his own with a special escort. It looked as though some boss had sent for him.

During my sleepless nights I reviewed mental pictures of recent, wartime years. How many imprisoned Germans (with Soviet citizenship) had been sent off like that on secret journeys, never to arrive at their undisclosed destination? True, by now the war was over. But who could trust the Kolyma officials? I visualized scenes of beatings, interrogations, and firing squads. I saw in my mind's eye Serpantinka, the prison out in the taiga of which no one knew a thing because not one person had ever returned from there.

Worst of all was the consciousness of my own helplessness. I could not even put in an official request to know what had become of him. I was not a relative of his. After some thought, I wrote to one of his four sisters in Kazakhstan, to where they had been exiled. I asked her to put in a formal inquiry on behalf of his family. She did so. There was no reply.

Meanwhile there had been appreciable changes in my circumstances. Soon after our return from Northern Artek, where I was given a certificate of merit, I was summoned before the head of children's establishments, Dr. Gorbatova. She started by saying how pleased she was with my work.

"You have everything—education, application, and devotion to the children. But . . ."

I felt a spasm in the pit of my stomach. The meaning of that "but" was clear. Doubtless, the personnel department was making her life a misery because she was employing a terrorist on the ideological front. And now the kindhearted woman was searching for words to soften the blow. Dear God, how would I be able to send anything to Vasya?

"No, no. No one is thinking of firing you!" Gorbatova exclaimed, reading what was plainly written on my face. "I simply want to take certain measures so as to make your position more secure. . . ."

It emerged that the job of music teacher in our kindergarten was about to fall vacant. Our head, who had combined the music teach-

ing with her administrative duties, was leaving to join Kindergarten
Number 1. This presented me with a wonderful opportunity.

"I'm told you play the piano well."

"Very indifferently. I studied it a long time ago, back in my
childhood days."

"No matter. If you practice a bit it'll all come back. Otherwise,
you see . . ."

And here Gorbatova could not have spoken more frankly if she
had been a convicted terrorist herself, instead of a senior official.

"Very shortly a number of teacher trainees will be arriving from
the Preschool Teacher Training College at Krasnoyarsk. At that
point it will be virtually impossible for me to keep you on in your
present post. But as a pianist . . . There aren't any pianists among
them. It will be an extra qualification and give you more protection.
Besides, 'pianist' has a more neutral sound to it, not too close to
ideology. . . . Well, do you agree? The salary is the same."

Her arguments were unanswerable. But I agreed reluctantly.
After all, this wasn't some remote place in the wilderness like
Taskan, where all that was needed was to rattle through *Songs for
Infants*. I would have to stage concerts for large audiences, and
play rousing marches in quick time. In other words, I would have to
recover my lost technique in a hurry.

I sent a telegram to my mother in Rybinsk. She had been evacuated there from Leningrad and stayed on after the war. Poor
Mother! She still imagined Rybinsk was a place in which I might be
allowed to settle. I asked her to send me some music, though I was
not very hopeful that she would be able to buy what I needed in
Rybinsk. But a package did arrive, and inside it I was flabbergasted
to find the piano music I had played as a child. How on earth had
she managed to preserve it, to rescue it from two blazing houses,
her own and mine? There it was, though. I was now holding in my
hand my old Hanon, at which I used to toil at the age of eight.
The yellowing sheets, repaired with glue, bore the heavily penciled
annotations of my music teacher; how well I remembered her large
hand, drawing purple circles around the notes I kept getting wrong.
On one of the pages there was an entry in a child's crooked handwriting: "I kan't manage the octave. My fingers won't reach."

Hanon! I looked at it with profound contrition. At one time this
particular book had symbolized for me all the hostile forces of the

old world. It was this book I had consigned to outer darkness when I put in my application to join Komsomol, and announced to my parents that I now had more important things to do. Let the daughters of the world bourgeoisie study Hanon!

Little did I think that some day the despised Hanon would make its way to the Far North to save me from dismissal, from hardship, from all sorts of evil happenings. Forgive me, Hanon. I beg your forgiveness, too, Czerny and Clementi.

I set about it with the force of desperation, sitting for many long hours in front of that tinny kindergarten piano. It was far from easy to restore flexibility to the fingers of yesterday's lumberjack and pick wielder. If only Mother could have seen how I stuck to my task, how diligently I sat at my instrument. What trouble she used to have with my music! But now my future, and that of Vasya too, depended on this book which I had so loathed as a child. I tried my hardest. And I was helped by the annotations of my long dead teacher.

Gorbatova was right: to the personnel department the word "pianist" sounded more neutral than "teacher." But she was mistaken in thinking that the music mistress of a kindergarten could keep her distance from the ideological front. On the contrary. It was the music expert who also had to write the scenarios and produce the children's special concerts, which were the main display wares. They were put on for the benefit of the authorities. They were organized seven times a year on high days and holidays. Our entire work with the children was judged by the success or failure of these concerts. So even in my new job the methodologists from the Preschool Methodology Center continued to watch vigilantly over each step I took.

I was to make my debut with the 1948 New Year's concert. It coincided with the black days when the struggle to arrange for Vasya to join me had completely drained my strength, when Anton's face haunted me—Anton tortured, perhaps to death. It was at this very time that I had to tie myself in knots trying to devise a show to surpass anything yet seen in Magadan—glittering New-Year merriment. I had not only to write the show but also to communicate its gaiety to the children and the teachers. The main thing—what was the point of concealing it from myself?—was to please the bosses who would be coming to see it.

What if I gave it all up and sought refuge in the haven of Julia's reprocessing workshop? If I did, I would earn only a third of what I was currently getting. And what if I then suddenly got permission to send for Vasya? I wouldn't be able to afford his fare. So I had to do all I could to create a good impression and to avoid being fired from a well-paid job.

The New Year's concert was an immense success, which was not all that hard to achieve. For the routine presentations of previous occasions were pretty dreary affairs, more or less the same, year in year out. The methodologists were impressed by the dramatization of the story. It provided valuable experience for the work of the Methodology Center. The parents laughed along with their children. Gorbatova shook my hand and said in a loud voice for Podushkin, the head of the personnel department, to hear: "We've never had a concert like it in our kindergartens before." Even the head of the Medical Administration, Shcherbakov, gave me a little smile and a nod.

How low can one sink! Was this me? Was I not better off, after all, in prison or in camp? There I did not have to curry favor with my superiors. And the rations were free. Yes, but while I was eating those free rations I had lost Alyosha. Now what I had to do was to save Vasya. Not, of course, at any price . . . Not regardless . . . After all, I had done nothing dishonorable. I had simply pretended to be merry, simply politely returned Shcherbakov's smile. . . . Such syllogisms tormented me day and night; the worst thing was that there was no point in so much as mentioning them to Julia. She was proud of my success and considered all the rest an intellectual's fancies.

It was a comfortless wintry January in Magadan. True, the temperature here did not descend to minus 50 degrees, as was often the case in Taskan or Elgen. But minus 30 to minus 35 degrees in Magadan was harder to bear than minus 50 in the taiga. The biting wind off the sea, the humidity of the air, and a special oppressiveness peculiar to Magadan got people down.

Each morning I wanted to die—chiefly so as to forget it all. But my passionate desire for oblivion fought and lost the daily battle. It lost out to my memory, which kept confronting me with the one word "Vasya." I had to get him out to me. And if I was unsuccessful in that, I had to send him money each month for his keep and his schooling.

On one of those days when I wanted to howl from desperation

like a wild animal but was instead obliged to accompany the children practicing "Stalin is with us everywhere and always / he is our guiding star," the door of the music room opened, just the merest fraction.

"You're wanted. . . . Someone from your house."

Julia stood in the doorway. Her look reflected some extraordinary occurrence. It could have been a miracle, or an earthquake. Alarm, joy, shock—all were there.

She clasped my hand and whispered:

"Tell them you're suddenly not feeling well. Or think up something else. . . . But insist on going home at once! He has only an hour to spare!"

"Who?"

"Anton Walter. He's sitting in our room."

I don't remember how we got there, don't remember running with the wind in our faces. I only remember that Julia said: "Stop and get your breath or you'll kill yourself. Then what will I say to him?"

He was standing right in the doorway, listening for movements in the corridor. He immediately recognized my footsteps and flung the door wide open. I threw myself straight into his arms.

Had I met him in the street, I would not have recognized him, for he now resembled any one of our Taskan goners. It was unbelievable that anyone could have grown so thin in less than a year. He seemed to have acquired a limp, and his leg was bandaged. There were black shadows under his eyes. The wrinkles on his cheeks could not have been more accentuated had he been an old man. But it was he. Alive. Or maybe only half alive. He kept feeling for my hand as if to assure himself that it was I—as though I, not he, had risen from the grave.

Now I got my answers to all my nightly conundrums: Where? How? Why?

At Shturmovoi things had been more or less tolerable at first. There was enough bread, and the behavior of the camp authorities was frigid but correct. But then a new chief disciplinary officer turned up. He was violently against the doctor from the outset, for a number of reasons: because of the latter's unconstrained way of speaking to the management; because the prisoner-doctor had once happened to see the chief improperly dressed when he had been taken ill as a result of imbibing too much pure alcohol; and because

Walter was a German, a Fritz who still needed to be taught a lesson, who needed to have the smile wiped off his face, the dirty
swine. . . .

He started bit by bit to harass the doctor. He forbade him to
write or receive letters. What relation is she of yours, this Ginzburg
woman? It's all a bit suspicious. . . . When you're free, then you
can write.

So Anton had fallen out of favor with his masters. But at this
very time in the metropolis of Magadan events were moving in the
opposite direction: the doctor had clearly won the favor of his
masters. What had happened was that the head of Dalstroi, General
Nikishov, had been in terrible pain with his liver. The attacks were
acute, and the general got angry with his doctors. Then one of his
entourage happened to mention that in Moscow in such cases homeopaths were found to be a great help.

"Well, don't we have any homeopaths among the zeks?"

"Yes, I've just remembered. There is one. But he's a German!"

"So much the better. The Germans are hot on science. Where is
he?"

"In Shturmovoi, the strict-regime camp."

"Bring him in!"

So one fine day the order arrived for the prisoner, Walter, Anton
Yakovlevich, to be escorted to Magadan. At Shturmovoi the master's anger had long ago reached the boiling point, so the order
was interpreted as a punitive measure against the hated German.
The chief disciplinary officer did not doubt that Anton was on his
way to being reinvestigated and retried. And since the German
had already been resentenced twice to the camps, in addition to the
original term of detention, what could lie in store for the dear
fellow? Only Serpantinka and the end. Or perhaps the end without
any change of prison. The last thing to enter the chief's head was
that the Kraut had been asked for by the big man. So he sent
Anton off by normal means of transport, that is, under guard in
short stages. Unfortunately, the order from Magadan had not contained the word urgent. So they had taken their time in delivering
Anton: the journey had lasted four months in all. He had done the
rounds of various ice-cold taiga prisons where they flung him into
cells populated with terrifying professional criminals. He had done
the entire journey through the taiga on foot. He had been given
virtually nothing to eat. Any complaints on his part were merely

sneered at. No one wastes words on those who are ready for the drop.

"True enough," Anton said, "my number was up. Irrespective of whether or not they meant to shoot me. Any fourth-year medical student could have arrived at that diagnosis. Especially when this trophic ulcer broke out on my leg."

So it was an ulcer that was causing him to limp. I thought he had broken his leg. . . . How often he had said to me at Taskan, when finding such ulcers on the legs of the goners: "It's the beginning of the end. Disintegration of the tissue."

"Don't get alarmed. It really would have been the end if General Nikishov's liver hadn't acted up. But now they need me. They'll fatten me up. The ulcer will heal."

(On that occasion he proved right. For many years after this there was just a persistent, small discoloration to show for what had been an open ulcer. It was not until late 1959, after the emotional stress and physical shock caused by his rehabilitation and return to the mainland, that by some mysterious law of nature the trophic ulcer opened up again and reestablished itself on Anton's leg. It was the brand that so many Kolyma prisoners bear when they depart this life. Within two days of his death, at the end of December 1959, lying in the Moscow Institute of Therapy, Anton was to say with a wry smile: "The inmates of Auschwitz and Dachau are known by the numbers branded on their wrists. The inmates of Kolyma can be recognized by this mark, tattooed on them by starvation.")

But in the late forties it was still a long time until that final blow. We were struggling for survival like birds caught in a double-glazed window, one pane of which has been left half open: caught between the fear of stifling and the hope of flying to freedom. There were now good grounds for hope, for we were together again, and he would soon receive a pass permitting him to go unescorted.

They had put Anton in special quarters—the so-called quarantine center, four kilometers out of town. They had assigned him to the free hospital; thus he had every opportunity of putting flesh back on his bones.

His first appearance before General Nikishov was accompanied by some unpleasantness. As part of the preparation of the doctor for a visit of such importance, the general's envoys brought along to the quarantine center a civilian suit of clothes—a shirt and tie, and real shoes. This infuriated Anton, who was still suffering the crippling effects of his forced marches. He refused point-blank to put the suit on. But why? For the simple reason that it didn't go with his general appearance or with his social position. Well, he couldn't present himself to the general in the rags he had on now, could he? Why not, if he could wear them at other times? . . . So that was it, was it! Was he perhaps refusing to treat the general? Not at all, it was a doctor's sacred obligation to treat anyone who turned to him for help. But he had no intention of taking part in a masquerade. It would do the general good to see how a prisoner-doctor looked, after four months tramping about the taiga from one punishment cell to the next.

The envoys had left, after suggesting to the doctor that he think it over until the following day. Julia, who had succumbed on sight to Anton's charm, did all she could be dissuade him from "digging in your heels over trifles," from "turning this idiotic suit into a matter of principle." I held my tongue. In the first place, I knew that it was useless to say anything; second, I was all knotted up inside at the thought of how I had set out to curry favor at New Year's. I kept quiet, even though I was dying of fright—they might hustle him away to some place still worse than Shturmovoi.

But it all passed over. The two sides settled for a new set of camp clothing, which the doctor wore when they took him along to see the general the following day. In the entrance hall the same underlings made him put on a white medical overall. But the camp boots and camp trousers still peeped out from underneath it.

As it happened, the general, who was going through hell with his pain, paid no attention to the doctor's external appearance. But he did have the latter's prescriptions to a homeopathic chemist sent off to Moscow immediately, by a special plane.

A new life began. It was no longer a wasteland of lonely despair, although each new day brought its full complement of acute foreboding. Whenever Anton was even a little late with his daily visit to us (and he made the journey simply to show us that he was still alive, then marched all those kilometers back to his quarantine center), I almost died from what I imagined might have happened. It wasn't just imagination! There were so many things that really could have happened to him. The possible disasters that most often occurred to me were these: he might have been posted again; he might have fallen down and frozen to death on the road from the quarantine center; or he might have been killed by some professional criminal whom he had refused to let off work.

What most tormented me was that not only was I powerless to help, I should never even get any definite news. He would simply fail to turn up one dreadful evening and disappear into thin air, as if he had never existed. . . . So I was rigid with fright until the moment I heard our agreed signal of three knocks at the door. He had come! He was alive! He was alive and with us today. And tomorrow was a long way off. . . .

Anton had to do a total of not less than ten kilometers on foot each day: from the quarantine center to the free hospital, from the hospital to us, and at night back again to the quarantine center. But, strange as it may seem, it was this physical activity and the heavy demands of his work that cured him and delivered him from the ranks of the goners. He was then under fifty, and his will to survive was enormous. The first outward sign of his getting better was that he started telling jokes and stories in which he took all the parts. Laughter was heard from our room in the evening, just as it had been in Taskan. New characters appeared in his stories. Before our eyes the holy martyr was turning into the jolly saint.

Nikishov, thank heaven, seemed to benefit from the homeopathic treatment, and he gave orders that the German was to be kept in Magadan, where he would be at hand if needed.

"Do you realize just what a gift from the gods it is, our being able to see each other every day?" Anton kept on repeating. "What were the odds against our meeting again? Maybe ten thousand to one! And presto, this one chance in ten thousand turns up! You'll see: Vasya will soon be here with us. But you'll have to make more of an effort."

More of an effort! I had already received nine refusals and sent in my tenth application. All our friends were advising me to go to see Gridasova if I was refused for the tenth time. All sorts of tales circulated about her. For example the story of the ballerina, Ira Mukhina, who had been on our penal draft. Ira had somehow cast such a spell on the omnipotent Gridasova that the latter had provided her with a perfectly clean passport, given her a complete set of clothing from her own wardrobe, and paid for her passage back to the mainland. They also said that anyone she took a dislike to might as well say his prayers.

In March I finally secured an appointment with Colonel Franko
in the Dalstroi personnel department. I had put my name down to
see him several times, but to no avail: he was elsewhere, or ill, or
not seeing anyone. But there I was at last, in front of an enormous,
polished desk, behind which there sat a very gallant and much
decorated officer. He did not ask me to sit down; while I haltingly
explained my business he sat frowning and impatiently tapping
the desk top with his fountain pen.

"The refusal you have received is in full accordance with the
existing regulations on the subject."

"But please understand! The boy has nowhere to live! He has
to go to school. . . ."

"I can't go into your family affairs."

"It's not a family affair but a public affair. The court did not
deprive me of my maternal rights. My elder son died of starvation
in Leningrad. By what law are you sentencing me to permanent
separation from my second and only son?"

My reference to rights and laws knocked the colonel off his balance. The master's wrath rained down on me. The colonel's neck
slowly reddened under his high collar, and the red gradually
spread to his cheeks.

"Your rights are extremely limited. Have you forgotten your five
years' deprivation of rights?"

"Of the right to vote. I have not been deprived of the right to be
a mother to my son."

"I have no intention of entering into an argument with you. The
interview is over."

By now he was furious, and he hissed these last words like an
enraged goose.

But I, too, was incensed. I had reached that pitch of emotion at
which people are no longer responsible for their actions.

Hurtling out of the Dalstroi personnel department, I crossed the
square at full speed under the hoods of the trucks and scuttled
through the open door of another institution—the Magadan Camp
Administration. Formally speaking, the MCA had no responsibility
for me—I was a free person now. But it was the seat of Comrade
Gridasova, my last recourse, the most powerful instance of all, the
one person who could return Vasya to me.

Paying no attention to the serpentine queue waiting outside the
door, I burst into the disinfecting room, as it was called—the office

of Gridasova's private secretary. Somehow no one in the queue said a word to me. Perhaps they just didn't have time to react as I flew past them like an arrow.

It was only when I had burst through to find myself staring at a black and gold door plate—HEAD OF MCA—that the secretary, dumbfounded at first by my unheard-of conduct, recovered her wits and came abruptly to the defense of her citadel.

"You're out of your mind. People have been waiting for months to be admitted. Get out of here at once!"

My heart was pounding. There was a fog gathering before my eyes. I could not make out the secretary's face. I was briefly aware only of a fiery mop of hair dyed bright red, cascading over a narrow forehead. She was, it seemed, taller and bigger than me. But I flung myself at her and shoved her away from the door. The unexpectedness and presumptuousness of my actions evidently took her by surprise. I burst into the office of the Queen of Kolyma, shouting and sobbing.

I realized later the risk I had taken. For the Queen—and this was the general consensus—knew not only how to pardon but also how to punish. It all depended on the occasion, on her mood, on what her magic mirror on the wall would say. Was she the fairest one of all?

What did I blurt out through my sobs? What words poured from me in response to that regal look of astonishment? I don't really remember. But in any case they were not about rights and laws. . . . I instinctively grasped that this theme was even more alien to the Queen than to Colonel Franko. Oddly enough, although I was at that moment undoubtedly in a state of shock, my mind was secretly at work. I found myself quite consciously selecting just the words that were capable of exerting an effect on this passionate devotee of slushy films, the former warden, Shurochka Gridasova. I found myself shouting out precisely the powerful clichés that could move her heart. A mother's tears . . . Nobody wants someone else's child. . . . An orphan can so easily go astray. . . .

Her vacuous, pretty face took on an increasingly compassionate look, until finally a soft little voice broke in on me. It spoke—no, cooed—straight into my ear:

"Calm yourself, my dear! Your little boy will be here with you. . . ."

What followed was like a delirious dream. She rang for her

secretary and told her to take paper and write, ignoring her complaints about my unheard-of insolence. The missive that she dictated was addressed to none other than Colonel Franko. Aleksandra Romanovna Gridasova, Deputy of the Magadan Town Soviet, had the honor of requesting the Dalstroi Personnel Department to assist in summoning from Kazan secondary schoolboy Aksyonov, Vasily Pavlovich.

"I dare not go back to Franko. A moment ago he virtually kicked me out of his office."

"Well, he'll change his tune now. Don't be afraid, my dear! No, don't thank me. I'm a woman myself. . . . I know what it is to have a mother's heart. . . ."

This "my dear," which she repeated several times, made her remarkably like a kindly lady of the manor talking to a serf girl whom she had befriended.

A quarter of an hour later I was standing once more, or rather sitting, in the bright-eyed Colonel Franko's presence, watching the expression on his face change miraculously as he read the note from the Magadan Town Soviet Deputy, A. R. Gridasova. The chromatic modulations of his voice reflected the changes in his face.

"What, you again? Didn't I tell you that . . . Another piece of paper? What is it this time? Hm . . . What are you standing for? Take a seat! Hm . . . hm . . . From Kazan? I know Kazan. It's a big city. With a university of its own. So your husband's name is Aksyonov? I seem to have heard something about him in the thirties. Is he alive? You don't know? Hm . . . Well, well! The secondary school here is a good one. The boy can keep up with his schooling. . . ."

After these few kind words the colonel brought out his fountain pen and very legibly wrote just one word across the corner of Gridasova's note. But what a word: "Implement!"

In the evening, when Anton arrived from the hospital, I re-enacted the whole scene for him and Julia. But that night it was some time before I managed to get to sleep. I kept peering into the darkness, imagining that I could discern my fortunes trembling in the balance. On one scale our masters' wrath, on the other their favor. A fickle, freakish, precarious favor, liable to give out at any minute.

I doubtless was—and still am—illogical. But while fully aware that our masters' favor was insufferably degrading, I nevertheless experienced then—as I still do now—a feeling of the most sincere gratitude to this Queen. Sentimentality is not, I suggest, the greatest danger of our time, and it was to the good that the mighty Gridasova was capable, if not of genuinely kindly feelings, at least of sentimentality.

Her later fate was a cruel one. After General Nikishov's dismissal from the service, and after the discovery of Aleksandra Romanovna's liaison with someone else, she found herself in Moscow with two or three children plus a drunkard of a husband on her hands. The fact that she had not stashed away any hoard of money from the period of her one-woman rule of Kolyma also speaks in her favor. In the sixties she often telephoned rehabilitated ex-prisoners to whom she had once shown mercy. Aleksandra Romanovna would ask for a small loan to tide her over until her husband's payday. And not one of the rehabilitated ever refused her.

7

· *"Don't cry in front of them"*

After Colonel Franko's magical order, arrangements for Vasya's journey went through other channels—channels in which the affairs of ex-prisoners were an insignificant part of the traffic. These channels were specially designed for bringing out to Kolyma people who were wanted and needed there. Now things moved much more quickly.

When the Kazan militia courteously handed over to Vasya a first-class set of documents assuring his entry into a secret, banned zone, the Aksyonovs were beside themselves with excitement. But they began to wonder: How could an outlaw who played the piano in a kindergarten procure such splendid documents? They sent me an embarrassed letter in which they congratulated me on my "comeback" but also changed their tune on the subject of Vasya. They were kindly people and in the ten years he had been with them they had become attached to the boy. Although over the past two years he had almost worn them down with his wayward behavior and they themselves had demanded that I take him off their hands, now that it had become a practical possibility they were afraid to send him on such a long journey.

"Why not let him finish school here?" they wrote.

A new obstacle had arisen unexpectedly. It would be the last straw if my reunion with Vasya were to be wrecked now, after the ordeals I had gone through to get him a travel permit. But my anxiety was superfluous. I had an ally in Vasya himself. For the first time since our parting twelve years before I started to receive letters from him in which I caught glimpses of my unknown son's personality. Instead of the terse little notes he had previously sent ("How are you? We are all right. How is the weather where you are? It's all right here," etc.), I began to get emphatic assertions that he had received the pass and would definitely be coming. Was it true that Kolyma was a stone's throw from Alaska? And was it the case that there were tribes in Kolyma related to the Iroquois?

I read and reread these sheets of paper covered with the unformed handwriting of a teenager, and I could vividly picture to myself my little boy tossing about at night on the couch in the Aksyonovs' dining room, dreaming of becoming an explorer like La Pérouse or Vasco da Gama, of sailing through meandering, green inlets between cliffs of basalt and pearl. I realized how ardently he longed for adventure on some distant voyage, he who had as yet seen nothing in his life other than an orphaned childhood in a family of not particularly close relatives and a dull, regimented school of the forties.

For the first time we were connected by a thin thread of unspoken understanding. Now I knew how to write to him: instead of reminiscing about our family life of long ago, about which he could remember nothing, I now dwelled on descriptions of Kolyma's exotic scenery, on the dangers of the journey by sea. I asked what means of transport he preferred, sea or air. . . . Anton got him a dagger made from a walrus tusk and decorated by Chukchi ivory carvers, and I gave Vasya a detailed description of the dagger and of the Chukchi way of life (of which I knew at the time only what others had told me). I got in reply every time the same impatient question: "When will it be?"

He was scheduled to arrive at the beginning of September so as not to miss out on the school year. With my heart in my mouth, I paid a visit to what was then the one and only secondary school in Magadan and had a talk with the director of studies; I explained that my son was to arrive shortly and asked whether they had a vacancy in the ninth class. . . . It was a sharp, prickly feeling of re-emerging from the land of nightmares into the land of ordinary, rational human activity. What a wonderful thing it was to be, just for a moment, someone like all the others. Not a prisoner in solitary, not in transit, not an accused before the Military Collegium, not a terrorist-detainee. Just a mother visiting a school to register her son.

But for the time being these were all pipe dreams. There were many hurdles yet before our reunion became a reality. First of all, I had to find the fare. Where was I to get it from? Plane fare would be three thousand rubles. Another question was: Who would accompany him? Although Vasya was nearly sixteen, and the journey out to Magadan had become somewhat easier over the years, especially for free persons, I was still in thrall to old notions: to my mind, my son was still an infant and the journey was still as hard as it had been when I had made it under escort. I simply could not entertain the thought of my child making such a journey all alone.

Julia undertook to find the money.

"I've already passed the word around among the people we know. We'll get it together. . . . After all, he'll be the first mainland child of an ex-prisoner to come out to Kolyma. What do you mean, charity? What rubbish! It's a loan, of course. I've told them all that we will pay it back in the course of the year."

But then something occurred that made the collection unnecessary. It suddenly emerged that one of Julia's helpers in the workshop was a secret millionaire. Well, not a millionaire but a "thousand-aire"—Aunt Dusya.

Aunt Dusya was an expert knitter of wool sweaters and had established a clientele among the Kolyma elite. Apart from that, her old mother had recently died, bequeathing to the sixty-year-old Dusya a stout log cabin with shutters. Some distant relatives had written to ask Dusya whether she would be coming to take possession of her legacy. If not, perhaps she would assign the house to them and they would see she didn't lose by this transaction. After a brief exchange of letters, Dusya had received a money order for five thousand rubles.

Julia was the only person to whom Aunt Dusya had confided all this. She had kept it a secret from the others since she was afraid of arousing their envy. Aunt Dusya kept her savings book in Julia's iron safe, which contained all the documentation of the workshop. In her everyday dealings Aunt Dusya was thrifty almost to the point of miserliness. For example, whenever a big pot of soup was made for everybody in the workshop, Aunt Dusya wouldn't let anyone skim it, because she maintained it was the scum that contained the most nourishing protein.

It was Aunt Dusya who became my principal creditor. She chose to visit us late at night, when all our neighbors were already sleeping, sat down on the bed in her quilted jacket, looked around at the thin walls through which the least sound from the adjoining matchboxes could be heard, and put her finger to her lips.

"Shh . . . shh . . . The main thing is to get it all settled nice and quietly, so people can't tittle-tattle," she whispered, rummaging in the recesses of her jacket. "Here, take it! Three, exactly, for the plane ticket. For all the odds and ends, you can borrow from somebody else. Only please don't tell anybody that I've handed out so much money. People'll start to get envious, and I don't like that."

Large hundred-ruble notes, colorful, imposing, brand-new, lay there in a solid wad on the rickety little table. Thirty of them. Radiant, resplendent, incredible. They troubled us.

"It's an awful lot, Aunt Dusya," said Julia. "Perhaps we'd do better to try and get everyone to chip in a bit, so that you're not the only one to carry the burden."

"What's the point of fooling around? Take it, since I've given it to you! It's not as if I'm throwing the money away—it's on loan."

"Of course! I'll pay it back within the year, Dusya. But perhaps you'd feel happier if I gave you a receipt," I ventured.

A look of mild irritation flitted across Aunt Dusya's face.

"You know the saying: 'Don't accept a blow; don't refuse a gift.' What would be the point of giving me a receipt? Birds of passage, that's what we are. Here today, gone tomorrow . . . If your lucky number comes up, you can let me have it sooner. You think I wouldn't take your word for it? We've known each other some time now. . . ."

Aunt Dusya counted the hundred-ruble notes again, patted them into a neat rectangle, and stroked the pile with a broad palm coarsened by tree felling.

"Surprised?" she again muttered indignantly. "You're thinking: Why has the old skinflint suddenly coughed up? Well, that just goes to show you how much you understand about people! Just because I won't give the girls money to go to the movies, you think I'm some sort of miser. What's the point of us going to the movies? A zek's life is a sight more interesting than anything you'd see in any movie. But this is something really important. The first time a zek's son is coming from the mainland. If mine were alive and coming here, you wouldn't refuse me a loan, would you? Well, that's how it is. . . . I have to go. . . . You get to bed now. . . ."

(Aunt Dusya's only son had been killed in the first year of the war. The most shameful thing was that when she was handing over the money neither I nor Julia had managed to remember this. Aunt Dusya never spoke of it. She had been unbearably hurt when the notification of his death had been addressed not to her—as if she were not her son's mother—but to some distant aunt. It seemed to her that this humiliation cast a shadow also on her son's memory.)

I now had the money for the ticket. There remained the matter of finding an escort. It was Anton who found a traveling companion. In the free hospital where he was working, one of the serious cardiac cases was a man named Kozyrev, the chief accountant at Dalstroi. His was a long, hopeless illness. By pure chance the free doctor went away, and for a short time Kozyrev was handed over to Anton's care. Anton had him for two weeks, during which time the patient got considerably better. No one could understand what caused the improvement. Perhaps a change in the atmospheric pressure? More likely, the influence of psychotherapy, at which Anton was without equal. (To tease him I used to say that he was more of a priest than a doctor.)

But then the free doctor in charge of the case returned and took over from Anton, and . . . the patient took a sharp turn for the worse. Kozyrev's wife, Nina Konstantinovna, a cashier in a food store, rushed around trying to persuade the administration to have her husband transferred to the ward for which Walter was responsible. They pointed out that there were only ex-zeks in that ward. They appealed to her political sense and tried to convince her that the transfer of a patient from a free doctor to a prisoner-doctor— and a German at that—might have undesirable political overtones. This wrangle was still in progress when the patient died. In all probability, even Anton could not have brought him back to health; at least that was what he thought himself. But no one could change the widow's mind: if her husband had remained in Dr. Walter's care, he would still be alive.

After the funeral the widow collapsed with grief. She decided not to go to the hospital for treatment; she had Anton attend her at home. He paid her daily visits. The sick woman recovered and became passionately devoted to the doctor. She would do anything for him. When he told her the story of our efforts to bring Vasya out, she categorically announced: "It so happens that I'm going on leave to the mainland. I'll bring him back."

She was a lean, nimble woman of fifty, with small, quick eyes. She never made a mistake in counting out the change at her cash desk. Her arithmetic, though, was better than her Russian. She spoke in the accent of the lower-middle-class suburbs of Moscow, and couldn't even get her own patronymic right: "Konstantinovna" became "Kiskinkinovna." But she had a tender heart and, still more important, a will of her own. She made up her own mind about who was good and who was bad, without having to consult their personal file. She didn't give a damn about Anton's articles, about his period of imprisonment, or even about his being a German. She knew just one thing: he had saved her, and he would indubitably have saved her husband if they had let him, the skunks! . . .

In the matter of bringing Vasya out to Kolyma she showed herself to be not only kindhearted but also determined. Her daughter Tamara was married to an MGB interrogator who strongly objected to his mother-in-law's getting mixed up with the son of someone who had a political record. But Nina Konstantinovna simply ignored these domestic complications and went her own way.

At this stage, when things seemed to be turning out so favorably, I became more nervous than ever. I was haunted night and day by the fear that some fatal mishap might prevent Vasya's arrival. Suppose he fell ill. . . . Suppose the Aksyonovs dug their heels in. . . . Suppose he changed his mind. . . . Suppose Kozyreva changed her mind. . . . But no, she stuck to her guns. In May she invited me to her apartment, choosing an hour when her son-in-law would be away at work. I went along at the appointed hour and handed over Dusya's three thousand rubles for Vasya's airfare.

"Right, then," she said, rapidly counting the notes and screwing up her small, inquisitive eyes at me. "Right! You can stop worrying. I said I'd bring him and I will. For the doctor's sake . . . How many years has it been since you've seen your boy? Twelve years? How on earth did you hold on? No one would guess to look at you that you had grieved for him so much. You look in pretty good shape."

In June I raised another thousand in small loans and sent it off to Mother in Rybinsk to enable her to go to Kazan, get Vasya fitted out, and take him to Moscow, where Kozyreva would be awaiting him. This was a year and a half before Mother's death. But she concealed from me how ill she was feeling, how difficult the journey was for her. It was only afterward that I recalled the part in her letter where she had written: "How I used to love the trips on the Volga! But lately I haven't been feeling too well, even when I travel by boat. But none of that matters. The important thing is for you and little Vasya to be together again."

In July I received news that Vasya was already in Moscow, in the Kozyrevs' apartment on Sretenka Street. Mother had handed him over personally to Nina Konstantinovna, and had gone home to Rybinsk. Vasya was enchanted with Moscow, with his own freedom, with his friendship with the unruly son of the Kozyrev family, Volodya, who had dropped out of school. He was now a taxi driver, and he was driving Vasya around Moscow to show him the sights. Vasya and Nina Konstantinovna would soon be taking the plane to Magadan.

But July and August passed, and all my phone calls to the MGB interrogator's apartment elicited one and the same answer: Nina Konstantinovna had been delayed for family reasons. In September I was due to leave town and go with the kindergarten to the health camp again. I felt quite desperate. He would arrive in my absence. . . . But October came around. School had begun a month before. I was back from the Northern Artek Pioneer camp, and still there was no sign of Nina Kozyreva and Vasya.

My nervous tension mounted. Vasya was so skimpily dressed that he would freeze, having to fly in late autumn. He might have to miss a year of school. . . . But all these reasonable daytime fears were nothing compared with my dark, nighttime forebodings, which were utterly irrational. Perhaps as a result of someone's evil designs I was doomed to lose both my children. Alyosha was no more. . . . And Vasya, the last spark of my now almost extinct life would either board the plane and perish somewhere up in the clouds or else simply disappear into thin air. And again, as during those sleepless nights at Elgen, I heard the formula of despair hammering in my ears: "No one will ever call me Mother again."

Both Anton and Julia daily expended a vast quantity of words, angry words and loving words, to bring me to my senses.

"It'll end up with his arriving and your not being here to greet him," Julia predicted gloomily. "You don't eat, drink, or sleep. . . . How much longer can it go on?"

"You're ungrateful," Anton said with fury. "You're the only ex-zek who's managed to get permission for her son to come out here, and all you do is . . ."

"Please don't say that. You'll bring me bad luck."

At this Anton mounted his hobbyhorse. He proclaimed that he had met no more superstitious people in the prisons and camps than the former Communists. They believed in literally anything, in any sort of sign or manifestation. . . . If only I believed in God as much as I did in all those idiocies. . . .

Here Julia broke in, and they both ignored me and started to argue among themselves. Julia, who almost from the cradle had had it drummed firmly into her head that religion was the opium of the people, could not bear hearing Anton hold forth on the difference between faith and superstition.

"It's quite extraordinary, Anton Yakovlevich, how you, a person with excellent training in biology, can repeat such fables."

"What is much stranger, Julia Pavlovna, is to find you, a person educated in philosophy, repeating the flattest of platitudes and refusing to draw conclusions from the lessons that we all learned in prison."

I left them to pursue their interminable argument and strolled off to the watchman's room in Julia's workshop next door, to phone the Kozyrevs.

"Tell me, please, has Nina Konstantinovna arrived?"

"No, not yet."

The receiver was slammed down directly in my ear, to cut short my questions. There followed a long succession of wearisome days, each of which began in hope and ended in despair.

Meanwhile Julia and I had moved into the new apartment. She had been given an official order entitling her to an entire fifteen square meters in view of the enlargement of the family: namely, Vasya's imminent arrival. Our new building was next door to the old one, but it was two stories high, and our apartment was on the second floor. There were at least twenty rooms along the corridor. Ours was one of the best—or perhaps that was only how it seemed to us at the time. In any event, it really did measure fifteen square meters, and it had a good window. Julia had somehow obtained a screen, and we used it to partition off a separate corner for Vasya. He had an iron bed, a chair, and a small table; on the table were an inkpot, paper, and textbooks for the ninth class. We had laid in for Vasya a woolen blanket and a real feather pillow, which Julia bore in as if it were a trophy, holding it above her head, her eyes flashing triumphantly. Anton had tucked under the pillow a set of new underwear, socks, and two shirts. He had obtained all this in exchange for a large number of his bread rations at the quarantine center.

And so Kolyma prepared to greet my schoolboy son with a first-rate set of standard camp clothing.

Far from thanking my faithful friends, I scolded them, seeking an outlet for my frustrated longing and my anxiety. At times I showered unjust accusations on them.

"Of course . . . it's easy for you to wait calmly. . . . It isn't *your* only remaining child who's missing."

They didn't take offense. They understood, and they put up with me.

But one day . . . I took the receiver off the hook and with a feeling of numb hopelessness began inquiring whether Nina Konstantinovna had arrived, making my voice sound as impersonal as that of the announcer of the correct time. Suddenly, instead of a blunt, peremptory no, I heard the cheerful, even overcheerful, voice of a tipsy man.

"Yes, she's arrived. We're celebrating. And drinking to her health."

"Oh . . . tell me, what about the boy? Was the boy from Kazan on the plane with her?"

"The boy?"

At that point in the conversation someone came up to whoever I was talking to and asked him something. His attention was diverted, and he began giving someone instructions about plates and dishes, in the same jolly voice. . . . He made a joke of it, and the other person laughed loudly in reply.

How long did that pause in our conversation last? A minute? An eternity? In any case, I had time enough to visualize with appalling clarity all the possible variants of Vasya's tragic end. All the cars in Moscow had combined to run him over. The entire criminal population of Vladivostok or Khabarovsk had robbed him and left him for dead. All the MGB personnel in all those towns had pulled him in for some careless word he had let drop. Any moment now and the same cheerful voice would be saying no, the boy had not arrived. . . .

"The boy? You mean the boy from Kazan? Yes, he's sitting here on the couch. He's worried that they're taking so long to come for him. . . . He's refused champagne, the little teetotaler. . . ."

Another burst of laughter. Then someone took the receiver from my merry interlocutor and said in a hard, hostile voice:

"Why don't you come and pick up your son, madam? He knows your address, but you can't expect him to find his way around in a strange place all at once. And there's nobody here to go with him. Anybody would think we'd done enough getting him here from the mainland."

"I'm on my way . . . this very moment. . . . I didn't know."

I put the receiver down. I wanted to run. But something strange had happened to me. My legs were glued to the floor; they felt weightless, as if made of cotton wool. As though from a great distance, I heard the voice of the watchman on duty:

"Dear me, dear me . . . What's the matter, lady? Looks like you're on your last legs!"

He stuck his head out of the inspection window and shouted across to someone:

"Run to Karepova! Tell her her relative's keeling over."

Julia arrived on the scene. Valerian drops and validol were administered.

"Pull yourself together. I'll go with you." Julia, too, was excited and flustered.

The scene that greeted our eyes in the Kozyrevs' flat was reminiscent of a shot from one of those early films showing White Guard officers having a debauch. We cooled our heels in the entrance hall, waiting for Nina Konstantinovna to come out, and through the half-open door we could see the glint of epaulettes and the flushed faces, and we heard the tinkling of glasses, bursts of laughter, and drunken shouts.

"Oh, it's you, is it? He's been waiting so long he's getting really miserable." She hospitably invited us in. "There are two of you, are there? I wonder whether he'll know which is his mother."

She was so eager to embellish what was bound to be an interest-ing and touching spectacle—a recognition scene, as she thought.

"Watch, Tamara," she called to her daughter, the interrogator's wife. "It'll be just like at the movies," and turning toward the couch, she went on:

"Look, Vasya, my pet. Do you see? Two làdies . . . One of them has to be your mother. You must choose: Which one?"

It was only then that my eyes found the person I had been vainly trying to pick out in the drunken hurly-burly. There he was! A thin teenager in a frayed jacket sitting awkwardly huddled up in one corner of a vast couch.

He rose to his feet. He seemed quite tall and broad in the shoul-ders. He bore no resemblance whatsoever to the tow-haired, four-year-old roly-poly who used to toddle around our large apartment in Kazan twelve years back. That child, with his fair hair and his blue eyes, had resembled the country children of the Ryazan branch of the Aksyonov family. But this one, the sixteen-year-old, had chestnut hair, and gray eyes that at a distance looked hazel like Alyosha's. Altogether, he was like Alyosha rather than his earlier self.

All these observations were registered by someone who existed quite independently of me. I myself, benumbed and incapable of articulate thought, had to direct all my efforts toward remaining upright and not crumpling up in a heap from the dull thudding of the blood rushing to my temples, my neck, my face. . . .

He did not hesitate between Julia and myself. He came up to me and self-consciously put his hand on my shoulder. And then I heard at long last the word that I had been afraid of never hearing again, that now came to me across a gulf of almost twelve years, from the time before all those courts, prisons, and penal drafts, before the death of my first-born, before all those nights in Elgen.

"Mother," said my son, Vasya.

"He recognized you," Kozyreva exclaimed in delight. "That's blood speaking. It always does. . . . You see, Tamara?"

His eyes were definitely not hazel. Not like Alyosha's. Alyosha's hazel eyes were closed forever. They could not come back again. And yet . . . How much he resembled Alyosha as he was then, at the age of ten—no, nearly eleven. My two sons had for an instant merged into one and the same image.

"Alyosha, my darling," I said in a whisper, almost involuntarily.

Suddenly I heard a deep, muffled voice: "No, Mamma. I'm not Alyosha. I'm Vasya."

And then in a rapid whisper into my ear:

"Don't cry in front of them. . . ."

Thereupon I took hold of myself. I looked at him in the way that those who are really close, who know everything about one another, who are members of the same family, look at one another. He understood my look. It was the most crucial moment in my life: the joining up of the broken links in our chain of time; the recapturing of our organic closeness severed by twelve years of separation, of living among strangers. My son! And he knew, even though I hadn't said a word to him, who *we* were and who *they* were. He appealed to me not to demean myself in their presence.

"Don't be afraid, my dear. . . . I won't cry," my look said to him. And aloud, in a matter-of-fact, almost calm voice:

"Say thank you to Nina Konstantinovna, Vasya, and let's go home. It's time."

Kozyreva looked at me with astonishment and unconcealed disappointment. Wasn't I going to sob my heart out, hugging my son to me? Shouldn't I tell her guests how I had suffered during our separation? Would I, or wouldn't I, touch the heartstrings of her son-in-law, who, although he had had a good deal to drink, was scowling all the same at the sight of these strange guests?

"What do you mean, go home? Sit down for a moment, and at least take a drink in honor of the occasion. What people you are! Made of iron . . . She didn't even shed one tear. . . . What do you say to that, Tamara?"

They pestered us for quite a while longer, pressing glasses of champagne into our hands, while the kindlier, or perhaps the tipsier, officers tried to make us join them at the table. It was Julia, the diplomatic mistress of the reprocessing workshop, who saved the situation: she sat down for a minute and even took a sip of the champagne to avoid giving offense. She explained, with a wave of the hand in the direction of Vasya and myself, that we were both quite worn out: he after his journey, and his mother from her long vigil.

All this happened on October 9, 1948. After an interval of eleven years and eight months I was again taking my second son down the street, his hand clasped firmly in mine.

But how fragile it is, this thread that has joined again past and future, how it trembles in the wind! It must not be allowed to snap again! Keep it from breaking, keep it from breaking at all costs. . . .

"Vasya, you have to know, you simply have to, that your mother achieved the well-nigh impossible," Julia hastened to explain. She subjected Vasya—who was unprepared for it—to a none-too-coherent account of all my trials and tribulations with the Dalstroi personnel department, my visit to Gridasova, of how I had set about collecting money for his journey, etc., etc.

But in essence she was right. I really had achieved the well-nigh impossible. And now here he was, walking by my side, taking broader strides than I, with his belongings clutched in his arms— a much-patched, much-washed rucksack resembling the packs we used to cart around in the camps. And the jacket on his back was the same kind we used to wear in Elgen. In my time nobody wore a jacket like that on the mainland. They must have made their appearance during the war. But I was terribly upset that nearly all that Vasya was wearing closely resembled camp clothing. . . . A huge new task loomed ahead—getting Vasya an overcoat.

We kept on walking, in silence, finding no words to express that which needed saying but was too overwhelming for words. The only one who was not at a loss for words was Julia. She spoke almost without stopping for the entire journey, giving Vasya an explanation of everything all at once: about how Magadan had grown and what it had been like before; about the fine secondary school; and about our big new room—all fifteen square meters of it!

But that night Julia—bless her—left the two of us alone and went off on the pretext of having to be on duty in her workshop. It was then we had our first talk. We didn't get a wink of sleep that night. Indeed, we refused even to think about sleep. We were in a hurry to learn about each other and were delighted that each of us recognized himself in the other. How astonishing, how really astounding are the laws of genetics! Magical! This child, who remembered neither his father nor his mother, resembled both of them not only in appearance but also in his tastes, his prejudices, and his habits. I trembled when he ran his hands through his hair with an Aksyonov gesture. I found myself catching my breath with joyful astonishment when that very first night he started to recite from memory the very poems that had been my constant companions during my fight for survival in the camps. Like me, he too found in poetry a bulwark against the inhumanity of the real world. Poetry was for him a form of resistance. That night of our first talk together we had Blok and

Pasternak and Akhmatova with us. And I was so glad to be able to offer him an abundance of those things that he looked to me to supply.

"Now I understand what a mother is . . . for the very first time. Before, especially when I was a small boy, it seemed to me that Aunt Xenia looked after me like a mother. And she did look after me, but . . ."

He paused for thought. The pause lasted several minutes. Then he came out with a fairly precise formulation:

"Mother means, above all, unselfishness. And another thing—you can recite your favorite verses to her, and if you stop she will go on from the line where you left off."

(The glow of our first talk in Magadan lit up my relations with my son through all the years that were to come. There were many ups and downs. His way ahead would be complicated: before him lay the temptations that beset a popular author, the trials of adverse —and far from unprejudiced—notices by time-serving critics, the intrusion into his life of persons who were fundamentally alien to me and, for that matter, to him too. When the difficult moments came, I always called to mind the clear, unsullied spring within him, which was revealed to me that first night he spent in Kolyma. And this always allayed my anxiety. I was always to know that inside him there remained the same pure depths. The rest was froth; it would disappear as soon as the river returned to its bed. I was proved right. Today my forty-three-year-old son is as much my friend and comforter as was that boy who arrived in Magadan with a small volume of Blok in a shabby rucksack.)

Prior to Vasya's arrival, the entire Magadan colony of former detainees had been heatedly debating how best to explain to the first mainland child to have penetrated Colonel Franko's protective screens the main questions in our lives: How had we got here? Was there even a particle of truth in the monstrous charges pressed against us? Who was to blame for the cruelties and injustices committed? To put it in a word: Was he to be told the *truth*? The whole truth?

It was odd, but many people inclined toward not putting irresolvable doubts into his young mind. Even Julia said: "He has to live. If you know the whole truth, life is harder. And more dangerous." There was only Anton to argue heatedly and passionately that you could not build a genuine relationship with your own son on lies or even on half-truths, that what should most concern us was not his worldly success but his integrity.

I gave all the various bits of advice I received on this score a reasonably patient hearing, but privately I had no doubts. The first time he asked me, "What was it for?" I replied, "It's not a question of What for; the question is Why." After that I told him with absolute candor and truthfulness about everything I had been through and what I had learned as a result. At that time, in 1948, I was far from understanding all of it. But there was much that I had understood.

However, even had I tried to hide the truth from him that night, I should not have succeeded. Because he understood it without being told. And the precious part of the relationship that grew up between us would have been unthinkable without confronting the truth. And so, on the night of October 9–10, when dawn was almost upon us, I gave him a verbal precis of the chapters of *Journey into the Whirlwind* as I had conceived them. He was my first listener.

8

· *The house of cards*

Some days after his arrival Vasya said, "Mamma, we ought to have something special in the house: a puppy or a kitten. . . ."

He did not know that such a modest wish presented great difficulties in the Magadan of that time. Even dogs (other than Alsatians), let alone cats, had to be imported. But after prolonged efforts I did succeed in procuring a mainland cat, Agafya, who was to be a member of our family for several years to come. Very elegant, capricious about her food, she in no way resembled her kin in Kolyma, who were the first generation to undergo domestication. (These creatures, wild cats only yesterday, were like little tigers. Some people we knew tried to tame them, but I found them repulsive.)

Agafya gave our home a very traditional look. She loved to install herself on the table, warming herself at the table lamp and purring like a patriarchal samovar. When Vasya sat down at the table to do his homework, she would change position and go over to drape herself around his shoulders like a luxurious fur trimming.

The vacancy for a grandfather was filled by Yakov Mikhailovich Umansky, who kept his promise to give Vasya math lessons. The old man always turned up punctually, rolling slowly along like a whale, but he would not leave until correct answers had been found to all the problems, which, alas, was something he could not always manage. Every time this happened Yakov Mikhailovich would begin by flying off the handle and maintaining that there must be a misprint in the textbook; then he would get depressed, complain of his sclerosis, and recall the time when he had found solving problems like these as easy as shelling peas. I remember several occasions when he nevertheless had to leave without having solved the problem in question. But each time this occurred, he would return around one or two in the morning, undeterred by distance or weather. He would appear on the threshold, calling, "Get up, Vasya, I've found the mistake." Vasya would groan sleepily and say, "Who the hell cares?" But the old man, muffled up in a balaclava helmet all covered with ice, would stand there like a ghost until Vasya got up and wrote down the correct solution.

After the departure of his best friend, Kuprianov, the old man grew extremely lonely and became a constant visitor to our household, even though he and Anton were always having heated arguments. They differed in their opinions on Thomas More, Aquinas, the side effects of sulphonamides, and the effectiveness of small doses of sublimate. They were a classic illustration of the clash of two diametrically opposed psychological types. Anton's passionate, committed way of thinking, his predilection for the absolute, ran up hard against the skeptical irony, the sorrowful unbelief of this kindly old man who doubted whether the human race was capable of acting for noble motives. These quarrels attained their maximum intensity whenever they concerned one of the two subjects on which Anton felt most strongly: Martin Luther, whom Anton considered to be the source of all this world's ills, and, conversely, Samuel Hahnemann, the founder of homeopathy, who was for Anton the savior of mankind.

But however heated the arguments and the stinging recriminations became, the old man had only to arrive late on one of his visits for Anton to start getting worried, to keep looking at his watch, and to talk about Yakov Mikhailovich's high blood pressure. Anton would relax only when he heard the familiar flip-flap of his visitor's capacious galoshes—the sort of vast, high, rubber overshoes that used to be worn by the rag-and-bone merchants in Kazan.

Vasya had grown very attached to Yakov Mikhailovich, even though he laughed rather disrespectfully at the old man's charming eccentricities. Umansky was always absorbed in some idea to the exclusion of everything else, and he was utterly absent-minded. He would address Agafya the tabby cat as "sir." "Agafya, come here, sir," he would say in all seriousness. "Here's a nice bit of venison for you. The fact is I can't manage it. It's too stringy for me. But I'm sure it presents no problem for you, dear sir, eh?"

Sometimes the old man would recite verses he had made up himself. They were from some never-ending poem that presented in chronological order the entire history of philosophy. Vasya and I committed to memory one verse of it about Lucretius, and we would declaim it to amuse each other and cheer ourselves up when we were depressed. I still remember that verse today:

The secrets of nature the first to unveil—
Lucretius Carus is worthy of praise.
He served at the altar of reason and light
And carried a torch lit with freedom's bright rays.

On one occasion Yakov Mikhailovich, much flattered by our attention, disclosed that he had been asked to translate "La Périchole's* Letter" from the French.

"It's for a vocal performance. A lady singer approached me on the subject. Her score has the text in French."

Vasya literally writhed on his bed, contorted with laughter, while Yakov Mikhailovich dramatically declaimed: "I am thy Périchole, who loves thee, even though I sob."

As you see, the house of cards we had built was outwardly an idyllic one. But not for one second were we unaware of the menacing, subterranean shocks that constantly caused the ground beneath our house of cards to tremble. For 1949 was almost upon us, and the

---

* Character in Merimée's *Carrosse du Saint Sacrement* and Offenbach's *La Périchole*.

gathering menace of a new catastrophe was all around. Each of us had privately noted the ever-increasing number of penal drafts arriving from the mainland and the dismissal of many former detainees from good jobs. Anton, moreover, knew of the steady tightening of the regime inside the camp. But it was taboo to speak of it. To avoid frightening Vasya; and to not cast a shadow over our period of grace, to live as though nothing were amiss.

And we went on living. Vasya, who was already displaying signs of literary talent, his acute power of observation, and his interest in people who were characters in their own right, was sometimes happy simply to listen to debates and conversations he hadn't had occasion to hear before. He had spent all his conscious life with the Aksyonov family, where they all spoke and thought of nothing but their daily bread. He was delighted with the sort of people he was meeting for the first time in his life in Kolyma, people who were stimulated by things outside themselves despite the scarcity of daily bread in their own lives.

We had friends come to visit us in our house of cards, as befitted a proper family household; for example, Professor Simorin and his wife, Tanya. They lived in a small shack opposite our building. Theirs, too, was a camp romance that had survived all the perils: official obstacles, separation, the impossibility of communicating while they were apart. Now they were both on this side of the barbed wire; they were no longer zeks but ex-zeks enjoying the luxury of having their own stove, as well as that of free cohabitation. Simorin, a brilliantly erudite man, a wit, and a former lady-killer, impressed Vasya with tales of his past before his arrest, in which there figured names that Vasya had come across only on the covers of textbooks. On a par with Simorin was Dr. Orlov, a colleague of Anton's. True, he was less communicative than Simorin, but sometimes he would come out with interesting paradoxes on all aspects of life.

Another of our visitors was Vera Shukhaeva, the artist, who used to tell us about Paris, about her meetings with Modigliani and Léger, and about the work of her husband. Now, on the brink of 1949, Vera Shukhaeva was working in the Magadan Dressmaking Workshop; she sometimes managed to make the fleshy matrons of Magadan society look quite well turned out.

Finally, we had a whole colony of Germans nesting in our corridor, who were constantly dropping into our apartment. There was

Hans Mangardt, an Austrian with a picturesque Father Christmas beard, a Communist of long standing, who since his arrival in Russia had been through all sorts of ups and downs that he was now "interpreting from the Marxist point of view." His wife, Johanna Wilke, had been a typist for the Berlin committee of the German Communist Party. In their wake came all their compatriots, who greatly moved Anton by their choral renderings of German songs.

Nathan Steinberger, our old acquaintance from Taskan, also made his appearance. He never stopped worrying about finding a job. He had now been joined by his genuine, mainland, wife who had been released from camp in Karaganda. She was a boisterous person who nagged her husband until Anton and I frequently felt nostalgic for the pleasant hours we had spent in Taskan in Nathan's company. Now that his wife was around it was impossible to have any calm, thoughtful conversation with him.

Another of our Germans was Gertrude Richter, who at that time played the piano with the orchestra of the Magadan House of Culture. She was still ailing, emaciated, and permanently hungry. She had a hospitable welcome in our household, and Anton gave her medical attention. Even then, a lot of what she said did not make sense; none the less, who could then have foreseen that later, in her native Leipzig, she would become a faithful swordbearer in Walter Ulbricht's Praetorian Guard?

I had acquaintances also among the free population—and not only colleagues at work. I attended, of course, parents' meetings at Vasya's school, and Anton introduced me to some of his free patients whom he trusted completely.

But we always had to keep our distance from the free population. We could have perfectly friendly chats with them on neutral territory: at school, in the street, in the park, in the foyer of the Gornyak Cinema. But it never entered our heads—or theirs—to invite such chance acquaintances home. The only free members of the population to visit our apartment were Vasya's classmates. But even they somehow tended to be children with flaws in their personal files. Yura Akimov's father had been in prison, and Yura and his mother had come out to join him when he was released. That was after Vasya's arrival. Yura Markelov's mother had come out under contract but had then married a former detainee, our old acquaintance from Taskan, Professor Pentegov.

Thanks to Vasya's friends I now had a new source of income. I started giving lessons to children who had fallen behind with their Russian. Despite this we were invariably short of money. So in addition to such traditional highbrow sources of additional income as cramming, Julia and I did not disdain what we laughingly called "involvement with the private sector." In the evenings we used to hem and embroider so-called handkerchiefs, which were squares of scrap material Julia had left over from her workshop. Every Saturday a suspicious-looking old gent, whom we nicknamed the Middleman, came to collect our wares. He would take delivery of the finished handkerchiefs and sell them in the Magadan flea market on Sundays. There was nothing remotely like them to be had in the Magadan shops at the time. On Mondays he would hand over whatever he had got for them, after deducting a pretty stiff commission for himself. I haven't the vaguest recollection of what our trading profits amounted to, but I do remember they played some sort of role in our budget, in our constant efforts to find enough food for our fairly substantial household and our numerous guests. In postwar Madagan things were always a bit difficult for those who did not receive the special pay increments for the Far North and who were without access to the many-tiered system of closed-distribution shops. What made it worse was that prices in the town market were marked up to take account of the enormous sums of money in circulation.

You might think that in these conditions of constant fear and want none of us would have been interested in adding to our family. And yet . . .

It happened soon after Vasya's arrival, on an ordinary working day. I had finished my music periods with the junior and middle groups. There remained the senior group, and I was hammering out a marching tune, as usual, which was their cue to enter the music room. Tripping along in time with the music, the children had to describe a circle and end up opposite their own little chairs. All of a sudden I spotted a little baby girl behind the skirt of the last girl in line. The little girl was not merely smaller than anyone in the senior class; she didn't even measure up to those in the junior class. The little girl had tears in her bright eyes, and the sort of downy fluff on her head you'd associate with a fledgling that had fallen out of its nest.

Their teacher explained to me in a rapid whisper that the child's mother, an ex-zek, had parked the little girl (who had been taken ill) in the hospital and then vanished into the blue, just abandoning her. . . . In the spring there was to be a children's convoy to the special children's home in Komsomolsk, on the Amur. Until then we were supposed to be looking after her. Apparently there was no vacancy in the crèches. . . . And we were assumed to be tough enough to cope with anything. . . . There were thirty-eight of them in the group as it was. . . . And the new one was the wrong age, and a terrible crybaby, too. They'd had about enough of her. . . . Couldn't she just sit around during the music period? It might take her mind off things.

And it did take Tonya's mind off things. She put her ear against the highly polished side of the piano and gave a happy peal of laughter when she heard the thrumming inside. When the other girls started practicing one of the standard Russian dances, she suddenly got to her feet and joined in the circle. She was then one year and ten months old. But she moved more rhythmically than the six-year-olds into whose midst she had so unexpectedly intruded.

And so it went on from that day forward. In the morning I had only to turn up in the so-called music room and the door of whichever classroom Tonya had been dumped in would fly open and she would rush out as fast as her legs would carry her, shouting en route, "The music's here! The music's here!" For someone of her age and background she spoke amazingly well. Not all our four-year-olds had a vocabulary or pronunciation as good as hers.

The nurses and teachers were only too happy to steer Tonya in my direction. She didn't cry, she didn't make a fuss; she just sat there beside the piano throughout all the periods with the various groups. She danced and sang with them all. But in her general behavior she was high-strung, sensitive, and tearful.

One Saturday, when the children were being handed over to their parents for the day off, I was kept back in the head's office for a meeting of some sort, and it was twilight in the music room by the time I got back there. This queer, low-ceilinged room with asymmetric windows looked more gloomy than ever in the half light with no one around. The only patch on its dirty gray walls, apart from the black silhouette of the piano, was an enormous portrait of the Generalissimo with his medals and red-striped trousers—quite out of proportion with the size of the room. At the foot of the portrait, on top of an improvised pedestal, there was always a vase of artificial flowers. They were very rough-and-ready imitations made out of pieces of silk, or, failing that, starched gauze. But the children had been taught to treat the altar with holy awe, and not even the most mischievous of them ever ventured to touch either the flowers or the portrait.

But at that moment someone was standing by the flowers. A diminutive figure was fingering the bunch of white gauze roses.

"Tonya? What are you doing there in the pitch dark?"

She gave me a straight answer.

"I'm crying. . . ."

Usually Tonya cried aloud. She would howl and sob and make a lot of noise. But in the twilight of that Saturday evening, when after the week's hustle and bustle the whole building had fallen silent, Tonya was crying noiselessly. She presumably had no strength left in her after all her howling fits. She had probably begun to cry when Saturday's hurly-burly was at its height, when the boys were sliding down the banisters, whooping as they went and performing gymnastic feats worthy of circus artists, and the girls were squealing and quarreling, looking for their mittens or their woolen tights in the general pile, while the supervisors shouted at children and parents alike. And the word "home" would be hanging over this chaos. All the children would be shouting it out; it was repeated by their parents and taken up by the supervisors. How could anyone hear Tonya's sobs?

Tonya echoed the word. "Home—what's that?"

How was she to know? And how could one possibly explain it to her? Her biography to date had not included this strange concept. She had been in the Elgen children's home, the hospital, our resident kindergarten. . . . And ahead of her was a children's draft to another special institution. Would it even be right to try to explain what "home" meant?

"Let's go to pets' corner and give the little rabbits some water," I suggested to her in an unnatural, wooden voice.

No, she wasn't interested in little rabbits, and she irritably dismissed my suggestion.

Then she announced with a precision almost incredible in one of her age:

"I haven't got a home. . . ."

That Saturday when—after arranging it with the head—I brought Tonya back with me to our room, no one was particularly surprised. I had on previous occasions brought back for the weekend one or another of the children who had been left behind. The only comment was Vasya's grumble: "She's awfully small. She'll interfere with my homework."

Tonya herself was so much at home from the moment she entered our apartment that after looking around the room her first question was: "But where's my bed?" She had (and still has) a great talent for instantly finding her bearings in an unfamiliar situation.

On Monday morning she flatly refused to return to the kindergarten. She liked it where she was; it was much nicer at home; and she would stay there with Mamma (a word she had immediately borrowed from Vasya). But Mamma had to go to work! Well, in that case Tonya agreed to go back to school just for the music lessons, as long as she could come straight home afterward.

The kindergarten head did not allow me to take her home with me on that Monday evening. On Saturdays, when there was no one around, by all means. But weekdays were out. The inspectors might turn up at any moment and demand that the child be handed over to them for dispatch to a children's home on the mainland.

That Monday night I made one strange discovery: I realized that on Saturday, when Tonya had been there, I had slept better and had been free of the nightmares about Alyosha's death which had continued to plague me even after Vasya's arrival. Every feeling connected with Vasya, even the happiest, also held suffering for me. This was because I kept seeing Vasya and Alyosha side by side, measuring them against each other, comparing their character, and torturing myself with fantasies about the three of us talking together. Alyosha was always there, an unseen presence at Vasya's side, especially at night, and I used to wake up in the morning completely drained by my silent ordeal. I dared not speak of it either to Anton (he considered my stubborn refusal to accept Alyosha's loss a terrible sin) or to Julia, and certainly not to Vasya.

The next Saturday Tonya was a long time getting to sleep. She kept tossing about and sighing. When I sat down on the edge of the couch she suddenly took my hand in both hers and tucked it under her cheek. I held my breath. . . . For this was Alyosha's gesture. After he had had measles with severe complications at the age of three, he had always demanded that I sit by him until he went to sleep, and he had used this selfsame gesture of taking my hand and laying his cheek on it.

For a moment I had the impression that even her gaze was like Alyosha's, although, objectively speaking, her gray-blue eyes were as different as could be from the hazel eyes of the son I had lost.

Now from one Saturday to the next I had yet another posting to dread. Before Tonya had come on the scene, my first thought on rising had been: Don't let them send Anton away when the head of Dalstroi no longer needs him. Now, on top of this, I felt faint with fear and anguish when I opened the door of the kindergarten, in case I should suddenly be told that the convoy of orphans for Komsomolsk had already left.

Nowadays it seems almost incredible, and yet it was a fact; two-year-old Tonya already knew the word "convoy." It flitted through the conversations of the nurses—ex-zeks—and the games of the older children—alumni of the Elgen children's home. One Sunday, sitting at table with us, Tonya suddenly made a pronouncement quite unrelated to the general conversation:

"Those who don't have a mamma—they're the ones who go with the convoy. . . . But I have a mamma. . . ."

As it happened, Tonya fell ill with diphtheria just two days before the departure of the orphans' convoy and was put in the hospital.

"So, your Tonya has missed the main draft. And the next one isn't for at least another year," the kindergarten head said to me.

I was not, of course, allowed inside the infectious diseases section of the hospital, so I stood on a mound under the closed window and made signs to Tonya, who was sobbing bitterly, to calm her down.

About a fortnight later the doctor announced that the little girl was almost well again, and could be discharged if she were a child with a home of her own. But she could not be transferred to somewhere where there was a group of children, for she was a virus carrier. Vasya had already had diphtheria so there was no reason why she could not come to us.

During the month and a half she spent with us, she completely forgot her past tribulations, began to cry less, and developed mentally to a remarkable extent.

And I noticed myself reacting in the same, odd way yet again. When the little girl was there, my grief for Alyosha became less heart-rending; the small, mechanical, humdrum tasks involved in looking after a little child seemed to drive it out of my mind. It was as though feeding her semolina, washing her garments, tucking her into bed, and dressing her brought back memories of the maternal feelings I had never been able to gratify fully and poured healing balm on my mortally wounded soul.

All the members of my household were up in arms at my proposal to adopt Tonya. Julia waxed particularly indignant:

"You really are a genius at inventing new forms of torture for yourself. You can't be satisfied with the troubles you've got already. . . . You said yourself we live in a house of cards. And you couldn't have said it better! So why burden yourself with a child as well? Someone else's child at that—and of unknown heredity! You can be sure that the mother who abandoned the child wouldn't have endowed her with particularly virtuous qualities. . . . And suppose they pick us up again? What will it do to her to be an orphan for the second time? Besides, she's a nice-looking little girl; some childless colonel's wife will be only too glad to take her over, and she'll soon be in her element."

Vasya, who treated Tonya with the same unthinking kindness as he did Agafya the cat, found it impossible to give the question serious attention. He stayed silent but I could see that he found Julia's arguments convincing.

Anton approached my proposal from a different angle:

"Have you considered whether we have the right to link the child's fate with our own, the fate of the doomed?"

It was all very distressing, but it did nothing to dissuade me. For they didn't know, couldn't know, that all their rational arguments were meaningless to me, that for me the appearance of Tonya in my life was not a matter-of-fact event: it had a hidden significance, connected almost mystically with Alyosha.

Having listened to all the objections, I went off the following day to the department in charge of guardianship and foster care. Total failure! It emerged that politically unreliable persons did not have the right to adopt children.

"You should be thankful that you haven't been deprived of maternal rights over your *own* children! Whatever gave you the idea you could adopt other people's?" This was the spiteful reaction of a female person with a desk in that department, who had obviously gone crazy from having nothing whatsoever to do. "You can put it right out of your head!" From under a tall hairdo her small ears protruded like a bat's. The pouting lips that ejected these fearsome words had been neatly lipsticked into a Cupid's bow.

That same evening, when Anton and I were alone, and after I had told him about my visit to the department that decided the fate of children, he saw how upset I was and started to speak of my kindness, of how the little girl would, of course, be better off with me, but . . .

"Heavens above! What's all this about kindness? It's not a question of kindness. . . . Can't you see that I need Tonya more than she needs me?"

When he heard this, Anton broke off short and ruminated. . . . He never said another word about the inadvisability of the action.

(Over the course of the next thirteen years he was more than a father to Tonya. Unfortunately, he died when Tonya was in her fifteenth year. I was left alone to help her over the rough patches and pitfalls of adolescence. Julia's prophecies about unknown heredity were to some extent borne out. There were moments when I succumbed to complete despair, not knowing how to cope with actions beyond my comprehension, alien to my mentality. But not once in all the twenty-seven years that she has been my daughter—at the time I write this she is twenty-nine and an actress at the Leningrad Comedy Theater—not once have I ever regretted adopting her. I have always accepted both the grief and the joy she has brought me as an organic part of my life. The feeling that I could not, should not, pass her by has remained with me.)

Meanwhile, 1949, twin brother of 1937, was advancing on our land, on the whole of Eastern Europe, and, before all else, on the places of prison and exile.

We sensed its dread approach. Instinctively and sometimes quite consciously, we listened for its step. But true to our principle of using our breathing space up to the very last minute, we lived in disregard of the threat. We even took part in the New Year's festivities. True, Anton was not allowed out of camp that evening. But the three of us—Julia, Vasya, and I—saw in that sinister year among decent people, surrounded by general good will and sympathy. I wrote a sketch for the employees of the various kindergartens and presented the program myself. Julia saw in the New Year in her workshop and Vasya in his school.

We never spoke aloud of impending troubles that seemed to grudge us our happiness. It was only at night—when sleeping and waking merge into one, when you lose control of words and thoughts, when the mainspring of long years of tension slackens—

only then did the monsters come into their own. They paraded before your eyes one after the other, they seized you by the throat with their tenacious sticky fingers. And then . . .

Anton, transferred to distant places, tried and retried. Myself or Julia, or both of us, rearrested. Vasya left all alone on this remote planet. Tonya packed off to Komsomolsk.

Would I preserve my contempt for fate? Would I preserve, when I faced these things, the stoutheartedness and proud endurance of my youth?

1949, 1949 . . .

9

· *In alphabetical order*

Sinister rumors coming from the mainland were the first we heard of it. It was said that the town of Aleksandrov in the Vladimir region (101 kilometers from Moscow), where a lot of former prisoners who had returned in 1947 had settled, was being systematically and relentlessly emptied of people. Each night a handful of people were taken away. Specific names were mentioned, many of them known to us.

At nighttime Julia and I discussed this frightening development in whispers, where Vasya could not hear us. In so doing, we never failed to compliment each other on our foresight. How right we had been to remain in Kolyma! Julia fervently hoped and sought to persuade me too that they wouldn't take anyone from our remote planet. We were isolated from the rest of the world as it was. Anyhow they couldn't possibly get by without the former prisoners! The entire industrial production of the area depended on them. . . .

But even our own experience—let alone other people's—fails to teach us anything. We were falling into our old habits of attempting to forecast our own future and the future of everyone else on the basis of rational assumptions. We had learned nothing in all our twelve years. The logic, or rather the illogic, of evil-doing was as much a closed book to us as ever. Or, perhaps, we deliberately banished grim forebodings so as to wrest for ourselves a further month, week, or day./ . . .

Evidently not only we but also the humbler of the free employees had no suspicion that a mass purge was in preparation. At the least, things proceeded peacefully, smoothly, almost idyllically at my place of work. The New Year's show in the kindergarten went off as expected. And then the concert to mark Soviet Army Day. The children marched onto the stage dressed in the uniforms of all branches of the services. Our methodologists frequently held conferences, at which I was invariably singled out for praise. I had in fact become skillful at writing scenarios for the matinees and at devising novelties that amused both children and parents. On one occasion I even performed with my children on the radio, and the announcer blurted out my name without thinking. The poor girl got severely reprimanded for it, but all our former detainees interpreted the slip as a meaningful symptom of liberalization.

And suddenly . . . one ill-starred day we all learned that right there in Magadan two of our people had been arrested all over again. The first of them, Antonov, had been working as an accountant somewhere or other. The second, Averback or Averbukh, had been living on the ground floor of our building. He was a quiet, self-contained person who would give you a polite good day but never stopped to talk.

The general alarm aroused by the rearrests was swiftly dispelled by various hypotheses and "reliable" rumors. It was said that Antonov was, after all, responsible for a substantial sum of money, so his arrest would, of course, be connected with an unaccounted-for deficit. And what of the second? He, it seems, had earlier been an active Zionist. With the recent creation of the State of Israel, Zionism had attracted much attention. They had probably decided to check up on his old contacts. Once they had checked, they would let him go. . . .

A short while later they hauled in Anya Vinogradova and Dr. Volberg, a physician who was very popular in the town. Once again, there was panic to begin with, followed by mutual reassurances: there must have been some unfortunate medical mishap. . . . Vinogradova was also in that line of business, as a medical assistant. They were being accused, presumably, of causing a patient's death.

No one wanted to believe that mass rearrests had started. At least no one wanted to acknowledge this, even to himself. When I look back on that frightening period, I marvel at people's willful blindness: How could we have failed to ponder over what was so obvious, over the fact that with each passing day the local administration of the new ministry—the MGB, a reorganized version of the NKVD—was spreading, putting down deeper roots, behaving more and more as though it owned Magadan, taking over the best buildings in town, not excluding such fortresses as the Maglag building. The terms "Red House" and "White House"—their two citadels—had become common currency. You may think that old hands like ourselves, with ten years in detention behind us and two years of "freedom" in Magadan, ought to have taken a closer look at the features and behavior of the young MGB officers who had appeared out of the blue and who scurried about the streets of the city with a proprietory look on their forceful, well-fed faces. The very fact of their constant increase in numbers should have led us to suspect that new sweeps were being planned. But we refused to notice any of it, let alone to reflect on what was everywhere to be seen.

It later emerged that the rearrests were in full spate and that we had failed to notice their scale because the sweep was being conducted throughout Kolyma on the basis of a single list. The tally for the town of Magadan itself accounted as yet for no more than a handful of individual cases. In one way or another, we survived happily up to the autumn of '49. Our house of cards stood firm right up to October. Vasya moved up into the tenth class. Tonya escaped the second mass convoy, because this time the order called for the dispatch of children aged five or over, and she was only three. And fate also treated us to four wonderful weeks in the Northern Artek Pioneer camp, to which I was permitted to take Vasya. Tonya went along with the other children in the kindergarten. Vasya liked the exotic scenery, went for long walks through the conical hills, filled out, and acquired a tan. Tonya profited from being allowed while on holiday to stay glued to my side. And September—the only month in Kolyma that shows the inhabitants any kindness—favored us with a gentle yellow sun, cobwebs, and cranberries.

I clung, oh, how I clung, to each of those days, sensing, or rather knowing with virtual certainty, that the life I had built up with such care was running out, seeping through my fingers. However meager, however impoverished and poisoned by constant fear, it was still life. With Vasya, Tonya, Anton, and Julia . . . But this period of grace was now also coming to its end. The crag hanging over us was liable at any moment to crash down on our heads.

In Northern Artek it was easier to put the MGB out of your mind; the rumors that were circulating in town did not reach so far. But in mid-September, when we returned to Magadan, it was impossible to remain in doubt of the impending catastrophe. All the former detainees were going about like lost souls; when they met in the street, instead of greeting one another they would exchange in a half-whisper the latest names of those to have been hauled in. Not one of those arrested had yet returned. Their fate was an impenetrable secret. The rationale and the purpose of the arrests remained undisclosed.

The first to solve the riddle was old Umansky. One evening when he had been helping Vasya with his algebra, he sat down on the couch, leaned back against the wall exhausted, closed his eyes, and suddenly asked:

"Do you have a pencil?"

After covering a sheet of his notepad with short lines of writing, Yakov Mikhailovich rose to his feet and exclaimed:

"Eureka! It's all quite clear! It's in alphabetical order. . . ."

We were all at home at the time. But we had stopped having the cozy talks around the table that we had had in '47. Instead, we stayed silent, each of us trying to avoid looking in another's eyes so as not to see the reflection of his own overpowering terror. Even Tonya sensed our depression and talked to her doll in whispers.

"What's in alphabetical order?"

"They're rearresting people in alphabetical order! Listen . . . I I have sorted them out. These are the names we know of in Magadan. . . ."

And he started to read them out: Antonov, Averbukh, Astafyev, Baturina, Berseneva, Blank, Venediktov, Vinogradova, Volberg . . .*

"Rubbish!" Anton exclaimed indignantly, darting angry warning glances at Umansky. "Pure coincidence!"

But I saw it all at once. A familiar, stifling spasm tore at my throat.

* Transliterated into English, the opening letters of the Russian alphabet are
A, B, V, G, D, E.

The culmination of my fear. *A . . . B . . . V . . .* In that case the next letter would be mine! Anton, too, had grasped this right away; that was why he was shouting at Umansky and signaling to him with his eyes—to avoid prematurely alarming Vasya.

"Stupid guesswork," Anton repeated exasperated. But I recalled that lately each time he came into our room in the evening he looked around anxiously and gave a sigh of relief when he saw me.

Someone was knocking at the door. In came our neighbor Johanna —as pale as death.

"They've taken Gertrude," she said, slumping into a chair as if she had fainted.

This was one shell that had burst too close for comfort. Gertrude was virtually our daily guest. Gertrude, an orthodox Party member, a former Berlin Ph.D., a past master at tortuous syllogisms directed toward explaining and theoretically justifying any action that Stalin the Genius might undertake.

"How can she have done anything wrong playing the piano in the House of Culture orchestra?" Julia said, distracted.

"How could you in your workshop, or your friend in the kindergarten? Nobody is guilty of anything; it's just that 'he' feels hungry," Umansky replied. "What odd questions from someone who has done so many years in camp. It's time you understood. It's a mass sweep. Rearrests of former detainees. In alphabetical order . . ."

"That just shows how badly your researches have let you down," Anton broke in angrily. "Gertrude's last name is Richter . . . spelled with an R. . . ."

Yes, of course! Straight from *B* to *R*. Perhaps Umansky really was mistaken. . . . But he replied calmly:

"I personally would be glad to be wrong, but, regretfully, I am right. The fact of the matter is that Gertrude has a double-barreled last name: Richter-Bartok. Or, more correctly, Bartok-Richter. . . . Obviously, she was listed under *B*."

From then on Vasya started asking me anxiously from time to time: "Mamma, aren't you frightened?" To this I replied, "God is merciful. . . ." He usually asked me this just before going to sleep. The thought of arrest was connected with the nighttime.

But as it happened, it was daytime, as in '37. I was giving the senior group their music lesson. The October holiday was approaching, and we had to give the children intensive coaching for their gala concert. The children were learning the song "And Stalin from his high tribune looks down on children with a smile" under their teacher's direction. The accompaniment was a bit difficult, and I had already twice played wrong notes.

At that point two men in civilian clothes, one young, the other a little older, wrenched open the door and strode into the music room without ceremony.

"No one's allowed in here. There's a music lesson on," six-year-old Bella Rubina said to them severely. She would soon be seven, and she set great store by her role as the oldest in the group.

But the new arrivals looked straight through the little girl as if she were made of air. They behaved just as if the thirty-eight children in the room were not there. They had eyes only for me. *I* was the one they wanted. The younger of the pair casually took from his side pocket a small card with gilt lettering and showed it briefly to me. I had just time to take in the word "security." His companion said in a low voice:

"Follow us!"

"Eugenia Semyonovna, don't go!" shouted out Edik Klimov, rising up from his seat.

The image of his anxious, flushed face was to pursue me in prison. The infallibility of a child's intuition! He had sensed the danger and was rushing headlong to meet it like a combative little sparrow—to rally, to defend, to ward off . . .

But at the same time the head came in. She too was flushed and she tried to avoid looking at me.

"Eugenia Semyonovna will be returning shortly," she told the children, "and I'll stay with you in the meantime."

Upstairs, in the head's office, they showed me a warrant for my arrest and a search warrant. It was all done according to the rules, with the Public Prosecutor's authorization.

"We'll just take a ride and look your apartment over," one of the knights-errant of the MGB told me.

"I won't take a step until you let me see my son. He's at school. He will be left behind out here at the end of the earth, all alone, with no means of support. I must talk to him before we are parted, and tell him where to go for help."

The older knight-errant shrugged his shoulders.

"Oh well, I suppose it's all right. . . . The school's right nearby. We've got a car. Let's go and pick him up."

Vasya told me later that he knew what it was all about as soon as the classroom door opened in the middle of the lesson and a commanding voice rang out: "Aksyonov! Outside!" Many of the other pupils understood too. There on the edge of the earth the White House didn't stand on ceremony, and its little habits (and those of the Red House too) were well known to the population.

A minute later there were four of us in a car with drawn silk curtains: I, the two knights-errant—fearlessly executing their dangerous mission of detaining a well-known terrorist—and my younger son, who at the age of seventeen was going through the ritual of seeing his mother off to prison for the second time. He was a very little boy now. His lips were trembling and he kept repeating: "Mamma dear . . . Mamma dear."

With a fearful effort of will I forced myself to concentrate on practical matters. I had to decide there and then, in the space of the few minutes remaining to me, what instructions to give Vasya. Should I tell him to send a telegram to the mainland, and as soon as he had money for the return fare, to return to Kazan? Or was I to say that he should remain here until he had finished the tenth-year class? After all, Julia's letter K would not be turning up for some time yet. There might be no change until spring. . . . But if they took Julia, they'd take away the room; and then Vasya would be not only without bread but without a roof over his head. What would Anton, a prisoner, be able to do for him? In this sense I didn't need to worry about Tonya—she would be fed and housed. It was a good thing I had taken her back to the kindergarten that day. . . .

The search was performed somewhat casually, as if their hearts were not in it. It was all over and done with in fifteen minutes, and I used that time to bundle some things together for myself and to show Vasya where his laundry and his clothes were. By ill fortune, there was absolutely no money in the kitty: my wages were due the following day. I wrote out a note authorizing Vasya to collect them, but I was by no means sure that they would hand the money over to him. If one were to judge by '37, nothing would come of it: in '37 we had lost our belongings, our books, our wages, and our royalties.

"Sign the search certificate," the knights-errant ordered. "Fourteen pages of materials have been confiscated. . . ."

Dear God, what sort of materials? They must be "Puss in Boots," the fairy tale I had dramatized for the puppet theater.

"Headquarters will decide what's for children and what's for adults," mysteriously pronounced the senior knight-errant. Then he suddenly began to chide Vasya, who had been unable to restrain his tears.

"Shame on you, young man! You're seventeen years old. At your age I already had to feed a family. . . ."

Vasya flew off the handle. He replied brusquely:

"With your profession, keeping a family is easy enough. But I was an orphan at four, and after all the trouble I've had getting back to my mother, you're taking her away again."

The younger knight-errant couldn't keep it up. A human instinct stirred in him.

"It's not for long," he muttered. "There's no need to get upset, it's not like '37. You'll be seeing in the new year together. And just you stay put, my boy! Finish your tenth-year class here or you'll lose a whole year. . . ."

Of course, I did not believe a word of what he was saying. In 1937 they had summoned people along "for forty minutes." But it was a good thing he chose to tell a well-meaning fib so as to reassure Vasya.

I finally decided what to tell Vasya to do. He must send my sister a telegram saying that I was gravely ill and asking for money for his return fare. But when the money arrived he was to put it in the savings bank and continue with his schooling in Magadan. The money would serve as a form of insurance, so that he would have the return fare in case of extreme need. He understood this reference to the possibility of Julia's being arrested and gave me a nod to show that he had understood. The young knight-errant growled, "He won't need to go anywhere. . . ."

We signed the search certificate recording the confiscation of "Puss in Boots." In so doing I learned the names of the two knights-errant. The younger was Chentsov, the older Palei.

I embraced Vasya. We went out into the corridor. Frightened faces peered out of the doors along it. Anna Feliksovna, an old German lady living in Johanna's apartment, whispered in astonishment: "Up to their old tricks again? Taking mothers from their children?"

In the car Palei sat beside me, and Chentsov beside the driver. I raised my eyes in the direction of our window and saw that Vasya had moved the table away and had his face glued to the glass. This image would haunt me in prison like a deathly visitation. Even now, after a period of so many years, I find it painful to write about. I will try to be brief.

We drew up outside the White House. A bad omen. The word from the zeks' bush telegraph was that the White House was for the select few. The Red House was a step down on the ladder: it was for the mass swoops. For yet bigger mass swoops! What made it still more painful was that the White House had been the premises of Maglag, where Gridasova had had her office and where the previous year I had succeeded in obtaining permission for Vasya to come out. For the sake of the new all-powerful ministry they had even eased out the Queen of Kolyma. With what hopes I had emerged from that building a year ago!

I was led into the typing pool, where my knights-errant had to complete some paper work about me. I sat down on a stool awaiting my dispatch to prison. The typist was inexperienced, could only type with two fingers, and was occasionally unsure of her spelling.

"Carried out—one *r* or two?" she asked Chentsov like a trustful child, and he cast an inquiring glance in my direction.

"Er . . . two," he said uncertainly, with an interrogative intonation. I confirmed this with a nod. "That's right, two."

I suddenly felt sorry for both Chentsov and the typist. Poor things! They knew nothing. . . . They couldn't spell, and they didn't know right from wrong. But this feeling of compassion gave way to one of exasperation with the typist's stupid, glazed blue eyes and with Chentsov's equally glazed black jackboots, ludicrously protruding from beneath his civilian overcoat. The sooner I could be off to prison, to a cell shared with people of my own kind, the better. . . .

The main office smelled of dust, tobacco, garlic, and damp overcoats. Some great hulking specimen with the face of an elderly, tired bulldog rummaged through my pockets and spent a long time pondering deeply over the leg that Tonya had wrenched off her baby doll and that I had dropped into my pocket with the thought of putting it back on later. The hulking specimen was supposed to draw up an inventory of "personal effects" taken from me on my going into prison. He had already written down "Hair pins—3 (three), indelible pencil—1 (one)." Then he was in trouble. How should he enter the doll's leg? He held it up to the light. "Nothing there—you can see through it." He licked his thumb and rubbed the object. Again nothing to show for it. . . . It didn't change its consistency. . . . Finally he asked, "What's this you've got here?" And gave a sigh of relief when he heard my reply: "A piece from a broken toy." This he could deal with in his listing.

But the procedure for ensuring the safety of the state was by no means finished. They also brought into play an unkempt wardress whose task it was to perform the personal search. I established that the procedure had not changed a bit over the past ten years, had not improved in the slightest. The wardress went about it just as her colleagues in Butyrki, Lefortovo, and Yaroslavl had. Except that she was perhaps a little cruder in her ways.

A short walk along the echoing, vaulted corridors. A rattle of keys. The squeal of the cell door. A horrible cell! Damp, cramped, and stinking. The stone floor gave off a penetrating cold that gripped my legs. The only movable object was a night bucket. A hideous window, a fairly large one though, which let the daylight in. The fiery globe of the sun's reflection affixed its seal to the barriers between ourselves and the land of the living.

"Eugenia! Eugenia!"

Women prisoners were crying out my name in unison and individually. They were all known to me, every single one of them. They were all rearrests, veterans of Elgen, like me. They kept on at me, eagerly demanding information. I told them briefly who had been hauled in during the last few days, what the weather was like outside, what was in the newspapers, what was on sale in the shops. But that didn't satisfy them. What they wanted above all to know was why we, and not others in the same "criminal" category, had been arrested. The interrogations to which they had been subjected had shed absolutely no light on this.

Interrupting one another, they put forward various profound hypotheses on this score. The most interesting suggestions were made by Gertrude. She laid down the law from an upper bunk like the prophet Moses from Mount Sinai. Not for nothing was she a Doctor of Philosophy and a true-blue German from Germany—a *Reichsdeutsche*. The Frau Doktor traced our arrests direct to the Marxist theory of cognition, Lenin's theory of imperialism, and also the latest meeting of the Italian and Afghan ministers of foreign affairs.

While she was delivering her sermon, I tested Umansky's clever conjecture. Yes . . . there were the *A*'s—Alimbekova and Artamanova, *B*'s—Bartok, Berseneva, *V*'s—Vasilyeva, Veis, Vinogradova, *G*'s—Gavrilova, Ginzburg . . .

"That's enough, Gertrude," I said, with a gesture of exhaustion. "Take a look around you and leave your theoretical generalizations behind; try to understand the world as it is, empirically."

She put her own interpretation on my words and whispered to me in German:

"If you know something important, don't say it out loud. There are all sorts of people here."

"Good Lord! Here we go again. . . . Thirteen years behind bars and you still imagine that you're surrounded by all sorts of odd people, that you are the only one who isn't odd. The only one to be trusted with confidential matters and state secrets."

"What do you mean?" Gertrude asked huffily.

"I mean that they're arresting us in alphabetical order. Don't look at me as if I were mad! They're rearresting people in alphabetical order! Look around you . . . *A, B, V, G* . . ."

At that moment the cell door opened again and we saw a pale, middle-aged woman, whom none of us knew, standing in the doorway.

"What's your name?" we asked, almost in unison.

"Golubyova," she answered softly. "Nina Golubyova from Orotukan."

Dead silence reigned in the cell.

10

· *Vaskov's House*

The most fearful thing is that evil becomes ordinary, part of a normal daily routine extending over decades. In '37 evil had assumed a monumental-tragic appearance. The Dragon breathed out red flames, hurled livid lightning bolts, struck down his victims with white-hot swords.

But in '49 the Georgian Serpent, yawning with repletion and

boredom, was drawing up at leisure an alphabetical list of those to be exterminated and did not disdain "Puss in Boots" as material evidence of terrorist activity.

Boredom prevailed not only on the surface of the Dragon's kingdom, where each day the minimum number of words and phrases needed to support life diminished further, but also in its subterranean dominions, its Hades, where total tedium also reigned supreme.

Twelve years earlier, being arrested had been like discovering a new world for the old faithfuls of the Red Guard who on February 15, 1937, crossed the threshold of Kazan's Black Lake Prison. An unknown and unsuspected underground region opened up to receive them. The almost atrophied need to find their own answers to vexing questions reawoke in them. Their ardent interest in these new discoveries had prevailed even over the acuteness of their personal suffering.

But by '49 I had no thirst for knowledge, no curiosity, no interest in the souls of the butchers and their victims. It was all clear. I now knew that it all conformed to a hackneyed pattern. I knew the stereotyped reactions of the persecutors and the persecuted.

In '37 when I had first come to realize my personal responsibility for it all, I used to dream of purging my guilt with suffering.

By '49 I already knew that suffering can only cleanse one up to a point. When it drags on for decades and becomes a matter of routine, it no longer cleanses; it simply dulls all sensation. I had nevertheless retained some spark of life in my free existence in Magadan; but after my second arrest I would surely turn into a thing of wood.

There I was lying on the upper row of plank bunks between Gertrude and Nastya Berseneva, and the only thing I felt was revulsion. Toward everything: our beggar's pittance—the bread ration shoved at us from behind the grille and the wooden shutter; the bumblings of Gertrude and the invective of Anya Vinogradova, who cursed the interrogators colorfully and elaborately morning, noon, and night. Toward myself, too. A feeling of total nausea.

For as much as a year before my arrest the very name of the place had set me trembling. When people said of someone, "He has been in Vaskov's House," it meant that he had been through a higher circle of the Inferno with which we were as yet unfamiliar. "Vaskov's House" had a sinister ring comparable only with "Serpantinka" —the prison out in the taiga.

But there I was lying on the plank bunk in Vaskov's House, and my feeling was not one of horror. Disgust, yes; but not horror. I was numb already, and past caring. I was shocked not so much by the situation as a whole as by minor details. The smell of herring, for example. I am allergic to it. However hungry I might be, I would never touch the salt herring they dished out in prison and camp. Whereas Gertrude and Nastya, between whom I lay like a match between two others, picked the herring off the bones with their fingers. This happened each morning. And their fingers, which were level with my face, reeked of stomach-turning fish oil all day and all night. To my mind, the worst thing about Vaskov's House was this smell of herring, aggravated by the stench from the night bucket.

The investigation? It was a very strange business. As phony as was the "phony war." It was swathed in clinging layers of clammy boredom like everything to do with Vaskov's House. The young investigator Gaidukov did not even try to conceal his boredom. He yawned openly, stretched, and sometimes, unable to stand it any longer, phoned his colleague in the next room and shared the latest soccer results with him. The walls in the White House, where I was taken to be questioned, were thin, and I needed no telephone to make out pretty well what Gaidukov's friend, the other young investigator, thought about the subject.

Gracious me, what on earth would my first lot of inquisitors—Tsarevsky, Vevers, and Yelshin—have said? They had carried out their interrogations so enthusiastically, so angrily, so craftily, and sometimes with such treacherous kindliness. And for what? Just so that an imperturbable and somewhat phlegmatic Gaidukov could write out their fiery protocols afresh in his copperplate handwriting twelve years later.

They confronted me with no new charges. They required no "confessions." Gaidukov compliantly wrote into the record all I said to him, without changing a thing. He even recorded my words about the illegal methods of investigation used in '37. At that time I had still to come across the expression "I couldn't care less"; no one could have cared less than Gaidukov.

On one occasion while I was signing something, I noticed inside the file the document authorizing my present arrest. I managed to take in the words: ". . . on suspicion of continuing her terrorist activity."

"What on earth is that?" I burst out. "Am I supposed to have continued with my terrorist activity in the kindergarten?"

Gaidukov scanned the document with an air of indifference and replied without raising his voice:

"That's just for the record. . . . What do you expect us to put down when your old article is 58, sections 8 and 11? Terrorist group . . . We couldn't put you down for espionage or sabotage, could we?"

Well, he was what you might call a harmless nonentity, a pen pusher. He allowed me to have parcels from home. And I received a package consisting entirely of edible symbols. Two camp doughnuts. Which meant that Anton was visiting Vasya. The doughnuts were an extra that Anton earned for his doctoring and brought home from the quarantine center. Two open sandwiches with hard-boiled eggs and sprats: the kind they sold in the school buffet. That meant Vasya was still attending school. Finally, some pastry straws—bits of dough fried in vegetable oil—Julia's specialty. A sign that Julia was still at home.

One day I had a rare stroke of luck. I was taken along to the interrogation not, as usual, at night but in broad daylight. As I emerged from the gates of Vaskov's House I caught a glimpse of my Vasya standing beside the guardhouse with a parcel under his arm. And he spotted me. I was gripped by a brief but intense spasm of joy. There he was, alive and well, and looking reasonably fit. He hadn't taken the plane back to the mainland, he hadn't lost his head, and he hadn't given up his last year at school. There he was, bringing his mother parcels, unafraid; if he was afraid, he was mastering his terror, even though they were probably giving him hell in his Komsomol organization.

I gave him a broad smile and waved as I took my place in the car. (When later we were reunited he couldn't get over my looking so cheerful!)

But the fleeting moment of comfort passed and I was plunged back into utter despair. Yet again a prisoner . . . Again the familiar nagging feeling of a guard dogging my steps. As if there had never been a letup. The restless thoughts that tormented me at night were like an endless obituary. I composed and recomposed my life, but however I set it out it led me down the one and only escape route— the path to death. After all, I couldn't allow myself to fall into their hands a second time and go through the inferno that was Elgen.

I had no thought at all of suicide, certainly not of any particular way of killing myself. I knew that would not be necessary. It would suffice to stop resisting death, and death would come.

As was later to emerge, we had been arrested merely in order to have our status regularized to that of permanent, lifelong exile by a decision of the MGB's Special Conference. What this involved was getting the old case file copied out, sending it by courier to Moscow, waiting for it to be rubber-stamped (and there was a nationwide waiting list), and finally taking delivery of the sentence from the same leisurely courier. It took some five to six months—half a year in Vaskov's House!

Ah, had we only known this! If only we had had an inkling of these humane intentions! Then we would have had strength to bear that cell. For exile is not camp. There's no guard, no barbed wire; one is allowed to live in one's own hovel, with one's own nearest and dearest around one. . . .

But the investigators had no right to tell us what was or was not to befall us. (The only exception was my young knight-errant, Chentsov of the MGB, who, on discovering during his search a copy of "Puss in Boots" in the possession of a notorious terrorist, had told Vasya and me that now it was not at all like '37. Taught by all those years of lies, I had not believed him at the time, but it had in fact turned out to be the truth. In retrospect, I am grateful to Chentsov for his humane attempt to give us some reassurance, and glad for him that his heart had stirred at the sight of my parting from Vasya.)

All this, however, would emerge later. In the meantime we, the unfortunate possessors of names beginning with the first letters of the alphabet—you might call us the first to jump through the 1949 hoop—were left to find out from what befell us what might be the aims of this replay. We were haunted by the vision of a new period of detention in camp. We were expecting a full repetition of the entire 1937 program, and that prospect was beyond human endurance.

I was therefore preparing myself for death during my nighttime vigils, reviewing the whole course of my life, my torments, my misfortunes, and my hurts. And my many and great offenses. I recited from memory, in German, the Catholic prayers that Anton had taught me. For the first time in my life I dreamed of the church as a place of refuge. How comforting it must be to enter a cathedral, to lean one's forehead against one of the pillars. The pillar is clean and cool to the touch. There's no one else in sight. But you can feel someone's unseen hand on your head. Thou alone, O Lord, knowest how weary I am.

The debate in our cell about what was to happen to us went on day and night. People spoke of monstrous new sentences. Twenty years . . . twenty-five years . . . Only Gertrude displayed any optimism. She maintained that ghettos would be created for former prisoners, something halfway between the camps and free settlement.

"*Zum Beispiel,* a collective farm called 'Red Beet,' " she said in her comic Russian. This had a certain pleasing humor to it; more important, everyone wanted it to be the truth. From then on the whole discussion about what was awaiting us could be summed up in the words "Elgen or the 'Red Beet.' "

The October Revolution holiday* was upon us. In accordance with the best traditions, the masters of Vaskov's House decided to mark it with a massive search. This accomplished, the investigators had three days off work, not one of us was called out, and the sickening boredom that gripped our hermetically sealed cell took on, as it were, a physical form, spreading across the floor in vast dirty patches.

And then without warning, in the midst of this funereal silence on the night of November 9, the lock grated and the cell door opened with a rusty creak. They'd come for me, to take me for interrogation!

A minute later I was already greedily inhaling the frosty November wind as I stood by the guardhouse waiting for the car to appear. (From Vaskov's House we were taken for interrogation by car.) I gave the handle that lowered the side window an imperceptible turn and had a lovely whiff of oxygen. The guard pretended not to have seen.

After the holiday period Gaidukov seemed rather puffy and more blasé than ever.

"Well, your position has now been regularized," he said magisterially, patting the fat pink file containing my case with the palm of his hand. It was the same file that had been instituted back in '37. But it had a new, glossy folder clearly stamped: "Not to be destroyed." Below this stamp was another stamp with a string of ab-

---

* October Revolution Day is celebrated on November 7–8. After the revolution calendar reform was imposed, shifting dates from the Julian to the Gregorian, a thirteen-day difference since 1900.

breviations: "VChK-OGPU-NKVD-MVD-MGB." Anyone with an author's eye would say the file ran to at least twenty printer's sheets.

"Is all that really about me?" I asked limply.

"Who else, do you suppose?" said Gaidukov, surprised.

Suddenly the telephone on his desk rang.

"Yes, yes," my interrogator replied, straightening up a little, "she's with me now. Certainly, Comrade Colonel . . . this very minute, Comrade Colonel . . ."

Turning to me, Gaidukov said:

"Our chief, Colonel Tsirulnitsky, wants to see you. Follow me!"

The colonel had a very imposing, almost patrician look about him. He was moderately tall and moderately portly, with a Roman nose and a picturesque streak of gray in his still abundant head of hair. A medieval cardinal's mantle would have gone well with his appearance. But the decorations that formed a tight multicolored cluster on his chest were a reminder that his services did not date from the Middle Ages.

"Sit down" (to me). "You can go" (to Gaidukov).

What happened next was something incredible and inexplicable! The colonel suddenly wiped the look of importance off his face and addressed me by my Christian name and patronymic, as if we were having tea together.

"What a fine boy you've got! He came here to get permission to send you parcels. I admired him. And how boldly he spoke to us! People are usually afraid of us. . . ."

He uttered these last words with an odd intonation. Not pompously, not smugly, but with a certain chagrin.

"Do you have only the one son?" he asked.

This was the one question I could not bear. I was silent for some time, mentally repeating to myself Vasya's plea: "Don't cry in front of them!" The pause dragged on. The colonel looked uncomprehendingly at me.

"There were two of them. People started interfering with my life, and then I had only one."

"Was it the war?"

"The blockade. Leningrad."

"But that could have happened even if you had been there."

"No. I would have dragged him out of the flames alive."

The colonel was now looking at me with undisguised but inexplicable compassion. I pulled myself up sharply. What was I doing?

Hadn't I seen enough of their ploys over the last twelve years? Any moment now he would be offering to release me—in exchange for certain services. So I answered his kindly look with one of wary hostility. The colonel smiled wryly.

"You don't like us. . . ."

"Why should I?" was the unguarded response that fell from my lips. Then I got scared. He had got what he wanted; he had made me talk out of turn. And now, once he found out that he could do nothing with me, the reprisals would start. I recalled the tales I had heard of the punishment cells in Vaskov's House.

But the colonel had no thought of turning nasty. He tapped his pencil on the glass table top and said, reflectively, as if thinking aloud:

"Yes, you have a wonderful son. I've got one just the same. . . . The same age, that is. But whether he would have the pluck to stand up for his father at the crucial moment and in such a terrifying place—that I don't know. So you see that every cloud has its silver lining. Now you know for sure how much your son loves you."

No, I had not yet turned completely into stone. The words about my son's love, from an MGB colonel in the White House, of all people, shattered me. I broke my vow to Vasya and let "them" see me cry.

The colonel got up from his chair with surprising agility, poured some water into a glass, and brought it over to me. I gulped it down feverishly, my teeth chattering against the glass. And suddenly I heard a totally unbelievable phrase coming from that quarter.

"I know that you are innocent. . . ."

What could it mean? Was this some utterly fiendish ploy? Or, or . . . Could it possibly be meant sincerely?

"Yes, I know that for a fact," said the colonel. "But it is beyond my powers to take the appropriate action. However, I can make things easier for you. And I will. Read this!"

He extracted a folder from the drawer and moved the table lamp closer to me.

I kept reading the words mechanically, unable in my confusion to make sense of the official jargon. The sentences turned into bubbles that burst, leaving no trace. But at last it became a bit clearer.

The communication was addressed to the Special Conference

Attached to the MGB, USSR. It was a copy of the one that had been sent to Moscow. "For the attention of . . . Case of . . . Accused of . . ." and so on. Well, that's just the special code used in the Georgian Serpent's realm. But here was the crux: "Banishment to a recognized place of exile." Forced settlement! The "Red Beet Collective Farm"! How wonderful! In other words, not Elgen, not the camps, not the barbed wire. . . . So I was to have the open sky over my head. . . .

I raised my shining eyes to the colonel.

"Settlement? Free settlement? Can I be with my family?"

"Yes. And you'll be leaving prison soon. Only a few more days to go."

He handed me another document. It was a copy of a letter he had sent to the Public Prosecutor. In it he recommended that the "preventive measures" taken with regard to me be changed, and that "detention be replaced by an undertaking not to leave the locality." He based his request on the argument that my infant son had been left without means of support.

"You see? I've turned your seventeen-year-old son into a child, so as to get you released."

"What about the Prosecutor?"

"He has agreed. I spoke to him today. But his decision isn't official yet. He's promised to let me have it tomorrow. Well, by the time the document has gone through all the official channels, that'll be another five days or so. So, you can count on being at home with your son in a week. Next time you're called out 'packed and ready' it will mean you're released. And you'll be back at work at your old place."

The thought flashed across my mind that I should ask him there and then to give me permission to adopt Tonya. But he had already pressed the button of the doorbell, and the guard who had come to take me was standing in the doorway.

"Take the prisoner away," the colonel ordered, hardly moving his lips. His face was haughty and inscrutable again. All that he had been saying to me a moment ago seemed like fantasy, a waking dream.

I returned to my cell at dawn. They were already handing out the hot water, bread, and herring. As I went across the prison yard, I filled my lungs with fresh November air, and after that the pungent smell of herring bowled me over. In other respects, too, the reality of the cell was even more unbearable after the ephemeral visions shown me by Colonel Tsirulnitsky.

"You're looking as white as a sheet," Gertrude said to me. "What did they say to you?"

"Later," I said, and refusing not only the herring but the bread, I lay down on the bunk and closed my eyes.

For fear of ruining the dream or inviting bad luck, I resolved to tell nobody about the colonel's strange behavior.

A day went by. . . . two days . . . three. Hope and despair. Despair and hope. People lay all around me, huddled together on the plank bunks like sardines, and I felt as lonely as a solitary street lamp on a deserted square.

The fourth day they brought me my regular food parcel, done up in a bundle. This was an omen of total defeat. If they had really been on the point of releasing me, they would not have accepted the parcel on my behalf. In other words, nothing had come of it. The Public Prosecutor had probably refused to sign.

Toward the end of the fifth day, when from sheer anguish I could feel the root of every hair on my head, I gave in: I woke up Gertrude and told her the whole story of my conversation with the colonel.

"*Ach, Genia, wie dumm Du bist!*" Gertrude exclaimed. She proceeded to deliver herself of a whole long speech in which she expressed astonishment that I could for a single moment have believed such statements coming from the colonel. It was perfectly clear: he had wanted to sound me out; to worm his way into my confidence; to convert me into an ally. "You say he asked nothing of you? Just you wait, he will. . . ."

I felt ashamed. How true—there were no limits to my stupid credulity. Even orthodox Gertrude took a realistic view of the "humanity" of our jailers. And yet . . . I had played the same record hundreds of times, going over and over in my mind everything the colonel had said. I hadn't dreamed it, after all. . . . All right, suppose he was lying. I had still read with my own eyes the document about "banishment to a recognized place of exile." But there again, they could so easily fabricate any sort of document.

Five more days went by. It was only on November 19—by which time I had finally and irrevocably succumbed to the semioblivion of the prison, with a scar across my soul—it was only then that I heard the words I had already ceased to expect: "Pack your things!"

I was not the only person to jump down from the bunks in reply. All my neighbors leapt to their feet one after the other. For this was an epoch-making event for all of us. Not one single person had left the cell packed until now; finally the fate of one of us had been decided. And this would be a bench mark for the rest.

The guard had stayed in the doorway until I had got my things together, so there was no opportunity to exchange messages. Nor was there any need to. The looks they gave me were sufficient: "Get us news somehow. . . ." "Please, if you can . . ."

Within a few minutes I was in the prison office. There sat the same hulking specimen who a month previously had drawn up the inventory of my personal effects. He was now meticulously laying them out in front of me: three hairpins, one indelible pencil, and—most important—the chubby, celluloid leg of Tonya's doll. How I adore the scrupulous observance of legal niceties!

"Sign!"

In came my investigator, Gaidukov. I had never suspected that he could look so kind and jolly.

"Well, that's it," he said. "You'll be home for supper. We just have to drop by the Prosecutor's office in the car, where I'll pick up a document for you, and then I'll drop you off and you can go wherever you like. Within the limits of Magadan, that is. . . ."

When I saw his mood of benevolence, a complicated plan occurred to me.

"Comrade Investigator! I've left my spectacles in the cell. I can't read without them."

This was a barefaced lie. At that stage I had not yet taken to wearing spectacles. Gaidukov sent the giant off to the cell to look for them; he returned, inevitably, empty-handed. The mythical spectacles couldn't be found.

"Could I please go there myself, just for a minute, with the guard? I promise not to say a word."

This was completely against the rules. But today Gaidukov wanted to be consistently kind. He went with me himself. He hurried me along frantically, but I managed, as I scrambled about on the upper bunks, to whisper to Gertrude our secret password, "The Red Beet." Now at least they wouldn't go in fear of being newly sentenced to the camps.

In the course of the ten minutes I spent waiting for Gaidukov in the car, parked outside the Public Prosecutor's office, all the old demons made frantic efforts to take over my mind. Dozens of premonitions, each one worse than the last. Any moment now Gaidukov would come out and say that the Prosecutor had said no. And then back to jail. Or he would inform me with a sly grin for just what diabolical ends Colonel Tsirulnitsky had been so kind to me. I could not begin to imagine what they might be, but it would doubtless be something abysmally horrid, cynical, and shameless. . . . And after that the only step remaining to me would be death.

"You can go home," said Gaidukov, opening the car door. And he said it in such a friendly voice that I went pink with shame at all my suppositions. What had I turned into? Life had so trampled on me that I had completely lost the ability to believe in anything good. And yet a miracle had occurred: I was on my way home. Home! Someone had helped me to climb out of the abyss; but instead of being grateful and pondering over the thought that even in the Georgian Serpent's main residence there were people in whom the sense of decency was not entirely dead, I was busily ferreting out traps and trip wires.

"Thank you," I said sincerely, addressing the words not to Gaidukov but to a point somewhere above his head.

"You're welcome." He smiled and said, "Come to the White House at one o'clock tomorrow, and ask for me so that we can get you to sign the undertaking not to leave the area."

The MGB car disappeared around the corner, and I remained there on the sidewalk with a large, ill-tied bundle in my arms. In their fear that I might suddenly be sent off into the wilds, the members of my household had brought all sorts of warm garments to the prison for me, and now I was drooping under the weight of this accumulation. Besides, I had grown unused to fresh air in the fetid atmosphere of Vaskov's House. I could hardly stagger along. My head swam, and my legs buckled under me.

Completely exhausted, I put my bundle down and paused to recover my breath. Suddenly I heard a quiet "Oh." Our methodology expert from the Preschool Methodology Center had stopped beside me. The selfsame Aleksandra Mikhailovna Shilnikova who used to lecture about the affecting love of the children for the Great and Wise One. She looked at me, and I saw, as if for the first time, her typically Ural face with its high forehead, gentle mouth, and large round eyes. A very human face it turned out to be, when the official overlay was removed from it.

"They've released you?" she asked. "Released you for good?"

"I can't be certain about the 'for good' part. But 'for the time being' is good enough. They've released me for the time being. I'm trying to get home. . . ."

"Let me help you carry your bundle. You must be very weak, I can see."

We slowly climbed the slope that led to our ghetto. Aleksandra Mikhailovna, from whom in the last two years I had heard so many fancy speeches about the goals of preschool training, carried my dusty prison bundle, offered to lend me money, and tucked all sorts of odds and ends from her own bag into my pocket. Her soul could still put out green shoots beneath the dead layer of crinkly paper flowers.

(After the Twentieth Congress, after the delivery of Khrushchev's special report, Aleksandra Mikhailovna came up to me and said, "Heavens, how blind I was! How I used to idealize that man!" She could no longer bring herself to utter the name that had so recently been sacred to her. "You who knew about it all must have considered me a hopeless case." "No," I answered, "the fur jacket spoke for you." "What fur jacket?" "Don't you remember the old fur jacket in which I had bundled up all my prison belongings . . . and which you helped carry?")

We were already in sight of our building when we came across Vasya. He was walking toward us in the company of his school friend, Felix Chernetsky. For a moment we were too surprised to throw ourselves into each other's arms.

(Later, Vasya told me that when Felix spotted me he had said, "That's your mother ahead of us." Vasya had taken this for a joke and retorted, "Aren't you ashamed to joke about things like that?")

"Vasya!"

Once more his face turned into that of a little child. As it had been when they came to take me away.

"Mamma darling!"

How wonderfully cozy was our sooty, crooked little corridor! What a blissfully domestic smell of fried onions it contained! And how dear to me were all those people clustered around our door!

Anton wouldn't be home until evening. He had to do a distance of eight kilometers on foot each day in order to hand over his prison supper to Vasya. So I thought I might as well run along to the kindergarten and pick up Tonya, so that we could all be together again in the evening. All together.

It was the rest period in the kindergarten. The children were all asleep. But the teachers, nannies, and nurses enveloped me in such genuine warmth and compassion that they purged my soul of all the accretions gathered in Vaskov's House. I learned that on the day of the November holiday they had taken presents to Vasya—pastries, candy . . . How good people were! The previous day's thoughts of death seemed to me remote, just as if they had never in fact entered my head.

One of the teachers from Tonya's group came up to ask to be forgiven. The little girl had howled so bitterly, calling for her mamma, that they had had to tell her a lie to the effect that Mamma had died and would not be coming back.

"We hadn't really expected you back. . . . Please forgive me. . . ."

On our way home Tonya, who was clinging to my arm with all her strength, chattered away, but every now and then inserted the question, "You won't be dying any more, will you?"

Julia was determined to give Anton a surprise: that evening, before Anton arrived, she instructed me to take Tonya in my arms and sit down on the other side of the screen. For my part, I would dearly have loved to greet Anton not in the room but in the corridor, but I could not refuse Julia. I let her have her joke.

I heard Anton come in and take off his galoshes by the door. He gave a deep sigh, put something down on the table, and reminded Vasya that tomorrow was the day for handing in the parcel at the prison. Suddenly Tonya couldn't keep the secret any longer.

"But Mamma is not going to die any more," she announced, jumping down from my knees and running out from behind the screen.

Anton tugged at the screen so hard that it fell over, making an appalling clatter. The neighbors rushed in again to see what the noise meant.

"You? You?" Anton said over and over again.

The neighbors around us wiped away their tears, but Anton and I did not cry. He kept saying, "How thin you've become!" and I said, "Never mind, I'll soon get better."

It was nighttime. Anton had gone back to his camp. Julia had returned to her workshop for the night shift. Tonya was sleeping on the couch. Vasya and I were left talking endlessly, lying in our beds. He had already wished me good night several times over, but our conversation kept picking up again.

Finally I fell asleep, savoring even in my sleep the deeply comforting feeling of the clean sheets and the blanket cover. I was awakened by Vasya's voice.

"Mamma, are you asleep?"

"Yes. What is it?"

"Nothing. I just wanted to say, Sleep well, Mother dear. . . ."

And half an hour later, again:

"Sleep well, Mother dear. . . ."

11

· *After the earthquake*

The first glow of joy after my release from prison had faded. The reaction had set in. I would wake up in the morning pale from lack of sleep, with swollen eyelids and a pain in my head. And there it was again, that same feeling of being doomed.

A December dawn in Kolyma was staring at me through the window. There was nowhere to hide from it. I had to go out into the street, mingle with my fellows, and learn what was in the news.

The news was distinguished by its unrelieved sameness. The strict alphabetical order was still being adhered to. Each day they hauled in a new batch of "repeaters." The only surprising thing was how they managed to pack so many people into the confined space of Vaskov's House. By now they would probably be occupying the floor space under the bunks, too. Each day the alphabet got closer to Julia's letter. Each evening, before going to sleep, Julia would issue instructions.

"If they come for me today, just remember: my fur gauntlets are being mended. So please pick them up at the shop and bring them with you. Don't bring any bread; the ration's enough. But don't forget to bring sugar. If I don't have sugar, I go crazy. . . ."

I had given up saying, "Don't talk such rubbish." I replied tersely, "All right. I'll do as you say."

For a while after my release everyone's morale was high, now that they had it first hand from me that they would only be subjected to compulsory settlement and that no one was being given a new term in camp. But somehow, with the immediate prospect of Vaskov's House for who knew how long before them, their radiant hopes began to pale.

Vasya went around looking gloomy. He had only six months to do before finishing his secondary school, and he had produced a crop of poor grades. Any attempt on my part to raise this particular subject caused his hackles to rise.

"I suppose the MGB is worrying about my marks, is that it?"

There was no point in answering. It was a fact that the MGB had become part of our daily life. You could turn a blind eye, if you wanted, to their previous, prearrest form of surveillance: that had been done in secret. But now they were watching me openly, and the shadow of the White House had fallen across our little house of cards, across our precarious family happiness. The first week after my discharge from prison I had had to go there three times: the first time to sign an undertaking not to leave the area, the second and third times to lodge a complaint against the personnel department, which was refusing to reinstate me in my job. And after that they had simply directed me to report to them twice a week until they received from Moscow a decision on my new case.

A telephone call from "you know where" sufficed to get me back my old job. I was now playing the piano again, but I could not help catching the pitying glances my colleagues directed at me, or overhearing snatches of their conversation about the head being on the lookout for a new music instructor. The head had become most reluctant to let Tonya accompany me home.

"The more she gets used to it, the harder it'll be for her to break the habit. . . ."

Anton, too, was not always successful in getting to visit us in the evening, because the regime in camp had been tightened up in connection with the approach of a historic date: the seventieth birthday of the Inspirer and Organizer of All Our Victories, the Great Philologist and Best Friend of Soviet Gymnasts—Generalissimo Stalin.

Julia insisted that the radio be kept permanently on. Her theory was: "We must listen to everything." And our loudspeaker blared away from morning to night, pouring out obsequious dithyrambs of hero-worship in honor of the Leader. The seventieth-birthday celebrations lasted almost an entire week. The orgies of ecstatic raving and declarations of love and devotion went on for hours at a time. Each national minority performed a witch dance of its own. The Central Asians rattled tambourines and clicked their tongues. The Siberians bellowed heart-rendingly about the wide-open spaces of their wonderful homeland, where they had supposedly devised their joyful song of praise to the Great Friend and Leader. The people of Ryazan and Voronezh put in some fast heel-and-toe work in honor of the Generalissimo, punctuating the strains of the accordion with wild cries. Then the radio transmitted the festivities on Red Square, with thunderous bands and choirs. This, too, was staged crescendo, and it looked as if the crescendo would never reach its peak.

It all seems hardly believable now. Did we not in fact dream up those dervishlike dances that accompanied the departure from the historic scene of that year of evil memory? Alas, no. Until quite recently the accuracy of our recollection was regularly confirmed, every time we twiddled the knob and came across the sound of those piercing, high soprano voices screeching out their superlatives, in paroxysms of love for the Great Helmsman.

On December 25, 1949, my mother died. My second arrest had been the final drop that filled her cup to overflowing. How she had scurried around, my poor mother, when she learned from Vasya's letter that he had again been left on his own, without me! How desperately she had tried, from so far away, to help, to come to the rescue! She had sent telegrams to unknown persons in Magadan, telegrams beginning with the words: "I beg you . . ."; she, a withered little old lady of almost seventy, in her flimsy overcoat trimmed with braid, had plucked up courage enough to cross the threshold of that fearful ministry, to try to make the sleek, clean-shaven duty officers understand that according to all the laws a mother had the right at least to know whether her daughter was alive or not, and, if alive, where she was.

Thank goodness my letter about my release from Vaskov's House had reached her in time. And I had also had her very last message, written on a badly ruled sheet of exercise paper. My mother's handwriting was now large and sprawling. She complained of her left eye. She could hardly see anything with it. But with her right eye she had made out my handwriting, and understood that I had got out alive again. She therefore wrote, "How happy I am!" But she wrote this only a week before her own death.

She was a quite ordinary, uncelebrated mother. The mother of a prisoner. She had accomplished her silent, unconscious feat of endurance in the years when she was an aged widow without a home of her own. But she was not daunted by illness, by age, or by chronic undernourishment. For her there was no such thing as the lost land beyond the horizon in our grotesque kingdom of the Georgian Serpent. All those long, thirteen years, day in, day out, she had never given up searching for me wherever I might have been put away. If her letters of those thirteen years were published they would make a human document of compelling force. But the letters had been taken away from me during searches, when I was in transit, and at the time of my second arrest.

I no longer have any letters of hers. But two photographs survive. One shows a dark-eyed, thoughtful high-school girl in 1902. The young lady was unobtrusively reading a not entirely comprehensible but prohibited and therefore intriguing volume, *Critique of the Gotha Program.* The other photograph shows a sorrowful old lady. She had studied every syllable of the rules for corresponding with prisoners, which were also not entirely comprehensible. As well she might, for from time to time she entered into single combat with the Great Slaughterer and, in her holy innocence, was genuinely amazed at his refusal to honor even the rules that he himself had made. In the innumerable petitions she had sent off, she had always written: "On the basis of Paragraph such-and-such of Decree such-and-such, I request permission to . . ."

They brought me the telegram with the news of Mother's death on December 26. The loudspeaker was still in the throes of obsequious jubilation. Someone gave an earsplitting yell, "Long live . . ." blotting out even the sound of the massed bands. Yes, "he" had lived to see his seventieth birthday. . . . But my mother had not. . . .

There was one blow after another. The decree of the MGB Special Conference on my new case had arrived. I had been sentenced to compulsory settlement for life within the confines of Eastern Siberia.

It was, of course, not the fact of lifelong exile that was lethal for me, for all of us. On the contrary, that was a lesser evil than the monstrous prospect of a new camp sentence. What was lethal about it was the address: Eastern Siberia. Going there would mean the total collapse of our house of cards. I would be taken away and Anton would be left behind in Kolyma to serve his last four years. And after that he, too, would be sentenced to permanent compulsory settlement, but in a different place from where I would be. Vasya would be left entirely on his own because Julia's letter in the alphabet—and with it Vaskov's House—was drawing inexorably nearer. In the spring Tonya would be sent off to a special children's home. Finally, by all accounts, the journey awaiting me was terrifying. Some people had already done it, and few of them had lived to tell the tale. One in particular who had recently fallen victim to such a journey was a friend of Umansky's—the young, talented Vasily Kuprianov.

The irony of it all was that this particular resettlement address was a concession I owed to the sympathy and leniency of Colonel Tsirulnitsky. He had wanted to make things easier for me, and in consequence my papers had been made out not for Kolyma, a "remote place of banishment," but for Eastern Siberia, a "less remote place. . . ." It was, after all, on the mainland. How could he have known all my circumstances?

After receiving the sentence, my investigator, Gaidukov, suggested I come along and register with him the following day. The convoy to Eastern Siberia had been put off for the time being owing to exceptionally severe frost, but it might be rescheduled at any time.

A bizarre life started for me. My bundle of possessions for the journey stood all ready in the corner of the room. Every time I had to report I said good-by to everyone in the morning as usual. But as soon as I had done my stint at the piano, playing heroic marches and lyrical songs, off I rushed—not home, but to the White House for registration. It was there, in the corridor, that one day Colonel Tsirulnitsky spotted me.

"What's wrong with you? Are you ill?" he asked, looking at my drawn, yellow face with black circles under my eyes.

"No, not ill. One can't regard despair as a form of illness."

"Why despair?" the colonel asked with exasperation. "You were given a relatively mild sentence. Not Kolyma with its permafrost, but Eastern Siberia. There they have a real summer, and vegetables and the railway. Your relatives can come and visit you."

The colonel was looking at me with undisguised annoyance. He had expected gratitude, not reproaches.

"I've already settled down here. I have a place to live, a job, and people who are near and dear to me. But out there, in Eastern Siberia, I'll have to begin all over again. I'll be at the mercy of all and sundry. . . ." I tried to explain the situation to him.

After a short pause the colonel swung open the door to his office.

"Come in! If you prefer Kolyma as a place of exile, put in an application to that effect to the Special Conference and we'll forward it to Moscow. Say you are too ill to make the journey."

"But what about the convoy?"

"We'll put it off until the answer comes through. . . ."

I was so excited that I was quite unable to compose the text of my application and the colonel had to dictate it to me. "In view of severe deterioration in my state of health . . . I could not possibly stand a long-distance convoy journey. . . . In view of the fact that my son is studying in the final class of the Magadan Secondary School . . ."

"And my daughter's only little," I suddenly added.

"What daughter?"

And then I launched into Tonya's history, for the colonel's benefit. Tonya was the one who wouldn't be able to stand a long journey. . . . And all this while she was on the list for Komsomolsk. Would the colonel like to take a look at the little girl? She was right here, sitting in the corridor, waiting for me.

"In this place? A little child?"

"Yes, I had either to bring her with me here or to return her to the kindergarten. I must take her to the baths today."

"Well, do you want to adopt her officially?"

"I tried to. But they refused. They said it couldn't be done in the case of 'repressed' persons."

This was three-year-old Tonya's first meeting with the all-powerful ministry. Her dialogue with the colonel ran roughly as follows:

"Hello, Tonya. Tell me, would you like to go to Moscow?"

"With Mamma?"

"No, with me. Mamma has to work. . . ."

"I won't go without Mamma."

"Hm . . . that's too bad. They have a circus in Moscow, with bears and monkeys and wolves. . . ."

"We've got Agafya, our cat, at home."

"Agafya, you say?" replied the colonel. He lifted the telephone receiver. After getting through to the Department of Guardianship and Foster Care attached to the Town Educational Authority, he said brusquely that he had recently been approached by deportee-resettler so-and-so. On the subject of the little girl Antonia. Well then, the view of the MGB was that the request should be granted.

I could just visualize how that must have bowled over the sharp-eared, batlike creature who had told me that I ought to have been deprived of my maternal rights even over my own children.

What, in fact, had come over the colonel? Why had he displayed feelings so totally at variance with his profession? This man, laden down with decorations for his service in "the Organization," had done so much for me. He had had me released from prison. (Others, while awaiting reregistration as permanent exiles, had had to wait in prison not one month, like me, but five or six months.) He had helped me get my job back in the face of the active opposition of the personnel department. He had undertaken to try and get my place of exile changed and meanwhile had postponed the convoy. And now he had also helped me over Tonya. . . .

At the time his mysterious conduct was a riddle to me. Only after the colonel's departure from Magadan did I hear that during my 1949 odyssey the colonel already knew he was shortly about to be retired. He was flabbergasted by this and inwardly confused, as he could find no explanation for the "injustice" done to him. Perhaps for the first time in his life he paused to think about what was happening to other people. I had simply chanced his way during the period when he was thoroughly mixed up.

What had happened to him was connected with another of the earthquakes of 1949, the epicenter of which was located on the mainland. We had only just begun to catch the first faint rumblings of the distant thunder. The difficulty in the colonel's case was that despite all his services to the Organization, he had something that told against him in his personal file—a fatal and ineradicable defect. It related to the fifth entry in his personal questionnaire, the one that dealt with national origin.

Be that as it may, within a few days of the meeting between
Tonya and the colonel, the two of us emerged from the Magadan
civil registration office, bearing a certificate in which my first
name, patronymic, and surname were listed in the column "Mother."
Although Julia continued to assert that it was a wild idea of mine
for which we would still have to pay, she too heaved a sigh of relief when she realized that we no longer had to fear the children's
draft, the threat of which had been hanging over us for the past
year and a half.

The reply to my application to the MGB Special Conference was
comparatively quick in arriving: it took about six weeks. I was
graciously allowed to remain in Kolyma for life. We celebrated
the event with a family banquet. It's a splendid thing, the theory of
the lesser evil. I joyfully accepted from the commandant's hands
the appropriate document—my substitute for an identity card, as it
were—which recorded that I was limited in my freedom of movement to within a radius of seven kilometers from Magadan, that I
was under the open surveillance of the MGB, and that I was obliged
to report to them twice a month. And that all this was *for life!*

My enthusiasm was genuine. For surely it is the lesser evil: to be
able to remain with your nearest and dearest in a hovel you have
made your own, to work in a kindergarten, to be surrounded by
comrades from prison and camp of many years standing. It might
have been the long march to Eastern Siberia, plagued by scurvy,
dysentery, and starvation, a journey like the one responsible for
the slow, agonizing death of Umansky's friend, Vasily Kuprianov.
It might have been some new, unknown wasteland where I would
have had to begin all over again without a roof over my head or a
friendly neighbor.

Nor did the "permanent" and "for life" tags induce any feeling
of desperation in me.

"It remains to be seen *whose* life is in question, mine or 'his,' "
I commented to my intimates. "And he's older than my mother,
anyway."

We were still rejoicing at the news of my permanent settlement
within the confines of Kolyma when another piece of good news
was heard. Good news, if interpreted according to the theory of
the lesser evil. In Vaskov's House what would today be called a
demographic explosion had taken place. As a result of the absolute
overcrowding of the prison, our local MGB authorities had secured

Moscow's permission to complete the registration of repeaters for compulsory life resettlement without preliminary incarceration. From then on all those scheduled for reprocessing as exiles no longer had to be arrested. They were simply summoned to the White House, where their passports were taken from them; they had to give a signed undertaking not to leave the district; and then they were allowed to go home. A month or two later, after their cases had been processed in Moscow, the people in question were summoned a second time and given in place of their passport the sort of document that I now owned. To our great joy, this beneficial reform had taken place at the stage when they had got to the letter *I*. And so they never did reach *K* and with it Julia's arrest.

In this peculiarly paradoxical way our house of cards not only withstood the earthquake of 1949 but emerged from it if anything a shade stronger.

Perhaps it would be more accurate to compare our one-room apartment with an ark floating on the waters of Creation. The fact remains that despite a heavy buffeting, our ark floated out into the new decade.

The fifties were with us. It was the spring of 1950. The scenes flashed past as in the cinema. Vasya was in his last days at school. But he was faced with a graduation certificate with a failing grade in physics! Having a testimonial like that on top of his biographical data, how would he ever get into a university?

The evening of the school graduation ceremony, I was sitting among the parents of the graduates alongside the colonels' wives and the generals' wives. I listened to an eager, long-nosed lady historian calling on her pupils not to forget our shining, golden Magadan, built by the hands of enthusiasts. They should be proud that they had studied in such a town.

I was in my best dress, one that Mamma had sent in her last parcel. It was from my sister Natasha's wardrobe and had seemed perfectly respectable to me up to that evening. But alongside the silks, the fox furs, and the abundance of jewelry I looked like the lowest of kitchen maids whose son had received an education thanks to her masters' charity.

(I am really being dreadfully ungrateful. These tastelessly overdressed matrons had shown their humanity and provided Vasya with free lunches at the expense of the parents' committee all the time I had been in Vaskov's House.)

That evening Vasya got drunk for the first time, and I had to drag him home through the dark streets, observing myself in this classically Russian role and sobbing bitterly as I went along. The next morning he begged forgiveness like a little boy and swore never to repeat the performance. But I cried inconsolably.

In fact, I was crying not over Vasya's debut in the art of drinking but because another fearful ordeal was approaching: the day of Vasya's departure for the mainland. How they had flown, our two years together! Now he was off again. And now that he had become mine, become ours, I would be grieving for him even more than I used to grieve for the four-year-old son from whom I had been parted.

For the first time it dawned on me that compulsory settlement for life—even in the Kolyma area—was not quite such a tasty dish, after all. Although my son promised to fly out for his holidays and I promised him, come what may, to put aside money for the journey, both of us had the same question in our minds: Was permanent separation in store for us?

The day came. Magadan Airport was still virtually deserted in those days. The free parents of Vasya's schoolmates had come, like myself, to see off their children but, unlike me, they were happily promising their children to come on leave to the mainland very soon.

Boarding. Our last embrace. Our final, ridiculous words. Something about galoshes, I think: Had he forgotten his galoshes? A small dot in the sky, buzzing like a bumblebee. It flew away, carrying from me my last son of my own flesh and blood, the only surviving offshoot of my real family. And I stood there all alone on the deserted airfield, looking fixedly into the sky, although there was no longer anything to be seen. Alone . . . Anton could not afford to be seen around in public places, so he had said good-by to Vasya the previous evening. Julia had done so at work. I hadn't taken Tonya with me for fear she would cry.

Vasya had flown off. As if he had existed only in a dream. I could barely drag my leaden feet back to the bus stop. Arriving home, I entered the room. That, too, would not be mine much longer. Tonya and I would have to leave because my Julia was getting married. I was glad for her and for her future husband. He was a very steady, thoughtful ex-teacher from Byelorussia, a former employee of the Minsk Education Department. He had served his sentence and was content to stay put. In Minsk, prior to his arrest, he had been married to a Jew. She had been killed by the Nazis during the occupation. At the same time they had also killed his two children, a boy and a girl, although they were registered as Byelorussians. A kind, gentle person, he had one peculiarity: he could not bear the sight of little girls. They all seemed to him like his murdered five-year-old daughter. "Please forgive me for not talking to your Tonya. I cannot. She reminds me of my daughter."

Yes, I was glad for Julia, but it was hard for me to have to leave this room, which was still so full of Vasya. I tried not to show my sadness to Julia, who was giving me so much help in my efforts to obtain new accommodations.

Finally our approaches were successful. On the ground floor of our building there was an enormous communal kitchen, the size of a barn. They allowed me to have eight square meters of it partitioned off with plywood.

It was not cozy in our new home. There was a constant smell of the remains of cabbage soup, burned milk, and fried fish. The kitchen came to life early in the morning. Fifteen women, several of them former common criminals, were constantly in and out of it, discussing their daily business, quarreling, singing—all at the top of their voices and in the choicest language.

When Anton looked in during the evening he tried to comfort me: he would soon be leaving camp and we would exchange this room for another. I responded with a tired smile, much as one might smile at a child who had promised to cut off the head of the Georgian Serpent. There were still two years to go before the end of his sentence. If they let him out at all. He was a German, after all. And these were bad times!

Certainly the times were just as unquiet as ever. For '50 was turning out to be no easier than '49. Ex-zeks like ourselves were being sentenced to permanent compulsory settlement at an ever-increasing rate. And many of them had not been allowed to remain in Magadan but had been sent off deeper into the taiga. Each day brought new tidings, all of the same order. Shura Sidorenko and Hans Stern had committed suicide. They had lived together for years and loved each other to distraction. When they had been sentenced to resettlement they had been dispatched to opposite ends of the Kolyma wilderness. They had been refused permission to register their marriage, which would have allowed them to live

together in exile: he was an Austrian subject. They had stoked up
the stove in their little shack, blocked off the chimney, and died
from suffocation. My old friend the physician from Belichye,
Kalambet, had hanged himself. Tina Keller had gone mad. Nor had
our Gertrude been allowed to stay in Magadan after her release
from Vaskov's House; she had been sent to Omsukchan, from where
she had been writing letters quite unlike her. She made very little
attempt at a theoretical justification of the "present stage" and instead complained bitterly about her own hardships.

The news reaching us from the mainland was sinister. Nothing
but tales of martyrdom and long lists of rearrested people. My fear
of Eastern Siberia had been well founded. Although it was considered a nonremote region, our people there were succumbing
to starvation since they were denied work, even manual labor. They
were also succumbing to grief since they were cut off from all the
friends who had shared their misfortunes for so many years. Everybody was shocked by the news of the suicide of Lipa Kaplan.
They all remembered her in the camp as the picture of health, always laughing, an irrepressible tomboy. The sight of her always
made Zimmerman angry: "You look as flourishing as if you were on
a vacation!" Afterward, when Zimmerman was in the offing, we
used to shout to Lipa: "Make yourself scare, or those rosy cheeks
will land you in Izvestkovaya!" And this red-cheeked, fun-loving
girl had taken poison when she was about to be rearrested.

Was there a single ray of hope to be seen through the impenetrable gloom? I was incredulous and almost annoyed when Anton
kept telling me that he now had hopes of early release. What was
the point of such childish talk? It would be quite something if he
avoided collecting an additional sentence! But again and again he
told me in some detail how he had succeeded in curing a very high-
placed official of his long-standing eczema. The man had considered
himself incurable and was now overjoyed to be well again. He
had sworn that he would get the doctor released before the expiry of
his sentence, even if he were a thousand per cent German. No, I
couldn't take all that seriously. It simply didn't fit in with what
was going on around us at the time.

But we lived in a land of paradoxes. One day, fairly late in the
evening when Tonya was already asleep and I was filling out,
between convulsive yawns, one of my endless programs of musical
exercises, there was a knock at our new plywood door. It was a

strange knock, victorious. It had the rhythm of the "Triumphal March" in *Aida*.

"Tell me, please, is this not the apartment of Dr. Walter?" asked Anton, hauling his wooden camp suitcase through the narrow door. "I believe this is the apartment of the free Dr. Walter. And you, in all probability, must be his wife, Frau Walter?"

He flashed his teeth, chuckling loudly. He woke up Tonya and rumpled her hair. He switched on the bright overhead bulb. Then he spread out his release certificate on the table. It was no dream. He really had been released early, two years prior to the expiration of his *third* sentence.

Now our eight square meters of ex-kitchen space had to accommodate a ménage of three. Anton now worked as a free doctor in the same hospital where he had just been practicing as a prisoner. But in order to have him registered for residence on my housing space allocation, we were asked to produce our marriage registration certificate. This was the only right accorded forced settlers: the right to "joint residence," as it was called, if they were officially married. However, this applied only to new marriages, contracted at the place of exile. People who had married on the mainland and had been separated in '37 were not to be reunited under any circumstances.

I did not particularly want to visit the civil registry. I had complicated, anguished feelings toward my mainland husband, Pavel Aksyonov, or rather, toward the memory of him. For, irrespective of whether he was alive or dead, I was firmly convinced that we would never meet again. In that other, first, life of mine, which now seemed like something that had come to me in a dream, we had loved and understood one another. I do not think that we would ever have parted if the Beloved Father and the Greatest Friend of Soviet Families had not taken a hand in the matter. And I had continued to love Pavel as one loves the dear departed. It was strange, but it seemed to me that he and Anton would have taken to each other. I often used to tell Vasya about his father in the presence of Anton, who happily joined in these conversations. I don't know whether this meant I was a criminal and a bigamist. I felt no twinge of conscience. But now that registration of my marriage to Anton had become a practical, immediate question, it suddenly seemed to me, by some inexplicable twist of logic, that for Pavel's sake I must not register this union. It was as if the involvement of the civil registry would be an insult to him.

Formally I was entitled to consider myself a widow because, back in '39, in answer to my written inquiry about the fate of my husband, I had been handed a certificate stating that he had died of pneumonia. But after that definitive notification, letters from him had continued to arrive. When Alyosha died, Mother had sent me a telegram: "You must stay alive for Vasya's sake. He has lost his father already." But even after that there were rumors that Pavel was alive and at Inta.

Anton, who had noticed that I kept putting off my visit to the civil registry, understood it all without words.

"But after all, it's just a police procedure. We have to do this to avoid unnecessary suffering. Otherwise we may end up like Shura and Hans. You'll be told to go west and I'll be ordered off in the opposite direction. . . ."

In the civil registry they didn't ask for any documentary proof of the death of my husband or of Anton's first wife. It appeared that there was a law permitting a new marriage in the event of ten years' absence without trace of one of the spouses. And all those who had been buried alive in one or other of the lands of the Georgian Serpent's kingdom were considered missing, both from the mainland and from the other corners of the kingdom.

In this way we became by the beginning of '51 the possessors of a number of weighty documents: a marriage certificate, Tonya's birth certificate, and Vasya's university entrance certificate. Despite his minimal marks, Vasya had managed to get accepted by the Medical Faculty and had sent us the certificate to this effect just in case.

However modest these documents, they nevertheless possessed a particle of the magic force that all papers exert in our country. They helped create some form of defense, however fragile, around our house of cards. At the very least we had ready official answers to suspicious persons who inquired, "What is she/he to you?"

The twists and turns of a prisoner's fate are beyond understanding! As things had worked out, our little house of cards had not only withstood the earthquake of '49–'50, but had acquired legal title.

Only, however, until the next subterranean tremor made itself felt.

12

A new wave of persecutions was not long in coming. This time the misfortune arose from my own righteous labors. As we were constantly short of money and I now had to send regular remittances to Vasya, I welcomed any opportunity for giving private lessons. And although on this particular occasion I was a little worried because the family offering me work was so high up in the official establishment, I nevertheless accepted.

They were, so to speak, the second-ranking family in the Kolyma official hierarchy. I had been asked to give lessons in the family of the head of the Dalstroi Political Administration, Shevchenko.

Shevchenko's wife—a handsome woman with a rather intelligent face—had seen me at work in our kindergarten. She used to come and visit us as a member of the women's committee. She had liked the music lessons and especially the dramatized fairy tales. We had been acting "The Wolf and the Seven Little Kids." Edik Klimov had been playing the liveliest, most ingenious seventh kid. All the nurses and cooks from the kitchen crowded in to watch him. He had also charmed our important visitor. During the break she asked me to give her fourteen-year-old son coaching in Russian, remarking bitterly that all the boy was interested in was soccer.

I had already heard various things about this woman from the prisoners employed in her service. They said she was quite different from the other bosses' wives. She read books, was interested in music, and, above all, displayed an extraordinary interest in those employed on her staff. A human interest. Shukhaeva, the designer, had told me that the woman in question not only came to examine the new styles in her women's dress shop, but also asked well-informed questions about painting and about her past life in Paris. She had inquired of her manicurist—a fat, cheerful, irrepressible Latvian known to us in Elgen by the nickname Sweet Little Alma—with an ironic smile just how she had managed to become a saboteur with a complexion like hers. She had said straight away to her laundress, Anya Shuralova, that she had known her husband, the former commander of the Moscow Military District, who had been shot in '37. It seemed likely that if the fiery breath of '37 had not singed her wings, it had passed close to her and caused her to tremble.

I started to visit the third floor of the local government apartments three times a week. I had to go past two armed guards—one on each floor—and show them the note from my employer: "Please let the teacher pass."

With my pupil I had a difficult time. He was a hopeless blockhead. He gave a cynical sneer when I voiced my fears that he was risking a second year in the same class. He screwed up his handsome eyes, just like his mother's, and boomed: "That would be more dangerous for the teachers than for me. They won't want to have Shevchenko's son getting bad marks."

"An insufferable child," his mother sighed. "Let him be, let's go and have a cup of coffee. . . ."

She clearly wanted me to become her companion. But I remained shy of her advances, mindful of the golden maxim about the danger of being in the master's good graces. But even my brief replies to her questions about the fate of my family, about my second arrest, about the court, the prison, and the camp brought tears to her eyes.

I very occasionally met the master in the corridor. He would give me a polite nod and disappear behind the door of his office. In his appearance, too, there was a certain incompatibility with the Kolyma stereotype. He had the face of an intelligent person.

One day, out of the blue, the Shevchenkos' maidservant arrived at the kindergarten with an envelope for me. It contained the money for the lessons I had given.

"The lady of the house told me to say that for the time being there is no need for you to come any more. The boy is ill."

She started going toward the door, then turned back, called me to one side, and spoke to me in a whisper, addressing me as servant to servant.

"I'll tell you the truth but you mustn't let on. I'm an ex-zek myself, so why should I tell lies to one of us? The boy's as fit as a fiddle. But the master has had a row with the head of Dalstroi, who said to him that his wife had surrounded herself with prisoners. The dressmaker and the laundress and the maid and the manicurist and even the teacher, he said, are all counter-revolutionaries. And the teacher is even an ex–prison inmate! It's not just a coincidence.

So my days there are also doubtless numbered. Just as long as they let you keep your job here, in the kindergarten! Anyhow, be careful. . . ."

I had long since heard that Mitrakov, the head of Dalstroi, who had replaced Nikishov on the latter's retirement, was at daggers drawn with Shevchenko, the head of the Political Administration. I don't know whether there was any issue of principle involved or whether it was simply a struggle for power within the confines of our remote planet, Kolyma. All that was known was that the hostility between the two top men of Kolyma had reached such a pitch that Mitrakov had started to look for excuses to get rid of Shevchenko. The partiality of the latter's wife to former prisoners was one possible excuse.

A number of different reports soon reached me to the effect that I had been the subject of discussion at a meeting of the Magadan Party activists and that my name had been mentioned with the epithet "well-known terrorist" attached to it. Mitrakov had apparently said something along the following lines: "We are here to protect you, Comrade Shevchenko, from possible attack by the counter-revolutionary elements that infest this region. You have a permanent armed guard posted on your staircase. But you invited a well-known terrorist to come as tutor to your son. In fact, your wife has surrounded herself with nothing but spies, saboteurs, and terrorists. . . ."

My fate was decided. I had become the lackey who gets a sore head whenever his masters fight. I was dismissed from my job. "Without any explanation," as my kindergarten head told me. She was very upset about it. She had paid several visits to the personnel department to plead my cause. She had begged them at least to put it off for two weeks or so, so as to fit in just one gala concert. Not a chance! "What can have happened?" she wondered. "Perhaps you know?"

I did know. But what was the point of telling the head about it? "We'll be lost without you," she went on. "Just when we've had such a success, too!"

By "success" she meant our recent radio performance of the same "Seven Little Kids" in one of the children's hour programs. I had always been both touched and depressed by the inability of ordinary, unsophisticated people to understand the basic modalities of our existence. Our head had been working there in the kindergarten, in the very epicenter of the earthquake, for some years past, and yet the logical connection between the "success" of an ex-prisoner in his or her work and that person's removal from that same work escaped her.

I, for my part, did understand this and, wise from my bitter experience, had entreated the radio employees in charge of the program not to mention my name. And they had not mentioned it. What they had said was: "You have been listening to a radio adaptation for children of 'The Wolf and the Seven Little Kids,' performed by children in the senior group of the Magadan Kindergarten. The adaptation was made by the kindergarten music instructor."

But a transparent incognito of that sort was powerless to save the situation. On the contrary, it had served to pour oil on the flames. In Mitrakov's report to the Party activists, the incident with the "Seven Little Kids" was presented as follows: "Thanks to the political irresponsibility of the radio employees as well as of those in charge of them, a barely disguised class enemy, who recently served a sentence for terrorist activity, was given access to the media. This is not the first occasion when, with the connivance of the corresponding organizations, the enemy has succeeded in infiltrating the ideological front." To what giddy political heights the seven poor little kids had been promoted!

I was in despair. This occurrence was just as much of a shock to me as my second arrest. It was no use for Anton, with his irrepressible optimism, to seek to assure me that things were not all that bad. Now, if it had happened while he was still in camp, it really would have put us in an acutely difficult position. But as it was, he was getting his hospital pay, so we wouldn't starve.

I found these reassurances of little comfort. It was not just a matter of money. I was oppressed by the thought that I was completely without rights, that I could be disposed of like a surplus object, that any hopes of obtaining even a little more independence (as compared with life in camp or prison) were illusory. They had only to indicate their wishes, and in a trice you were flung out of the children's collective where you had grown close to everyone over the four years you had spent working there and where every child was a part of your life. They, our very experienced prisoners' children, had, of course, seen through it. Not for one moment did they believe in the official version—that I had fallen ill. I slipped back to the kindergarten to sign the discharge form, trying to avoid meeting the children. But they caught me, clung to me, howled for all they were worth, and chanted: "Our Eugenia Semyonovna is off to camp again!" They didn't ask me to stay with them, for they knew all too well that it was not in my power to do so. Only Edik whispered fiercely into my ear that I wouldn't have to suffer it much longer: he would soon be grown up—he'd be going to school in a month—and then he would take revenge on all who had harmed me.

I had to run the gauntlet with this wretched discharge form and face up to cross-examination, expressions of sympathy, and various hypotheses. But finally the day came when, after accompanying Anton to his work and Tonya to the kindergarten, I returned to our den, with the plywood partition dividing it from the kitchen, and realized with pitiless clarity that I had nowhere to rush off to, and no need to think up new spectacles, to write out degrading reports and work plans, or to learn new marches and songs for the children. In other words, for the first time since reaching the age of fourteen—not counting my time in prison—I was an unemployed person, a dependent. My existence became gray and monotonous. I could not even find strength to look for another job.

To rescue me from my torpor, Anton accomplished the impossible. It was a real miracle! He bought me a piano. A genuine Red October piano, with a smooth lacquer finish and gilded pedals. When they brought it along to our building on the truck, the entire population of our two floors turned out on the street. In 1951 in Magadan the total number of pianos was quite limited, especially those in private hands. It went without saying that in our ghetto the appearance of a piano was regarded as a phenomenon belonging to some other solar system.

To help me recover from my state of depression, Anton had displayed fantastic persistence. He had used all his connections among his free patients and gone into debt for the next three years. But now, when he got back from work, he would pause in the doorway for a minute or two, smiling happily and admiring the piano's glossy black shine; he stood with his back against the partition, which did little to separate us from the foul-mouthed squabbling and the stench of cooking that continued throughout the day. The creamy-white keys of the piano appeared to smile back at him. It seemed like a vision from another world alongside the trestle bed, the stools, and the cotton-wool pillows in gray camp pillow-cases tied with tapes. Sometimes Anton would sit down at the piano himself and play a few slow chords, making it sound like an organ or a harmonium.

If the purchase of the piano was a miracle, it was no less of a miracle that he had managed to install it in the eight square meters that housed all three of us and where, quite apart from our sleeping places, the stools, and the tables, we had already accumulated a lot of bookshelves.

Anton found me a number of students. This gave me some income but failed to rescue me from my feeling of alienation, of being spurned by life. Only now that I had lost my job did I fully realize what a joy it was to be able to forget for a few hours each day that I was a pariah. That was what I had got from the kindergarten where I was needed by the entire collective, where they respected me, loved me, and looked forward to my arrival. But now . . . There was something infinitely degrading in having to frequent these apartments bursting at the seams with material comforts, having to wipe your feet carefully before venturing onto the overpolished parquet floor, having to chat with the lady of the house about the successes of her idolized infant. And these wives were totally unlike Shevchenko's wife: every gesture or word of theirs served to underline the favor they had done by permitting me to earn a livelihood.

Against the gray background of my existence there were still two dark, black-letter days that stood out: the first and fifteenth day of each month. These were the dates for my so-called reporting, when I had to go along for registration to MGB headquarters. It was located in a small house on the square, between the MGB's White House and the MVD's Red House. From early in the morning, we deportee-resettlers formed up into an enormously long queue, blocking the narrow corridor and filling it with anxious whispering, nervous coughs, and clouds of tobacco smoke.

The reporting procedure was, on the face of it, quite simple. It was just a matter of having a date stamped in the "wolf's ticket," which did duty for an internal passport, and of ticking the personal-entry card kept in the drawer of the commandant's desk. But those responsible for the compulsory settlement of former prisoners were still a long way from the end of the alphabet. New exiles were arriving all the time. Meanwhile, the commandant got the cards mixed up and spent ages looking for the right one, sometimes failing to find it and ordering those concerned to come back the following day. All in all, one had sometimes to stand in line in the corridor for a very long time indeed before passing through the shabby door.

Two or three days before the first and the fifteenth I began to feel depressed at the prospect of the imminent visit to the shrine. It was no use my attempting to rationalize it—a mere formality, I would tell myself. And Anton's reassurances were of even less use: they were not particularly sincere, because one could sense the alarm behind the optimistic words that were based on the lesser evil theory. The fact was that after each reporting session something always happened to someone. Someone was sent from Magadan out to the taiga. Someone was interrogated as to where he was working and a few days later dismissed from his job. And some of us were simply invited to "step this way," taken out to the back courtyard of the MGB premises, and from there sent off to an unknown destination. Then everyone was overwhelmed by the Great Fear, the feeling of fright that had become an integral part of our consciousness and that was so familiar from all our Butyrkis, from Lefortovo, from Yaroslavl, from Vaskov's House. . . . We all started trying to reassure one another that there could be no question of anyone getting shot, and yet our temples throbbed, there was that horrible sinking feeling in the pit of the stomach, and all those around us turned into wraithlike figures and swirled before our eyes like shadows projected on the wall.

Were we all cowards? Hardly. It was merely a nervous reflex from times past. Those who have not been through all the circles we went through do not understand. Even now, twenty years since the time when I visited the MGB headquarters in Magadan, I am exasperated beyond measure when I hear the sort of arguments put forward by free people, those who have never been inside: "What have you got to be afraid of? You've been through far worse than that!" That is just the point. We have been through it. You merely picture it all in your mind's eye, but we *know*.

And so twice a month we crowded into the stuffy little corridor, prey to one and the same torment, brought together in kinship by one and the same wounds. Each one who left the commandant's office, closing the squeaky door carefully behind him and carefully folding up his residence permit as he went along, was fortune's favorite. The fact of having had the permit stamped meant condi-tional liberty for a whole fifteen days. Each one about to enter this door, hurriedly unfolding his document as he went, was a diver plunging into a bottomless gulf. His head was tucked well into his shoulders, ready to receive yet another blow.

The first and the fifteenth of each month Anton and I said good-by as though it was forever. He suffered a lot from not having to report. He felt guilty that things were worse for me than for him. He would have liked to accompany me to the MGB headquarters but he had to be at work on the dot. He could only walk me as far as the entrance to our building, where he would say, "Forgive me, Genia my dear, if I have ever done anything to hurt you." And I would reply, "And you, too . . . Be sure to look after Tonya."

Once I had the stamped permit in my pocket, and nothing—thank God!—had happened, I would rush off somewhere to call him at the hospital. "Everything's all right. I'm going home." The whole episode repeated itself on the first and fifteenth of every month.

At the beginning of 1952 we managed to change apartments. Instead of our little, eight-square-meter birdcage we were now given no less than fifteen square meters in one of the new barracks at the small settlement of Nagaevo. It was not far away from the bay of that name; you could smell the sea air, and the buildings were not as filthy as in our old Sangorodok. The residents here were a mixed lot. The basic mass of prisoners and deportees with their families was diluted with some of the poorer free inhabitants—those who had recently arrived from the mainland and had not yet received their supplementary pay.

Our pleasure was spoiled by the knowledge that it derived from someone else's misfortune. The talented deported artist, Isaac Sher-man, had just died from a coronary in what had become our new room. His wife, Marina, who had shared all his ups and downs with him, had not wanted, had not been able for a moment, to stay on in a house where everything reminded her of her husband. She had agreed to take over our hovel, had wanted to get the ex-change over and done with as soon as possible, and had been grateful to Anton for taking all the arrangements onto his shoulders.

Our new quarters were close to the hospital where Anton was working, but in order to get to the center of town we had to go across an extensive, snow-covered vacant site exposed to the wind, almost unlit, and very convenient for criminals plying their evening trade. And they plied it to good effect. The entire activity of the White House and the Red House was directed at us, the enemies of the people, terrorists, spies, saboteurs, and traitors. It did not normally extend to the professional riffraff. The authorities had second thoughts only every now and then, when special occurrences forced their hand. During the dark winter evenings Anton would not allow me to go across that particular plot of land alone and always tried to bring Tonya home from the kindergarten himself. But there were days when he was on duty for twenty-four hours at a stretch, and I had to go and get her myself. I went there and back, scanning everyone I came across apprehensively.

I had good reason to do so. I remember one tragicomic incident. It was only about seven o'clock in the evening, but our wasteland looked like some arctic tract at midnight. Tonya and I were scurrying along the path between the banks of snow. It was Tonya who first noticed the figure of a man bounding toward us across the drifts.

"Is he a good man or a nasty one? Why is he bathing in the snow?"

He was plunging into the snow in order to overtake us on a parallel course. I was familiar with this wolflike tactic of the professional riffraff: to go parallel to the intended victim, and then, with one sudden bound, to block the way and confront him. No sooner had I thought of it than it happened. Just as I had expected, he jumped. He also had another startling trick: he flicked a large cigarette lighter so that a blue flame flashed in my eyes. Tonya screamed and burst into tears.

"Tell the kid to shut up!" he said in an unexpectedly resonant baritone voice. "And don't you start yelling or you'll make it worse for yourself. Now listen here: don't be afraid, it's not your money I'm after, and not your furs."

He poked a contemptuous finger at my collar, which, as it happened, was of real fox fur. A Chukchi hunter who had been Anton's patient had offered him a small fur for a token sum, and Anton had gratified his secret hankering after a life of luxury. He had bought the fox fur. It was a long time before I stopped berating him for it.

"I don't need your bit of fox," said our highway companion, "but what I do need is a clean passport for a woman. . . . I'm on the run. Get it? I've made myself one but I need another for my

woman. So hand over your passport and get the hell out of here
with that kid of yours. I won't touch you. . . . You'll only be
fined a hundred or so for losing the passport. Your colonel won't
miss that!"

I had my deportee's identification with me. I wasn't at all afraid
of the prospect of parting with it. As the saying goes, it's the sort
of document it's worse to find than to lose. But I nevertheless tried
to make my interlocutor see reason.

"But listen, your wife is probably quite young, I'm over forty.
The date of birth won't fit."

"That's not your problem! Provided the document's in decent
shape, someone will fix the date. Hand it over, I say, or you'll
be sorry. . . ."

"In fact, my passport is of no possible use to you. You wouldn't
get far on it." He bellowed angrily and unmistakably raised his arm
to strike me. Tonya howled even louder.

"Get the kid to shut up, or I'll do it myself. . . ."

I hastily produced my document from my bag.

"What've you got there? I want the passport!"

"That's what I have in place of a passport. Use your lighter and
read who I am."

He took a long time reading it, his thick, fever-cracked lips
forming the words.

"Re-strict-ed in move-ment rights . . . Under open sur-veil-
lance of MGB au-thor-it-ies."

And then he ran quite assuredly through the obviously familiar
words: "To report on the first and fifteenth of each month."

He blew the lighter out and suddenly burst into a peal of quite
good-natured, almost schoolboyish laughter.

"Well, lady, it looks as if you're also in need of a clean one, eh?"

Thereupon all three of us saw the humor of the situation. The
icy frog in the pit of my stomach disappeared. Tonya jumped up
and down and shouted: "He's not a nasty man. He's a kind one,
isn't he?"

The "kind man" explained clearly that it was the fox fur that
had caused the confusion. He had taken me for a colonel's wife.

"Colonels' wives don't live in Nagaevo," was my rational reply.
"They live on Stalin Street and on the Kolyma Highway."

When he learned that he had been dealing with the wife and
daughter of Dr. Walter, our new acquaintance was genuinely upset.

He told me that under the professionals' unwritten code the doctor was someone who enjoyed personal immunity, since he had given the professionals treatment at his quarantine center camp. Had I only told him who I was, he wouldn't have dreamed of scaring me!

"There is one thing: you mustn't be seen around here with the kid in the dark. It's Lenny the Strangler's home ground. He's a psycho. He'd go for you—and it'd be too late to prove that you were Dr. Walter's wife. Let me take you home so you don't come to any more harm. . . ."

He took Tonya by the hand and me by the arm. In those spots where the ground wind had exposed the icy surface underneath, he kept warning us, touchingly: "Look out. Careful . . . It's slippery here." He took us right up to the door of the hut and handed us over to Anton, after repeating his warning about the psycho Lenny the Strangler.

In point of fact, although our living conditions definitely had improved—fifteen meters is an advance over eight, after all—the Nagaevo area, which was fraught with encounters of that kind, somehow helped to close the circle of desperation more tightly around me. Those impenetrably dark winter evenings, the icy wasteland on the route to the town center—it all tended to isolate us still more from the normal rhythm of life, from the prospect of daily employment for which I increasingly yearned.

All of a sudden there was a ray of hope. Oddly enough, it came from the direction of those selfsame Seven Little Kids who had so brazenly penetrated the ideological front.

One Sunday afternoon in Nagaevo we had a visit from an unknown lady. She was one of the free citizenry: well-dressed, energetic, and full of ideas. "Don't you recognize me?" she asked. "We used to meet in the Preschool Methodology Center. I am Kraevskaya, Lyubov Pavlovna Kraevskaya, head of Kindergarten Number 2. I had great difficulty finding you. And when I got into your corridor I only just managed to make my way through the three-wheeled traffic jam."

She was referring to the seventeen children inhabiting our corridor. They were constantly pedaling up and down on their tricycles, ringing their bells furiously and shouting at one another. A large consignment of tricycles recently received by the Magadan Department Store had been sold out within the hour. But I had got there in time. Our Tonya was a pretty aggressive tricyclist.

After her little joke about the cyclists, Kraevskaya told me without beating about the bush that she was proposing to apply for me to fill the post of music assistant at her kindergarten. She had come to get my consent. I told her bitterly the entire story of the lessons in the Shevchenkos' apartment, the radio broadcast about the Seven Little Kids, and Mitrakov's speech to the Party activists. The personnel department would never agree to her plan. . . .

"You surprise me," Lyubov Pavlovna interjected cheerfully and impetuously. "You occupied, it seems, a responsible Party position in your previous career outside. In that case how can you fail to understand the workings of the system? Don't you realize that Mitrakov is completely indifferent to you as a person and that all he cares about is getting at Shevchenko? They simply assembled the dossier he required. . . . I am sure that over the past two months he's even forgotten your name. . . ."

It further emerged that Kraevskaya's husband was the chief architect of Magadan and had good connections. He would help. . . .

"Tell me," I asked, "who put in a good word for me? What could induce you to take all this trouble on my behalf? Was it simply that you wanted to help someone down on her luck?"

"Again, you surprise me," she replied calmly, looking straight at me with cheerful, ironic eyes. "Don't you understand the system? The main thing is to be able to display your wares. And in the operation of a kindergarten, the main thing is the festival shows and gala concerts. All the higher-ups come and watch them. That's what they judge the school by. . . . You ask who put in a good word for you? Your 'Seven Little Kids,' of course! It was such a wonderful show. . . ."

She got up, gave her nose a dab of powder in the mirror, and added, with a laugh: "You don't know your own worth. . . . Not only are you a musician, but you are also an adapter and producer. As soon as I heard the 'Seven Little Kids' on the radio, I said to myself, 'My name's not Kraevskaya if I don't get that woman onto my staff. . . .'"

Within two weeks of her visit I was already sitting at the piano in Kindergarten Number 2. My new head did not confide to me the details of her efforts to get me appointed. She merely said that the matter had gone through "six instances." At one point even Mitrakov's deputy's chauffeur had played a part. In one way or another, the Seven Little Kids had again penetrated the ideological front and taken over the platform. The affair of the Little Cockroach was by no means so easily settled. But that belongs to the next chapter.

13

· *The Little Cockroach*

The deprivation of civil rights, to which I had been sentenced by the Moscow Military Collegium in 1937, ended in February 1952.

I would have completely overlooked this. After experiencing rearrest, compulsory settlement for life, and dismissal from my job, it was hardly likely that I would be particularly exercised about my "deprivation." If anything, the reverse applied. It was something of an advantage—with election campaigning at the national, republic, and local levels a pretty frequent occurrence—not to be bothered by the innumerable agitators. When we heard them knocking at the door of our lodgings, we answered, correctly and to the point: "There are no voters here. Only people deprived of their rights." The answer was nothing to be surprised about in Kolyma, and the agitators retreated in silence after putting down on their list some sort of mark next to the number of our room.

But this time our standard formula failed to discourage the agitator.

"No," she countered as she came in, "your deprivation of rights ended on the fifteenth of February of this year. I am the agitator for this district, and I want to talk to you."

She was a first-class example, a paragon of a free Kolyma lady: one of the civic-minded; the wife of neither a top-ranking nor yet of an entirely junior member of the establishment. She was enveloped in a haze of the fashionable perfume White Lilac. She glittered, from her mother-of-pearl manicure to the gold crowns of

her teeth. And the rest of her inventory was equally adequate to
the occasion: her dark blue cardigan, her fox fur, and her Chukchi
beaded moccasins.

"I want first of all to congratulate you," she said, stretching out
her hand to me, "and to welcome you back with all my heart to
the family of the workers."

I had a nasty taste in my mouth. These were the same unforgettable words that had embellished the gates at Elgen: "Our selfless
labor will restore us to the family of the workers."

"You are mistaken," I barked out. "I am sentenced to compulsory
settlement for life."

"Not so, my dear, I am not mistaken. According to regulations,
deportees enjoy voting rights."

She sat down on the edge of my bed in the most democratic way
imaginable, and immediately started to tell me about the productivity feats of the distinguished free miner for whom we were due
to cast our vote.

She was a Stalinist of the effusively emotional variety. She simply
oozed enthusiastic benevolence, and a fervent desire to induct me,
a heathen, into that harmonious world in which she lived so fruit-
fully. She spoke to me more or less in the manner in which gentle,
patient missionaries doubtless address primitive African tribesmen.

"So, I assume you have understood me? Deportees enjoy the
right to elect . . ."

"And to be elected?"

"What do you mean?" she inquired with curiosity.

"Well, let's say . . . suppose suddenly someone put me up at
the pre-election meeting as a candidate for the local Soviet. Can I
run?"

The agitator burst into a ripple of pure, childlike laughter.

"One can see just how cut off from life you have been. Can you
really think that everyone gets up and says what comes into his
head at the pre-election meeting? After all, the lists have already
been processed in the Party organs. It doesn't matter that much.
You can come along to our agitation center and you'll gradually
get back into the swing. . . . You must really have been quite
young when it happened to you."

"What 'happened'?" I countered obdurately.

"Well, when you got caught up in a counter-revolutionary or-

ganization, you were just a young thing. You didn't understand. . . .
And they took advantage of that. . . . They crawl into any
crack. . . ."

"Who crawls into what crack?" I asked with still greater obduracy.

"Well, these foreign agents! From the intelligence services . . .
the ones who recruited you. But you mustn't get upset. It's long
over and done with. And the Soviet regime wants to put back on
the right path those who lost their bearings when they were young
and inexperienced."

"What a beautiful ring you have," I said, not taking my eyes off
the sapphire stone on her finger.

"Do you like it?" she replied in turn. "The main thing is that it
goes with this outfit. . . . And, people say, with my eyes, too . . ."

She darted a brief, diffident glance at the mirror. Her eyes were,
in fact, of an impeccable light blue.

In parting she rewarded me with a resplendent smile, and even
presented me with a colored postcard of incredible beauty. Across
a gorgeous scarlet rose there snaked a golden ribbon that was
inscribed: "Everyone to the polls!" followed by an appeal to me
from the entire agitators' collective: "Please do not be late for the
election, register your vote as early as possible, and display the
highest degree of political awareness from the very first step you
take in your new life."

Getting up early was indeed one of the rules of the election game.
It was assumed that their highly developed civic sense would not
allow people to get a wink of sleep the night before election day,
and that with the first rays of dawn they would tumble out of
their beds and rush off to the polling booths, which opened at six
in the morning. (For that matter, the "first rays of dawn," which
constantly figured in the Kolyma paper were, of course, the purest
figment of the imagination. At that time of year the dawn sky in
Kolyma hardly began to turn a faint blue before about ten o'clock.)

"Genia, for God's sake, please say yes!" my neighbor, Claudia
Trifonovna Firsova, entreated me. "Let's go and be the first to
vote." She, like me, was newly restored to the family of the
workers.

Claudia, who had done eight years for failure to denounce someone or other, was now the wife of a free driver, Stepan Gusyev.
It was an exceptionally happy marriage. It was sheer joy to observe

them. Stepan was a unique specimen—a nondrinking Kolyma driver.
He used to return from a long journey on the central highway
as sober as a judge and shout out for the entire corridor to hear:
"Has anyone seen my Claudia?" He would be encumbered with
an entire frozen fish, or an enormous hunk of venison that he had
lugged along for her. Claudia, who was never tired, would start
cooking, washing, and cleaning floors immediately after work, lest
Stepan—heaven forbid—experience any discomfort. Their room was
full of little rugs, antimacassars, and cushion covers embellished
with swans, kittens, water sprites, and deer hunters. The base of their
magnificent bed was trimmed with a lace frieze made on her days
off by Claudia with her bobbins. There was only one thing that got
Claudia down: the difference between them in social standing.

"You see, Genia," she said, opening her heart to me while we
were doing our laundry together in the kitchen shared by all of us,
"you see I'm not a match for him. His record is tremendously
clean. His father's a Party member. His mother's a deputy in the
local Soviet. How can I show myself to them? A former citizen
. . . deprived of civil rights. The shame of it . . ."

Stepan certainly was what they called a distinguished citizen.
You could count on the fingers of one hand the Kolyma drivers
who had never done time, and you'd still risk exaggerating. Stepan
had been a favorite of the local newspaper reporters for the past
two years; they used him as material for feature articles about the
"conquerors of the wild taiga."

"Let's be the first to get there," Claudia whispered ardently to
me. "The first to arrive are always the ones to be photographed;
their photos are put up on the honor board and then published
in the paper. And I can take that photo with me when we go
and visit Stepan's parents on the mainland. Then I can say I'm not
just a nobody, that I've been in the papers, too."

Her pleasant, kindly face shone at the thought, and she was so
proud of her stratagem that I didn't have the heart to tell her that
the newspapers have special controls to make sure that prisoners
don't get in while no one is looking, whether as authors or as heroes.
I agreed for the sake of voter Firsova's family happiness to get up
in the middle of the night.

Anton was on duty at the hospital that night. The "conqueror
of the wild taiga," Stepan, was on one of his long journeys. Claudia
and I ran like greyhounds through the icy mist of our wasteland.

In fact there was no cause to be afraid: that particular night, the one before the election, there were hordes of militiamen patrolling the area.

We were the first to deposit our voting slips. And—what joy—the photographer did take Claudia's picture, and wrote down her name and place of work. She walked back home, quiet and happy, and kept repeating: "How nice it feels! Just like getting back from morning service!"

All the greater was her disillusionment the following day when Claudia read in the newspaper that the first person in our electoral district to cast her vote for the Communist and non-Party bloc had been Comrade Tamara Vasilevna Kozikhina, an employee of the Consumer Service Combine. There was a picture of Kozikhina dropping her voting paper into the box and smiling like a Hollywood star.

"How can they say she was first?" exclaimed Claudia in childish despair. "Tamara, the hairdresser! You remember, we had already voted and were on our way out when we bumped into her in the doorway. She had only just removed her overshoes and was shaking off the snow. Why do they tell such lies? And they call themselves journalists. . . . No, really, there's no truth in this world. . . ."

It was both touching and comic that this woman, who had done eight years for nondenunciation of something or other about which she hadn't even heard at the time, had only now, since her return to the "family of the workers," discovered the existence of lies. As a consequence, she was burning with indignation.

"At the time I thought it was just a blooper. I thought they'd made a mistake and taken me for someone else. . . . But in this case . . . They knew exactly what the story was, and then they printed one lie after another. And people read it and think it's the truth. . . . It was in the paper, wasn't it, so it must be right."

That evening our quiet Claudia tore the newspaper out of the hands of her Stepan and, weeping, flung herself onto their majestic bed, crumpling the newly starched frieze in the process.

Stepan was aggrieved and puzzled. " 'Don't look at that old haybag,' she says. It's a picture of Tamara, the hairdresser, voting first thing in the morning. 'She's just a pain in the neck to me,' I tell her. There she was like the Queen of the May, swanking around the ballot box. Why am I supposed to care? Do you think Claudia's sick? I've never known her to yell at me like that, or to be jealous."

"It's not jealousy," I said to Stepan, "it's envy of Tamara's civic status, of her having all her rights as a citizen. And she's upset by the reporter's lies. In actual fact it wasn't Tamara but Claudia who was the first to vote."

"Ah, what a silly girl my Claudia is," said the teetotal miracle of a driver, affectionately summing up the position. "What a thing to be envious about. Who knows what may happen to that same Tamara tomorrow? With us it's a matter of dialectics: today a promotee, tomorrow a deportee."

There was certainly more than enough dialectics in the social make-up of our distant planet! We even had deportees who had not been expelled from the Party. These Party members were all German nationals. They had no special privileges: they used to report to MGB headquarters twice a month like the rest of us; in place of an internal passport they had a certificate similar to mine which limited their freedom of movement to within a radius of seven kilometers from their place of resettlement. Sometimes their visits to the MGB premises coincided with Party meetings, in which case the Germans, after waiting their turn in the lengthy queue to have their residence permit stamped, would hurry off to their Party meeting, at which they would vote unanimously in favor of heightening Bolshevik vigilance in view of the sharpening of the class struggle as we advanced toward Communism.

Our "Old Man," Yakov Mikhailovich Umansky, who now had a lot more time on his hands since Vasya's departure and the termination of the math lessons, even supplied a model for "The Social and Political Structure of Kolyma." According to it, there were no fewer than nine social classes to be taken into account: zeks, ex-zeks without civil rights, ex-zeks with civil rights, deportees for a fixed period of time, compulsory settlers for a fixed period of time, deportee-settlers for life, settlers with special status for a fixed period of time, and settlers with special status for life. At the apex of this pyramid stood the Germans who were simultaneously compulsory settlers and Party members.

He headed his model "The Thorny Path to the Classless Society." Everyone smiled and teased the old man. They knew him, they said, as a doctor, a philosopher, a poet, and a mathematician, but now they would have to add "sociologist" to the list.

But all this was a week before his death. We saw him for the last time on Sunday as usual. On Sundays we used to organize a traditional lunch for such of our deportee friends as lived here on their own. One of those usually present was Yuri Konstantinovich Milonov, an Old Bolshevik from as far back as '12 or '13. Another one was Aleksandr Milchakov, a former Secretary of the Central Committee of the Komsomol. There was also Takhavi Ayupov, whom I had known in Kazan, a former Secretary of the Tartar Central Executive Committee. And Yakov Mikhailovich never missed a single one of these Sunday lunches.

On what was to be his last visit he was merry and animated; he repeated several times his favorite prophecy: "Just wait. The time will come when we will all proudly wear a 'political prisoner' badge." And in addition: "Surely I will live to read 'his' obituary, won't I? He and I are the same age. But I have my hopes. I live my life in the open air and I watch my diet, but he is doubtless putting on weight. Moreover I undergo less nervous strain than he does. For I have nothing to lose, and I have absolutely no enemies."

That Sunday evening when Anton and I were seeing him out, he suddenly said with subdued sadness: "What do you think? Is it possible that my little Liza has forgotten me?" This was a wound that never healed. His daughters never wrote to him, fearing any connection with an enemy of the people. He, for his part, while never spending anything on himself, was busy putting away money for his daughters in the savings bank, so that they should know their father had been thinking of them.

The next week, on Saturday, Tanya Simorina came rushing in and said agitatedly: "Go to the morgue. He's there."

He lay there at peace, younger looking, and rather majestic. It was the morgue at the free hospital in which Yakov Mikhailovich had worked for several years as pathologist; two of the morgue technicians, both former common criminals, were standing beside his corpse, both of them looking pale and downcast. They had pinned an artificial but skillfully fashioned carnation to the lapel of the old man's jacket. I thought of his words about a political prisoner badge.

We gave him a good burial, on a high place, with a headstone and an enclosure. And I wrote a letter to his Liza and Susanna in which I not only gave them the number of the savings bank book he had bequeathed them but also told them in detail the sort of man their father had been. I said not a word about the suffering they had caused him, or about how hurt he had been by their silence. Some of our circle urged me to hint at it so that the daughters would at least in retrospect recognize their cruelty. But I did not agree. There was no question of cruelty: it was the same Great Fear. And if the former tribunes, leaders, and prophets had taken part in the devilish spectacle and carried out to the letter all the instructions of Public Prosecutor Vyshinsky, its producer, what more could you expect from two unfortunate, ordinary housewives terrorized by the vigilant whispers emanating from the communal kitchen?

I was proved right. For at that moment of acute grief the image of their much loved father ousted all their fears. We received a letter written from the heart which began with the words: "Dear unknown friends, standing beside the grave of our beloved father! God will reward you for your goodness. . . ."

Our entire deportee colony mourned for Yakov Mikhailovich. After his death we learned of the existence of a great many people, unknown to us but linked to the old man by the various services he had done them. In one case it was a loan, in another he had given free treatment; he had helped correct the manuscript of a third and done some translations for yet another. . . . Among these people there were some unworthy ones who had exploited the absent-mindedness, unworldliness, and absolute impracticality in everyday affairs of the eccentric doctor.

It was the use of his name ("The late Dr. Umansky sent me") that first unlocked our door to a man who brought us a lot of grief and left behind him in our apartment the filthy footprints of a *provocateur*. For that matter, we had no way of knowing whether Yakov Mikhailovich had indeed been planning just before his death to introduce Engineer Krivoshei to us. His reference to the dead man may have been simply the most convenient way of penetrating our house and worming his way into our confidence.

Engineer Krivoshei presented himself to us as a political, recently released from camp. This was the first lie. It later emerged that he was a common criminal, sentenced either for embezzlement or criminal negligence. In addition, he made himself out to be a sick man who had recently undergone a major operation and needed Anton's help. (Whereupon the scar of the operation was exhibited.) But the thing that most inspired trust in this new acquaintance was that he was so well educated—and what is more, in matters that bore no relation to his profession as an engineer. He loved poetry, of which he had an extensive knowledge, and used to recite Blok, Akhmatova, and Pasternak from memory. He had new and original things to say about politics, economics, and history. I remember how interesting it was to listen to his analysis of half-forgotten pages of Klyuchevsky and Solovyov.* He had, it was true, a somewhat flowery, archaic way of expressing himself, but this tallied well enough with the image of a hereditary intellectual from St. Petersburg, which was how he presented himself.

Bit by bit he became one of our regulars and took over the place vacated by Yakov Mikhailovich at our Sunday lunches. Everyone took to our new acquaintance. They all gladly tolerated his inexhaustible garrulity. For his stories were interesting ones. He had in his repertoire a number of humorous tales, which he was always happy to serve up as an encore, amid peals of laughter all around. His best piece was called "Wallace's Monologue."

We were all familiar with the story of how the American Henry Wallace† had managed to travel through Kolyma and observe only the Potemkin villages that the authorities had decided to show him. But Krivoshei, when he delivered "Wallace's Monologue," impersonated the perspicacious traveler and imitated his accent so well that the old story glowed with fresh color.

"The tall, sturdy boys from Central Russia are determined to conquer this wild region," Krivoshei would say, imitating Wallace. Then he would comment in a whispered aside: "Three picked squads of armed guards, disguised in overalls of American manufacture." Then back to Wallace: "Pioneers of progress. The founders of new cities." Then it was the women's turn: "During the long winter evenings the women and girls sought one another's company and dedicated themselves to the art of embroidering Gobelin tapestries. This is an old Russian art: Gobelinwirkerei." And then the corresponding aside: "Needlework in a camp workshop, women dressed up in decent wool jackets—one of those workshops where our womenfolk went blind over their 'wirkerei.' "

In the intervals between fragments of his "Wallace's Monologue," Krivoshei would slip in an intermezzo: he would make it appear

* Vasily Klyuchevsky (1841–1911): historian, writer of a multivolume history of Russia. Sergei Solovyov (1820–1879): writer of books on Russian history.
† Henry Wallace (1888–1965): Vice President of the U.S. from 1940–1944, visited Magadan in 1944. He reported on his visit in Soviet Asia Mission (1946).

that he was actually telling it all to the Kolyma drivers who were
guffawing and praising the Americans for being such donkeys—
and in particular for bringing in supplies of antifreeze. Our gallant
drivers consumed this preparation with a bite of blubber to help
it down, despite the fact that the containers were labeled "Poison"
in Russian and in English. This, the story went, was death to the
spindle-shanked Americans but an hour of blissful oblivion as far
as our lads were concerned!

So Krivoshei became the life and soul of the company. Though
sometimes Anton and I did wonder, particularly when we realized
that our new acquaintance suddenly ceased to be charming as soon
as he stopped talking. You would notice all of a sudden how
tightly he pursed his wide, toadlike lips. And behind the spectacles
his eyes had taken on an evasive look—he was good at averting
them and avoiding the eyes of whomever he was talking to.

But perhaps we recalled this only later, when we had learned
what he was like. At the time, if we had entertained any doubts,
they were dispelled for good and all when we visited him at his
place and saw for ourselves his seven-square-meter birdcage stuffed
to bursting with books. The bookshelves reached right up to the
ceiling. Apart from books, his den held nothing but two stools and
a bedside table on which he ate and wrote. A camp bed stood in
the corridor behind the door and was unfolded only at night.

What rare, tempting morsels there were to be found on the
roughly carpentered shelves: Baudelaire's *Les Fleurs du Mal;* a full
edition of Goethe in German; several entire sets of the journal
Vestnik Evropy for the early years of the century; the almanacs
Vesy and *Shipovnik.** It would have been impossible to name them
all. . . . My heart thumped when I heard the master of the house
solemnly announce that although he never lent books to anyone, he
would make an exception for us and we could select—now, if we
liked—two books each. He could see that books were as much a
treasure to us as to him and that we would be punctilious about
returning them.

Breathless with enthusiasm, he told us the history of some of the
books. This one he had exchanged in camp for two bread rations.

* *Vestnik Evropy* was published monthly in Moscow from 1866 through 1915.
Vesy, a literary monthly published in Leningrad, served as a vehicle for the
symbolists. *Shipovnik* was a literary-artistic journal published in Leningrad
from 1906 through 1918.

Those others had come to him from a deportee friend of his who had died in a remote taiga settlement. And these here he had, would you believe it, bought at the Magadan open-air market. They had been lying alongside the crabs at the back of the stall.

Even his hands trembled at the thought of his luck. The jealous greed with which he observed our movements when we took a volume from the shelves marked him down as a genuine bibliophile, or rather a bibliomaniac. Was it possible to associate this with anything bad? Anyone who traded his camp bread ration for a book could not be a nasty person.

As it turned out, he could. That, however, emerged later, at the beginning of 1953. Throughout 1952 we and Engineer Krivoshei were the closest of friends. We enthusiastically quoted his witty sayings, listened entranced to his tales, and were profoundly grateful for the use of his unique library. During that cheerless year when the news from the mainland became increasingly sinister and the newspapers increasingly strident, we really opened our hearts to our cultivated friend. I was acting out the words of the popular song: "The little bird plays with the cat / She cannot see the harm in that."

For New Year's 1953 Krivoshei presented each of us with a book. I got a volume of Akhmatova's poems in a prerevolutionary edition, Anton got Shelenin's textbook on therapy, and Tonya got a collection of Chukovsky's stories for children. We were particularly pleased with this third gift, for the fact was that our new friend liked animals but did not like children. Each time he came to see us he would pick up Agafya the cat and keep stroking her until he left. He usually paid not the slightest attention to Tonya, never smiled at her, and even frowned with annoyance when her questions distracted me from our conversation. At times I used to ask him why he was so unforthcoming with the child. He replied with a tone of sincerity that life had knocked out of him the feeling of tenderness which is an absolute necessity when talking to children. He was incapable of playing the hypocrite. Moreover, he took such a gloomy view of the future of our civilization that he was simply astounded at people who were ready to plunge new unfortunates into this chaos.

These arguments caused us pain. When he looked through Tonya, as if through an empty space, it seemed to us not to go with the image we had of an acutely intelligent and sensitive person. We were thus all the more pleased when he smiled at Tonya and handed her a volume of Chukovsky's stories.

I knew nearly all these stories by heart and often used to tell them to the children in the kindergarten, where none of Chukovsky's books were available. But on this occasion, to give Krivoshei pleasure, I immediately started to read them out loud from the book, turning over the handsome, glossy pages. And then we came to "The Little Cockroach," with which we were, of course, already familiar, although we had never tried to get inside the sense of it. . . . I started reading:

"And the cockroach became the victor and the master of the seas and forests. The animals bowed and scraped before Mr. Whiskers, hoping the wretch would perish." Suddenly we were all struck by the double entendre. I started laughing. Anton simultaneously started laughing. Yet Krivoshei became deadly serious. The lenses of his glasses flashed and sparkled.

"What is it you're thinking?" he exclaimed with unusual emotion ". . . surely not! Surely Chukovsky would not have dared!"

Instead of answering, I read on, putting more expression into it: "And he went around among the animals, stroking his gilded breastplate. . . . Bring me your young, my darling animals, and I will eat them for my supper."

"Surely Chukovsky would not have dared!" Krivoshei repeated, now more keyed up than we had ever seen him before.

I wasn't slow in answering. ("The little bird plays with the cat.")

"I don't know whether Chukovsky intended it. Probably not. But objectively, that's the only way to take it. Just listen to the description of the animals' reaction: 'They sit and tremble under the bushes, hiding behind the green hummocks. All you can see of them is their ears quivering, all you can hear is their teeth chattering.' Or take this sentence: 'The wolves were so frightened that they ate each other up.' "

Krivoshei walked around the room without pausing for an instant. He squeezed his hands together so tightly that the knuckles showed white.

"A brilliant piece of political satire! It can't be that no one has noticed it. . . . It must simply be that everyone is scared to admit that such a thing could have entered his head. . . . Such a . . ."

After our guest's departure, Anton said unhappily:

"I'm left with a nasty feeling about it. Why did he get so worked up? You shouldn't have read the one about the cockroach. If there's one thing we don't need it's to be accused of *lèse majesté*. Of course Krivoshei won't tell anybody, but all the same . . . Let's agree not to say another word about it to anyone."

These words of caution from Anton, who never thought twice about what he said, made an impression on me. After that I never repeated my conjectures about the cockroach to a single living soul.

Meanwhile 1953 arrived. In my new kindergarten we saw it in with a splendid children's party around the Christmas tree. It was a magnificent success and I was publicly thanked for organizing it.

However, exactly two days after receiving this commendation I was abruptly removed from my job without explanation. The head, who a year previously had fought so energetically on my behalf, behaved strangely. She wouldn't look me in the eye and could only drop mysterious hints that the Special Sector was somehow involved. It was evident that she knew something and that this something presaged a bad end for me. She talked to me as members of the family talk to patients who do not know that they are suffering from cancer. She hoped I would get better. She even mumbled something about the following year. The main thing, she said, was to let some time elapse. . . . Maybe later on . . .

The following day our acquaintance Engineer Krivoshei came along to express his sympathy. Neither Anton nor Tonya were at home. The visitor sat down by the table. Agafya ensconced herself on his knees and purred luxuriantly. Krivoshei started upbraiding me for my excessive trustfulness. Take our friend Milonov, for instance: the other day Krivoshei had himself seen Milonov emerging from the White House late at night. What business could he have had there?

"What do you mean!" I exclaimed indignantly. "Life isn't worth living if you suspect your closest friends of treachery! We know Milonov. . . . He's an honorable man. . . ."

Krivoshei gave a strange sneer. I suddenly felt scared. For I hadn't yet asked myself who was the real traitor who had wormed his way into our house. But at that moment I noticed as if for the first time that his face wore a mask from behind which his real self occasionally emerged without benefit of dissimulation. It was a look utterly alien to the sort of inner world we had attributed to him. I hadn't quite seen through him, but I had an inkling of what I would soon know.

My guest was preparing to go when Anton came, or rather burst, into the room. He looked like death. I had never seen him so upset. With the barest of nods to Krivoshei, he said perfunctorily to me:

"Let's go out into the corridor for a minute. . . ."

This was so unlike his normal courteous self that I realized at once: what he was about to tell me had to do precisely with this incessant chatterbox, this connoisseur of Russian literature and passionate animal lover.

"What is it?" I asked, already anticipating the answer.

"He's the one. You were dismissed from your job because he informed on you. He told them about your reading 'The Little Cockroach' and your commentary on it."

One of the nurses who had worked with Anton in the polyclinic, after getting him to swear that he would never tell anyone of their conversation, had exclaimed: "Dear God! What's going to happen to you both? What has your Eugenia gone and done? To have called Comrade Stalin a spider!"

That is what they had been told at a closed Party meeting. And they had also had explained to them just what the consequences of such sacrilege were.

I listened, cold with fright, to what Anton had to say. The mechanics of the incident were now quite clear to me. No one, not a single living soul other than Krivoshei, had heard my audacious conjectures about the cockroach. The confusion between arachnid and insect was evidently to be explained by the defective education of the functionaries in the White House and also by the unconscious, subcortical processes that substituted the very real, sinister, and far from comic bloodsucking spider for the grotesque, semicomic cockroach.

"Give the informer one in the teeth and kick him out the door," I urged.

"There's always time for that. One must never show a *provocateur* straight away that he's been detected. Let's keep a watch on him for a few days. We'll warn the others. . . ."

Such astonishing discretion from quick-tempered Anton was to be explained, as he told me later, by his having noticed on his way in a number of militiamen in the street near our building. They were hovering there because there had been a brawl in one of the rooms inhabited by truck drivers. Krivoshei might appeal to them for the protection of the law, and that might hasten the course of events.

We somehow managed to return to our room where our treasured guest was sitting in the same idyllic posture, with the cat on his knees as if nothing were wrong.

I did not feel strong enough to sit there looking at him; without making any excuses, I dashed to the other side of the screen, where we had an electric plate on a night table amid what passed for a kitchen. Once there I began feverishly peeling potatoes while I listened to Anton deal with the situation.

"Eugenia Semyonovna overreacts," Krivoshei volunteered kindly, as if he were speaking to someone who was sick. "After all, she's been through much worse. It'll pass over this time too."

"Uh-huh." Anton impatiently drummed on the table.

"Before you arrived I was in fact saying that she ought to be more discriminating and less trusting in her choice of friends," our guest continued in the same majestic tone, stroking the cat's front paws with two fingers.

"Uh-huh . . ." Anton all but snarled, "*that's* the truth."

Fortunately, the conversation did not go on for long. One of the neighbors knocked at the door and started talking to Anton about his ailments. This gave Krivoshei the opportunity to bring his visit to an end with due decorum. He would be on his way, he would not come between the patient and his doctor. He evidently acted on the principle "the more impudent, the better," for he made a point of sticking his head behind the screen to urge me, "Go easy on your nerves." He held out his hand to say good-by.

"Forgive me—dirty hands, you know," I said equivocally, hiding my hands behind my back.

But it was not part of his technique to take hints. He smiled sweetly, and without losing his composure, simply gave me a friendly wave of his hand, which had remained suspended in the air.

That evening (for there was now nothing to lose), I again read "The Little Cockroach" aloud to Tonya.

"Poor, poor animals! They cry, they sob, they howl / In every den, in every lair, they curse the glutton foul."

14

When I opened the newspaper the next morning, I saw the announcement about the Doctors' Plot, about the "murderers in white coats."*

The sequel was unlike anything Kolyma had yet experienced. It was the first time this pestilence had penetrated our distant planet. Until then we had been, as far as the authorities were concerned, a single, uniform mass. They had made no attempt to single out from the generality of the martyrs either Gentile or Jew. Even the "cosmopolitan" campaign of '49 had somehow passed us by. At that time our local authorities had had other things to think about; their own particular concerns tended to exclude these nationwide affairs. They'd been up to their eyes with the mass rearrests, the business of deportation and permanent resettlement, the enlargement of the MGB network. . . . And besides that . . .

How our own community, the zeks and deportees, felt about it goes without saying. Preponderant among us were the Komsomols of the twenties and thirties who had been well and truly pickled in the ideas and categories drummed into them in their youth. We simply had no idea of how robust the "friendship of the peoples" had grown back there on the mainland while we were in limbo.

So in that sense Kolyma was shamefully backward. It was only in 1953 that the administrators pulled themselves together and, started to "regularize the nationality mix." The head of the Medical Administration, Shcherbakov, who was certainly neither heartless nor stupid, rushed around the hospital courtyard as if he had suddenly gone out of his mind, exclaiming: "Isn't Gorin a Jew? Isn't Walter a Jew? Well, where are the Jews around here?"

"Perhaps I'd better send for a racial purity certificate from Germany," Anton joked morosely.

The joke had some basis in fact. Through newly arrived prisoners

---

* A group of Jewish doctors was accused in a *Pravda* article in January 1953 of having procured the murder of several leading Soviet functionaries. The furor died down after Stalin's death.

who had been in captivity in Germany, Anton had somehow learned of the fate of his brother, who had found himself in Germany together with other *Volksdeutsche*. There he had been subjected to a "racial investigation," after which he had received a document certifying that the Walter family for five generations back had been pure-blooded Teutons to a man.

But Teuton blood didn't help Anton. He, too, was dismissed from his job. True, Podushkin, the head of personnel, gave a sympathetic hearing to Anton's explanation that he was not a Jew.

"No one is accusing you of *that*." The head rejected the false accusation. "But you can be accused of something else."

He made transparent hints about not letting one's tongue run away with one and about not joining in counter-revolutionary gossip. Of course, it would have been ridiculous to expect our good friend Krivoshei to conceal from the White House Anton's participation in that discussion of Kornei Chukovsky's work.

Anyway, by the beginning of February 1953, he, like me, was out of a job and without hope of one. Just to complete the picture, they also turned Tonya away from the kindergarten.

"It's because you're not working, Mamma. Marya Ivanovna said that now you had time to look after me."

Yes, I had any amount of time on my hands now. But soon I no longer had the means to feed Tonya as generously and as well as she had been fed in the kindergarten.

When you have lived for years on end without any sense of the future or any real feeling for the reality of the morrow, the whole idea of putting something aside, of saving, goes clean out of your head. There had been periods when we had been earning quite a lot of money. We could have saved up for a rainy day. But when every day is rainy, you somehow don't think about it. And now we were ourselves astonished at where all the money had gone; all at once we were without means.

Our friends naturally came to our aid. They once again found us private pupils and private patients. We gave the former lessons and the latter treatment, as if in a dream, almost mechanically. Because by now our feeling of doom, our expectation of a final catastrophe, had reached its apogee. We realized that the whole process had now relocated itself on a different time scale—to be calculated in days, hours, and, perhaps, even minutes. The powerful radiation emanating from the White House had penetrated us through and through. Day and night we lived in expectation of arrest for the third time.

I feel guilty vis-à-vis the reader. It's so monotonous! Here we are again, awaiting arrest! Not another round of those nightmares!

But anyone who has himself experienced this morbid tension of the nerves, anyone who has felt like a duck with the hunter's gun trained on him, will not condemn me. He will know that the second arrest is far more terrifying than the first one, and the third one far worse than the second. Yes, by the time you have tottered as far as the seventh circle of hell, the first seems utter paradise.

And February 1953 was a time of tempests. They groaned and howled so, those familiar Scythian blizzards outside our window, during our sleepless nights. And for some reason they kept chanting an idiotic doggerel contributed by some newspaper to the case of the doctor-assassins: "And the serpent's hand could not strike the eagle's noble heart."

But the serpent has no hands! That is what makes it so terrifying, that it has no hands. . . . It wriggles, and it unerringly sinks its fangs deep into one's heart. It would surely never strike at the noble eagle, but *my* heart would be an easy target. . . .

Steps in the corridor! We had such a long corrridor—fifteen rooms on one side and fifteen on the other. The slightest sound from the corridor was audible in any room. Steps . . . They're here! My whole body cringes, right down to my toes. I won't let them take me! Not again! I've had enough!

But what was I to do? It was quite simple—I would die. Could I bring myself to do it? Of course! It would happen if I wanted it badly enough. Provided I no longer cared about saying good-by to these ground mists, to these chanting blizzards. If I could simply entrust myself to death's care with a light heart. It alone could release me. The main thing was that it would extinguish memory. I had grown so weak that I could no longer bear the recollection of past sufferings, let alone the thought of new sufferings to come.

Anton tried to rescue me from my state of numbness, from the pitiful immobility of a rabbit hypnotized by a snake. He suggested that I should set to energetically and get our affairs in order. What affairs? "Well, what about your belongings?" he said. "Just so that the White House won't get them. We have children, remember. . . ."

He was, of course, right. We worked feverishly to dispose of our possessions. After all, we did have something of value: the piano. We lugged it into the room of Stepan and Claudia Gusyev. They handed over six thousand rubles in cash for it. And Stepan muttered that it was a provisional transaction, and as soon as things quieted down—and that was bound to happen, surely—he could roll the piano straight back again, since we were only next door.

On this occasion Claudia was able to think more clearly than her husband. She shook her head, blew her nose, and promised to bring us parcels.

With the help of the practical-minded Julia we sold our old bric-a-brac quite profitably, and emerged with a substantial sum of money—eleven thousand rubles. Half of that sum we sent off to Vasya: "Put it in your savings book, but don't touch it until you hear for certain that I am no more." This was what I wrote on the counterfoil of the money order. At that time Vasya's higher education was still an obsession for me. If Vasya had to leave the Institute it would be almost as much of a tragedy for me as my own extermination. I would have scratched out the eyes of anyone who predicted that Vasya would not make use of his medical degree and that his life would take an entirely different course. That was the blood of my unknown ancestors speaking—people who had been ready to go without soup as long as they could raise learned children.

Tonya was in a worse position than any of us. It was dreadful to think that she would land in a children's home once more after having had a real home with Mamma and Papa. Our present, odd behavior was very much to her liking. No one went rushing off anywhere, no one had to go to work. She woke up as merry as a grig and started singing in her bed, clapping her hands together and shouting, "Papa's at home! Mamma's at home!"

I was racked with remorse! How could I ever have linked the child to my life, a life preyed on by demons? It had been sheer egoism on my part. I had needed a substitute for Alyosha. No, not a substitute; there could be no substitute for him, not even Vasya. Not a substitute for him, but a constant reminder of him. Not one that tore me to shreds, but a gentle reminder. . . . And look what the result was now. . . .

I felt a little better when we received a letter from Anton's sisters in Kazakhstan, where they were living as deportees. They wrote that they were ready to take on the little girl, whom they considered a member of the family, if—heaven forbid—anything should happen to us. Apparently, Anton had written to them without telling me about it. Julia promised to send the child off to the sisters at once in the company of some reliable free person returning to the mainland.

So it was all done, everything was provided for. Now we could only wait. And we waited. Our friends, too, waited. When they came across us in the street, they were delighted: "They're still around!" When they came to visit us, they first knocked at the Gusyevs' door to check whether our room had been sealed off. We didn't mind. We ourselves were paralyzed with fear. We imagined *agents provocateurs* or people from the White House everywhere. After burning our fingers on the poetry lover, Krivoshei, we now treated anyone we did not know with suspicion.

I remember how scared we were when we received a visit from an unknown young man who announced himself to be a distant relative of one of Anton's free colleagues at the hospital, Dr. Chernov. Just before that Chernov had left on a visit to the mainland. It seemed to us frightfully suspicious that our visitor, who according to his account had just arrived from the mainland, should be so very like a camp inmate. He had sharp, prominent cheekbones, with dry, scaly skin stretched tightly over them; a skimpy jacket; down-at-the-heel felt boots; and a Siberian-type fur hat that had seen better days. It all reminded us of the types we had come across in the taiga. Not until much later did we, who had seen nothing of wartime Russia, learn that in those years—the "fatal forties"—it was quite normal to see people looking like that in our towns and villages. In addition to all this, Gleb—as the young man was called—was a deserter from a collective farm and had been on the run for two years. He had found a way out of his troubles in the Dalstroi Personnel Department, where he had been taken on as a mechanical-digger operator for the Kolyma gold mines. The need for workers with that specialty was so great that the personnel department turned a blind eye to Gleb's tarnished curriculum vitae.

Because he was in constant fear of the avenging arm, in addition to being underfed and homeless, a certain animal glint crept into Gleb's eyes from time to time—not so much the look of a wolf, more that of a stray dog surrounded by his pursuers. But he had soft, rather slack lips. They revealed him as someone to be pitied. Gleb ate with the voracity of someone who appreciated having food to eat. Over his third mug of tea, he recovered from his initial embarrassment, unbuttoned his jacket, and started to give us a highly realistic description of life on the collective farms.

"I'm telling you everything quite frankly, because I've been told to look on you as friends."

We exchanged glances. "I look on you as friends" was the expression that our friend Krivoshei had liked using. And he used to sit at the table in precisely the same place Gleb was sitting in now. And we used to entertain him just as hospitably. So a bizarre dialogue ensued.

GLEB. When the kids started swelling with hunger, I made up my mind. I'll get out of here, I thought, and earn a few kopecks somehow to send to them. I couldn't bear to look at them.

WE   [*After a pause, with downcast eyes and speaking like automatons*].
Do you have many children?

GLEB   [*Not noticing our state of fright*].
Three of them . . . The wife had to work like a horse while I was away at the war. And now the authorities, instead of saying thank you . . .

WE   [*With the false intonation of inexperienced liars*].
Where are you staying in Magadan?

I have written at length of this casual encounter to show to what depths we descended in our persecution mania. I could already see in my mind's eye the crisp formulations about slandering the collective farm system which would be lying in the latest additions to our White House dossiers, next to a few lines on the affair of the cockroach. For a moment or two I was sure almost beyond doubt that Gleb had been sent to us to obtain additional confirmation of Krivoshei's depositions. And yet only our persecution mania made us mistake this eternal underdog from the village of Lost-in-the-Mud for a *provocateur* and allowed us to see anything ambiguous or contrived in his ingenuous lamentations.

That was the sort of black thought we allowed into our hearts. Our tea-drinking session with Gleb was always to remain with me as one of my shameful memories. Even today I feel ashamed when his face floats in front of me with a look of painful bewilderment in his eyes. In his mind he must have been comparing the good things Dr. Chernov had said about us with what he had encountered that day.

"F-f-forgive me, if there's s-s-something wrong," he stammered, getting to his feet. "I only, you see . . . I only meant . . . And then they kept telling me that . . ."

When he had gone we had a quarrel over some trifle. Then I burst into tears and said:

"I'm an utter worm!"

"The thing is that they would never bother to send anybody else now. After all, they've already got more than enough material on us," Anton said. He added, "Let's go out for a walk."

We always went for a walk when things became too much. We went out whatever the weather—what did we care about blizzards or snow storms? We used to roam around the town and then wander in the direction of Marchekan or toward the sugar-loaf hill. The reward for our exertions was total physical exhaustion. Having achieved a state of complete collapse, we were then able to get some sleep, for however short a period, and despite the fearful nightmares. All that mattered was to get to sleep!

But incidents like our treatment of Gleb happened to Anton less frequently than they did to me. The main thing was that he was still as kind as ever; he would never refuse to dash off, at any hour of the night or day, to see anyone who was ill and had called for his help. At times he was a prey to a sort of condemned man's frenetic jollity. He would start to make jokes, tell funny stories, and suggest we go to the cinema.

"Let's go! It's perfect peace of mind for at least two hours. They wouldn't dream of arresting us in the cinema. They don't want to cause any disturbance."

And we frequently did go to the cinema. We sat in our seats, holding hands, encouraged by the fact that the glances directed at us contained neither dread nor cruelty. They held nothing but curiosity. For the entire town knew the German doctor. They all knew that he had just been removed from his job. And nearly all of them—including those at the top—were unhappy about it. They all needed him.

The last day in February there was some Italian film on at the Gornyak Cinema.

"I'll pick up some tickets," said Anton. He went out, leaving me alone with my pupil. I was coaching a girl who had got dismally bad marks in Russian.

Suddenly there was a knock at the door. He had come. The man we had been expecting. I immediately realized this by some sixth sense.

"What's wrong with you?" shouted the thirteen-year-old. She told me later that I had gone as white as a sheet.

Without waiting for an answer to his knock, he opened the door. He gave it a powerful jab with his white felt boot, and it yielded submissively. It was someone in civilian clothes. He was only given away by his standard-issue boots and by the piping on the high uniform collar that just protruded above the fur collar of his overcoat. Not that it mattered! Had he come in royal regalia, or dressed up as a musketeer, I would have known him at a glance. One of *them!*

"Where is Walter?" he asked without any preamble. And in the same voice. With the same intonation. The Butyrki-Lubyanka-Elgen-Vaskov's House voice.

"I don't know. . . ."

"What do you mean, you don't know? He's your husband, isn't he?"

"He didn't say where he was going. He may have gone to see a patient. . . ."

"How can he go to see a patient when he was dismissed from his post a month ago?"

He appeared to have no interest in me personally. But he scrutinized the room carefully. He strode around it as though he owned the place, his boots leaving large wet imprints on the floor. He glanced at the young lady's exercise book and read with some slight interest the rule on the spelling of a participle with a negative prefix. Then he looked at his watch.

"If he gets back soon, he's to come straight away to the Red House, Room Number 17. But if he's not back within the hour, then he's to come tomorrow by 9 A.M. Remember, not the White House but the Red House, is that clear?"

By 9 A.M. I heaved a sigh of relief. So we had been granted one extra night. I mustn't forget all the things I had to say to Anton. The most important things. For after the arrest of someone close to you, just like after his death, it always turns out that you have forgotten to tell him the one thing that matters. . . . Oh, if only this man would go away before Anton returns, if only he can avoid meeting him in the corridor!

I strained every muscle, trying to project the thought into the other's mind: Go away, go away for heaven's sake! But he was in no hurry. He glanced at his watch again. Oh, horror! He was sitting down!

No . . . only adjusting the puttee that had detached itself from his right boot. He rose to his feet. . . .

"So, at nine sharp! Is that clear?"

I wanted to follow him out into the corridor but my backward pupil, who had fully grasped the meaning of this entire episode (a real native of Kolyma!) pushed me back and tiptoed after the white felt boots. The seconds went by endlessly.

"He's gone . . ." my pupil whispered, and there were tears in her short-sighted eyes. "He's gone down the hill toward the bay. . . . Anton Yakovlevich is just coming from the town. . . . But from the other direction . . . No, no, they didn't meet!"

Anton took just one look at me from the doorway, and knew all that had happened.

"They came for me?"

I told him briefly what had happened.

"We mustn't be separated for a moment," he said. "They might have come for you first . . . and hauled you off in my absence. . . ."

For several minutes we discussed—with the active participation of my pupil—the very important detail that he was ordered to report to the Red House rather than to the White House. It gave grounds for hope.

"In the Red House they deal with exile and resettlement," explained our thirteen-year-old young lady from Kolyma, whose father was another Mr. Felt Boots. "If it were a new sentence, then it would have to be the White House." On this subject she could score top marks. She might not know when to write a participle and the preceding negative as one word, but she knew all about this.

After sitting on the stool for a short while, just as he was, in his fur hat and overcoat, Anton got up decisively.

"We mustn't be late for the cinema, Genia. . . . Of course we're going. . . . We're not going to spend our last free evening moping around here like martyrs! We might as well amuse ourselves. . . ."

We took Tonya over to Julia's; and once again we found ourselves sitting hands clasped in our favorite seats, in the last row but
one, near the side aisle.

In the course of the Italian film, they showed part of a Catholic
mass. Anton was overjoyed.

"Dear me, what a primitive savage you still are, Genia," he
whispered, "a real Communist Hottentot! Just to think, you've never
heard that, or anything like it. But then you have all that joy ahead
of you. . . ."

And suddenly we both distinctly heard from behind me a girl
in an expensive astrakhan jacket, saying to her neighbor with a
sigh:

"Fancy that, how they used to worship God! Just as if he were
Stalin!"

The night went by amazingly quickly. It was strange, but that
night I did manage to get to sleep. We reasoned that since the
summons was for nine in the morning they were hardly likely to
come that night. But after we woke up, at about six o'clock, the
hours rushed by at a furious rate. Once again we hadn't managed
to say the things that mattered most, and Anton was already standing in the doorway in his overcoat and fur hat. Once again, he said:

"Forgive me if I've done anything to hurt you."

"Shh! shh! How many hours should I wait before giving up hope
that you'll come back?"

"About four, at least four. I'll have to go through the documentation point . . . then wait around outside offices. So don't abandon
hope until one o'clock, understand? And if I don't return, we will
be together again sometime."

To work off my fearful state of emotional tension, to find some
outlet for the turmoil inside me, I started to wash the floor. I
scrubbed frantically at those spots where there were still traces of
yesterday's felt boots. And then I furiously soaped the floorcloth, as
if I seriously intended to restore it to its original state.

A knock at the door. It was all right, it was only our friend
Mikhail Frantsevich Heiss, one of Anton's fellow countrymen, also
a German "colonist" from the Crimea. He looked not only worried
but also badly shaken up, and this reinforced my sense of despair.

"You've already heard?" I asked.

"Yes. Have you heard too?"

I was momentarily surprised by his strange question; how could

I, of all people, not know? Then I began to question him: What was the outlook for someone who had been summoned not to the White House but to the Red House? Could we possibly hope that . . . ?

"Yes, we can," he declared, with what sounded like absurd solemnity. "We may indeed hope now."

And then he added, quite inconsequentially:

"Why have you turned the radio off? Turn it on!"

"Heavens above! What's the matter with you? Don't you realize that Anton has been summoned to the Red House?"

Without answering, he went over to the wall and plugged in the radio. Suddenly, through all the crackling, I heard . . . Dear Lord, what was I hearing?

"There has been a deterioration. . . . Intermittent heartbeat . . . pulse barely detectable."

The announcer's voice, tense as a violin string, throbbed with suppressed grief. A wild, improbable surmise flashed through my mind like a bolt of forked lightning, but I could not bring myself to trust in it. I stood in front of Heiss, my eyes popping out; I was still clutching the floorcloth, from which water was dripping onto the floor.

"We have just broadcast a bulletin on the health . . ."

The din in my head—as if the noise of the high tide had entered the room all the way from the bay—prevented me from hearing the long list of ranks and titles. But then, loud and clear, I heard:

"Iosif Vissarionovich Stalin."

The clean floorcloth fell from my hands and plopped into the bucket of dirty water. Then silence . . . In the silence I quite distinctly heard Anton's rapid footsteps in the corridor.

"He's back!"

"They've taken my identity card," Anton proclaimed in a euphoric voice, as if he were announcing good tidings. "They suddenly realized that I was not down on the lists of exiles or of deportees. They'll simply change my status to that of compulsory settlement."

"Who knows whether they will or not?" responded Heiss mysteriously.

Anton was on the point of telling us about what they had said in the Red House when the loudspeaker again blared out for all it was worth. "We are broadcasting the latest bulletin on . . ."

"Anton, dearest," I insisted, clutching at Anton's hand. "Anton . . . But what if . . . what if he gets better?"

"Don't talk nonsense, Genia," Anton almost shouted at me in his excitement. "I tell you as a doctor: recovery is impossible. Do you hear? 'Cheyne-Stokes respiration'—that means he's in his death throes."

"You are simply babes in arms!" Heiss said in an icy tone of voice. "Do you really think that if there were any hope of his recovery, they would have told the people about this illness? Most likely he is already dead."

I collapsed on the table, sobbing loudly. My body shook. It was my unwinding, not only for these last months spent awaiting my third arrest; I was also weeping for two lost decades. In the space of a minute the whole procession of events swept by before my eyes. All the tortures and all the prison cells. All the long files of those who had suffered the final penalty, and the countless legions of those who had been made to suffer. And my own life destroyed by his diabolical will. And my boy, my dead son . . .

Somewhere over the hill and far away in a Moscow that had become unreal to us, the blood-stained graven idol of our century had breathed his last. That was an event of overwhelming importance for millions whose suffering had not yet reached its term, for those nearest and dearest to them, and for each small, individual life.

I must confess that I was sobbing not for the monumental historical tragedy alone, but most of all for myself. What this man had done to me, to my spirit, to my children, to my mother . . .

"What time is it?" asked Heiss.

"Midnight," answered Anton. "The twelfth hour has struck. Soon we will all be free. . . ."

· *They're playing Bach on the radio*

Both up to and after March 5, in the harrowing days of the funeral rites of the Great and Wise One, Bach ruled supreme on the air. Music occupied an unprecedented, colossal place in the radio broadcasts of that brief period. Majestic musical phrases, slow and luminous, rolled forth from all the loudspeakers in our building, drowning out the clatter of children's feet in the corridor and the hysterical sobbing of the women.

Yes, in our building, inhabited by the down and outs of Kolyma society, women diligently wailed for the deceased, crying, "Who will look after us now that you are gone?" They knew what was right, our womenfolk, and they did not want to be upstaged by their neighbors. The whole of Magadan was sobbing; they sobbed too.

But then there were moments when they came together in the kitchen, suddenly broke off their wild lament, and exchanged matter-of-fact opinions as to what *would* happen to us orphans now. Regarding foreign affairs, they all agreed that there was no escaping war because now there was no one to stand up for us. But as for internal affairs, some optimistic notes were to be heard through their sobs: maybe things would be a little easier now. . . . Maybe some of us might manage to move to the mainland.

"Why aren't you crying, Mamma?" asked Tonya. "All the other Mammas are crying except you. . . ."

"Mamma has already cried once," Anton patiently explained to her. "But you weren't there. You were with Aunt Julia."

During the period of mourning Anton suddenly found himself with an enormous clientele on his hands. The higher-ups kept sending for him to visit them. Many of them had been taken ill from their feelings of distress, from their state of complete emotional confusion, and from their fears for the future. And they remembered the existence of the disgraced and dismissed German doctor who had had to hand in his passport at the Red House, but who was nevertheless a skillful practitioner, damn it!

Confusion had overtaken the Kolyma V.I.P.'s even before the announcement of the fatal outcome of the illness of our Leader and Friend. The preliminary news bulletins had already plunged the authorities into a state of agonized incomprehension. For they had completely overlooked the strange fact that the Generalissimo was made of the same imperfect flesh and blood as we sinful mortals. The very fact of his illness was a crack in the structure of that happy, intelligible, harmonious planet of which they were the denizens and the masters and which they so skillfully controlled. Blood pressure . . . albuminates in the urine . . . Damn it, that sort of stuff was all very well for ordinary mortals, but what could such base matters possibly have to do with *him?*

The ancient Slavs would doubtless have been equally offended in their noblest feelings if they had been suddenly informed that Perun's blood pressure had gone up; likewise the Egyptians, if they had suddenly learned that their god Osiris had albuminates in his urine.

The effect of his death on the Kolyma bosses was even more destructive. It was no wonder that during those few days many of them had heart attacks or dangerously high blood pressure. For all the realism of their outlook, these people could not accept the vulgar notion that the Genius, Leader, Father, Creator, Inspirer, Organizer, Best Friend, Coryphaeus, etc., etc., was subject to the same base laws of biology as any prisoner or special resettler. The audacity of Death intruding upon that giant system, so beautifully constructed, so thoroughly planned, was beyond belief. Moreover, they had all become used to the idea that persons of note could die only if Stalin personally gave the order. And suddenly . . . No, really, there was something scandalous, something indecent about it. . . .

Johann Sebastian Bach's measured music was called on to prop up the tottering pillars of majesty.

There were not a few heart attacks and nervous breakdowns at the same time among our political deportees, too. Deprived of hope for decades on end, we were bowled over by the first flicker of distant lightning. Accustomed as we had grown to slavery, we almost went into a dead faint when the thought of freedom first dawned on us. Chained to our icy prison, we felt ill as memories of trains, ships, and planes were reborn in us. . . .

Not one of us could bear to stay put in those days. We used to roam the streets. We would stop every time we met one of *us*. With a cautious look to each side, we exchanged a secret twinkle, an excited whisper. It was as if we were all drunk. Everyone's head was spinning with the expectation of imminent change. And although no one yet knew that Ehrenburg's facile pen would shortly launch the springtime word "thaw," we seemed to hear already the creaking sound of the ice floes freeing themselves from their long immobilization, and we had already taken to repeating in jest Ostap Bender's phrase, "The ice is on the move, gentlemen of the jury!"

"They say it'll be Molotov."

"Hardly . . . He's an ass. . . . He can only repeat the old tricks."

"Well, that's all that's needed. . . ."

"More likely Beria . . ."

"If so, things may get even rougher, I think."

"But there must be some sort of document . . . a will naming his successor."

"In any event they'll do away with forced settlement—you'll see!"

"Not to mention twenty-five year sentences . . ."

From time to time some completely bewildered voice was to be heard saying, "Just so long as it doesn't get any worse. . . ."

But any such person was loudly and instantly squashed. The old debates about the role of the individual in history were renewed. There were still orthodox Marxists to be found among the deportees; they mumbled through their cracked and colorless lips things they had once learned by rote at lectures on dialectical materialism.

But the vast majority of deportees had clearly registered the shock caused to the state when it lost its sovereign at the close of his thirtieth year on the throne; they had witnessed the confusion and panic of its servants, high and low, when "the finger that for so many years had pushed the most important button of the whole administrative machine" had ceased to exist.

On the fourth day of the funeral music, when I got home from Magadan, I observed that our piano was back in its old place. A smiling Stepan Gusyev, our miraculous teetotaler driver, had this time broken his pledge. He and Anton were both sitting at the table sipping champagne—our Kolyma substitute for lemonade and for mineral water—from mugs.

"You're safe now," said Stepan, giving me a friendly wink. "They won't touch you now."

He found a third mug in the cupboard, filled it for me, and pronounced:

"Well . . . To freedom!"

"The voice of the people is the voice of God," Anton commented.

In actual fact there were not as yet any concrete signs that the danger for us was over. Strictly speaking, the possibility that the White House would take action on Krivoshei's denunciation was in no way excluded. But we felt intuitively that this would not happen. Without any joint decision on the matter, without ever discussing it, we stopped expecting a third arrest. It was as if a millstone had fallen from around our necks. One major contribution to this newly acquired sense of life was made by music, the music of Bach, which day and night continued to pour out of the radio. It served to remind us that he who had personified madness and cruelty was no more.

I could not have explained precisely what it was I expected from the near future. But I waited in passionate expectation. Each morning now began for me with the thrilling feeling that everything had quaked, shifted, changed position. We were at the headwaters of a new epoch. Of course, disquiet was our constant companion. It lured us out into the street. There was a need to see people and hear their opinions on our future and on the country's future. And how wonderful it was to find that nearly all of "our people" shared these feelings!

One time Julia and I were walking along the central street of Magadan. We met Aleksei Alekseevich Astakhov. He was a friend of Anton's from his stint in the gold mine. He was glowing all over. His splendid Alexander II–type black beard gleamed, as did his hazel eyes, and his teeth, which were white and indestructible like Anton's. He was the most picturesque person imaginable: tall, elegant, and handsome. And it was pure joy to hear him speak. He was such a witty, amusing, brilliant talker. And all this despite long years of imprisonment.

"I wish you great joy on this happy day of resurrection!" cried Aleksei Alekseevich. For a moment his voice drowned out even the funeral music, which was still in full spate over the radio, from every loudspeaker within hearing. . . . Astakhov had gone deaf at the mine and now he was not always successful in adjusting the volume of his booming voice to suit the ears of his interlocutor.

Cautious Julia was in a panic. She looked around at the passers-by. Then she shouted out equally loudly, straight into Astakhov's ear:

"I didn't realize Easter was so early this year."

She gave me a look of triumph. Look how I've dealt with this embarrassing situation! Then, so as to be absolutely certain, Julia added feelingly:

"The most probable thing is that Lavrenti Pavlovich . . . will become General Secretary. . . . That would be the most sensible solution. . . ."

My dear Julia, what a conspirator you would have made. But your efforts were wasted! Not one of the passers-by was paying the slightest attention to us. They all had a mass of new problems, new worries on their minds. In this new situation each one was only beginning to feel his own way along.

Two other deportees came up to us: again a cross fire of forecasts, theories, and apprehensions. The dazzling word "rehabilitation" had not yet entered into our conversations, but talk of "amnesty"—we thought of it as a humiliation, yet longed for it—was already in the air. And there were already quite a few comrades in the know who were forecasting exactly what articles would come within the scope of this good-will act of the new government.

In all this talk there was a great deal that was comic, silly, or touching. People who had been cut off from life on the mainland for decades could not fail to make some mistakes in their judgments. But we were all united in our certainty that whoever now ascended the Moscow throne (and somehow no one doubted that the dictatorship would be a one-man affair) would be less cruel than the deceased. Because even by satanic, let alone human, standards it was impossible to be more cruel.

Our optimistic speculations first began to assume flesh within ten days of the end of the Generalissimo: on March 15, the day for the next reporting-in of the deportees and resettlers. As I went into the long, narrow corridor where we usually stood in an endless file leading up to the doors of the commandant's office, I noticed that there was a bench along the notorious wall.

A bench! Quite a comfortable one with a back, like a garden seat. A long one, seating about ten people. There were four people on it already. They all had shining eyes and broad smiles. For after all, we had been standing here for years, waiting our turn, propping up with our backs and sides the dirty gray wall, which left whitish marks on our clothes. For years we had shifted from one leg to the other, waiting for the magic door to open, allowing the sullen commandant to stamp our documents without raising his eyes, thereby prolonging our existence for another two weeks. And suddenly a bench had materialized on this spot, a bench with a back. . . .

"Sit down, my dear," an old man in a gray padded jacket with blue elbow patches said to me: "Sit down and have a rest! The commandant doesn't want you to tire yourself unnecessarily."

He winked merrily at me with his bloodshot sclerotic eye, and the other three guffawed. Laughter in the commandant's office!

Within ten minutes or so the bench was filled, but those for whom there was no room were quite happy and stared lovingly at those already on it.

And then a second miracle occurred. Both our commandants hurried into the building, closing the door behind them to keep out the draughts and . . . smiled at us. To tell the truth, their smiles were a bit forced, a bit uncertain, with an underlying hint of apprehensiveness. But the fact remained: the commandants had been seen to smile. The same commandants—and we had seen a large number of them come and go—who had invariably walked past us, slamming the street door behind them without actually shutting it and so letting all the cold drafts into the corridor, without even glancing in our direction, and with faces of rock as if we were not living creatures but parts of the building.

"In you come, comrades," said one of the commandants. "The two of us will get you stamped in half the time. . . . Five of you at a time. And the rest of you take a seat on the bench over there; you won't have long to wait."

"I thought he said 'comrades.' Or did I hear wrongly?" asked Golubyova, one of the resettlers, whom I knew from Vaskov's House.

"No, you heard correctly," replied the old man with the blue elbow patches.

"If we're entitled to the bench, what's to stop us being called comrades?" Smacking his lips, he added, "It's what you might call socialist humanism!"

A friendly chorus of laughter greeted his sally.

The days flew by, and bit by bit the funeral music began to give way to the usual talks and discussions. We now kept our radio permanently plugged in. For the first time you could actually expect real news amid the usual torrent of nonsense from the little box.

And one day we really did hear something that astounded not merely the whole world but even the old Kolyma hands. It was at the beginning of April.

"Listen!" shrieked Claudia Gusyev, flying into the kitchen. "Listen to the radio!"

The radio in the kitchen was kept permanently on, but it was always drowned out by the sputtering of gas primuses and kerosene burners and by the sound of women's voices. But this time there was instantaneous and complete silence. In the sudden silence we listened to the reading of the official announcement on the termination of the Doctors' Case—"the assassins in white gowns." The text obviously gave the announcer a lot of bother. His voice, so used to reciting triumphal achievements and heroic moments, sounded odd. His had been the voice of the Infallible State. But now, for the first time in the memory of the listeners, it was having to speak of its own errors. And not only of errors, but also of "illegal methods of investigation"! True, these strange words were pronounced somewhat indistinctly, as if they had to be forced out through the teeth, and with obvious effort. None the less, they were uttered. To our way of thinking this was the beginning of a new era.

"Illegal methods of investigation." Just think of it! They had come out with it at last. These four words became a vaccine injected under the skin of millions of Kolyma deportees and prisoners and produced irrepressible excitement—in all of them together and in each one of them individually. People stopped sleeping. They grew haggard with the strain, with the expectation of unheard-of changes at any minute. They talked themselves hoarse, telling and retelling one another, as if in a sort of fever, the same old stories of interrogation that they had related a thousand and one times before now over those long, long years. All the wounds of '37 and '49 were reopened, tingled unbearably, and demanded relief. They were no longer to be borne after the appearance in the press, even in the newspaper *Sovietskaya Kolyma* of those four words—"illegal methods of investigation."

Gradually, excesses started to crystallize from the formless ferment. One of the deportees threw his identity card in the commandant's

face and shouted out: "I'm not coming again! I'm too old to have
to come and pay my respects to you every two weeks and wheedle
a stamp out of you. If you want me, you can come and get me!
But I'm not coming here again!" The important point is that nothing
happened to him. A few days later he received his identity card
back through the mail. And it had been stamped for the two weeks
in question and for another two weeks ahead after that. . . .

At the Magadan men's transit camp the work force kicked up
merry hell over some soup that had gone sour. Some of them even
flung their bowls onto the floor. And again the authorities bore
with them. No one was put in the punishment cells. And they were
each issued two ladlefuls of *kasha* in place of the sour soup.

One sunny April morning it was suddenly discovered that an
unknown malefactor had jammed a rusty night bucket on top of
Comrade Stalin's statue—the one in the Magadan Park of Rest and
Culture—right on top of his head.

Simultaneously there were rumors of mutinies in the camps. Not
in our area—somewhere around Vorkuta and Igarka. The information about the disturbance was vague and fragmentary, as if relat-
ing to some distant underground tremors. But their echo was certainly heard; it went the round of our tenements like a distant roll
of thunder. Unheard-of changes . . . unprecedented mutinies.

Now, when I look back, I can see that those were happy days
for us. We achieved some release from our fear; an instinctive feeling of relief as yet, not based on facts or on a sober analysis of
them. But nevertheless . . . Our muscles suddenly tensed; our
spiritual energies rallied; it was as if we had been thrust under a
magic shower. It had stripped away the apathy that had seemingly
suffused every pore of our body. We grew young again. I became
fantastically full of energy. I felt twenty years old.

I launched a number of assaults on the authorities. First and fore-
most I sent in a petition for my rehabilitation. For the very first
time. I had never before succumbed to the mass psychosis of sending
off petitions, which had affected so many people. Often enough in
Elgen, after the evening roll call, taking care that the wardens did
not see, people would write by the dim light of oil lamps petition
after petition, varying only the address. Sometimes it was the
Procurator General, sometimes the Ministry of State Security, sometimes the Chairman of the Council of Ministers, sometimes the
Central Committee. But more often than not the addressee would be

Comrade Stalin. Some people tossed off several hundred petitions during their period in camp. The answer was always the same: "There are no grounds for a review of sentence."

I had never indulged in this sort of thing. I knew for a fact that as long as the Children's Best Friend was on the throne, not a single Kolyma mother would return to her children.

I was now writing a petition in the belief that there was a chance of getting a favorable answer to it. I addressed it to Voroshilov, because I had once met him in my youth. I included a brief reminder of myself, informed him of my fate and asked him to intervene. He could do so; and *now* he had the opportunity of doing so. I was in no doubt that the tyrant's death had freed not only us, but all those who had stood behind him in the role of his nearest comrades in arms.

Of course, in my aspirations and hopes at that time there was little room for sober analysis of the situation or of the peculiarities of the system as a whole. In the state of general euphoria in which we then all found ourselves the emotions got the upper hand. The feeling of almost physical rebirth which we then experienced prevented us from reasoning things out, assessing them, or weighing them.

Just how far my hopes for the start of a new era had gone was evident from the mere fact that I dashed off various letters to the mainland requesting copies (or better) of my academic documents. At the very least, a copy of my university diploma. Julia assured me that I might equally well ask them to send me a star from the sky. She took it for granted that the one thing left over from our previous life would be the same pink folder marked: "To be permanently retained."

But the miracles continued. The sister of Aksyonov (my husband) succeeded in obtaining from the records office a copy of my university diploma and sent it out to me. At that point I took one further step, bold enough to astound not merely the authorities but even many of my comrades in exile. I wrote to the Dalstroi Political Administration, asking them to indicate on what means I was supposed to exist in exile if I was not allowed to work. I asked for employment to fit my qualifications—as a teacher. As if to underline my challenge, I added, "As there are no institutions of higher learning in Magadan, I am prepared to teach in a secondary school."

"You're out of your mind!" exclaimed Julia. "Do you really want

to call attention to yourself by such demands? They still haven't
dealt with Krivoshei's denunciations of you."

Astakhov made a little joke of it. He even composed a pamphlet,
"From Bench to Chair," in which he related in verse how in my
excitement at seeing the bench in front of the commandant's office
I had asked to be given a professorial chair, whereupon someone
in felt boots had given me a thorough shaking so as to dispel once
and for all any more mad ideas of that kind.

But I stuck to my guns. "Laugh away," I said. "I know what
they'll answer: 'We would be happy to take you on, but you don't
have your diploma or your teacher's license.' Then I'll whisk out
my little diploma and show it to them. We'll see what tune they sing
then. In my view, they'll have had the ground cut from under
their feet."

Anton pretended to sigh at my unreasonableness and remarked
jokingly that the Seven Little Kids hadn't taught me a thing. I was
graduating from ideological-diversionary work among six-year-olds
to its equivalent among sixteen-year-olds.

But these were all jokes. On the serious plane I could see that he
entirely approved of my energetic actions and was himself in the
same state of elation as I.

Not even Beria's amnesty, announced shortly afterward, could
extinguish this mood. Although, of course, it distressed us greatly
and reduced some to complete despair once more. It was an amnesty
solely for common criminals. It hardly affected the politicals because its terms covered only those with sentences of up to five
years. And there were none such among the politicals. Even those
with eight-year sentences were an insignificant minority.

Not only was this amnesty a disappointment; it also brought
along a host of everyday calamities. While waiting for transport
back to the mainland, the professional riffraff released from the
camps terrorized Magadan. The militia could not cope with the
cases of public theft. The audacity of these criminals left us with
the idea, or rather the anxious presentiment, that orgiastic pogroms
were imminent. When darkness fell we were virtually under
blockade in Nagaevo. You were taking your life in your hands if
you crossed the empty site behind the hospital after dark.

Happily, spring came at last even to Kolyma and the rivers were
navigable once again. They started to embark the new free citizens,
the "friends of the people"—Beria's beneficiaries—onto the steam-

ships in small groups. The steamships sailed to Nakhodka Bay and from there to Vladivostok, where their passengers were loaded into freight cars. The train that bore off these packs of desperadoes was nicknamed the Merry Five Hundred. The criminals who had been amnestied were known as the Merrymakers, after the train. We were still hearing rumors a long time afterward about the feats of the Merrymakers in Vladivostok, Khabarovsk, and the Siberian towns along the route to the capital.

At the beginning of the summer Anton was finally offered work. He was taken on by the state insurance organization as a doctor to certify the health of those taking out insurance policies. It was a dull and soulless job from which he returned home each day more out of sorts and a little grayer. But there could be no question of turning it down. For this miserable state insurance job did help rescue us from the state of constant penury which had gone on so long.

"How are you going to formalize my appointment?" Anton inquired of his new bosses. "My passport's been confiscated and I don't have any deportee papers at the moment."

"No matter, it's all been squared with the proper authorities." Such was the evasive, hasty, and even somewhat shamefaced answer he received.

Then I too was offered a job—playing the piano in the Marchekan kindergarten. It was very far away, and very difficult to get to. Moreover, in the changed circumstances, it seemed insufferable to me to have to perform the same drudgery as before. After all, the Head Torturer was no more. Could I really not obtain intellectual work, even in the simplest, most elementary form? Now that fear for our very lives had somewhat receded, deprivation of real work caused me acute suffering. To write and teach. To teach and write. That was what I had been waiting for, that was what I had been thinking about day and night, drawing up in my head outlines of my first lectures. I could not bring myself to commit them to paper for fear of putting the evil eye on them or scaring away my stubborn optimism, which almost no one shared. And yet the unexpected continued to happen. It was as if history was finally starting to operate in our favor.

I was in the kitchen—boiling a repulsively ugly crab under the direction of Aunt Zina, who was on duty that day—at the moment when our permanently plugged-in radio suddenly started regaling us with details from Lavrenti Beria's biography. On hearing that he was an agent of the Tsarist secret police, an English spy, and an arrant enemy of the people, Aunt Zina and I left the boiling crab to the mercies of fate and stared at each other in mute disbelief.

"Aunt Zina," I said, "Aunt Zina, would you please repeat what you just heard over the radio?"

"Why me? What do you think you heard?" she shouted, advancing on me almost aggressively.

"I didn't quite catch it. . . . Or perhaps I misheard it. . . ."

"Well, I haven't been able to make sense of it all for a long time now. You're educated folk, you read newspapers and talk on the telephone. . . . It's not for me to repeat things like that. We're simple folk, we didn't go to no university."

I quickly got ready and rushed off to see Anton at his new place of work.

"Did you hear?"

"Shh, shh," he replied, "Let's say nothing for the moment. I'll finish off here and we'll look in at the post office and check. . . ."

I immediately realized what he had in mind. At the post office, above the registered-correspondence section, hung a portrait of Lavrenti Beria: a very intellectual face; a pince-nez; regular, in fact rather fine, features; and a thoughtful look.

Quite out of breath, we ran into the spacious hall of the post office. Above the head of the young lady who was dealing with registered letters, a large, dark, square, empty space yawned provocatively, almost cynically. It was apparent that the paint on the wall around had faded over the years.

Within a few days of this occurrence Anton was informed in an unprecedentedly courteous way that Colonel Shevelyov of the Red House would like to meet Dr. Walter. No, the colonel was not insisting on any specific time. Whenever the doctor had an hour or so free, would he please phone such-and-such a number.

The meeting took place. The interlocutors, seated cozily side by side on a soft leather settee, discussed with perfect mutual understanding the misbehavior of the colonel's liver, agreed on a diet, summoned the courier—who was flying to Moscow the following day—and handed him there and then a prescription for the homeopathic pharmacy in Moscow. It was only when he had accompanied the doctor to the door and given him a grateful handshake that the colonel suddenly recalled:

"Oh yes, I almost forgot . . . Just one moment, doctor. . . . Your passport has been lying around in my desk. Please take it with you."

A wind usually sprang up as the summer sun went down in Magadan. It would never enter your head to take your overcoat off when you were climbing the rise from the town center to the wasteland by the hospital. Even returning downhill you still felt the cold bite of the wind.

That particular evening when we decided to celebrate the return of Anton's passport, it was all somehow different. You would probably not get a day like that once or twice in the entire summer. Even on the steep slope the air was still, clear, and slightly transparent. We stopped for a moment to look at the bay spread out before us.

"How marvelous it is today!" Anton exclaimed. "It isn't Nagaevo, it's more like Naples. . . ."

White ships, delicately moving aside to make way for one another, were clustered around the jetties. The setting sun, not scarlet as usual but a soft peach color, was nestling gently down onto the dark blue expanse of the sea.

We stopped, unable to tear our eyes away from the undreamed-of beauty exposed to our gaze.

"Naples, did you say?" I retorted. "Well, maybe we'll be able to see Naples too. . . . I feel that life is starting all over again. . . . We're not old yet. . . ."

A time of mad expectation! Of crazy hopes that the lives stolen from us might be restored. Of mysterious, barely audible inner voices.

Well, let us pause to take in this wondrously beautiful sea, to whose beauty we are now alive for the first time in many years. Let us pause to enjoy our illusions a little longer, and put off the descent to reality. The illusions can be left to refute themselves with no help from us. If the Dragon has been killed, it means that the good and brave Prince Ivan, the Tsar's Son, at the head of his noble army, is coming to our rescue.

Let us pause. How can we have failed to notice how picturesque our bay is! We have failed to distinguish between its harsh, primitive beauty and the dirty flotsam of gray jerkins, hideous rope sandals, and vicious yells from convoy guards disgorged by its waters. . . .

Captivated by the weather, the entire population of our building turned out onto the empty site. People had a smoke, called after their children, stroked their knotted, exhausted legs, combed out their hair, or chewed cedar nuts. Just like in a Voronezh or Penza village.

There was unusual silence in the corridor. But you could hear music coming out of the loudspeakers from behind the thirty closed doors (fifteen on either side).

"It's Bach again, I think," said Anton, listening intently.

"That's good. It's a good omen. They always play Bach when they're at a loss for what to say next. . . ."

This was how Johann Sebastian Bach came to be drawn into the secular affairs of us poor sinners.

16

· *The commandants study the classics*

In the middle of August I received an official communication through the mail. The Magadan Department of Education invited me to come and discuss with them the question of my employment. The letter arrived on Friday and I was due to go there on Monday. So I had three full days in which to vacillate between the fear of bringing bad luck on myself and an irresistible desire to show the contents to those who had predicted failure for my foolhardy venture.

I succumbed, and did show it to them. The fabulous letter was passed from hand to hand, read and reread, and discussed at length. "Good gracious, they're summoning you to the Education Department! Can you beat that, a deportee for life being given an interview by the Education Department! . . ." Their passion for extrapolating sweeping generalizations from isolated facts caused our former prisoners to interpret this paper as the surest possible sign of early rehabilitation. Certain inveterate skeptics commented with curled lips: "It's some sort of ruse! It just can't happen."

It was, in fact, difficult to take on trust. Of course, the Education Department was not an institution on a par with the Ministry or the Political Administration, palatial in appearance and surrounded with armed guards. But all the same, the Education Department too was one of the islets of the free world. The caste of untouchables had no right whatsoever to enter. It was not in the same category as our Medical Administration, which employed a whole crowd of ex-zeks and resettlers.

I was the first among us to enter these portals. While I was finding my way along the unfamiliar corridors I couldn't help feeling that some unexpected blow was about to descend on me. In the personnel department office a flashily dressed woman with an imposing bust occupied the foreground. Toward the rear of the room, with his back to the door, sat a man immersed in his files. In silence I handed my treasured certificate to the woman. She lengthily scrutinized it, with such concentration that it might have been in Chinese.

"This person is you?" she finally asked.

Then she went across to a safe as big as a church, took some forms out of it, and put them down in front of me.

"Fill these in!"

A personal questionnaire. The questionnaire for persons embarking on an educational career in this thrice-blessed region of the north. The only one I ever had to deal with. In the thirties such things did not yet exist, while after the Twentieth Congress and my return to the mainland they had already ceased to exist. The forms made an indelible impression on me. Even now I remember individual questions. Your first husband's mother's maiden name . . . And, in parentheses, ditto for second, third . . . State the addresses and places of employment of your brothers, their wives, your sisters and their husbands. . . . Dear God, dear God! What am I getting into? Would it not have been better for me to stay in the world of the Seven Little Kids, where no one teased me with questions like these? But my retreat had been cut off.

"Sit down at the table over there and fill it in legibly without alterations," the good lady ordered, busying herself with some particularly handsome, multicolored folders.

When after working on them for a long time I laid the duly completed sheets before her, her face was a study. And, in human terms, it was easy enough to understand her reaction. She—whose job it was to ferret out every last great aunt with a kulak past, every husband's brother's wife with a non-Russian name—she, who had been trained for such subtle tasks, suddenly found dumped on her desk these cynically frank admissions: imprisonment for terrorist activity (under articles of the criminal code which carried the death penalty), trial by the Military Collegium, forced resettlement for life, two political prisoner husbands, a whole crowd of repressed relatives on Anton's side. Not to mention the plethora of German surnames, which the Orthodox Aksyonovs could not trump, as Pavel had had only one sister and one brother, while Anton had four sisters and four brothers, two of whom, moreover, were living in West Germany.

"Andrei Ivanovich," the good lady called out in a faint voice, "could you come here for just a moment?"

She was summoning help even though she was aware that for some unfathomable reason it had been decided on high to admit me to the teaching profession and that there were orders to process me. But she simply couldn't control her own reactions. Her reflexes, conditioned over the years, paralyzed her. She was like a hunting dog that for some unknown reason is made to release the game it has caught.

The young man sitting with his back to us got up and came across to the good lady's desk. His appearance was of the sort one does not easily forget. Something after the style of a prerevolutionary schoolmaster with a chalk-white forehead. He was patently intelligent. It was apparent from his attentive eyes and his wide, tautly compressed lips that, unlike his superior, he had taken in a number of things during the period since the fifth of March and had in any case learned not to express surprise. With an inscrutable gaze he read through the list of my crimes and the details of my genealogy, and said:

"Splendid!"

The good lady shuddered.

"Splendid!" he repeated. "Now, if you would just write out an application for the vacant post of Russian language and literature teacher in the school for adults. And please attach your academic certificates."

The good lady came to life and seized at this straw.

"But, of course, you don't have your certificates with you, do you?" she inquired.

"Why not? Here they are. Copies, of course. But certified in order."

Unpleasantly surprised, she started to read my diplomas. Her neatly plucked eyebrows rose higher and higher. The poor thing was having a terrible time in reconciling this sort of diploma with *that sort* of biography. But her colleague rose immediately to the occasion.

"What a good thing it is that you'll be working with adults. That will be more like what you're used to as a university teacher than working in a school for children."

What I was used to! Good Lord! Had I ever been that fledgling teacher? Somewhere in the dim past beyond recall—beyond the valleys and the hills, the prisons and the camps—there was a flickering image in the recesses of my memory of a certain young simpleton who used to deliver well-memorized lectures from the podium with complete self-assurance.

For a moment I was gripped with panic. What was I getting myself into? What was I going to teach them? Perhaps I'd forgotten it all. Perhaps they wouldn't want to listen.

"There you are, all signed, sealed, and delivered," the young man stoutly declared, returning with my papers from his superiors. "I'll let you have the relevant extract from your letter of appointment, and you can get in touch with the director of the school."

The day before September 1 I lost my voice from excitement. It didn't go completely, but it was a hoarse drunkard's croak.

"Nervous laryngitis," Anton diagnosed. He gave me a homeopathic preparation made from clover, nicknamed Professor Jack. I don't know whether it helped Jack, but it certainly didn't help me. Jack, presumably, did not have to return to the university after the sort of marathon travels I had undertaken.

"Ordinary medicines are no help in unique situations," I said to Anton, making him very angry. "I'll get better myself!"

I really did get better, just as suddenly as I had contracted the complaint in the first instance. From astonishment. From an unexpected shock.

"Here are your pupils," said the director of the school, leading me into the classroom.

What was this? In front of me I saw officers with brilliant gold epaulettes and beautifully polished boots. One solid mass of officers. Forty of them. Among them I spotted faces I knew. These were our commandants! Both past and present, young ones and older ones. Later on it was explained to me that with change in the air officers were required to have reached a certain educational level; they had to hurry off to adult school to acquire the now essential graduation certificate.

I had been picturing my pupils as workers from the car repair factory and the airport, and perhaps stevedores from the port at Nagaevo. I had visualized worthy, industrious people among whom there would be many of my comrades in misfortune. I had dreamed of making friends with them, of earning their gratitude for what I would give them. And now . . .

"Your Russian language and literature teacher." This was how the director introduced me, and I saw in the eyes of the commandants acute curiosity, derision, perhaps even hostility. Nevertheless they all rose to their feet and barked out in proper military fashion:

"Good day, Comrade Teacher."

"Good day, comrades," I replied, finding to my astonishment that my voice had returned to me. I had been cured, I repeat, by the very unexpectedness of the blow. One had to credit the powers that be with a sense of irony. If there were special reasons for their accepting such a suspect character for pedagogical duties, at least vigilance would be ensured, given the composition of the class. And this was certainly the case: in the looks directed at me vigilance was very much in evidence, whereas of good will and the desire to get from me something new, something hitherto unknown to them, there was little or no trace.

"Well, well, well . . . How am I going to establish a relationship with them when Gorokhov, my commandant, is sitting in the front row? The man who endorses my documents with a violet stamp twice a month . . ."

"Don't you remember, you used to tell me how all the notices he posted up were chock full of mistakes. . . . Go ahead and teach him Russian grammar," Anton calmly reassured me.

"But I have to queue up to see him. . . . He—in fact, each of them—regards me as a criminal."

"I doubt it. The majority of them are just peasant boys. They almost certainly have a sense of reality. . . . And if they can do a year's study they'll become quite different people. . . . The one important thing is to forget all about their epaulettes and ranks. Address them as you would normal pupils. . . ."

Easy enough to say! But it's not so easy breaking firmly established conditioned reflexes! Those jackboots, those smoothly shaven cheekbones and the piping on their collars aroused a persecution complex in me. I peered endlessly into their faces and saw only arrogance in them or, at best, the sort of grins to be expected of a captive audience. I would go into the classroom and almost physically sense the emanations of morose distrust. Some of them were doubtless keeping their ears pricked in case I should start to sneak in something ideologically suspect. Others evidently did not believe that I had plumbed the depths of learning. They endlessly needled me with questions about dates, place names, titles of works—openly consulting their textbooks to check up on my answers.

Relations got still worse after our first dictation test. It reaped a vast harvest of failing grades. An oppressive atmosphere descended on the classroom. These people, who hitherto had been against me on, so to speak, general grounds, had now been personally insulted by me. The more intelligent among them merely concealed their hostility, but those who could not reconcile themselves either to their new role or, for that matter, to the winds of change, went to the school authorities to complain.

After their complaint the director of studies came to the class. He explained to them lengthily and cogently that the comrade officers were not to think that marks were assigned at the whim of the teacher. There was a scale approved by the ministry according to which four spelling mistakes and four mistakes in punctuation resulted in failure.

They could not, of course, answer back in the face of words such as "scale," "ministry," and "approved," but they remained annoyed with me. Captain Epifanov had particular difficulty simmering down. He was a bowlegged, tubby individual, like an actor from the Young Spectator's Theater made up to play the Hedgehog. He did have some vague notion of spelling, but he was immovable on the question of punctuation. Even commas got under his skin, not to mention colons and hyphens. He simply couldn't entertain the thought that serious people would worry about such trivialities.

After the second piece of dictation, for which I unhesitatingly failed him again, he headed a full-blown opposition group that tried to interrupt my explanations by asking provocative questions. During our lessons on syntax I would catch him giving me prickly glances out of his little hedgehog eyes.

So then I resorted to a time-hallowed example, described by Veresaev in his recollections of his own prerevolutionary high school. I wrote down on the blackboard a construction without any punctuation marks. It was Nicholas II's decree on the petition of a criminal under sentence of death: "Execution impossible reprieve." Then I asked Epifanov the question: "Would the condemned man be executed on the basis of the decree?" My restive pupil hummed and hawed, looking sullenly at the blackboard. Finally he gestured dismissively:

"Nicholas II was a well-known idiot! You can read what he wrote one way or the other."

"How about now?" I asked, putting a comma after the word "execution."

"Hmm . . . Now they'll shoot him. . . ."

"And what about this?" I rubbed out the existing comma and put in a new one after the word "impossible."

"He's reprieved!" the whole class shouted out.

"Now you see, Comrade Epifanov, that a man's life may depend on a single misplaced or omitted comma."

My unsophisticated pupils were clearly tickled by this hoary old grammatical curiosity. They clustered around me during the break, trying me out with various casuistical questions about punctuation marks, quoting examples and arguing with each other.

Another episode through which the ice between them and me was partially broken involved First Lieutenant Nasredinov. I had long since marked him down as someone anxious to learn, someone who reminded me of my evening-class students in Kazan long ago. On his side I sensed a relatively friendly attitude toward me. Nasredinov spoke Russian very badly and wrote it even worse, but he never took offense at being given low marks, and studied hard.

On one occasion he had to stand up and say his piece in front of the whole class. The subject was Mayakovsky and his poem "To Comrade Nette."* The poor lieutenant was simply drenched in sweat from his efforts to reproduce the capricious lines. And every-

* The poem commemorates Teodor Ivanovich Nette (1896–1921), who commanded a Red Army battalion during the civil war and died in Latvia while serving as a Soviet diplomatic courier.

one heaved a sigh of relief when he announced that he was now
going to analyze the ideological content of the poem.

"Just a moment, Comrade Teacher . . . the answer's coming. . . ."

Nasredinov then explained that the phrase "bound by an iron
oath" meant that we live in capitalist encirclement; that "you riddle
with bullets" meant "stay where you are or I'll fire!" And as to the
phrase "For its sake you take up your cross" . . .

Nasredinov, head bent, puffed out his cheeks and went red in the
face from the effort to unravel the riddle.

"Just a moment, Comrade Teacher . . . it's coming. . . ."

Then suddenly a radiant smile. He'd got it!

"Aha! I see! 'For its sake you take up your cross.' . . . Russians
put a cross on their graves. So it means 'Stay where you are or we'll
fire and give you a grave with a cross on it.' "

The merry laughter that ran through the class brought a wave
of human warmth with it and dispelled the feeling of tension. What
can be better than genuine good humor to help people uncover the
primary, childlike element in them, free from the incrustations of
cruel, adult experience?

The days flew by, and bit by bit I began to distinguish the different psychological types among my officers. Lieutenant Sumoch-
kin, for example: his opinion of the literary craft and of those who
engaged in it was quite unequivocal. According to him, no particular
skill was needed. Any person who was literate could manage it,
especially in prose. You just described things as they were and
shoved in descriptions of nature from time to time. The person next
to him at the desk supported him, merely adding that ideological
correctitude had to be observed. So long as the ideas were correct,
the writing part was something anyone could do.

No effort on my part could shift them from their adopted stance
of rocklike, militant stupidity. It could be detected in all they said
as unmistakably as a Vyatka or an Odessa accent.

There were also the incorrigibly argumentative types in our
class. They, too, profoundly despised scribblers, pen pushers, and
highbrows, but they expressed their feelings in a lively way—challenging others, inviting objections or altercations. I was not so dis-
couraged by them. The very fact of their assertiveness, their keen-
ness to argue, had a human element to it. There was a hope of
making contact with them, of getting through the protective fatty

tissue to their innermost hearts, where, possibly, something might
be hiding.

"Forgive me for saying so, but why do you need to do it at all,
to get through to the hearts of the likes of them? And what can you
possibly discover in the depths of a gendarme's heart?"

This was the interjection with which Mikhail Frantsevich Heiss
—the same person who had been the first to bring us the news of the
death of the Great and Wise One—broke sharply into my flood of
eloquence during one of our Sunday get-togethers. Heiss was implacable where his recollection of the sufferings he had endured
was concerned. He made no distinction between the Organizer and
the tens of thousands of country clods who had to stamp our deportee documents. From the very beginning he had advised me to
turn down my work in the school, because "They have fobbed you
off with assassins in lieu of pupils." Once I had taken the job, he said:

"Very well, let us assume it was very difficult for you to refuse
a job in your own profession, for which you had been waiting so
long. But why not just teach them what you're supposed to teach
them? Why put your heart into it? Save it for better times. They're
not all that far off. . . ."

Heiss seized on the slightest sign of thaw with extraordinary enthusiasm, looking for far-reaching consequences; thoughts of revenge
on the "butchers" played no small part in his dreams about better
times to come. Almost every Sunday he would try to bring me down
to earth as I told them about my work at school. These confronta-
tions left me with a bitter aftertaste, the more so as I did not as yet
have a fully thought out view with which to counter his own precisely formulated position. It was only when I was alone with Anton
that I felt able to voice my tentative retort to the line Heiss was
taking.

"That way there'll never be an end to it, will there? They'll get
us, then it'll be our turn, and after that . . . How long is all the
hatred going to persist? I'm not, of course, talking about the principal villains—they must be judged according to the magnitude of
their crimes—but just to take our commandants . . . How often
did we manage to survive in the camps thanks to decent convoy
guards? And don't forget Timoshkin! And do you know what happened the day before yesterday after a lesson on Pushkin? Lieutenant
Pogorelko came up to me during the break and asked me to read
just once more—or, as he put it, to tell him once more—Pushkin's

poem 'The Faded Merriment of Madcap Years.' And when I said to
him that the bell had already gone off, didn't he want to go out for
a smoke, he replied that he could always have a cigarette but you
didn't hear verses like that every day. I spent the whole of the long
break reciting Pushkin to them. And they—Pogorelko and about five
others—did without their smoke and listened. And how they listened!
Despise me if you want, but at that moment I saw them not as commandants but as my pupils. And I was desperately anxious that they
should like the very poems I liked."

At one of the regular sessions of the teachers' council the director
of studies said restrainedly that the officers were content with my
lessons. And a week after that I was approached by the class monitor,
Captain Razuvaev, who put forward the idea that now that it was
late autumn the evenings had become very windy and dark. It was
not safe to return home after lessons were over at 11 P.M. and also
to have to cross the vacant site in Nagaevo. So the class had decided
to introduce a duty rota. Each day one of the officers would accompany me all the way home.

Usually Anton met me, but those evenings he was on night duty
(he was now back at work in the hospital) I really did have a difficult time of it. So I accepted the officers' proposal with pleasure.
From now on, each day when I went downstairs to get my coat
from the cloakroom, one of my armed pupils was already waiting
for me there, and under his protection I would make my way securely back to Nagaevo.

I had done my fair share of journeys under guard, but this unusual
form of escort was something quite new to me. We kept in step,
and where there were potholes or humps my companion delicately
supported me by the elbow. There could be a great deal of conversation or very little during these journeys home, depending on
the character of my duty escort, but we observed one unwritten
law: we never spoke about politics even though events were feverishly piling up on us and each day brought with it new impressions,
hopes, and disappointments.

We nearly always spoke about literature, about the classics we
were studying in class. Often this was, on their side, a polite gesture
and a way of passing the time. But on occasion signs of unfeigned
interest in books would suddenly emerge. I sometimes used the
time to give them some extra teaching as we went along. My memory then was very good and I could remember the individual mis-

takes of each one and explain them to him as we made our way across the famous no man's land.

One day it was the turn of my own commandant, Gorokhov, to accompany me. The entire walk I kept on at him about the correct spelling of adjectival suffixes, and it wasn't until we were already going down the hill to Nagaevo that I suddenly remembered aloud:

"Oh yes, tomorrow is the fifteenth! So I'll be coming to see you in your office to get my documents stamped. . . ."

Gorokhov (a young, quite handsome blond of the type you get around Yaroslavl) halted, stared at me, and suddenly asked:

"Do you know Molotov?"

"Of course. Not personally, that is, but well enough. I've followed his career."

"Well, his wife is in the same position as you. . . . She has to register. I don't mean in our office, but she has to do it."

I was not particularly surprised, as I had already heard this. I was much more interested in trying to follow Gorokhov's train of thought.

"In the same position . . . in the same . . ." he repeated thoughtfully and finally broke off decisively, adding:

"I expect it'll soon be all over."

I stayed diplomatically silent. As he said good-by at the entrance, he thanked me jokingly "for the extra lesson while we walked," and said that I should come along the following day ten minutes before his office opened. He would make a point of arriving early and get the stamping over and done with quickly, as he was always uncomfortable at the thought of keeping such an educated lady standing—or, for that matter, sitting—in his office corridor.

"I don't know about being 'educated,'" I said, so as not to lose a chance of steering him toward illicit thoughts. "You've got any number of important scholars on your hands. Take old man Grebenshchikov, for example. He was behind me in the queue last time. He's an eminent geophysicist. A Corresponding Member of the Academy of Science."

"The one with the bad cough?"

"Yes, that's him. He works as hut warden with the builders' brigade."

Meanwhile the question of whether it was possible and admissible to adopt a benevolent attitude toward such bizarre pupils as those I had was a permanent feature on the agenda at our Sunday lunches. My relationship with Heiss got distinctly worse. I was furious with myself for failing to find sufficiently convincing objections to put up against his implacable reasoning, though I was inwardly convinced that I was right. Heiss took the offensive. He waxed sarcastic.

"So in fact they're splendid chaps, these officers from a certain ministry? And it's really quite pleasant to have them to teach classical literature to? And besides, you so much wanted to get back to your own profession. . . ."

"Leave that side of the question out of it. Yes, for many years I've been longing to get back to my own work. I kept dreaming avidly of being able to teach and write. . . . All those years while I was sawing, hoeing, scything, scrubbing floors, changing dressings, etc., etc. . . . Do you consider that a crime on my part? Does it mean that I have no principles?"

"Yes, since you ended up giving lessons to your jailers."

"But does it not occur to you that among the rank and file of the Army of Evil there are people, many people, who can be won over to the side of Good?"

And then the inspiration came to me. I started saying that ours was an age in which events affected such huge numbers of people, and the dividing lines between butchers and their victims were so blurred (think of all the people who had been only too ready to put others through Stalin's mincing machine, before slipping into it themselves!), that barricades such as that which in 1905, for example, divided *them* from *us* no longer existed. The systematic corruption of people's souls by means of the Great Lie, which resembled nothing ever known before, had resulted in thousands and thousands of ordinary people being caught up in the charade. Well then, were we to revenge ourselves on all of them? Should we rival the tyrant in cruelty? Was the ritual of hate to be prolonged indefinitely?

"Yes, but it's obviously no good trying to sow all that is reasonable, all that is good, and all that never dies on such rocky ground as the ordinary MGB district office!"

"Please, Mikhail Frantsevich," Professor Simorin, one of our Sunday regulars, suddenly broke into the conversation. "Let's look at the question in practical terms. At the moment we're all impatiently expecting radical changes in our society; time will tell whether our hopes have any foundation. Suppose we went back to the original ideal? What do you think would become of the countless petty commandants, guard officers, convoy guards? One enormous Nuremberg trial, is that what you have in mind?"

"Yes! Dozens, even hundreds of such trials!" Heiss heatedly exclaimed. "Pitiless vengeance! No, not vengeance, but retribution on all the accomplices and satraps of the tyrant! Let every small cog in that murderous machine receive its just deserts!"

I saw that Heiss had let himself be carried away, that he was now saying more than he really thought or felt. I called to mind how much he had suffered, and I even felt pity for him that he was prey to such bitterness. I very much wanted to quote aloud the words that stand as epigraph to *Anna Karenina:* "Vengeance is mine; I will repay, saith the Lord." . . . But I hadn't the courage to speak up. I was still very inhibited, not so much by the ideas as by the subconscious reflexes implanted in me by my unnatural training. I could not bring myself to voice my thoughts about the eternal and the transient, about the Whole and the human beings who were small, helpless particles of the Whole—the thoughts I used to confide to my prison bunk in Vaskov's House. And instead of this bare and unanswerable Biblical truth, I answered Heiss with a multitude of other, much less cogent, words.

"You say that if one were to leave the malefactors unpunished, they would end up tearing the world into shreds. You are probably right as far as the main agitators, the "inspirers and organizers," are concerned. But if we proceed against everyone who unthinkingly, or from cowardice, greed, simplemindedness, or ignorance, has done wrong; if we give fresh encouragement to bestial cruelty, even if the victims are yesterday's cogs in the complex machinery of evil-doing, where will it all end? What will happen to all of us in this sad and fearful world? We shall end up growing tusks and hair instead of skin! We shall find ourselves back on all fours!"

Anton, who had been watching us and listening to our argument with obvious disquiet, thought he would bring the conversation to a halt with a joke.

"Come on, admit it, you just aren't very good at hating. You lack training. . . . You don't know how to. . . . Your metabolism is all wrong. . . ."

"Not at all. I profoundly hate two of my contemporaries. Fortunately neither is still alive."

"Who's the second one?" inquired Simorin, with a smile.

"Who do you think? Hitler, of course!"

But Heiss would not be put off by jokes. He remained as morose as ever. He now addressed Anton.

"Suppose we stop trying to turn it into a joke and give serious answers instead. Do you approve of your wife's teaching activities?"

"In my view the one thing that these commandants need is to be taught. Theirs is a case of unmitigated ignorance. And we don't know how they would respond if only just a little light were to penetrate into their souls."

Then Anton paused for a moment and added, very quietly indeed:

"In fact, it seems to me that we all need educating and healing. . . ."

The guests went their various ways. It was after midnight and I had not yet corrected my pupils' work. I switched on the desk lamp and opened First Lieutenant Nasredinov's exercise book. He had written an essay on "The character of Nilovna in Gorky's novel *Mother.*" "In her young years Nilovna, like all the other girls, loved going for some walks and some excursions. . . ." Poor boy, he had got into an awful mess with his use of "some." But I was still too upset by the conversation. I put the exercise books aside for morning and went to bed. Anton and Tonya were breathing peacefully. But I was still upset and on edge, although I felt that I, not Heiss, was right.

17

· *Before the dawn*

It was probably a period not unlike the first months of the revolution. The adults of that time must also have lived in a constant, childlike expectation of miracles or horrors. And their expectations were not unjustified. The unexpected, unheard-of, startled them for a moment and then became ordinary. And life, chaotic and merciless, would sweep them along. It whisked them away like scraps of paper in a rushing wind. . . . Thrash about as much as you like, but it makes no difference!

The year 1954 equaled this early period in terms of oscillation between the two antipodes. Our masters now opened their newspapers with the same feeling of apprehension as we had. They listened as attentively as we did not only to what was announced over the radio but also to the various rumors that kept cropping up. They had their own rumors: staff was to be cut; institutions were to be reorganized; the special Kolyma allowances and the substantial monetary increments were to be terminated.

The management's nervousness made itself felt at every step. The more intelligent bosses realized that they must change their tune to suit the times. They became studiously polite and considerate toward us, and sometimes even allowed themselves heretical jokes. But many of them—those who were hopelessly, monumentally stupid—still clung to the old spiteful ways, which had become automatic. For example, the Education Department's accountant persisted in paying me at the lowest possible rate for a teacher.

"Deportees are not eligible for special allowances," he barked, not bothering to look at me.

"I'm not talking about the bonus for working in the far north. Why don't I get paid at the rate appropriate to my qualifications and experience?"

"Deportees have limited rights in all respects." He cut me off short, pronouncing the word "deportee" as if it were the equivalent of "plague carrier" or "pariah."

Portraits of the Generalissimo were still hanging up everywhere, solid as a rock, framed with black ribbons. Public speakers still invariably rounded off their speeches with the standard incantation: ". . . under the leadership of the Party of Lenin and Stalin." But new shoots were breaking through the soil, in one place after another, however stubborn the resistance. The Central Committee had held its famous plenum on agriculture. Nikita Khrushchev had begun to make himself felt. Rumors of Abakumov's impending trial* got through to us.

Old links with the mainland were renewed. Lydia Seifulina, the writer, wrote to Galya Voronskaya offering to help in obtaining

* Viktor Abakumov (1897–1954): Minister of State Security from 1947 to 1952. Executed after Stalin's death.

the posthumous rehabilitation of "dear Aleksandr Konstantinovich." The former Secretary of the Komsomol Central Committee, Aleksandr Milchakov, had received several letters from old friends who had preserved their freedom and maintained a stubborn silence all those years.

On the fifth of March—the first anniversary—commemorative articles appeared in the press. They still contained the sacramental formula: "Exactly a year ago, his heart beat its last, the heart of him who . . ." and so forth. But what struck everyone was the subdued tone of the proceedings. Especially by contrast with Women's Day on March 8, when the free women of Magadan forgot their nagging worries in an extraordinary round of jollifications.

"Do you remember how worried the womenfolk were last year that Women's Day might now be spoiled forever?" I asked Anton. "They were afraid that the shadow of the great death would make any festivity on the eighth unseemly. . . ."

"Earthly fame is transient," Anton sighed happily.

Those highly placed personages, my pupils, were very punctilious in wishing me a happy Women's Day, and I had the impression that their stereotyped speeches did contain a hint of good will to me personally. One individual note of greeting arrived by post from Lieutenant Nasredinov, the one who was keen on Mayakovsky. He sent me all sorts of good wishes and especially his hopes for my "early rebilitation."

The following day he came up to me in the school corridor and said with embarrassment:

"I made another mistake. I know now. It isn't 'rebilitation,' it's 'rehabilitation.' "

"Who corrected you?"

"I spotted it myself. The word comes into nearly every official document."

It was true: this astonishing, this intoxicating word was in our Kolyma air, winging its way from mouth to mouth.

The stories of the first rehabilitations were like the English children's tale about the small princess Sarah Crewe, who after all the horrors of growing up an orphan had inherited a rich diamond mine. If one were to believe the euphoric talk about them, the first people to be rehabilitated had moved into the very apartments from which they had once been taken to the cellars of the MGB. They had, allegedly, been given back the same senior Party posts and their accumulated salary in their old grade for all the years they had spent inside. True, no one as yet knew the names of these lucky people. But that such stories were told at all was a sign of the times.

In the spring of 1954 they did away with special entry passes for Kolyma. This brought me one unexpected joy. Vasya, who was by now in his fourth year at the medical institute, suddenly descended on us, posted to the Magadan hospital to walk the wards as an intern. For the entire summer! It was a surprise present from Anton. He had arranged it with the hospital and had sent Vasya his fare.

The plane arrived before the telegram from Khabarovsk, and I met my son, after a second, four years' absence, proceeding in the direction of our building. He was strolling along (as if he had never left) bareheaded—braving the weather—swinging a small, multi-colored rucksack. He was wearing an impossibly loud checked jacket.

The way he looked and the way he behaved seemed to suggest that the mainland had ceased to be another world, remote as the stars from Kolyma. The mainland had somehow come close to us. Vasya had simply bought his ticket, grabbed his little rucksack, and jumped on the plane, forgetting his cap in the process. For entry into Kolyma, as into any other area of the country, was now unre-stricted. My trials and tribulations when I was trying to get Vasya out there in the late forties now looked like ancient history. A day's journey, and there he was in front of me, my little boy! I could see him, speak to him, ruffle his beautiful, fair, wavy hair—but why was it so long?

And suddenly the whole force of my love burst out in a strange exclamation:

"What a ridiculous jacket you've got on! And what sort of a hair-cut is that?"

These were my first glimpses of "the new look." I ought to have been overjoyed that over these past years my child, son of a re-pressed family, had shaken off his tragic feeling of doom-laden hopelessness and that a youthful appetite for life had awakened in him, even if it was expressed in a cockatoo-colored jacket. But the Komsomol-Quaker reflexes implanted in me from childhood took over and I found myself saying angrily:

"You must go to the hairdresser and get some of that hair cut off. I'll buy you a normal jacket tomorrow. And we'll use the one you've got on to make Tonya a little coat for the summer."

"Over my dead body," Vasya retorted sullenly. "It's the most fashionable color."

He wasn't joking. And I held my tongue, shocked into realizing that it was all a lot more serious than it seemed and that our silly exchange represented my first brush with the second half of the century. The new generation was so incensed with the generation of their fathers that they did not want in any way to resemble it: not in habits, not in manners, not even in the color and cut of their jackets. And least of all in their outlook on life.

Meanwhile, events kept moving. Neither malice nor stupidity, neither obscurantism nor inertia could arrest the melting, in the hidden depths, of the age-old ice. The shock had been a powerful one; we were constantly aware of the seething waters down below, and at times, hardly daring to believe our eyes, we even saw rivulets breaking through to the surface.

In August 1954 deportation was commuted to resettlement. That meant the end of commandants' offices. There was anxious whispering among my officer pupils who were affected by this unprecedented reduction of staff. For us it meant that we could roam at the end of a longer leash. Instead of the seven-kilometer radius around Magadan which our deportee papers had conceded us, we were now to have the giddy possibility of crossing the Sea of Okhotsk and wandering about the mainland—provided, of course, we kept well clear of the towns and settlements specified in Clause Number 39 of the passport law.

I must give Gorokhov, my commandant-pupil, his due. Although the liquidation of the commandant's office must have upset his normal, smooth routine and threatened him with displacement and with other problems, he managed to set aside his personal worries and issue us with our stamped certificates for the militia with a genuinely friendly smile. We dashed out of his office and stood around in the street, twittering like a bunch of sparrows or schoolboys on their midday break. We kept interrupting one another, arguing about this miserable Clause Number 39, which, as we already knew, was written into all of our passports. Some people maintained that this meant "minus the capitals of all the republics," others made out that the prohibition extended to provincial capitals. But everyone agreed that the minuses didn't matter a damn. As long as they could travel, look around, and decide for themselves where they should live and what they should do. All the minuses were obliterated by the buffeting wind of freedom.

Small, localized changes followed in the wake of the big ones. For example, the rumor went around that the Bureau for the Special Checking of Information, which operated inside the editorial offices of our Magadan newspaper, had been abolished, because any ex-prison detainee or deportee could now get into print. I decided to check up on this. It took me two evenings to write an article on an entirely neutral theme. The subject was the corruption of the Russian language and the specific dialect of Kolyma. I quoted a few amusing examples, and described how teachers tried to combat this tendency in class. I signed it with my own name.

I set off for the newspaper office with a sinking heart again, just as I had on my first visit to the school. My second profession was no less dear to me than my first. I desperately wanted to write. My head swam when I thought of those editorial corridors and the smell of printers' ink.

The newspaper had now changed its name from *Sovietskaya Kolyma* to *Magadanskaya Pravda*. The editorial offices were located on the central square, where all the main institutions of the city were to be found. In the cultural department sat a very young man wearing a thick sweater with deer scampering across it. A pipe hung from his lips, and it was obvious from the show he made with it that he was indeed very young. After perusing the article, he exclaimed with pleasure:

"A fresh subject! And well written. Have you written before?"

"I used to write, and my work was frequently published. But that was a long time ago, in my youth. I've been repressed ever since 1937. I've only just been released from permanent exile within the Kolyma area."

The pipe fell from his lips. In his year and a bit he hadn't yet got used to such occurrences. His bright eyes clouded over with infantile panic, as if he had seen a bogeyman. And he mumbled something inarticulate to the effect that, in fact, he was not head of the department or even deputy head; just a staff writer. He didn't really have any authority at all.

But I continued with my offensive.

"I hear that the ban on contributions to the press from former prisoners has been completely lifted. What are you so surprised at? Times have changed, you know. I'm allowed to teach in a school, for instance. Be so good as to show the article to someone in authority. To the deputy editor, if no one else. I'll wait."

He was overjoyed at the opportunity to make his getaway. Off he went and told everyone, of course, about the sensational occurrence; the door started creaking, various people flitted in and out, darting curious glances at me while they rummaged for something or other among the papers on the desk. Then I was invited to see the deputy editor. He stood up from behind his desk and held out his hand to me! Now that showed how much the times had changed: What would he have said to me had I appeared before him a year earlier? But now he began muttering that he had heard about my interesting work in the school for adults. They would decide about the article within the next few days. He would just make a note of my address, and they'd let me know by mail.

I did not receive any written notification. I did receive a copy of the newspaper carrying my article, with my name in full underneath it.

More unholy commotion among the people in our circle. They thought up all sorts of hypotheses. . . . People were actually publishing *us!* Who could ask for a clearer indication that we were to be returned to the land of the living? Questions and more questions, general elation and happy laughter . . . We were intoxicated with that blissful feeling of good times to come, with the constant expectation of miracles, with the electric atmosphere that was giving off brilliant sparks all around us. Any moment now the gates of all the banned zones would open wide; any moment now all the planes and all the ships in Nagaevo Bay would form up in line abreast at the service of their improbable passengers.

True, this dazzling sudden reversal did not, in the event, materialize. The twisted skein unwound itself awkwardly, slowly, cautiously, with many a knot and many a tangle. But unwind it did.

The first rehabilitation in Magadan to attract widespread comment was that of Aleksandr Ivanovich Milchakov, the former Secretary of the Komsomol Central Committee. It could be said that they had their priorities right. No one had been as firmly convinced that this moment would come as was Sasha Milchakov. Throughout all the long years, he had existed in Kolyma expecting them to arrange at any moment for him to fly back to the mainland, resume his old post, and rejoin Marusya and the children. He spoke of Marusya in the tone one might use of someone who had slipped out to market and would return any moment now. . . . Other women did not exist for him, and he had steered well clear of Kolyma romances. He was waiting for Marusya. It was touching. But on the other hand, there was a sort of demonstrative aloofness about him, a consciousness that he was born to occupy positions of authority, and this put a lot of people on their guard. For example, while he behaved well enough toward Anton, who was in constant attendance on him, he would jokingly emphasize each time that the doctor was a "non-Party comrade."

I have an enduring memory of the day Milchakov boarded the plane for Moscow to report back for rehabilitation. By chance I witnessed his last steps on Kolyma soil. (The reason was that my Vasya was returning by the same plane after two months with us.)

I was struck by the fact that no one had come along to see Milchakov off. He stood there on the edge of the airstrip, taut and keyed up as though preparing to jump, his narrowed eyes riveted on some remote point invisible to us. He had become a "cat that walks by itself." Along with his prison clothes he had discarded any relationship with us—all memory of that extra morsel on the bread ration, the horrible propinquity of the plank bunks, the tags fastened to the arms of the dead. . . . This was not the same Sasha Milchakov who had come to see us to exchange news and conjectures, to complain to Anton about his digestive disorders, and to laugh at the latest jokes. This was a man who had neatly repaired the broken thread of his life. He had knotted the two ends together securely, joined up '37 and '54 and thrown away everything in between. Now he was on his way back to the appropriate "listed" job, to recommence the climb up Jacob's ladder, from which he had been accidentally toppled. They had done it in error, having mistaken him for someone else, of an entirely different kind. . . .

Aleksandr Ivanovich said a polite good-by to me. He even expressed confidence that we too would be taking a plane to the same destination. But the words rang false. He didn't even bother to pretend that he had any interest in whatever he was leaving behind.

Anton at first did not believe me and said that I was a past master at "inventing subtexts." But in Moscow three years later, in 1957, he was to remember my account of Milchakov's departure and to acknowledge—not for the first time—that I did have moments of insight.

(What happened in 1957 was as follows. "Why don't you call up

Sasha Milchakov?" asked Anton. "He'll be so pleased to hear we're in Moscow at last!" I phoned him. "Sasha," I said all excited, "Sasha, we're here in Moscow! Don't you recognize my voice? It's Genia. Genia and Anton." I was expecting confused exclamations of delight, suggestions about meeting right away. . . . And suddenly I heard a rasping, Karenin-like voice, inquiring in measured terms after my health, the health of the doctor. . . . I was so taken aback that I handed the receiver to Anton: "Speak to him yourself." Anton listened for some minutes to this unfamiliar voice, with its haughty, patronizing tone, and his face grew more and more set. Finally he said, "I wish you luck," and put the receiver down. To me he added, "Yes, what you sensed back there, at Magadan airport, turns out to be absolutely right.")

Yes, it was then, on Milchakov's last day in Kolyma, that I first encountered that astounding readiness to forget everything, to pull up the past by the roots and return to where one had left off—without any reappraisal of values in the light of cruel experience, with no regrets for those whom wounds like their own had only yesterday made their kin. How many varieties of the species I was to meet later, back on the mainland.

One can understand, and forgive, those who were permanently haunted by fear, who were unable to master their own nervous reflexes. (I too still sometimes relapse into the old state of terror—though not to the point of renouncing my past, or my friends, or this book—when the doorbell rings at night or when I hear the key turning on the other side of the lock.)

But how can one find understanding for those who for the sake of worldly success, for the sake of Vanity Fair, want to forget everything, to suppress in themselves all that they have learned through suffering, and to continue as if nothing had ever happened to the career that prison had interrupted, to the life in which glory and the mass execution of friends and acquaintances once went together. All this in the pursuit of phantoms, of trinkets, of diabolical folly. And yet we have so little time left to us in which to live. As I write this, Sasha Milchakov, our good friend in Kolyma, is no more.

No, the dream he had carried with him through eighteen years of suffering was not to be. After rehabilitation, he was not summoned to stand at the helm of the Ship of State. The Party directive was applied to him just as rigidly as to other rehabilitated persons. A well-deserved rest? Yes. A personal pension? By all means! Accommodation? It's yours! Publication of memoirs about his glorious revolutionary past? That's all right, you go ahead and publish them. . . . But that was it. For the conduct of today's affairs a new hierarchy of office holders had already been installed. Nurtured and licked into shape while you were sitting it out in Kolyma, Pechora, and Solovki. Not overburdened by an unduly extensive knowledge of history.

So Aleksandr Ivanovich Milchakov, with his burning desire to get into the action, to organize people, to make policy, to exercise his cramped hands, feet, and brain, was—alas—offered one outlet and one only: to share with the readers of the journal *Yunost* his reminiscences of the first years of the Komosol, of its splendid leaders, fighters, and revolutionary martyrs. But even in this "Lives of the Saints" Sasha was not able to tell all that had happened to his first comrades in arms, the Komsomol leaders of the early years of the revolution. The martyrdom of these heroes, shot in '37, was a forbidden theme if ever there was one. And whereas at the beginning of the sixties it was still possible to write, "He became a victim of infringements of revolutionary legality," by the mid-sixties you were required to end on an optimistic note, leaving in complete obscurity the question of how these incomparable heroes and knights of the revolution had departed this life.

Perhaps it was because of the collapse of his hopes that Sasha Milchakov died comparatively early, mourned by a devoted family, by the editorial board of the journal *Yunost*, and by us, his friends in harder times, who forgot our hurt and forgot that he had wanted to keep us at arm's length so as not to compromise himself by dangerous connections. We remembered Sasha as he had been in Magadan, not as the person he became in Moscow.

The thaw continued. In the school year 1954–55 I was able to give up the officers' class and take on two ordinary classes in the evening school for adults. My pupils now were pilots and workers from the car repair factory. Among them there were a number of former prisoners accepted for further education in these liberal times. I was invited to give refresher courses for teachers at the pedagogical institute; my evening classes were sometimes attended by the head of the town education authority, Trubchenko, no less, and by a yet greater none-other, the head of the regional education authority, Zhelezkov. They invited me to give a number of open lectures for teachers who wanted to "benefit" from my experience.

After these visits came manna from heaven: I was invited to the town housing department to "discuss an improvement in your accommodations."

The two-story wooden house on Commune Street—within a stone's throw of the school—seemed to us like the palace of Versailles. We were given a room of twenty square meters in an apartment where, apart from ourselves, there were only two other families. And this was after living in the barrack in Nagaevo where there had been thirty of us! The new apartment had a good kitchen, a bathroom, and a heated lavatory. Not daring to believe our own eyes, Anton and I tried out the taps in the bathroom and gingerly fingered the glazed tiles of the kitchen stove. We listened to the lavatory flush as though it were a signal from the other world: we had seen all sorts of things in the last two decades, but a lavatory with all modern conveniences was emphatically not among them.

The final improbable miracle of miracles was the appearance of a telephone on our table. It was installed after Anton was put in charge of a private ward for senior officials. I still remember to this day the number of that telephone, the first in the life that had begun for me on March 5, 1953: 22–71. There was no automatic exchange in Magadan in those days, and instead of a soulless buzz you heard a melodious little voice, saying conspiratorially, "I am putting you through. . . ." The first few days Anton and I used to play games with the telephone. We would call each other up at home from our respective places of work several times a day, and bubbling over with laughter, would indulge in quite nonsensical but delicious exchanges:

"Is that the Elgen state farm?"

"No, what do you want?"

"The Burkhala Mine?"

"Certainly not!"

"Can it be Vaskov's House?"

"Citizen, this is a private apartment, the residence of a very popular doctor, who is also a homeopathic charlatan."

"Really? I thought it was the apartment of an eminent expert on courses in belles-lettres for KGB commandants. . . ."

This was all for fun. But our delight in our new apartment was serious enough. We relished our newly acquired freedom from fear, keenly, sensuously, greedily. We locked the door at bedtime calmly and confidently, and fell asleep knowing that we need expect no ring or knock during the night. Our private room . . . In short: my home is my castle.

Around the New Year I received, one after another, two encouraging bits of paper from Moscow. The first told me that my rehabilitation petition, addressed to Voroshilov, had been passed on to the USSR General Prosecutor's office; and the second, that the petition had been sent on from the Prosecutor's office to the Supreme Court. Those in the know assured me that this was an excellent sign. What worried me was that Anton had not yet received any answer. On New Years' Eve Tonya put a picture postcard on top of his bedside table; in it she wished him "health, happiness, and a clean passport soon." At the age of eight she already understood perfectly well what a clean passport meant to anyone.

Then came the spring of 1955. My colleagues at the evening school for adults were having an animated discussion in the teachers' common room about holidays. They were trying to work out how many extra days' leave they were entitled to under the Kolyma regulations, comparing the relative attractions of the Crimea and the Caucasus, and showing one another the new outfits they had bought for their travels.

I had long ago learned to check by an act of will the bitterness that welled up in me when I overheard conversations like these! But I could keep it up no longer. The pounding tide of ordinary life awakened muffled echoes in my head.

At last the unbelievable moment came when the director of the school casually asked me the quite simple question:

"Why aren't you putting in an application for mainland leave?"

"Me? Leave on the mainland?"

"Why not?" the director asked in a bored voice. "It's been cleared with the personnel department. Your deportation order has been annulled. You're free to travel."

The director was a good woman. At least she had no appetite for evil. It was merely that the outlines of her face and figure reminded one of a large carp; as also did her dull, phlegmatic disposition. She goggled at me with profound astonishment when I embraced her and whispered Pushkin's lines into her ear:

There is balm yet for my sore heart,
I shall no more my God upbraid.
Consoled if it but be my part
To free one creature He hath made.

It was midnight. I was returning home from school. There was nothing to be afraid of now; it was just around the corner. The sea air from the bay reached us there, too. And the stars were the same as in Nagaevo. The holiday feeling persisted. Long-forgotten feelings, the smell of the earth in springtime, fragments of poems, a sense of oneness with the whole of creation . . . As if it were Easter, and as if I were fourteen again. . . .

Many years would go by, and one day I would remember my mood that night of the springtime thaw and feel deeply ashamed. That was to happen in the very early seventies when Arthur London's book *The Confession* came into my hands. From this staggering volume I learned that on what was for me a blissful night, when I thought that the end of our sufferings—our, not merely my, sufferings—had come, investigation of the Slansky affair* was going full steam ahead next door in Czechoslovakia. And those were the very days when foolish euphoria, as I enjoyed in advance my return to life, robbed me of the ability to think, to read the papers, to compare facts, to draw conclusions, and to look ahead; at that very time, when I all but believed that the golden age was upon us, people were still being subtly tormented and forced to play out the humiliating farce of a trial scripted in advance. . . . People were still being hanged for nothing, despite being guilty of nothing. . . . And their ashes were scattered to the four winds. . . . And that night, so imbued with the illusion of total freedom in the offing, was for many people who were no different from me—for those Czechs, for instance—brimful of the despair I had known of old.

But at that moment I knew nothing of this. The thaw had completely deprived me of the ability to look ahead and foresee things. I was possessed, almost unconsciously, by the foolish idea of the compensation that fate owed me for the sufferings I had endured. It befuddled me. I said to myself that I was still meant to be happy. I was not yet old. I still had time to do many things, read many books, time to write my own.

I stayed outside for quite a while, standing by the doorway and looking at the starry Kolyma sky, a cold sky but springlike. I was not thinking, just listening to a passionate and gentle voice within me. Yes, it was Blok's voice.

* Rudolf Slansky, General Secretary of the Communist Party in Czechoslovakia from 1945, was executed in 1952. In 1963 he was posthumously rehabilitated.

> I want, I want madly, to live
> To immortalize all else that lives,
> Make human all that is faceless,
> Make real again dreams that have faded . . .

Today I want to beg forgiveness of Arthur London and his comrades for my happiness on that particular night in 1955. And for having entitled this chapter "Before the dawn." But I will not alter the heading. To do that would be to depart from the truth about my perception of events at the time.

18

· *"In the absence of any corpus delicti"*

I was sitting in a comfortable Ilyushin 14, and the clouds beneath me were over the Sea of Okhotsk. It was not a dream. It was the fantastic reality of the mid-fifties. I had been ferried out to Kolyma in the hold of the *S.S. Dzhurma:* I was now being ferried back to the mainland in the lap of luxury, and the air hostess was saying, "Madam, please fasten your little girl's seat belt!" Madam! Could she mean me?

It was easier for nine-year-old Tonya to adapt to the strangeness of the situation than for me. She had no past. She was the personification of the future and bursting with curiosity. She bombarded me with questions, which I answered mechanically.

The keen feeling of being airborne, the astringent joy of movement, were overcast for me by the memory of Anton's eyes as he remained there on the airfield. Anton had not yet been rehabilitated and he had therefore refused to travel—actually, even to apply for permission to visit the mainland. But then neither had I been rehabilitated. He said that my case was different: "The suggestion came from them." He could not rid himself of the feeling that he was hopelessly discriminated against because of his origin.

I sensed that he had another reason for wanting me to leave without him this first time. He wanted me to be able to decide about our future together without feeling that I was under pressure. We now knew for sure that my first husband was alive.

Tonya and I were already seated and the plane ready to take off when Baranov—a pilot whom I had taught in my evening class—came in and asked me to go to the exit for a moment. Anton Yakovlevich wanted to say to me something that he had evidently forgotten when we said good-by. I went to the door, and Anton swiftly climbed up the gangway, which was still in place.

"Listen, you must do what your conscience tells you to. But please do remember . . ."

Just at that point he was hurried away. It was time to remove the gangway.

My conscience had long since told me what to do. I would return. Although I already knew that I was about to get my rehabilitation (I had received several papers that brought it some stages nearer for me), I had firmly resolved that I would not leave Kolyma as long as Anton was tied to it. Tonya and I would definitely be returning there in six months, when my leave was up. But . . . now . . . now I was flying to the mainland, and my whole being was not merely receptive but wide open to the cotton-wool clouds, the iridescent air stream, the stray sparks rushing out from underneath the wing. I was eager to welcome things half-forgotten, longed for, glimpsed at a distance in dreams—to welcome what we call *life*.

My answers to the innumerable questions with which Tonya showered me became more and more erratic. The passenger sitting immediately in front of me turned around and snorted loudly when he heard me explain the technicalities of flight. But I was not in the least offended. I chuckled with him and confided to him that I had never done well in physics.

"But can't the plane fall into the sea?" Tonya inquired anxiously.

"No, it can't."

My answer had a confident, categoric ring to it. Because it was not meant solely to reassure the little child; it was my own deep conviction. The plane could not fall. For it would be senseless to die in a plane crash after having survived Yaroslavl and Elgen, Izvestkovaya and Vaskov's House. It would mean that the world was haphazard and pointless. And I, for my part, in these years, the mid-fifties, was deeply convinced that the world was rational and that there was a higher meaning in things, convinced that God perceived the truth, though he might be slow to speak.

That was twenty years ago. How my heart has cooled off in the intervening years!

It took that 1955 plane a whole seven hours of sedate flying to cross the Sea of Okhotsk. At times I dozed off, dulled by the white glow given off by the windows. But each time, I jerked myself back into reality with the indignant thought: How dare I go to sleep when I was flying—I was afraid to utter the word—flying to Moscow! I might just as well be flying to Mars. I looked with astonishment at the person sitting behind me. Someone I knew, also a former prisoner, flying back to the mainland for the first time after eighteen years in camp. He was fast asleep and utterly oblivious to the world around him. His flattened, creased face exuded profound physical contentment; I remembered that his name was Fyodor Reshyotnikov and that he had twice been a goner and twice crawled back from the brink. His long-suffering bones had gathered new flesh around them. But this new flesh, the product of the benevolent attentions of the camp convalescent center, was the same wrinkled, yellowish dough from which his face had been molded as if from modeling paste. I remembered how he had boarded the plane with no sign of pleasurable excitement, without a smile, with a look of blank indifference.

I told myself again that I was not only fortunate, but infinitely fortunate. It was not only arms and legs, eyes and ears that I was taking with me aboard this Ilyushin relatively intact: my soul, too, had come through it all more or less unscathed; it had not lost the ability to love and to hate, to despair and to exult. I was possessed by a feeling of gratitude. Dear Lord, it is not a dream. Thou hast led me out of Kolyma. . . .

Gratitude is among the rarest of gifts. I am no exception. We all furiously cry "help" when we are in peril, but once the peril is past, we very seldom remember the source from which help has come. On my road to Calvary I had seen dozens, even hundreds of supereducated Marxists, dyed-in-the-wool orthodox Communists, who in their terror-stricken moments turned their tortured features toward Him whose existence they had so authoritatively denied for so many years in so many talks and lectures. But those who managed to survive addressed their thanks not to God but, at best, to Nikita Khrushchev. Or to no one at all. Such is our nature.

This is why I have remembered my first flight over the Sea of Okhotsk as a rare moment of illumination, when my soul was truly thankful for every blade of grass in the field and every star in the sky. And when I started dozing off, rocked by the air pockets—even then, in the gathering darkness, at the last frontier of consciousness—this otherworldly feeling stayed with me. I never experienced it again. It went for good amid the daily hubbub.

Khabarovsk. Landing. With a feeling of awe I walked on the gravel-strewn asphalt. . . . It was my first contact with mainland soil.

"Mamma dear! Look, look what a lot of nightingales!" Tonya exclaimed, transfixed with ecstasy at the sight of a flock of sparrows, twittering shrilly above a small heap of manure.

"There's a Kolyma kid for you! Never seen a sparrow before?" retorted a red-faced individual, clearly a member of the tribe of semicriminal Kolyma conquistadors, as he passed by. He turned out to be our neighbor at lunch in the restaurant. He flung a number of brand-new hundred-ruble notes down onto the table by way of a challenge, and demanded that the waitress bring him the "whole program" at once. He had taken a liking to Tonya, and kept educating her.

"What's this here? Don't you know? It's called an olive. It's like a plum, see. . . . But you wouldn't know what a plum was like, would you?"

Well, of course we had seen no plums where we came from. Tonya had never seen them in her life; I had seen them but forgotten all about them. But Tonya and I were like fellow conspirators. We merely exchanged meaningful glances. She already understood that it was best not to advertise her astonishment and draw attention to her rustic ignorance. Her sharp eye took everything in. A special little cruet for mustard and pepper. A suitcase with an elegant zipper fastening. Miracles, all around.

As we neared Irkutsk, the weather suddenly broke up. At first the snowy whiteness of the clouds was spattered with dark spots until it resembled an ermine robe. After that there was some sort of blizzard visible through the windows, and we were tossed about unmercifully. The passengers shifted uneasily in their reclining seats. A fat young lady with a red fringe coming right down to her brows grumbled audibly about what a fool she had been to be seduced by a free pass to a Sochi sanatorium when she had a husband and a decent room in South Sakhalin. Over eighteen square meters. The only one who slumbered on undisturbed was the former prison detainee, Fyodor Reshyotnikov. He slept like a babe, making up for all that lost time spent on night shifts in camp.

It took our pilot half an hour of maneuvering before he could land. The bump we had been longing for came at last. We were on terra firma. There was a general sigh of relief. The passengers cheered up immediately, exchanged jokes, combed their hair, rearranged their clothes, and remembered that it was long past dinnertime. And they all joined in the laughter when Fyodor Reshyotnikov woke up at last from his lethargic sleep and said in a surly growl:

"Those who're born to crawl aren't meant to fly. . . ."

"And indeed we won't be flying yet awhile," our stewardess retorted. "It's not flying weather. You can have a nice, cozy rest in Irkutsk."

The Aeroflot Hotel at Irkutsk astounded Tonya and me even more than the restaurant at Khabarovsk. Its public rooms were of the sort you could only associate with Count Frederick and Countess Elvira in one of the tales of high romance so beloved of the criminal riffraff. Massive, wine-colored velvet curtains hung from golden rings right down to the gleaming varnished floors. Crystal chandeliers tinkled softly. In a luxuriously upholstered armchair sat an elaborately dressed manager, busy with her paperwork. And over all this magnificence there proudly hung a curt typed notice: "No vacancies." However, after lengthy explanations, requests, and entreaties, the philanthropic management took pity on us, and the whole population of several stranded planes was accommodated higgledy-piggledy on the floor of the corridor to the right of the vestibule.

By the time night came the humaneness of those in charge extended to issuing us with a number of old mattresses, so that the children could now be installed on the floor with some degree of comfort. Their elders had to face a night on stools in the same corridor, underneath the loudspeakers that never got around to broadcasting the words we were waiting to hear: "The departure is announced of flight . . ."

And then all of a sudden one of the female passengers, a tiny, darting creature of forty or so, brought us a sensational piece of information. Apparently there were any number of vacant rooms in the hotel.

"They're all for the Chinese. They're not for us; we're second-class citizens. We've got the wrong sort of money. There's a whole floor completely empty, while we're lying around on the floor here. They're reserving them. But for whom?"

"What do you mean, 'for whom?'" the manager fumed. "This is the main Moscow–Peking route, don't you understand? The rooms are reserved for our Chinese comrades."

"And just when are they going to appear, these Chinese comrades? You can't fly in this weather. Irkutsk airport is closed. And by morning, if visibility improves, we'll be off and away ourselves."

But the manager continued to insist obtusely:

"You're not going to make your own laws here! This is an international route. . . ."

There was mutiny. The director of the hotel appeared on the scene: a delicate, pale individual, every line of him fine-drawn and elongated. His voice reminded one of oversweetened apple jelly. Calling on the passengers to be calm, he expressed a wish to see our papers. The manager nodded toward our internal passports, which were lying in a heap on her desk. The director quickly sorted them into three piles and started to call out our names, together with the numbers of our rooms.

My usual conditioned reflexes went into action. I decided that Tonya and I would either be given no room at all, or else some poky little attic. But suddenly we were assigned Room Number 17 on the second floor. At first I thought there must have been some mistake. My passport with its "minuses" and its "Clause Number 39" in no way qualified me to be the beneficiary of such "export-only" treatment. Could it be me to whom this white-uniformed maid was saying please? Could these enormous mirrors, these satin covers, this monumental wardrobe, be meant for us? All doubts were resolved by the appearance of the hotel director.

"Will it suit you?" he inquired, as if doling out another large portion of apple jelly. "We understand the historical process, you know. Yesterday's political prisoners are tomorrow's bosses. In our own particular case, in our particular ministry, a new comrade has been given one of the top jobs. He's one of those who have been going around in camp uniform since '37. You have to understand what it means. . . . It's all a matter of dialectical development. . . . I wish you a good night!"

So Tonya and I, thanks to the dialectical reasoning of the director of the Irkutsk hotel (which was not, however, justified by subsequent events, at least as far as the great careers he foresaw for rehabilitated prisoners were concerned), slept like two Dalai Lamas, under Chinese satin covers in beds with feet shaped like lions' heads.

The next morning was sunny. And once again we were flying, over Siberia and then over the Urals. With stops in Novosibirsk and Sverdlovsk. Only when we got to Sverdlovsk did I really feel that I was on my way back to the mainland. Our proximity to Moscow became more evident with each half hour that passed. The trees, the meadows, the birds, the color of the sky—it all came back to me, it all began to resemble the sights I used to treasure, but which had for so long been unrecoverable and unreal. I told Tonya the name of tree after tree, and felt as proud as if I had planted them myself, as if I were inducting her into her own inherited estate.

"We had birch trees in our Northern Artek camp. But they were different. . . ."

"They were just dwarfs. . . ."

All in all, Tonya coped better than I in the new surroundings. She was not distracted by the sweet, searing pain I felt in my chest, was not a victim of confusing associations, which made me forget what had happened when. I was even taken unaware by the stop at Kazan. I did not immediately realize that I was back on the spot where it all began—just as if I had come to look at my own grave.

I started when I heard the high, resonant, girlish voice. It was not so much the voice itself as the strong Tartar accent.

"Kazan airport. Are you all well, comrades?"

The ruddy-faced girl with furry eyebrows and a first-aid satchel over her shoulder again upset my sense of the passage of time. I had an odd feeling: Surely it couldn't be seventeen years since I had taught her to speak Russian? How my allotted span had trickled through my fingers like water, how the prime years of my life had been wasted on unbearable and monotonous suffering.

I would not, must not, give way to this corrosive bitterness. . . . For there I was, on my way back again. Starting a whole new, long chapter in my life. And it would be a fruitful one. . . .

"Look, Tonya, what a fine airport Kazan has. . . ."

I was upset to find Tonya unimpressed by the new airport building. She had never seen the tumble-down hut that stood there in the thirties, and she calmly pronounced the airport to be just the same as the one in Sverdlovsk.

Another two hours of somnolence, rocked by the plane, then at last . . . the miracle happened. A bump as we landed, another bump deep inside me. This was my Mars, my unattainable planet! This was the land whose contours had been all but obliterated for me, for all of us. . . .

"Moscow."

It was the voice of our air hostess. She was giving us instructions on landing procedure and telling us what form of city transportation to use.

I scarcely understood a word of what she was saying. I had decided that we should be last out of the plane, although Tonya was tugging me toward the exit with all her strength. She couldn't wait to get out. But I was playing for time, trying to check the rush of blood to my temples. Mechanically, feeling that it was all happening in my wild imagination, I went through the necessary motions: carrying my suitcase; waiting for the bus; answering Tonya's questions.

The day was never ending. I, who was used to the prolonged ordeal of penal convoys, to endless waiting at camp gates and in KGB office queues, felt that I would never get through that twenty-four-hour period which began in Sverdlovsk and was continuing here in Moscow, in the Taganka district. Why Taganka? I could not bring myself to turn to any of my old acquaintances for shelter. It still seemed to me—a strange visitor from the land of evil dreams with a pack across her shoulders—unthinkable to inflict such a burden on anyone. So I got one of my Magadan free acquaintances to give me a note to a Taganka landlady who made a business of letting out rooms or parts of rooms to visiting "freedmen" from Kolyma with money to burn.

The apartment turned out to be a damp semibasement, though it was equipped with a television set and a refrigerator. In exchange for our crisp new hundred-ruble notes, our rapacious landlady, as sleek and friendly as a well-fed cat, let us have a shabby double bed with a ragged blanket and shapeless, leaking, flattened pillows. We went to bed early, while it was still light, so as somehow to bring this eventful day to an end.

I dozed off instantaneously, but was awakened by an elated squeak.

"Mamma, look, the lady has her own little cinema!"

I opened my eyes, and Tonya and I, like two Kolyma country

cousins, watched a television program for the first time in our lives.

In the morning the kindly landlady of the Kolyma Traveler's Resthouse offered us coffee and sat down with us at the table. She had been without lodgers for a whole week, had had her fill of silence, and was longing for company—rather, for somebody to listen to her monologue. Her interlocutor was of no importance as far as she was concerned: what she wanted was a good uninterrupted chin-wag. At no time in her life had she ever traveled beyond Taganka, but she had a complete and detailed mastery of Magadan's problems. She knew who received what increments and whether it paid to work in the north or in the south. I gave her only half my attention and contributed occasional meaningless interjections. But all of a sudden she quizzically screwed up her still-undimmed eyes, with their shaggy eyebrows and prickly eyelashes, and put to me a mystifying question:

"You haven't forgotten how to get to Kirov Street, have you?"

Number 41 Kirov Street was the address of the USSR General Prosecutor's office, the first port of call for my rehabilitation. But how did our fat and feline landlady know of this? I hadn't breathed a word of it when talking to her, nor was there anything about it in the note that had served as my letter of recommendation.

"You get there by trolley bus; go as far as the Red Gates stop. Did the trolley bus run there in your time? I don't remember. . . ."

"Yes, it did. How do you know about me?"

"I wasn't born yesterday! I can see from your suitcase, from how you're dressed, and from the way you look, too. Leave the little girl with me. I'll look after her. And I won't charge you much."

But Tonya had the idea that the "Possecutor's" office (as she pronounced it) was yet another Moscow marvel like television. She turned stubborn, burst into tears, and insisted on going. So I gave in and took her with me.

On the way I tried to get a good look at Moscow through the trolley bus window, and to establish in what way it had changed over the intervening eighteen years. But I didn't succeed, because I could see my own reflection in the window, and I scrutinized it, trying to understand how it was that the first Muscovite I had met, our landlady, had immediately recognized me for an ex-convict of recent date. Wresting my gaze away from the window, I looked around me like an animal at bay; in each fellow passenger I saw a person of consequence, the proud possessor of a Moscow residence permit, a patent of nobility denied to me.

The doors of the gloomy gray granite building were hard to open, although people were constantly going in and out of them. I tugged hard at the doorknob. Tonya nimbly slipped in first and pulled me after her. I looked around and stood still, dumbfounded. What was this? I thought I had left Kolyma, but there it was, following me around. The vestibule was packed with our people. The same people, whom I would know amid thousands of others, with their work-scarred, gnarled hands, their teeth loosened by scurvy—and in their eyes the same expression of omniscience and extreme exhaustion which cannot be conveyed in words. This expression of theirs was not affected by the state of pleasurable excitement that possessed them all.

Nearly everyone was talking at the same time. They kept on talking and talking, but in hushed voices and with the usual sidelong glances at the men in uniform who darted about among the crowd, papers in hand. They were all talking about their wanderings, instructing one another as to the proper order in which to tackle the offices, desks, and counters of this gray granite building. The vestibule of the Prosecutor's office at Number 41 Kirov Street buzzed like . . . no, not like a beehive. Like a transit camp. Like the Vladivostok transit camp. I closed my eyes for a second. I felt shaky and queasy at the sharp twinge of memory, at this further disturbance of the time sequence.

"Mamma! Why is everyone in the Possecutor's gray-haired?" Tonya asked in a loud voice; friendly chuckles could be heard around us.

A minute later first one person, then another, then yet another, called out my name. By now I had recognized several of the individual faces. My extended family: sisters from Butyrki and brothers from the sea crossing; daughters from Elgen; and even mothers and fathers, for there were a lot of seventy-year-olds there. They were still alive then, in 1955. Their snow-white heads dotted about among the clientele of the gray granite building created the illusion that "they're all gray-haired at the Possecutor's."

Our people . . . from the same nether world in which I had lived for almost two decades. How terrifying their faces were in the pitiless light of a Moscow summer's day! But how dear they were to me, and how quickly their presence dissipated the sense of alienation that had never left me since the moment of my arrival in the capital.

Friendly arms reached out to me in greeting. Anastasya Fyodorovna, my cellmate from the Butyrki transit prison, quickly took charge of Tonya. And Ivan Sinitsyn, whom Anton and I used to have as one of our patients in the Taskan prisoners' hospital, escorted me to the correct window. In those days we had regarded him as a goner, but despite that, he had lived to be fifty, and to join the crowd at Number 41 Kirov Street.

On our way there, Ivan warned me to prepare myself for the inevitable red tape.

"The main thing is to remember that they're going to have to rehabilitate you sooner or later. So don't get desperate when they start saying: 'Come back in a day or two.' They can't help it, after all. One has to feel sorry for them, too—you can imagine the oceans of paper they're floundering in! And the sea of lies!"

But I was unbelievably fortunate. I had only to wait a few minutes at the counter after giving my name to the polite officer who was on the other side of the window.

"It's all in order," he said briefly but courteously, bending over his card index. "The Prosecutor has lodged an appeal against your sentence. So where you need to go is not here but the Supreme Court. On Vorovsky Street. You'll be given the final decision on your case there."

From 1 P.M. to 2 P.M. the Prosecutor's office had its lunch break; Ivan and I, and Anastasya Fyodorovna and two other "graybeards" I knew, who had done a full stretch inside, set off for the Lily of the Valley Café, which I remembered from my postgraduate days. I particularly remembered the taste of the Siberian-style piroshki that I used to eat in this café twenty years and more ago.

We had a table to ourselves. And we couldn't stop talking. We thought we were speaking in whispers, but evidently we were no longer in control of our voices. I noted that the people at the next table were listening to us, listening attentively. Young people—two boys and a girl. Probably students. Intelligent young people. It was so long since I had seen or heard young people like that. And yet how close we sat to one another! I was seized by a pang of anguish: how disgraced, how degraded we were in their eyes! How many decades would it take to erase from their minds the distrust of yesterday's "spies, saboteurs, and terrorists"?

But we already seemed to be of great interest to them. They had stopped talking altogether and were listening avidly to what we were saying. Finally, one of them got decisively to his feet, came across to us, and asked, very excitedly:

"Are you from there? From exile? Forgive me, it's not just idle curiosity."

"Yes," answered Nikolai Stepanovich Mordvinov, one of our graybeards, former geologist, former inmate of the Verkhneuralsk special political prison, former prisoner in the Ukhta camp, and formerly a handsome man.

"Yes, we're from 'those' places. Very remote ones. Victims of '37."

The young people were so shattered by this meeting that for some time they sat saying nothing, staring at us as if we were ghosts. Then the girl said, "Just one moment!" and rushed head-long toward the door. Within a short while she was back, carrying two bunches of gladioli wrapped in cellophane. She held out the flowers to Anastasya Fyodorovna and me. I noticed that the girl's eyes were full of tears and the spectacles of one of the young men were also glistening. We were silent. Then old Mordvinov gave a cough and said hoarsely:

"I repeat: we are victims. Victims, not heroes . . ."

"But you had the courage to endure it all," objected the student with the spectacles.

"The flowers must be a compliment to our powers of survival" was Anastasya Fyodorovna's unsubtle joke.

Our encounter with the unknown young people was something I was to remember for many long years. It was the first evidence that not everyone, by no means everyone, had believed in the great lie, and that many hearts—particularly young people's—secretly cherished sympathy for the innocent sufferers.

About three days later I had another eloquent confirmation of how right Yevtushenko had been when he wrote in the fine verse of his youthful years: "Fears are dying off in Russia." They were dying off before our eyes. Only fear, not belief in the calumny that had surrounded our names for nearly two decades, had made us outcasts.

Within a few days I received further convincing confirmation that by no means all those who had remained outside had taken what they were told about "spies, saboteurs, and terrorists" on trust. One day, early in the morning, unannounced and unexpected, Tonya Ivanova, my old friend from our days with the Komsomol, put in an appearance at our Taganka semibasement. How on earth had she discovered that I was in Moscow and in Taganka?

"My heart told me," she joked. "How could you bring yourself to squat in such a nasty little cellar? As if you had no friends left in Moscow! Off we go, if you don't mind!"

Within an hour we found ourselves in a comfortable two-room apartment on Chkalov Street, where Tonya's brother, Petya Ivanov, a journalist well known in the thirties, whom I had known since I was a young girl—and my so-called Party godfather, who had once put me up for Party membership—was expecting me. It gave me great satisfaction to hear his story of how he had succeeded in escaping arrest in '37 (he was then working for *Pravda*). He had displayed initiative. One fine night he had upped and left Moscow for an unknown destination, abandoning his family, his work, and his apartment. He had vanished into the wide-open spaces of our native land, to reappear in Moscow only with the partial turn of the tide after Yezhov's dismissal. Petya's choice of words, his little jokes and asides, left me in no doubt at all that he knew perfectly well what it was all about. It was a great comfort for me to discover like-minded people among the free Muscovites, among those who had come off lucky. It was only now that I, who had grown used to the superorthodoxy of their Kolyma free counterparts, began to realize how relative was the good fortune of the intelligentsia who had slipped clear of the net cast over them. I now understood that they, who had been able to sleep all those years in their own clean, comfortable beds, had been prey to the same great fears as we lesser mortals. Toward evening Xenia Krylova, one of my oldest friends, of whom I hadn't heard anything all these years, turned up! Her appearance provided yet another tenuous connection between my earlier life and the past eighteen years. The links between time present and time past were being reestablished. My little Tonya later gave a very amusing account of our meeting:

"They just looked at each other and cried. And each of them spoke just one word. Auntie said 'Genia' and Mamma said 'Xenia.' And they started crying again."

The switch from Kirov Street to Vorovsky Street signified the next step on the road to rehabilitation for each of us. So you would have expected morale to be higher in consequence. But logic notwithstanding, the atmosphere in the Supreme Court building on Vorovsky Street was infinitely more tense than in the Prosecutor's office on Kirov Street. There everyone was still exhilarated by the return to Moscow, the explosion of hope, and the fantastic plans for a new life which went with it. But by the time people got to Vorovsky Street they were worn out with queues, and the counter windows through which they had to squeeze their head for a sight of the officer's immaculate part as he bent his head over the documents, and the sound of his oracular voice as he pronounced (for the umpteenth time): "The protest has not yet been lodged!" or even, "Your case is in the hands of the Supreme Court!"

Those who had already got as far as Vorovsky Street were well and truly fed up with all of this.

"They were quick enough with the paper work when they gave me ten years in '37. There wasn't any bureaucratic red tape then! But now . . . You really have to hand it to these priests of Themis! All that paper to prove that I am not an agent of Madagascar, and that I didn't organize an espionage network in Penza on behalf of Ceylon!"

The old man who had uttered this heavily sarcastic tirade looked familiar. I had met him somewhere, but where? I remembered only when he said, with a wave of his hand, "Only a fool expects an answer. . . ." I had come across him in Magadan on my arrival at the hostel for ex–prison inmates employed at the hospital. In those days he had been notably cautious, taciturn, had carefully avoided seditious conversations, and invariably answered all rhetorical questions about the whys and wherefores with the same phrase he had just used: "Only a fool expects an answer. . . ."

Where had his cautious reserve now vanished to? Why had he become so bold when he was within days of getting his freedom? I found that this was typical. After a few days' queuing at Vorovsky Street, I came to one conclusion: it was precisely at this point, when they had only a little longer to wait, that people's patience simply gave out. They grew more and more irritable with the officers; and insolent retorts increasingly became the order of the day. I well remember, for example, a tall woman, so gaunt that it was impossible to say how old she was. Biding her time until one of the officers came right up to her, she said very loudly, pointing to a half-length portrait of Stalin still adorning the Supreme Court's anteroom:

"Why did they hang *him* up there? So that people won't forget who caused it all?"

The officer said not a word. In fact, the officers at Vorovsky Street were even more impassive than those at the Prosecutor's office. It was as if they had all plugged their ears with cotton wool. They threaded their way through our queues, excusing themselves in toneless, mechanical voices. In reply to direct questions they simply gave the number of the appropriate room or window. That was the full extent of their conversational stock in trade.

By and large the atmosphere of that institution in those days was an eloquent expression of the uncertainty, the sense of impermanence, of marking time, that characterized the whole country. One could readily imagine that one fine day these polite, monosyllabic officers would suddenly start banging their desks and vomiting obscenities, as their senior colleagues had in '37. But one could equally readily visualize the reverse: that one fine day their tongues would get the better of them, and they would start to demonstrate convincingly that they personally had had nothing to do with the crimes of '37—when they had been mere innocent children. And that they were aghast at the illegalities committed then.

I had spent more than ten days milling around inside the building, so when I was invited to look in "some time next week" I decided to pay a visit to Leningrad to see my sister and to visit my mother's grave; I would leave Tonya, who had been worn out by all the queuing and jostling, with my sister at her country cottage.

When I told the old man from Vorkuta, with whom I had struck up a friendship during our endless queuing at the windows, of my decision to this effect, he nobly offered to inquire daily about the progress of my case while he was checking up on his own. If need be, he would send me a telegram.

My sister turned out to be a complete stranger. With all her ardent family love for me, and her complete willingness to come to my aid in whatever way she could, she displayed an organic indifference to everything that was a matter of burning, consuming concern to me, all that for me and for all of *us* mattered most for the rest of our days. She listened to me distractedly, clearly preoccupied with her own thoughts, and rounded off all my stories with

the invariable rejoinder: "How horrible! It's best forgotten!" After
which she got back to her own affairs, the daily round, the common
task. I found this the more astounding in that her first husband,
Shura Korolyov, a graduate of the Institute of Red Professors and
the father of her only son, had been shot in 1937, and I had been
waiting for her to question me about our world, the world in which
he had perished. But there it was: our exchanges were increasingly
confined to reminiscences about our parents' family and old friends.
At the same time she was remarkably kind and generous, and
readily took over responsibility for Tonya, whom I was leaving
with her for the time being.

And then, at long last:

"A telegram for you!"

From my heavily pounding heart, I knew at once what the bearer
of good tidings, whose message came to me in the corridor of my
sister's communal apartment building, had to tell.

"Leave at once, collect rehabilitation certificate." The dear old
man from Vorkuta, my comrade-in-suffering whom I had known
for but a few days, had honorably carried out his undertaking.

The day arrived. How often over the endless years had I dreamed
of it, had I tried to picture the exact circumstances of this moment,
the moment of complete liberation, of final escape from the oppressive right hand that had borne down on and sought to crush me?
Our dreams had taken different forms but were invariably associated
with the idea of some sort of cataclysm, of a tempest that would
sweep away the monstrous, inhuman received truths; with the idea
of a *noble* someone who would open the doors of the prisons and
camps for us so that we would hurtle out to freedom, into the wind
of change.

The last thing I could possibly have imagined was that we would
receive our long-dreamed-of freedom through the establishment,
as it is called nowadays; that we would have to stand in enormous
queues to get this freedom, choking in a sea of documentation
drafted by the same sluggish bureaucrats, the best of whom were
apathetic, while the worst scarcely concealed their resentment of
these unforeseen, eccentric reforms.

And yet that was exactly how it was. It was a warm summer's
day. There were more than two hundred people sitting, standing
or shifting from leg to leg in a queue to see the colonel responsible
for issuing rehabilitation certificates. What with the foul air and

my own impatience I felt quite dizzy. There were minutes when I forgot the difference between this epoch-making certificate and the violet stamp of the Magadan KGB office which had served to extend my lease of life by another two weeks. I did my best to keep my spirits up by thinking about freedom, but the feeling of bitterness persisted. Was this really the way in which freedom comes?

By the time I had squeezed my way to within ten places of the door it was almost evening. We went in, all ten of us at once. With a weary gesture, the colonel bade us be seated on a bench by the wall and called each of us over by his last name. This elderly man—the boss in charge of rehabilitation certificates—was no less exhausted than we were. He was extremely hot. We were all skimpily dressed, but he was in full uniform, buttoned right up to the neck. The sweat poured off his bald forehead; now and then he had to break off to wipe his forehead with a handkerchief. He had to ask my last name three times, as if he were deaf.

"Here." He handed me the certificate. "Read it carefully. Please note that if you lose it, it will not be replaced."

In addition to the certificate, which I did not have time to read through, he gave me a page from a scratch pad with a telephone number written on it.

"What's this?"

"It's the phone number of the Party Control Commission. You will call them to ask about your reinstatement in the Party."

"Wh . . . what?"

I was so flabbergasted by this unexpected turn of affairs, and my face expressed such bewilderment, that the colonel perked up a bit and began to look at me as if I was actually alive.

"Surely you want Party rehabilitation?"

"I . . . I . . ."

I simply couldn't believe my ears. They were inviting me, a pariah only yesterday, to return to the ranks of the ruling Party. I didn't know what to say.

"Otherwise what will you put in your curriculum vitae when you are offered a job?" the colonel asked. By now he was treating me as an equal.

"Supposing I put . . . 'non-Party'?"

"But you're not non-Party. You were expelled from the Party. And the next question on the form will be: 'Were you ever a member of the Party and, if so, when and how did you leave it?'

And then you'll have to use the formula recorded in your case file: 'Expelled from the Party for counter-revolutionary Trotskyite terrorist activitity.' So I suggest you phone this number!"

As each person emerged from the colonel's office he was immediately surrounded by the crowd waiting in the vestibule. They literally wrenched from his hands the document he had just received, compared the wording with that of others, and exchanged various profound conjectures as to whether this or that formula meant full or qualified rehabilitation. Some of these barrack-room lawyers were a match for the authors of the certificates themselves. They insisted that there was a big difference between the two formulas: "In the absence of any corpus delicti," and "Since the charges are not proven."

My certificate was of the first type: "In the absence of any corpus delicti." The connoisseurs congratulated me. There were also, to be sure, doubting Thomases who held the paper up to the light to look for special watermarks, coded numbers, and serial letters. . . . I didn't pay too much attention to all this. What I was most afraid of was that they would make a mess of my certificate, or even—God forbid—tear it. "If you lose it, it will not be replaced."

But then new faces emerged from the colonel's office, attention was diverted from me, and my precious document was returned to my hands. Now I found myself stumbling along Vorovsky Street (yes, of course, it was what used to be Povarskaya Street. . . . I'd only just realized it), completely exhausted. In fact, ever since I had left Tonya in Leningrad, I had somehow begun to lose my grip, to tire easily, to eat less and less frequently, and had taken to endless and pointless wandering around the streets. I made an effort of will. I had to take myself in hand. I had to go at once to see Tonya Ivanova. They would all be on tenterhooks, waiting to see me and my certificate. I must show it to them immediately.

But what was her address? I was suddenly petrified. I came to a stop in the middle of Arbat Square, opened my handbag, and started feverishly to rummage inside it. The certificate was not there! I rapidly shuffled through receipts a year old and more (I had a dreadful habit of cramming every bit of paper into my handbag and turning it out only once a year!). . . . No certificate there. I was done for. . . . Standing in the middle of the square, my heart hammering wildly, I went through the accumulation of papers in my handbag all over again. What could have happened?

I was rescued from this state by the frantic screech of brakes and the furious imprecations of a truck driver. Preoccupied with the search for the certificate, I had without realizing it almost come to an untimely end under the wheels of one of those lumbering, mud-spattered juggernauts that used to cross the old Arbat Square in the mid-fifties.

"You such-and-such and so-and-so!" yelled the driver, utterly furious. "You country yokel! Why don't you stay down on the farm? They come to town and they don't even know how to walk down a street. You might have been just a nasty little wet spot, and I'd have ended up in the cooler! Damn and blast you!"

But I accepted even his stronger expressions—which I am here omitting—with total humility and a blissful smile. In the first place, he was right. I had flagrantly violated all pedestrian rules, and had not so much as glanced at the lights. And in the second place, what did any of it matter when my certificate had turned up? I hadn't put it into my handbag; I had put it where for the past eighteen years I had been in the habit of hiding everything of any value to me—inside my bodice, next to my heart.

I kept feeling myself to hear the heavenly crackle of my precious document on the other side of my undershirt, and mumbling apologies in the wake of the truck driver. Completely drained of strength, I made my way to the fountain outside the entrance to the Arbat subway station and collapsed on the bench, to rest with the old men bowed over their prerevolutionary walking sticks and the mothers of children playing ball beside the fountain. I took out my certificate and started reading it through with total concentration. Ah, hah! That's the crux of the matter! It says here: "In the light of newly discovered circumstances. . . ." It would be interesting to know what circumstances had been newly discovered by my incorruptible judges. Perhaps they had found the real terrorist and discovered that he, not I, had killed . . . Killed whom? After all, despite the millions of terrorists, no one, absolutely *no one* had been killed. . . . Only Kirov . . . And all of us in the camps knew the name of his murderer perfectly well.

Well, let's read on: "The case is closed in the absence of any corpus delicti." The favorite phrase, with which our more humane jailers had sought to comfort us and calm us down, came to mind: "They'll sort it out. If you're not guilty, they'll sort it out and let you go." And so they had. It had taken less than twenty years for the Supreme Court itself to pronounce magisterially: no corpus delicti!

I couldn't summon strength to get up from the bench and go into the subway. Suddenly two country cousins came over to me—a man and a woman with heavy suitcases in their hands and rucksacks over their shoulders.

"Would you please tell us, young lady, how we get to the Kazan station?"

This apparently trivial happening immediately put me in a good mood again. For one thing, they had called me "young lady." So, even in my late fifties, I didn't look like an old woman. And for another, they had asked me how to get to the Kazan station. Not to Mylga, not to Elgen, not to Vaskov's House, and not to Lefortovo, but simply to the Kazan station. And I did my very best to explain to them in detail where to change trains and where to cross the street.

I remembered that while I was rummaging in my handbag, looking for my mislaid certificate, I had seen in the depths a square of chocolate. I ate it with relish and rose resolutely from the bench. I looked around me. The well-nourished Moscow pigeons, which had not yet gone out of fashion, were deep in conversation with one another. A little girl in a red dress was busily skipping. A constant stream of people was pouring into the subway. I was about to join them. I would merge with the general stream. Could I really do that? I was just like everyone else!

"In the absence of any corpus deliciti . . ."

Epilogue

In effect this book has been with me for more than thirty years. At first it was just an idea, then a succession of constantly rewritten drafts, as I crossed out entire long sections of the text, and searched for more accurate words, more carefully considered judgments.

This applies particularly to the part of the book not included in the volume published in the West in 1967. For life continues, and although the path I have had to tread over the past two decades has become less precipitous, it remains a rather painful one. Besides, I am now reaching the end of my days. At that time of life, the awareness that everything personal is spent, the bleak and merciless certainty that for you there is no tomorrow, gives you priceless advantages: objectivity of judgment and, most important of all, gradual liberation from the Great Fear that accompanied my generation throughout its conscious life.

When in the twilight of your days you read through the unpublished part of the book still lying in your desk, you feel an irresistible need to change it again and again (to alter not the facts, of course, but the selection, treatment, and, above all, your judgments on them). On the one hand, this is a source of gratification: a sign that your mind has not yet ossified, is still capable of developing, of understanding new phenomena. But, on the other hand, these incessant alterations (the sad fate of all manuscripts lying around in drawers) damage the work to some extent, and may change its inflection for the worse.

I have therefore decided to make no more changes. Not even stylistic improvements. Let it remain as it is, as I have set it down, for even the imperfections of style reflect the particular state of mind in which I wrote it.

Readers often ask me: "How could you keep such a mass of names, facts, place names, and poems in your memory?"

Very simply: because just remembering it all to record it later had been the main object of my life throughout those eighteen years. The collection of material for this book began from the moment when I first crossed the threshold of the NKVD's Inner Prison in Kazan. All those years I had no opportunity to write anything down, to prepare any preliminary sketches for a future book. All that I have set down has been written from memory. When I began to work on the book, the only landmarks in the labyrinth of the past were my own poems, also composed without benefit of pencil or paper, but, thanks to the efficiency of my memory where poetry is concerned, clearly imprinted on my brain. I am fully aware of the homemade, amateur quality of my prison verses. But to a certain extent, they did duty for the notebooks I did not possess. And that is their justification.

I started to write the chapters, in sequence, back in 1959 in Transcarpathia, where we were living in a country cottage. I used to sit on a stump under a large walnut tree and write in pencil, holding a school exercise book on my knees. I was able to read the first chapters to Anton. He was already incurably ill. I first sensed the imminence of his death when he burst into tears on hearing my chapter "Butyrki Nights," and cold fingers gripped at my heart.

After his death, on December 27, 1959, I wrote in fits and starts. I would drop it for months on end, then work like a maniac night after night. (The daytime I spent writing for my bread and butter: run-of-the-mill articles and essays for journals, especially the educational ones.)

By 1962 I had become the author of an extensive manuscript of some 400 typescript pages. This bore little resemblance to what the many readers of *Journey into the Whirlwind* are now familiar with. This first version, written in the state of anguished lucidity which occurs after the loss of people close to you, was full of my most secret thoughts, which I had entrusted to no one but now committed to paper. The epigraph to this version was Blok's lines "The twentieth century—more homeless still, a haze where terrors hide beyond our ken." My own internal censor had not yet gone into action, since it did not occur to me that there could be any question of publication. I simply wrote because I had to.

But then came the Twenty-second Congress. It revived all my most impractical hopes. The well-thumbed folder that had hitherto been my companion, my confidant, suddenly acquired new importance in my own eyes. It seemed to me that the longed-for, hoped-for time had now at last come when I could speak out, when my truthful testimony would help those who genuinely wanted to avoid a repetition of our nation's shameful and dreadful past.

I read my first version, crammed with poems and emotional passages, over and over again, until I came to see that this was not a book but only the raw material for one. I set to work again, ruthlessly scrapping entire pages that I had treasured only yesterday. I crossed out the Blok epigraph committing me to a general, philosophical treatment of the subject beyond my powers, and adopted from Yevtushenko's poetry a new one, which shifted the emphasis to the concrete struggle against Stalin's crimes.

My long years of struggle with the housing authorities came to an end, and I was given a one-room apartment of my own in a cooperatively owned building. I burned the old folder, which I had had to keep shifting from one hiding place to another when I shared an apartment. Sometimes I feel sorry that I destroyed it, sorry to lose all the emotional outpourings and soul baring, which might have won my readers' hearts. But at the same time I know there was a great deal that was superfluous, haphazard, and too loosely put together.

I now worked regularly for several hours at a stretch, no longer too lazy to settle down with the typewriter after a tiring day at the office of the journal I was working for. I had assigned myself a specific aim: to offer the manuscript to the major journals. Perhaps to *Yunost*, where I had already published some of my pieces. Or— you never know your luck—even to *Novy Mir*, which by that time had already published *Ivan Denisovich*.

Alas, together with my hopes of publication the missing inner editor came into being. He carped at every paragraph: "You won't get that past the censor." I started looking for more streamlined formulations, and I not infrequently spoiled passages that had come out well, comforting myself with the thought that, after all, a sentence or so was not much sacrifice for the sake of publication, of reaching people at last.

All this had a considerable effect on the first part and the beginning of the second part of *Whirlwind*.

No sooner did the manuscript reach the editorial board of Moscow's two most popular literary journals, than it began a five-year voyage over the stormy waves of *samizdat*. The manuscript, of which dozens or even hundreds of copies had been made, repro-

duced itself with fantastic rapidity and passed beyond the boundaries
of Moscow. When I started receiving readers' letters from Leningrad and Krasnoyarsk, from Saratov and Odessa, I realized that I
had completely lost control over the astonishing life of my unpublished book.

I need hardly say how reassuring it was to discover in letters from
unknown people their reaction to inner secrets that for long years
had been cherished in silence. These letters, especially the ones from
young people, helped dispel my long-standing terror of the hypnotic
power of the monstrous accusations brought against us. I saw now
that the younger generation revered the memory of my comrades
who had perished in the dungeons, and they were grateful to me
for the fragments of the truth which they had gleaned from my
book.

I shortly started receiving letters from writers. Not only letters
but autographed copies of their books with touching inscriptions. I
received letters and books from Ehrenburg, Paustovsky, Kaverin,
Chukovsky, Solzhenitsyn, Yevtushenko, Voznesensky, Vigdorova,
Panova, Burstein, and many, many others. Encouraging verbal messages from scientists—from Academician Tamm, for example—were
relayed to me. The young historian, Roy Medvedev, whose father
had died among us in Kolyma, came to make my acquaintance.
Another group of historians presented me with their book, a collection of essays, inscribed: "To one who has stolen a march on
historians in her understanding of historic events."

It was perfectly clear to me that I owed this not to any special
literary merit in the book but solely to its truthfulness. People who
had been totally starved of the simple, unsophisticated truth were
grateful to anyone who would take the trouble of telling them,
de profundis, how it all really was.

I do want once more to assure my readers that I have written
nothing but the truth. There may, of course, be inaccuracies or
mistakes in the text of this book where my memory has rearranged
dates. But there are no lies, no politically appropriate sophisms, no
conscious suppressions. At my present age, when you look at life
from a certain distance, as it were, there is no point in making things
up. So I have written down the truth. Not the *whole truth* (for that
I could hardly have hoped to know) but *nothing but the truth*.

To be able to encompass the *whole truth* I had neither the range
of information, nor the skill, nor the depth of understanding. All

I could do was to resist subordinating my story to nimble sophisms
about what was and what was not expedient, to calculations about
what was called for by the needs of the moment. I took as my point
of departure the simple idea that truth does not need to be justified
by expediency. It is simply the *truth*. Expediency should take its
cue from truth, and not the other way around.

The more I wrote, the more I became convinced of this. The fact
that I had lost all hope of seeing the book published in my own
country was no doubt a help in this respect. And whereas the hand
of my own inner editor is visible in the first volume and in the
introduction to it,* I was not hampered by any ulterior considerations in what followed.

Meanwhile, as I was working on the ending of the book, the
number of copies in *samizdat* of the first part of it grew in a steady
geometrical progression. One Leningrad professor—an expert on
the history of literature that had bypassed the censorship in Russia—
told me that, from what his experienced eye had seen, my book
had beaten the *samizdat* publication record not only of our time
but of the nineteenth century too.

There were also, however, people who disliked my book. To
my great chagrin, Tvardovsky† was one of them. Whereas the
prose editors of *Novy Mir* showed sympathy and understanding
for my work, the chief editor was for some reason clearly preju-
diced against it. I was told that he had said: "She only noticed that
there was something wrong when they started jailing Communists.
She thought it quite natural when they were exterminating the
Russian peasantry."

A grave and unjust accusation. Of course, I had a very limited
understanding of events before '37, and I have written of this with
complete frankness. But when I heard of Tvardovsky's reaction to
my book, my immediate thought was that he had probably not
read it, that he had simply leafed through it. Otherwise he could
not have failed to notice that the question of the personal responsibility of each one of us is my greatest heartache, my greatest
source of anguish. I write of this in detail in the chapter headed
"Mea culpa." But Tvardovsky did not even spot that heading.

---

* Published as Epilogue in the English-language editions.
† Aleksandr Tvardovsky (1910–1971); editor, poet. Editor of *Novy Mir* from
1950 to 1954 and from 1958 to 1970; resigned in February 1970 after failing to
gain permission to publish Solzhenitsyn's *Cancer Ward*.

In the *Yunost* editorial offices, where I was given real grounds for hope, my manuscript also got stuck. And time was not on my side. It was becoming increasingly clear that a veto had been imposed on the subject. Finally, one day in a conversation with me, Polevoy, the chief editor, exclaimed, "Surely you didn't seriously hope that we would publish it?" After that *Yunost* forwarded my manuscript for safekeeping to the Marx-Engels-Lenin Institute, where, as the covering note put it, "It might serve as material on the history of the Party."

Accordingly, by the end of 1966 all hopes of publication, other than in *samizdat* form, had been buried. For me the sequel was not only unexpected but unbelievable.

Our various paths cross in an unforeseeable way in this world. Suddenly I saw that my book (or, rather, the first volume and part of the second) had been published in Italy. I, a long-term denizen of those icy holes in the ground for convicts—localities mostly written with a hard *Y* as in Myngakh, Khattynnakh—had been published in a city with the soft liquid *l* of Milan. And then I saw it coming out in Paris, London, Munich, New York, Stockholm, and many other places. I managed to see and actually handle many of these different editions. Some of them were brought back from abroad for me by the late Ilya Ehrenburg.

The state of mind of the author of such publications is an entirely new subject, thrown up by the strange times we live in. He is torn by conflicting feelings. On the one hand, he cannot suppress a natural feeling of delight at seeing his manuscript transformed into a book. On the other hand, he has not been able to correct it, has had no part in editing it. There was no chance to correct typographical errors (the Russian edition is full of spelling and punctuation mistakes). It is as if foreigners had rescued your child from death, but in so doing had wrested him from you forever. Yet meanwhile your own fellow countrymen have made it plain to you, the unfortunate mother, that you are to blame not only for having given birth to a child unwelcome to the authorities, but also for failing to keep it under lock and key.

One way or another the book had entered upon a new phase in its existence: from a pre-Gutenberg sample of our special homemade brand of *samizdat* literature, it had changed into the elegant, multilingual offspring of the publishing houses; had wandered into a world of luxurious, glossy paper, of gilt edging, of garish jackets.

The total alienation of the product from its author had been accomplished. The book had become a grown-up daughter off .on her continental tour, without so much as a look over her shoulder or a thought to spare for her old mother left to fend for herself at home.

But what will become of the other, as yet unpublished part of the book? Is it fated to remain a mere exercise book? And if it does, on what shall I put my hopes? On the thought that "manuscripts do not burn"? Whatever happens, I consider it my duty to finish the book. Not so much because I want to record the facts about my later years in camp and exile as to reveal to the reader the heroine's spiritual evolution, the gradual transformation of a naïve young Communist idealist into someone who had tasted unforgettably the fruits of the tree of the knowledge of good and evil, a human being who amid all her setbacks and sufferings also had moments (however brief) of fresh insight in her search for truth. It is this cruel journey of the soul and not just the chronology of my sufferings that I want to bring home to the reader.

And yet . . . yet I would like to hope that if not I, and if not my son, then perhaps my grandson will be able to read this book in full, published in our own land. . . .